I Speak for This Child

I Speak for This Child

True Stories of a Child Advocate

GAY COURTER

Crown Publishers, Inc.
New York

The events described in this book are true. These are real cases presented as accurately as possible. Some of the individuals in this book are composites and, except for nationally publicized cases, all names and identifying characteristics of people and places have been changed to assure their anonymity.

Exerpt from "The Change" in OPENINGS, copyright © 1968 by Wendell Berry, reprinted by permission of Harcourt Brace & Company.

"Listen to the Mustn'ts" from WHERE THE SIDEWALK ENDS by Shel Silverstein. Copyright © 1974 by Evil Eye Music, Inc. By permission of Edite Kroll Literary Agency.

From THE POETRY OF ROBERT FROST. Copyright © 1928, 1930, 1939, 1949, 1969 by Henry Holt and Co., Inc. Reprinted by permission of Henry Holt and Co., Inc.

Published by Crown Publishers, Inc., 201 East 50th Street, New York, New York 10022. Member of the Crown Publishing Group.
Random House, Inc. New York, Toronto, London, Sydney, Auckland
CROWN is a trademark of Crown Publishers, Inc.

Manufactured in the United States of America

Design by Deborah Kerner

Library of Congress Cataloging-in-Publication Data
Courter, Gay.
I speak for this child : true stories of a child advocate /
Gay Courter. — 1st ed.
p. cm.
Includes index.
1. Abused children—Services for—Florida—Case studies.
2. Children—Legal status, laws, etc.—Florida—Case studies.
3. Child welfare—Florida—Case studies. I. Title.
HV6626.53.F6C68 1995
362.7'68'09759—dc20   94-20936
                                                          CIP
ISBN 0-517-59541-9
10 9 8 7 6 5 4 3 2 1
First Edition

For Philip,
who showed me not only how to care,
but to love

For my sons, Blake and Joshua,
who taught me how
to listen to and respect children

For my mother and father,
who made me feel like
the most important person in the world

For my guardian children,
may all their dreams come true

Contents

Acknowledgments

Due to my vows of confidentiality, I cannot thank by name everyone who has helped me with this book.

However, I cannot leave out some of the experts and mentors and assistants who have contributed mightily to the project, including Jolene Cazzola, Betty Duermeier, Kathleen Cossey, Wayne Black, Ph.D., Pat Barton, Bradford Bobbitt, Esq., Elsie Weisman, Robin Madden, M.D., Ph.D., Mary Alisi, Debbie Rector, Mary Ann Boline, and Mary Wanke.

Donald Cutler, my perceptive agent, and Erica Marcus and Betty Prashker, at Crown Publishing, all had faith in the value of speaking out for a child even before children's rights became a popular national issue.

*The injustice done to an individual is
sometimes of service to the public.*
  —JUNIUS

*In this little world where children have their
existence, whosoever brings them up, there is
nothing so finely perceived and so finely felt,
as injustice.*
  —CHARLES DICKENS

*The solution of adult problems tomorrow
depends in large measure upon the way our
children grow up today. There is no greater
insight into the future than recognizing when
we save our children, we save ourselves.*
  —MARGARET MEAD

*For these are all our children. . . . We will all
profit by, or pay for whatever they become.*
  —JAMES BALDWIN

Children Are Waiting

*Many things we need can wait, the child cannot. Now is the
time his bones are being formed, his blood is being made,
his mind is being developed. To him we cannot say tomorrow,
his name is today.*
—GABRIELA MISTRAL

THE COVER STORY OF THE JULY 31, 1988, edition of *Parade*, "Who
Speaks for the Lost Children?" caught my eye. By the time I finished
it, I was incensed that foster care had become a dumping ground for
American children who never found their way back to their original
families or were not adopted into permanent homes. The article indicated
that there were ways to improve the system and that individuals on citizen review boards or working as volunteer advocates could benefit these
children. Now that is something I could do, I thought, and clipped the
story, even highlighting the reference to the nationwide Court Appointed
Special Advocate (CASA) program, which uses volunteers to speak out
for the best interests of foster children in court. After a few days, though,
I placed it in a file.

For a long time I had been looking for a way to contribute to our
community. Ever since my teen years, when I worked with the American
Friends Service Committee in a migrant workers village in California
and in a gang violence reduction project in East Harlem, I wanted to be
useful. At Antioch College in the 1960s there were frequent opportunities
not only to demonstrate against injustice, but also to participate in so-
cially beneficial works. For a long time I used my career as a filmmaker
and a writer to propagandize for issues in which I believed. To this end
my film director husband, Philip, and I produced documentary and educational films championing natural childbirth, parent-infant bonding,
breastfeeding, early childhood education for disadvantaged children in
urban and rural locations, and environmental concerns. We made com-
mercials to help political candidates win elections or to keep worthy

endeavors funded. My novels also explored social themes, but I was no longer active in community service.

Shortly after reading the article in *Parade*, our elder son, Blake, entered Groton School in Massachusetts. Soon he became active in community service projects there and told me the school's motto was *Cui Servire Est Regnare*, putting service above all. I was reminded again of how I was neglecting direct work in our locale, yet my forays into parent-teacher organizations, volunteering in the schools, and similar committee activities had been unsatisfying.

Even before reading the article, though, I had voiced strong opinions about children and legal issues, which had come to a head during the Baby M. surrogate mother case. Most everyone I knew felt the father, William Stern, who had contracted for the baby born in 1985, had every right to claim her, while Mary Beth Whitehead, the birth mother, had lost her chance to change her mind by agreeing to the conception. I knew that the mother-infant bond had a physical and hormonal basis that often superseded a logical one, and that a contract signed in early pregnancy before this attachment took place should not be enforced. In fact, when I read the published details on the contract, I became convinced that the surrogate mother's rights had been horridly compromised, if only because she had not received legal representation before she signed the highly questionable, and one-sided, document. To me, if it was illegal to sell a baby after it was born, it should be illegal to sell it before it was born. And yes, while Baby M. had bonded to her adoptive family, she had been yanked from her mother's breast under protest. At last the interests of Baby M. were considered when a Guardian ad Litem, an attorney, was appointed by the court. In discussing the case informally, I had argued for some sort of joint custody quite similar to the final outcome after an appeal. Of course this was theoretical. At that time I never thought that the opinion of someone without a law degree would matter—let alone make a difference—in these situations. The idea that a nonprofessional volunteer could champion a child had intrigued me, but like so many others, I lacked the time and motivation to actually become involved.

The catalyst that finally pushed me to act was the news reports about Bradley McGee, a two-year-old child living in foster care in Lakeland, Florida, who was murdered by his stepfather. The product of a rape, little Bradley was living with his teenage mother and her boyfriend. The mother had abandoned Bradley at a mall at the age of four months. After a placement with a relative didn't work out, he was moved to the Kirklands' foster home. His mother had not contacted him for six months, but when the Kirklands offered to adopt him, his mother reappeared, signed up for parenting classes, and received visitation rights. Even though Bradley's mother did not always comply with her agreements, the caseworkers wrote positive reports about the toddler's adjustment when he was with her. The foster parents, though, noticed that Bradley seemed traumatized by the visits and pleaded with the judge not to return the child to his mother. On July 25, 1989, the judge extended Bradley's stay with his mother and her new husband. Three days later he was dead from a brain hemorrhage after his stepfather dunked him repeatedly headfirst in a toilet as punishment for soiling his pants. Subsequent articles on the sensational case mentioned that ever since Bradley had come to the attention of the social service agency as an infant, he had been waiting to be assigned a Guardian ad Litem. Because of a shortage of advocates, there was nobody to convey the problems the foster parents saw to the judge. If only I had become a guardian a year earlier . . .

That did it. I got on the phone. Eight connections later Lillian Elliott, the Guardian ad Litem case coordinator, explained that our area was served by a very active program. Training began in September. Ten weeks after Bradley McGee's murder, I was assigned my first case. Since then, I have advocated for more than a dozen children and have sat in courtrooms with my heart beating rapidly as I awaited a judge's life-changing decision. Will an abusive parent regain custody of a frightened child? Will a family be split up? Will a mother who made a mistake be given a second chance? Will a sexual pervert be jailed? I am not merely a bystander but an active participant in the process. What I say carries weight because I have personally investigated the case and speak for the children involved.

Introduction

License to Care

*Success is to laugh often and much; to win the respect of
intelligent people and the affection of children; to earn the
appreciation of honest critics; to endure the betrayal of false
friends; to appreciate beauty; to find the best in others; to
leave the world a bit better whether by a healthy child, a
garden patch, or a redeemed social condition; to know even
one life has breathed easier because you have lived.
This is to have succeeded.*

—RALPH WALDO EMERSON

MY LIFE CHANGES THE MOMENT I OPEN THE ENVELOPE. It all begins
with an official document appointing me to the case. The paper heralds
its importance by its eight-and-a-half-by-fourteen-inch legal size. It arrives in an official envelope from the judicial circuit court. "In the interest of . . ." followed by the name and birth date of a child is typed at
the top of the page. The first paragraph states: "I, Gay Courter, a duly
qualified volunteer of the State of Florida Guardian ad Litem Program
have been nominated by the program and hereby give notice that I will
accept appointment as a Guardian ad Litem in this cause." This notice
of acceptance of the Guardian ad Litem is attached to the order appointing the Guardian ad Litem program to represent the best interests of this
particular child, who is involved in a court proceeding, usually because
that child is a victim of abuse or neglect.

Even though I already may have been told the general history of the
case and have given my tentative approval to accept the assignment
before these orders are sent, everything changes the moment I read the
name of the child one line above my own. A few minutes earlier this
child was a stranger living his life in another time and place than mine.
Intellectually I realize there are millions of children who live in poverty,
suffer serious health problems, are victims of crimes, neglect, and abuse.
I see their images in the newspapers and on television. I read articles
about their plight. I can rail against the societal woes that have given

the rich and powerful democratic United States appalling statistics about the health and welfare of our children. I can pontificate and quote. Yet this is the abstract. Anytime I want I can turn the page, change the topic, switch the channel. Anytime, that is, until the papers arrive.

As I stare at the document a former nonentity metamorphoses into a person with a name, a birth date, a beating heart, and blinking eyes. This is a living breathing child, who has been assigned to me. I am not an attorney or caseworker. I have no higher education in psychology or law or social science. I am a writer and filmmaker who has volunteered to be this child's voice in court.

If I sign this document, I am agreeing to perform the responsibilities of the Guardian ad Litem until termination of the jurisdiction of the court or discharge or release by the court or circuit director of the program. My involvement might be for several months only, but more likely it is a commitment that will span years. I also pledge to maintain any information received as confidential and will disclose the same only to parties to the cause or their counsel.

Before I consent, I peruse whatever has arrived in the file, although none of those documents—no matter how pathetic or sensational—has ever deterred me. For, from the moment I see my name below the child's, I know we are inexorably bound to travel a twisting road together—hand in hand, heart to heart—striving to win victories: some slight, others stupendous. No matter what happens I will champion that child's cause until he has a safe, stable place to live; until he is given the legal, psychological, educational, and medical services he deserves to have; until justice is served and the child is settled and better off than he would have been without my intervention.

While I may ignore the anonymous, I cannot circumvent this assignment.

For this is my License to Care.

Guardian ad Litem, sometimes abbreviated as GAL, is the legal title for a child advocate in the state of Florida. Other systems refer to their counterparts as court appointed special advocates (CASAs) as well as other, similar names. Also, different districts confer upon their advocates a varying range of powers and responsibilities. My experience rests entirely on the laws of Florida, which mandate in both legislative and administrative orders that there is a need for independent advocacy for children in abuse and neglect judicial proceedings. Chapter 415 of the Florida statutes—as well as the Rules of Juvenile Procedure of the Supreme Court of Florida, Rule 8.215—requires appointment of a Guardian ad Litem in any of these proceedings, and the state has appropriated funds for the Guardian ad Litem program to be administered through the state court system. Because of this legal mandate, guardians have party status in courtroom proceedings. *Party*, in legal parlance, refers to those by or against whom a legal suit is brought. Why, though, is there a need for a nonprofessional, unpaid person to become involved in a complicated court process when there are many other qualified specialists working on an abuse case?

At first it was thought that a child's interest was safeguarded during the judicial process. A neutral judge supervised the proceedings and attorneys represented the parents, the social services agencies, and the state. But are those assumptions true? Usually the person making the formal complaint of abuse and neglect is the local social services department. In Florida, this entity is called the Department of Health and Rehabilitative Services (HRS). HRS files a petition on behalf of the child and is represented by either the state attorney's office, if it is a criminal case, or an HRS staff lawyer, if it is a child abuse case. At first glance it would seem that this attorney would act in the child's best interests. Not necessarily so. The attorney's primary concern is to establish whether or not the child was harmed by the alleged perpetrator. But the child has needs that transcend merely proving the abuse occurred.

Then what about the respondent's attorney? In an abuse case, the respondent is often the child's parent. Because they have a client-attorney relationship, the lawyer is obligated to represent ardently the wishes of the parent. If this means tearing apart the prosecutor's case due to weak evidence or faulty procedure, he will do so, despite the fact that the parent may have actually abused the child. Even worse, protecting a parent-client sometimes means challenging a child's credibility. Thus the parent's interests and the child's interests can be in direct conflict because defending the client means denying the charges. Yet, if the parent is exonerated, he is free to abuse the child again.

How about the judge? Can he advocate for the rights of the child while remaining impartial during the adversarial process? No, he must listen to each side and hand down a fair decision based on the merits of the case, not what he believes is right for an individual.

What are social workers for if not professionally to represent the best interests of the child? The caseworkers do much of the direct contact work with the family and try to offer services to the injured child, but even in the finest department, heavy caseloads and cumbersome regulations created to manage standards and conduct make it difficult to spend the amount of time necessary to thoroughly handle each case. Also, these employees of large agencies have to weigh an individual's needs against management policy and budgeted resources. If there are six children vying for a single psychiatric bed or other prime placement, five will lose out, and only one will have his needs met. Who decides which child gets chosen?

Just as every child ideally has a parent who goes to bat for her own offspring, every child in the throes of a court dispute deserves an independent advocate who does not care about rules or policy or budgets or beds for the population in general, but only how she might best serve the child assigned to her. If your own child desperately needed a rare medication, you would not concern yourself with those who would be denied it so yours might recover. Likewise, a Guardian ad Litem will try to insure that her guardian child is first on the list for whatever he needs.

One by one, advocate by advocate, this program stretches across the United States, making a difference daily in the lives of thousands of children. Most of the guardians are volunteers. Most are not lawyers. And yet they have official clout to change a child's life. The fact that the child advocate model was conceived, exists, and thrives in a legal system so hidebound by procedures and traditions is remarkable.

Court appointed advocates for children, such as Guardians ad Litem, are relatively new in American justice. The idea is an innovative and controversial way to keep children from falling through the cracks. Even though there are now programs in every state, only about twenty-five percent of children in the court process are assigned guardians because there are not enough to go around. Some are paid, professional guardians, while others are attorneys who either receive fees or donate their time. More and more they are volunteers. They range in age from eighteen to eighty and many are professionals who take time out from their busy schedules to work with these children. In our area we have a dynamic group of retired guardians. About twenty percent are men.

How it works, why it works, and my involvement in the system is what this book is about. I am one volunteer and I speak from my personal experience. Until I had my first case, I had only been in a courtroom once and had never even observed a trial. My expectations when I started were far different from what they are now. My idealism remains but is filtered by my experiences, and so the choices and decisions I make today are not necessarily done in the order, manner, or style that I might have employed several years ago. More than ever, though, I understand that when I accept a case, I have nothing to lose. It cannot directly affect my career, my finances, or my family. I have nothing to gain either, at least nothing that can be quantified, although I know that I receive far more from each child than I expend.

My mission is pure: to make something that has gone terribly wrong a little better, phone call by phone call, visit by visit, meeting by meeting, court appearance by court appearance, report by report. I don't have to worry about my personal needs or those of the other adults: parents, agency workers, attorneys. Whenever there is a question or problem or decision, I weigh the alternatives and ask: what is in this child's best interests? The answer is not always simple, but it is made easier if the fog of confusion, paperwork, and hysteria surrounding the case is blown away and the child alone is the focus.

Confidentiality is the main covenant of trust between a guardian and her children. To enable the advocate to assess the factors in a child's life, almost unparalleled access is given to obtain records, including files from social services and economic services; child support enforcement; aging, adult, and Medicaid services; child-caring and public health facilities; medical and other health professionals from doctors to nurses, psychologists, psychiatrists, and counselors; educational institutions; law enforcement agencies and the Department of Corrections. Without further consent of the child or parents or authorities, the court order authorizes the guardian to inspect and copy any records relating to the child (including those pertaining to the parents, relatives, siblings, suspected perpetrators and their household members or any other adults involved with the child) with the proviso that the information received will not be disclosed except in reports to the court and other parties to the cause. Thus, as a Guardian ad Litem, I have been able to access records that are legally unavailable to police, lawyers, social service agencies, schools, and the families themselves. Information helps an advocate develop a picture of what is going on that is far more inclusive than the viewpoints of many others involved in a case.

For instance, I learned about a murder that a father committed, which had not been previously known to anyone else involved with the case; I discovered arrest records (but not convictions) for rape; medical reports on previous victims and stepchildren assaulted by a father accused of incest; psychological records on a sex offender showing a pattern to his crimes; and a wide variety of privileged papers that have greatly influenced my recommendations to the court. This aspect of a guardian's power is often the most shocking to people who have been led to believe that certain documents—such as psychiatric reports—are utterly confidential and can never be used against them. When it comes to the protection of a child, though, there are exceptions. I have had difficulty obtaining some files, but a doctor could be in contempt of court for not revealing them to me. A physician would not have to give me his notes, but he would be required to release the results of testing, historical information, his diagnosis, and opinions. I cannot show these to anyone except the judge, and they become a part of the permanent judicial record. Also they cannot be used to indict or convict the alleged perpetrator. But I can—and have—said to the court in a hearing to decide where a child should be placed, "According to the psychological records that I have reviewed, this man should not have custody of this child." This is an influential statement, one not made lightly, and one that holds much weight with the court, but it is an example of how a child can be protected without having to prove beyond a reasonable doubt that the child should not live somewhere that could be dangerous.

Yes, this power does create enemies. Emotions surrounding custody and family issues are sometimes explosive. In order to protect themselves, guardians are urged to preserve privacy by not revealing their home addresses, phone numbers, or involving their guardian families in their personal lives.

Privileged information is both a blessing and a curse. When it is used to protect the fragile rights of individuals and the anonymity of innocent victims, it is well employed. But often confidentiality is used as a veil to protect those who failed to serve a child in a proper or timely manner. New administrators of the state social service department are beginning to question the confidentiality of their cases because sealed files shield incompetent workers from inspection and accountability.

Still, I have sworn an oath to guard the secrets of my cases. Great care has been taken to camouflage the identities of the children in this book. Their names and ages and locations and almost every identifying fact about their families and backgrounds has been altered. Professions and histories of their relatives are as different as they can be while still reflecting the emotional truths of the stories. Despite these adjustments, I have tried to portray honestly and factually my involvement in the Guardian ad Litem program from the training phases through the various court hearings and decisions. The legal groundwork and placement situations have not been changed nor have the specific crimes against the children. Every professional person and foster family has been made into a fictional character, again with distinctive changes. Because there were often several social workers managing a case over time, different judges on the bench, various lawyers representing the parties (and because portraying all of these people would probably confuse the reader), some of these characters actually are composites. Of course I cannot recall every word of a conversation that may have happened many years ago. I never taped interviews (except in one case mentioned in the book), nor did I attempt to take verbatim notes. I did keep extensive field notes and jotted down phrases from pertinent telephone conversations, which were then typed into my journals and handed in monthly to my supervisor. Nevertheless, I sometimes quote actual dialogue to the best of my recollection. If the words are not precise, the meaning and the results are as accurate as possible. Other times I use the device of dialogue to tell the story more as it was lived, recreating only those scenes in which I participated. Some of the events are rather preposterous with strange coincidences, bizarre decisions and outcomes—the whole "truth is stranger than fiction" phenomenon. Many of the cases have convolutions, surprises, and legal maneuvers that cannot be eliminated if the impact on a child's life is to be understood. Though I have been tempted to modify the truth so it will seem more "real," I have adhered to the actual flow of events as much as possible, changing only a few situations, usually by leaving out extraneous incidents and characters, to make them comprehensible. But the girl's love of Robert Frost, the search for a missing mother, the child's marriage, and the swift appearance of adoptive parents are stunningly true.

As part of the record keeping required of a guardian, I kept daily time logs of every phone call (even those unanswered), every meeting, and every hour volunteered. Most guardians in our district volunteer ten to twenty hours per month on an average of two active cases. One full-time volunteer carries nine cases and donates two hundred hours per month. I typically spend twenty to forty hours each month, which I juggle between my writing, film work, and family life. My written logs have been invaluable in recreating events. Looking back after many months on a case, I have a very different perception than I did as the situation unfolded. As much as possible, I have attempted to tell the stories in chronological order forward in each case so a reader can follow my path as I waded through reams of perplexing material, made complex decisions, and lived through the consequences of my actions. The locations cover a wide geographical area in Florida, but no county or city is correctly identified, and the circuit court districts and other pertinent places have not been specified. Any town mentioned is definitely not the one involved. Much of the procedure for Guardians ad Litem is specific to Florida and does not apply in other parts of the country, where the roles and rules governing the conduct, responsibility, and power of advocates vary considerably.

Child rights cases have exploded in the media in the past few years, and several of these celebrated cases have impacted on me directly as well as the work of advocates everywhere. For a while I wrestled with whether or not to respect the confidentiality of these children and have decided that—for better or worse—they have become public record. Since those charged with protecting their confidentiality have chosen to break that silence, I do not feel obligated to protect it either. Only those families whose names and stories have been splashed across headlines and whose legal battles have made case law or serve as historical landmarks (such as Gregory K., Baby Jessica, and Kimberly Mays) are identified correctly. Also, the names of the members of my immediate family and associates have not been altered, since it would be illogical to do so.

Despite these restrictions, my guardian children are real, their chronicles are true. They need not only to be told, but also to be heard. Since I am a writer, I have decided that I must continue to speak for them through the medium I know best. "I want people to know what happened to me" was one girl's response when I asked if she wanted me to tell her story. Another said, "Maybe my story will make someone else's life better." I asked those children whom I could still locate to select their own pseudonyms for this book, and these are the names I have used. In some cases the real adults have also picked their aliases as a way of actively participating in the process of revealing the complex world of troubled families. These very private lives become the backdrop for a courtroom struggle to fortify children from violence and neglect as well as to provide them with what they are entitled to have under our Constitution: a permanent, safe place where they can not only survive, but thrive.

I Speak
for
This
Child

1

The Girl Who Loved
Robert Frost

Lydia's Story

❖

When will justice come? When those who are not injured
become as indignant as those who are.
—LEO TOLSTOY

I HAVE A FILE HERE WITH YOUR NAME ON IT," said Lillian Elliott, the district Guardian ad Litem case coordinator, in response to my call. "Saw this young woman in court and knew she needed a special friend. I've been holding it open just for you," she added warmly.

Whether or not this was true, I wasn't sure, but Lillian did have a way of selling a case. "Tell me more about her," I prompted. "Where is she living?"

"Very near you," she said to interest me further.

"Is she in a safe place?" I wondered, because sometimes a child remained in a potentially dangerous home if there had not been enough evidence to remove her.

"Yes, very, and she's not going anywhere for a while."

"Why is that?"

"She's been ordered there by the court. You see, this case is a bit different from the usual: the child is also the perpetrator." Lillian paused for me to absorb her meaning.

The children assigned to volunteers were almost always the victims, not the accused. "Why does the girl need a guardian?"

"The court has determined she's a CINS kid herself, a child in need of services"—Lillian hesitated for a moment—"because she put her baby sister in a microwave oven."

"Is that the horrendous case that was in the newspaper?"

"Yes, but why don't you read the file and then decide?" Lillian suggested. "In fact, maybe before you agree to take her on, you should meet her. If you don't feel comfortable with her, I'll find someone else."

"I told you I'd take anything you thought I could handle."

1

Already during my first year as a volunteer Guardian ad Litem, I had been through a complicated case and a criminal trial, so I was fairly confident that I could manage most situations, but I had been putting off accepting responsibility for a new child because I was completing a book. Finally, though, my desk was clear. I had delivered my latest novel and had many weeks to wait before I received the revisions from my editor. Our two sons were back in school. The bills were paid, the accounting files organized, so I had picked up the phone and called Lillian.

There is no traditional way a Guardian ad Litem receives a new case. There are always more children needing guardians than there are volunteers, and when an urgent one comes along, the coordinators will initially attempt to match a particular guardian with a child. When necessary, though, they parcel out a file to whoever will agree to accept it. Or, if a volunteer has time for a new case, there is almost always one ready and waiting.

"Let me send you the file," Lillian said. "We'll talk again after you've read it."

When I became a guardian in October 1989, our circuit court district—one of twenty in Florida—consisted of a central Guardian ad Litem program office with a small, dynamic professional staff that included Nancy Hastedt, the circuit director; Lillian Elliott, the administrative assistant who coordinated the volunteers; and Helen Bonito, the office manager. An attorney worked on a contract basis to advise the approximately forty volunteers responsible for a five-county district covering 4,231 square miles with a population of 573,144. Only 8.9 percent of the district's population is classified as people of color. With an average of 135 people per square mile, this is a sparsely settled area with one major urban center, a few medium-size towns, and much land given over to citrus groves, vegetable farming, cattle and goat ranching, horse raising, forests, recreational centers along rivers and seacoast, planned housing developments, and retirement communities. People over sixty-five make up 26.5 percent of the population, the largest group, while 17.3 percent are children under fifteen and 10.1 percent range from age fifteen to twenty-four.

Although guardians are supposed to be appointed for every child in the dependency court system, only 16 percent of the cases were covered at that time. When I finished training, I was the eleventh guardian in my county. In the beginning most of the people I met in the community had never heard of the program, and the initial part of every conversation was relegated to explaining what a Guardian ad Litem was. Four years later, as of September 1994, the paid staff had increased by three full-time case coordinator positions and we had opened two additional satellite offices. A half-time attorney was available to consult with 196 Guardians ad Litem, who were covering 409 active cases, which represented 57 percent of the children in the court system. Now most of the people I meet have at least heard about our work.

There has also been parallel growth in child advocacy throughout the United States. In 1977 Judge David Soukup of King County, Washington, was kept up at night by the Solomon-like decisions he had to hand down in family court without really knowing what was best for the child in question. Frustrated, he asked his bailiff to round up some volunteers who might help gather information for him about the status of these abused and neglected children. When fifty people showed up for his first informal brown bag lunch to discuss the issue, he knew he was on to a workable idea. Sixteen years later, this one judge's concept has spread nationwide and now there are approximately 37,000 people in all fifty states, including the District of Columbia, representing more than 116,000 children in court, in this the fastest-growing movement for their protection. Florida, where I live, has a model statewide program and representation available to children in every circuit court district.

A few days later the packet containing my next case arrived. I opened the legal folder and saw my guardian appointment papers with the name Lydia Ryan and her date of birth next to my name. Lydia was sixteen. I almost signed the acceptance papers at once, but considering the seriousness of the crime, I decided that it would be prudent to read the file first.

The most recent document was from the division of Children, Youth and Families stating that Lydia had been detained in the juvenile jail until the judge ordered her release, but her parents had refused to allow her to return home. One long sheet was filled in with the attempts made to contact Lydia's family, her parents' adamant refusal to take her in, as well as the investigator's attempts to find Lydia a bed for the night. This "lockout" constituted parental neglect. The next pages were computer printouts from the Florida protective services abuse hotline reporting system. All calls to this central registry were filed in this computer. An abuse complaint on Lydia's lockout had been entered against the parents. On it were listed two other children in the Ryan home: a ten-year-old sister, Audrey, and a seven-year-old brother, Mark.

Also attached was the shelter petition saying that there was no available parent, legal custodian, or responsible adult relative to provide supervision and care because "to wit: It has been alleged that Lydia's parents are refusing to pick her up from the detention center. The parents are also refusing to make any plans for Lydia's care." This document helped make Lydia a dependent of the state and was the reason why a guardian had been appointed. At the bottom it stated that "Lydia was charged with aggravated battery on her sister in May."

Her sister. I rechecked the official printout. Only two children were mentioned. The sister was ten. How could you put a ten-year-old in a microwave oven? Maybe there was a stepsister or the relationship was wrong. With multiple marriages and partners as well as children from various alliances, family kinships were sometimes confusing. Nothing in the file clarified this for me, nor did it explain where Lydia was presently living.

Our training had emphasized that the first chore of the Guardian ad Litem was to become a skilled investigator. We were not supposed to rely on—or duplicate—the previous work of caseworkers or law enforcement but rather locate and examine every relevant fact in the case. By applying creative insights we hope to evaluate and integrate our data with that of others to determine what action might be best for the child. Working back from the immediate crisis, we were to scrutinize other major turning points in that child's background, delve into the family circumstances as well as what had influenced the parents to make the decisions they had, also to analyze community and extended family resources.

Essential to this duty was the ability of the guardian not to jump to conclusions about the innocence or guilt of the perpetrator in cases of abuse. Actually the guardian was advised not to interview the child about the immediate incidents leading to the case because this was to be left to professionals, who understood how to minimize damage to the child as she relived the event. This policy also avoided having the guardian called as a witness. We had been told that if we used good listening skills the child would eventually tell most of the relevant details without being quizzed, but I wondered if this might be the case if Lydia had something to hide.

Anxious to locate the child herself, I contacted Mona Archibald, the HRS protective investigator assigned to the case. "Where is Lydia now?" I asked after the usual introductions.

"She was placed by her parents, with the approval of the agency and the court, at the Tabernacle Home for Girls,'' Mona said. ''Have you heard of it?''

''Actually, I have,'' I replied. Knowing that I was the guardian of several teen girls, a friend in the community had given me their brochure.

''Then you know it has a religious orientation.''

''Yes, but a sheltered environment might be better than a foster care home for a hostile and confused young woman. What I don't understand, though, is why she can't go home again?''

''Her parents believe she poses a risk to their other children.''

''Do you think she'll be there for a while?''

''The judge ordered her not to run from this placement or she will be returned to juvenile detention.''

''Then I guess I'd better see her there,'' I said, and thanked Mona Archibald for her help.

''Tabernacle Home,'' said the sunny voice on the phone when I called for an appointment to visit Lydia. I introduced myself and was told I was speaking with Marjorie Hoffman, one of the counselors. I explained that I had been assigned as Lydia's Guardian ad Litem and wished to meet her as soon as possible.

''Are you a Christian?'' Marjorie asked.

After a pause, I decided to be utterly frank. ''No, I am Jewish.''

''Well,'' Marjorie said with exaggerated politeness, ''we really cannot permit a non-Christian person to interfere with Lydia's program. She is a very vulnerable child, and until she is stabilized, we must be selective about who influences her.''

''I understand that,'' I replied coolly, ''however, I have been asked by the court to monitor this placement. I would be happy to come to discuss my role with you, and I believe you will find that we should not be in conflict, since we both have Lydia's best interests at heart.''

''Any policy change would have to be approved by the directors of our program, Pastor and Mrs. Shaw.''

''Fine. When might they meet with me?''

''They're unavailable until next Wednesday.'' Reluctantly I had to agree to wait until then.

I immediately contacted Lillian and explained my predicament. ''Perhaps you would prefer another volunteer, one more acceptable in terms of religion.''

''Never!'' Lillian huffed. ''What about separation of church and state?''

''What if they won't permit a non-Christian to visit her?''

"You are her court-appointed guardian and nobody can prevent you from seeing her."

"Shall I tell them that?"

"It shouldn't be necessary," Lillian said with conviction.

The Guardian ad Litem training classes compressed a minicourse in child welfare and legal issues into a three-day class for volunteers from other fields. Before being accepted for the program, our applications were vetted, thorough background checks were made, and references were carefully checked. But there were no special requirements. We were a diverse group of professionals, blue-collar workers, homemakers, retired people, students, teachers, nurses, and even writers. We came from a wide range of ages, races, backgrounds, and interests. Some were single, some were parents and grandparents, some were childless. Our reasons for wanting to volunteer were equally complex. A few had been from or knew of abusive families. Others, like me, had been galvanized by the Bradley McGee case and other horrifying press reports. Many worked in fields like education or medicine and saw the results of injury to children. Frustrated, they believed they could make a difference with their guardian work, if only to one child at a time.

When I completed the classes, I felt that I had neither absorbed the complex material nor was even remotely ready for any case, but in retrospect, I see that the preparation was much better than I realized. Nancy Hastedt, the circuit director, gave an excellent overview of the program, while Lillian Elliott, the case coordinator, instructed us on the rights and responsibilities of being an advocate. The staff attorney delivered a concise, yet thorough, outline of dependency law. A psychologist discussed milestones of child development, the cycles of abuse that permeate dysfunctional families, and the essential issues of attachment, separation, loss, and permanency. Sexual and physical abuse were covered by an unflinching presenter, who had slides and films to introduce the revolting ways children are injured by their disturbed caretakers. There were also lessons in communications, interviewing, and writing reports for both the program office and the court. A staff member of the Department of Health and Rehabilitative Services explained their rules, regulations, and partnership with guardians. A seasoned guardian offered vivid examples of what the volunteer job entailed from her personal experience.

When I accepted the Ryan case more than a year after the training and after having worked intensively as a guardian, I felt more secure in my role, and yet nothing I had been taught or learned in the field had prepared me for a confrontation with people who mistrusted me because I did not share their belief system.

The Tabernacle Home for Girls was set on the banks of a quiet curve in a meandering river that fed into the Gulf of Mexico. Directions took me through a pine forest, past live oaks draped in Spanish moss, down a bumpy dirt lane, to an old colonial house that had been recently repainted. A shiny van with the home's name on the side was in the driveway. I entered through the door marked OFFICE and met Marjorie Hoffman, a heavyset woman dressed entirely in white. The small room held two desks, a new computer system with a laser printer, a copy machine, and a small library. Every surface gleamed and materials were stacked in tidy piles. A girl knocked at the door and her request was dealt with. She was wearing a loose plaid pinafore hemmed at midcalf. Her long hair was pulled back with a matching ribbon and her freshly scrubbed face was devoid of makeup. In her hands she clasped a Bible, and when she replied to Marjorie, she looked down and said, "Yes, ma'am," then backed away.

"That's Tiffany," Marjorie explained. "She came to us six months ago after living for more than a year on the streets. She's one of our success stories," Marjorie continued as she ushered me into Mrs. Shaw's private office. This room overlooking the cove had been recently redecorated in pinks and blues, with oriental prints, silk flowers, and a couch with embroidered throw pillows.

After a few introductory remarks, Marjorie left me alone with Alice Shaw. Mrs. Shaw, in a tailored teal suit, silk blouse, and stockings, was formally dressed for Florida on a sizzling day.

"I had heard that this was a lovely facility," I commented, "but it is even nicer than I imagined."

"Then you probably know that we are all volunteers. We receive no compensation nor do we accept any state or federal funding. We survive on the generous donations from Christians, who believe in our work, and therefore we are free to run our program without any governmental interference." She stared at me challengingly.

"Tell me about Lydia. How long has she been here?"

Mrs. Shaw pointed to the file on my lap. "That must be in your paperwork."

"I know it was in June, but not the exact date or how she came here."

"Because of confidentiality rules I really cannot be that specific."

"I apologize for not giving you this sooner," I said, fumbling for a

copy of my court order. "Guardians are privy to all records on a child."
I handed her the document and read the pertinent sentence. " 'Upon
presentation of this Order to any agency, hospital, organization, school,
person or office . . . Lillian Elliott, Gay Courter, and the Circuit Director
are hereby authorized to inspect and/or copy, any records relating to the
above-named child without consent of said child and parents of said child
and records relating to her parents including any drug/alcohol records
and any routine progress reports relating to therapeutic goals, without
any further consent of any party to this action.' "

Alice Shaw held the paper as though she found it distasteful. "My
husband will have to study this."

My patience was waning, but I tried another tack. "I'm very interested
in learning more about your mission."

Mrs. Shaw allowed herself a small smile. "Currently we have five
girls in our program. We have a rigorous approach that works because
it offers the girls discipline for the first time in their lives. Initially a girl
like Lydia is shown how to ask Jesus to forgive her sins and to accept
him as her personal savior. Then she is introduced to the scriptures and
learns how the Lord's word impacts on every aspect of her daily life."

"What sort of routine do they have?"

"We wake them at five-thirty in the morning and they are in bed by
nine-thirty in the evening. Every moment is accounted for with Bible
study, exercise, and one hour of chores."

"What about school?"

"They receive a religious education."

"What about regular schooling?"

"It takes a year before the girls are ready to accept anything besides
the teachings of Christ. At the proper time they will be tested to see
where they are in school, and then an individualized program is designed.
Since the longest anyone has been with us is nine months, we are not
teaching school yet."

"Isn't that illegal?"

"These girls have already dropped out of school, so we are listed as
a remedial, therapeutic facility preparing their minds and hearts to accept
and appreciate an education when the time comes."

"Why does everyone have to lose an entire year?"

"We do not deviate from a well-established program that works."

"How long have you been doing this?"

"At this home, only eleven months, but it is based on a national
program called Teen Crisis Care."

"Is there any counseling?"

"The entire program is one of spiritual training, but we do have a Christian therapist who works with us."

"A psychologist?"

"She is trained by the church." Mrs. Shaw shook her head like a teacher annoyed with a slow student.

"How is Lydia adjusting?"

"Extremely well considering everything she has done."

"Actually, the records I have are somewhat confusing as to exactly what it is she did."

"In what way?" Alice Shaw asked in a helpful tone.

"Well, this business with the microwave oven for one. Was it her sister she injured?"

"Not exactly."

"Then what did happen?"

"We're aware that Lydia, like most of these girls, lies and cheats and manipulates to make herself sound better, but her mother has corroborated these facts. Lydia's boyfriend came over when the Ryans were not home. Her sister warned that if Lydia wouldn't let her do something she was not supposed to do, she would tattle to their parents. Lydia's boyfriend then threatened the sister that he would 'cut her up in pieces and put her in a microwave oven' if she called her mother. The poor child was so frightened she ran to a neighbor and the police were called."

"That's why Lydia spent three months in juvenile detention?"

"Lydia did not protect the child who had been left in her care."

"What happened to the boy?"

"His parents got him off, but the Ryans wanted Lydia to learn her lesson once and for all."

"What had she done to deserve a jail sentence?"

"Let me just say that she was no darling angel."

Two more girls in plaid pinafores strolled by the window. I asked, "May I see Lydia now?"

"Lydia does not have visitor privileges yet."

"I'm not a visitor. I am her court-appointed guardian and I have been directed by the judge to see her," I replied softly, but forcefully.

"We cannot make an exception. Before the girls can learn constructive ways to manage their lives, they must be isolated from the old destructive influences. For their own protection they have no money, receive no mail or phone calls. Nor do we allow any contact with the outside world, and they only see their parents once a month under supervised conditions."

"But I need to see Lydia so I can make an official report on her welfare."

"Unfortunately the other girls would not be able to separate a guardian visit from other special attention. Besides, Lydia's HRS worker is satisfied that she is under good care. As you can see, this is a safe, hygienic facility."

"I don't work for HRS, and as congenial as this home appears, I need to know how Lydia feels about living here."

"That's precisely why you cannot see her. Lydia could say anything, tell all sorts of tales to get released. She is a chronic runaway who escaped from her last shelter placement, and if she leaves here, she will be remanded to the juvenile delinquency center."

"I understand your point of view," I tried again, "but maybe I can explain it another way. Let's say Lydia was in a foster home, but the foster parents would not permit the Guardian ad Litem to visit. Might you not think they had something to hide? If I don't talk with her, I won't be able to attest to the fact that everything is fine."

"Just look around," Alice Shaw gestured. "Does this look like an abusive home?"

"Not at all," I allowed, "but I still need to see Lydia, and this court order gives me access to her."

"We won't be bullied by the court when we know we are right," Mrs. Shaw said, rising. Then she turned and gave a thin smile. "However, because you have gone out of your way to visit Lydia, and Marjorie may not have prepared you for our rules, I will arrange for you to meet with her briefly. Since she is legally our responsibility, I cannot grant you an unsupervised visit."

I was taken aback. Only known abusers were ever subjected to supervision when visiting a child. Seeing my offense, Mrs. Shaw's voice became honey-smooth. "Believe me, I am thinking of your protection as much as our own. These girls will do anything to get their way, even if it means unfairly accusing someone of improprieties. This is a delicate time because while Lydia has taken Jesus into her heart, she does not yet have the strength to fight off her demons."

Alice Shaw took some keys from her desk drawer. "One more thing. At this stage it is unhealthy for someone as fragile as Lydia to dredge up her past. Girls in this phase are filled with negative thinking that has to be erased. I am sure you know that the glass is better half-full than half-empty. We are teaching our girls to look at every day as a fresh start. I trust you won't violate this."

"I am here to introduce myself, to explain my role and, if she is amenable, to ask her a few questions so I can better understand her present situation."

"Yes, well . . . ," she murmured distractedly. Then she made eye contact with me. "Please consider that she is in a strictly controlled program and we can't confuse her by having her new values compromised by another counselor with a different set of doctrines."

"Guardians are not counselors, however we do try to be certain that our children are receiving every necessary service."

I watched Alice Shaw purse her lips with disapproval. "Are you suggesting that we might not be taking adequate care of her?"

I resented having my words twisted to put me on the defensive. I took a deep breath and continued. "No matter what Lydia has done, or what facility she lives in, she is still an American citizen with legal rights, just as even convicted criminals have rights. And one of her rights is to speak freely to her appointed Guardian ad Litem. I will abide by your rules now, and since this situation is different than any I have encountered, I will see her without demanding privacy. But because this goes against my directives as well as the Guardian ad Litem guidelines, I will have to check with my supervisor about whether or not I will be required to speak with Lydia alone next time."

"When might you wish to return?"

"In a week or so, or sooner if Lydia wishes."

"Our rules say visitors cannot come more often than once a month."

"Why don't we discuss that later? Right now I am anxious to meet Lydia."

Alice Shaw opened her mouth, then decided against further comment. She went into Marjorie's office and asked her to locate Lydia. In the meantime she gave me a tour of the downstairs, unlocking the chapel, the dining room, and well-equipped kitchen. "There are no sodas, candy, cakes or other sweets permitted because we must detoxify the children from their dependence on refined sugars and drugs."

Here was something with which I could wholeheartedly agree, and we talked about nutrition until Lydia was led into the empty classroom.

Lydia stared at her feet until she was introduced, then looked at me as though she were going to have to undergo an upsetting medical procedure.

"Hi," I said but did not approach her or offer my hand.

If Mrs. Shaw had said anything accurate about Lydia, the word "fragile" certainly described her. I had been expecting a tough cookie, a girl who could bully her sister and seem a real threat to her younger siblings, someone who needed a few months in jail to soften her hardened nature. But Lydia was a delicate, fine-boned young woman with streaky strawberry blonde hair and huge light-brown expressive eyes. She was dressed in a plaid pinafore with pink knit shirt, red socks, immaculate white sneakers. Lydia returned my smile with one of her own that seemed to slip out unexpectedly.

"This is Miss Gay," Marjorie said, then handed her a Bible to hold during the meeting. The counselor pulled out a chair from one of the student study carrels. "Why don't you sit here," she said to me. "I'm very busy so I won't be able to stay with you." With her chin she indicated Mrs. Shaw's office and her expression seemed to conspire with me slightly. I was certain this was with Mrs. Shaw's knowledge and felt they were playing some version of good cop/bad cop. "But I'll be in and out," she said, and went to the other side of the partition where we could not see her, though if she hovered nearby, she could hear us.

I introduced myself to Lydia as her Guardian ad Litem. "Have you ever heard of that before?"

"I've been in lots of programs and am used to all sorts of people messing with me so what difference does one more make?" she said without masking her irritation.

"What sorts of people?"

"You know, HRS people, public defenders, police, social workers, therapists. They all want to *help* me, but now that I have been saved I know that only Jesus can do that." Lydia's eyes shone with conviction.

"Jesus must be making a big difference in your life," I said softly. "I also can understand that I must look like one more in a long line of people you would rather not meet, but I'm different."

"Like how?"

"First, I will be here for you until you are eighteen, no matter where you live, even if you run away again or go back to the juvenile detention center."

"I'm not running away or going back to JDC ever again!"

"Good. But no matter what you do, I will still try to help you." I handed her my card with the GAL office numbers, told her how to place a collect call.

"I'm not allowed to use the phone here."

"Mrs. Shaw and I will have to work out who will be permitted to call whom and when. In the meantime, I will phone you at least once a week to check on you. And I will be visiting you too."

"They won't even let my mom in. She came twice and brought me clothes from home, but we couldn't see each other."

"Would you like to see your mother?"

"Yes, but not my father. He isn't my real father anyway."

I handed Lydia the Guardian ad Litem brochure. "Here are other ways I might assist you," I said and read aloud from the pamphlet. " 'The Guardian ad Litem protects the child from insensitive questioning and the often harmful effects of being embroiled in the adversary court process.' " I waited a beat. "That means a fight in court where two sides have different opinions."

"I've had my own lawyer already," she said with a superior sniff. "But I thought that lady from HRS was my legal guardian?"

Lydia was not the only one who misunderstood this point. HRS, represented by the caseworker Mona Archibald, was indeed Lydia's legal guardian under the courts. An HRS employee was the one who could sign her medical papers or withdraw her from school, while I, by representing her in the court proceedings, had other responsibilities, including making certain HRS did their job.

"I realize it is confusing, but yes, Mrs. Archibald works for HRS and will be in charge of your case for the social service agency, but I will be the person who represents what you want and need." I lowered my voice. "For instance, if you did not wish to stay here, I could help find you another placement."

"But I want to stay here!" Lydia responded loudly enough to have been overheard in Mrs. Shaw's office. "I know it's going to be tough, but they think I have what it takes to make it in the program."

I changed the subject. "What grade were you in when you left school?"

"I dropped out twice, so I never finished ninth."

"Didn't you like school?"

"Some of it was okay."

"What subjects do you prefer?"

"English. I want to be a writer."

When I grinned in response, Lydia gave me a challenging look. "Don't you think I can write?"

"Sure. It's just surprising because that is what I do. I'm a writer."

"Really? Do you write poetry?"

"Not much. I write books. But I like poetry. Who's your favorite poet?"

"Robert Frost. I had a book of his poems and I read about his life too."

"When I was your age, I memorized his poems."

"Do remember the one about the boy who died?"

"You mean 'Out, Out—'?"

Lydia's bright eyes glinted behind a film of tears. "Do you still know it by heart?"

"Some of it," I replied reluctantly because Mrs. Shaw would surely see any reference to this depressing poem as evidence of my leading Lydia to see the glass as half-empty.

"Say it," Lydia replied as a challenge.

"I think it begins, 'The buzz saw snarled and rattled in the yard/And made dust and dropped stove-length sticks of wood.' "

"You *do* know it!" Lydia's mouth gaped. "The part I like is when they say, 'And then—the watcher at his pulse took fright./No one believed. They listened at his heart.' " Her voice quavered.

" 'Little—less—nothing!—and that ended it,' " I filled in.

Lydia skipped the next line and whispered the last one. " 'And they, since they were not the one dead, turned to their affairs.' " There was the briefest pause, then Lydia blurted, "I guess you know about Teddy."

"Teddy? No, who is he?"

"My boyfriend. He was killed."

"Do you mean Teddy Kirby?" I asked very slowly as the grisly story came back to me. "The boy who disappeared and whose body was found a few months ago in the state forest?"

"How do you know so much about him?"

"It was in the papers," I said, recalling how many of us who had sons around the same age had been shocked by the case. In fact, my husband had assisted Teddy's father in transcribing some tape recordings to help the police find the murderer, who so far had eluded everyone. I decided against mentioning this coincidence to Lydia.

"I loved him." Lydia motioned for me to lean closer to her. "I was pregnant with his baby," she whispered, "but they made me get rid of it. You know . . ."

"An abortion," I filled in and she nodded. "Who made you?"

"My parents."

"And you didn't want to?"

"I suppose I did at the time, but if I had known what would happen to Teddy, or if I had known that it was a sin, I never would have agreed."

Just then Marjorie appeared from the other side of the room. "Lunch is almost over, Lydia. If you don't join the others, you won't get anything to eat."

My eyes locked with Lydia's. "I'll either call or see you next week."

Clasping the Bible to her chest, Lydia backed away from me, then hurried to the dining room. As I found my way out the back door, I saw Pastor Shaw interviewing a possible new admission, a girl whose arms were tattooed with snakes.

My next call was to Mona Archibald, the protective service worker at HRS assigned to Lydia's case. Mona said she had visited the Tabernacle Home once, knew it was religious oriented, and was satisfied with the facility. "Pastor Shaw estimated the cost of keeping a girl there at around a thousand a month."

"Is it true HRS pays nothing?"

"Yes, it is supported entirely by private donations."

"Do her parents contribute?"

"No, they can't afford to. Last year they had Lydia admitted to Valley View Hospital, a private mental health facility. Her hospitalization cost more than seventy thousand dollars, but when she stayed longer than the insurance allowed, her parents became responsible, and now they owe almost twenty thousand dollars. And that was before she got in trouble by putting the baby in the microwave oven."

"She never put a baby in a microwave." I explained what I had been told.

"That's what the paperwork says," Mona replied.

"I know, but the sister is a ten-year-old. Why didn't anyone question how she fit in a microwave?"

"Do you know about the knife or being tied to a fence?" This stopped me. "Then I suggest you read my file," Mona said.

"Okay, I will, but even so, don't her parents have a legal obligation to care for her?" I questioned. "I can't call up the state or a religious group and say that I am tired of supporting my teenagers because they are bratty or defiant or won't do their chores, or even because I already owe too much money for their bills."

"If Lydia had been placed by the court in HRS foster care, we could take legal action to force her parents to pay for her upkeep, but since she is in a private facility, we can't do that. Besides, this placement is saving the state a considerable amount of money."

"Do you know why Lydia was treated at Valley View?"

"Depression and drugs."

"Was this before or after her boyfriend disappeared?"

"Before," Mona replied. "Who told you about Teddy?"

"Lydia."

"Teddy and his crowd were into satanic rituals, which probably has something to do with the kid's murder. Fortunately, the people at the Tabernacle Home know how to deal with the results of those evil influences."

Since I hardly knew Mona, I tried to skirt the struggle between Satan and God that characterized the belief systems of many churches in the district. "I am mainly concerned that they aren't giving Lydia an education. If she were in foster care or at home, she could attend school."

"She dropped out of school before she went to the Tabernacle Home."

"Why can't she be reconciled with her family?"

"They are afraid she might harm the younger children again."

"But she never harmed anyone!" I protested.

"Well, you had better talk to Mrs. Ryan about that," Mona replied.

"I'm still uncomfortable with Lydia's lack of freedom at the Tabernacle Home as well as their secretiveness, which is preventing me from having a confidential relationship with her."

"The important factor is that she is safe and not able to cause any trouble."

"And not costing the state any money."

"We can't take over the care of every confused child who doesn't get along with her parents," Mona retorted, then said she had to take a call on the other line.

In order to investigate the Tabernacle Home, I turned to friends, the Brandons, a physician and his wife who are devout Christians. Darlene Brandon, who had been a teacher in several Christian academies, said she had met the Shaws but was reluctant to say anything about them until I explained they were in charge of a child for whom I bore a responsibility.

"I wouldn't allow either of them to walk my baby across the street," Darlene snapped. "You had better ask Harvey about them."

That evening Harvey Brandon began the discussion of the Tabernacle Home by mentioning their precarious financial situation. "They travel from church to church seeking donations and are always behind in their payments," he said.

"Would you trust them with disturbed young women?"

"I do have some concerns about their approach," Harvey began judiciously, then related a story about Pastor John Shaw. "I had a patient who was experiencing cardiac pains, but I never could find anything wrong with his heart. Then he told me that Pastor Shaw warned him that the Lord was going to punish him with a heart attack if he didn't shape up, thus creating psychosomatic symptoms. The next time I saw Shaw I asked him about it. He admitted saying it but did not feel he had done anything wrong by passing on God's 'message.'"

The next day I drove to the HRS office to acquire a complete copy of Lydia's file, something every Guardian ad Litem is entitled to have. The copy machine was outside the office of the department's attorney, Calvin Reynolds, and he stepped out to ask what case I was working on.

"Lydia Ryan," I responded without looking up from the pile of papers I was sorting.

"Oh, the microwave oven case," he said with a grunt to indicate his distaste.

I spun around. "She *never* put anyone in any microwave oven!"

"Then why was she in the juvenile detention center?"

"I don't know. You tell me! How can they put a kid in JDC for something she did not do, then when she has served time for no reason, place her in another kind of religious jail?"

Calvin, who was accustomed to the indignation of self-righteous guardians, tilted his head indulgently. "Have you been to the Tabernacle Home?"

"I was there yesterday."

Something in his expression made me realize he might not be as sold on the place as Mona. "From what the caseworker says it sounds almost too good to be true, but we could use some alternatives to foster care or group homes. In fact, we have three other teenage girls who might do well there. What's it like?"

"I have a few concerns . . ." I began cautiously. "For instance, the children's movements are restricted and they do not attend school."

"Come into my office for a moment," Calvin said softly. "I want to tell you about something that worried me."

After Calvin closed the door, he explained that before going to the Tabernacle Home, Lydia had run away from the HRS shelter to Jason's—that's her new boyfriend—house. Jason's mother suggested the Tabernacle Home, which was only a few miles away from where they lived. Lydia agreed to try it because she knew that if she got caught, she would be sent back to juvenile detention. After a few days, the Tabernacle Home persuaded Lydia's parents to sign the admission papers, but because she was technically a runaway from an HRS shelter, she had to appear in juvenile court.

"When Tabernacle Home received the subpoena for Lydia to appear for her hearing, Pastor Shaw telephoned me and said he was concerned that Lydia might run away again," Calvin explained. "He then asked my permission to restrain Lydia so he could guarantee her court appearance. I asked how they would do that, and he said, 'in handcuffs and shackles.' "

"What!" I exclaimed. "Are you serious?"

Calvin shook his head somberly. "Of course I told him absolutely not, but later I wondered how they would have acquired that sort of equipment."

"Now I can see why they don't want me to speak with her alone," I muttered.

Since my first phone call I had felt ill at ease with the Tabernacle Home, and nothing I had heard since had modified that sentiment. Now my antennae were fully extended. This girl needed my protection and nobody was going to deny it, even if I had to see the judge.

Since it was difficult for me to understand the strong religious underpinnings of the situation, I asked my husband, Phil, who had been brought up as a Christian and attended a fundamentalist university, for his perspective.

"First, don't jump to conclusions," Phil warned. "Even though they are restrictive, they might be offering her something she really needs: an accepting family. Also, by the simple act of being saved, she could be relieved of vast stores of guilt for past misdeeds."

"I still can't shake the sense that there is something wrong." I told him about some of the Tabernacle Home's rules.

"You say she has been saved?"

"Yes, and she is happy there, or claims she is."

"The control doesn't make sense from a spiritual point of view. The moment she accepted Jesus she was saved from transgression." He was thoughtful for a moment, then replied, "I'd be worried there might be something less savory going on there."

Even though it sounds as if I sail through the churning seas of my cases solo, I check every turn of the wheel, every course correction, with the professionals in the Guardian ad Litem office. Every letter that goes out in my name is first sent to the main office for approval and is cosigned by a staff member. Within days of completing the training course and other requirements, I was assigned my first case, which was managed by Lillian Elliott. When she wasn't there, her superior, Nancy Hastedt, was available to answer questions. I never made a move without their guidance then, and even now, I frequently check with them. Almost always they give me the green light to proceed on the course I think is best, but since there are legal consequences to my actions, it is always prudent to have a second opinion. More essential is the guidance and support they provide in helping to analyze the reactions of the players and deciding how to proceed.

Lillian, a young and feisty grandmother who has a shelf filled with tennis and golf trophies, is a woman with uncommon sensitivities to what motivates people. Raised to be a southern lady by her mother, a doyenne of Atlanta's elite society, she is always immaculately dressed. Although I've never seen her in white gloves and a straw hat, she wears them in my mental portrait of her. After raising her four children, Lillian expanded on the many volunteer activities she had undertaken as wife of a prominent banker by accepting supervisory positions in charity programs. Her interest in children's issues led her to become one of the first members of the Guardian ad Litem staff when an office opened in her city.

On the phone Lillian's voice has a molasses-rich drawl and her words are always genteel. Yet there is no indirectness, no beating around the bush to her instructions. I have never accustomed myself to her forthright way of piercing the core of a question. ''When was the last time you had sexual relations with your daughter?'' or ''Are you going to get tested today for drug abuse and tell me the results?'' or ''Do you think she is telling you the truth about the rape?'' are the types of inquiries Lillian makes softly, gently, yet with such persistence everyone—including me—feels compelled to answer forthrightly, even adding ''ma'am'' at the end of the sentence.

Twenty years younger than Lillian, Nancy Hastedt comes from a family of liberal educators in Detroit. As an idealistic teenager she worked on inner city youth councils and took a degree in education at the University of Michigan. Her distaste for northern winters convinced her to apply to a Florida school for her MBA, where she met her husband and settled down. She thought the best way to make a meaningful contribution was as a foster care caseworker for HRS, so she worked in that department for five years. Frustrated by a bureaucracy that was systems-oriented rather than people-centered, Nancy tried to establish reforms from within. When the circuit director of the local Guardian ad Litem program resigned to move out of state, Nancy applied for and won the job, which placed her on the other side of the table from her previous cohorts. Nancy's insider's view of the social service system gives her the perspective she needs to represent the children under her jurisdiction.

Nancy's style is flamboyant, especially compared to Lillian's gentility. With the broad shoulders and narrow hips of a Nolan Miller model, she has a wardrobe more suitable for an appearance on "Dynasty" than in a courtroom, yet she never seems inappropriately dressed. Her hair, a mass of dark short curls that defies the authority of the comb, is the antithesis of Lillian's sleek silver page boy. Yet there are no clashes between the two women. With varying styles—and great élan—each takes up the battle cry to give every child the chance he deserves.

In the early months when I looked to them for direction, they'd always first ask me how I perceived the problem and how I thought it best could be handled. Not a team player by nature, I was hesitant to state my nonconformist ideas. Each time, though, I was pushed much further in the direction I had been heading than I ever thought I would be allowed to go. When some of these maneuvers were successful, I concocted bolder plans, and soon I would ask myself: what is the fastest, best, easiest way to accomplish what this child needs? Then I would check with the office, which acted more like the cheering section than the umpire, and proceed to act on my scheme.

After my initial hostile visit to the Tabernacle Home and discovery that Lydia may have been wrongly accused, I suspected I was going to need more than a modicum of their wisdom and assistance to serve this child's best interests.

Anxious to hear the story from Lydia's parents, I telephoned her home and spoke to her mother, Catherine Ryan. After explaining my role, I asked to set up an appointment.

"I don't get off from my job as a bookkeeper until after five and then I am taking a college class two nights a week. I also have Scouts one night, my husband is fixing the roof for his aunt, and we have relatives coming."

"Isn't there an hour we can squeeze in somewhere?"

"I don't see what good it would do. My husband says Didi made her own bed, so now she can lie in it."

My jaw clenched. "Mrs. Ryan," I began in a purposefully deeper tone of voice, "I may not have explained my role to you sufficiently.

The judge has requested a thorough investigation of this situation. The rules require that I speak to Lydia's parents. So your cooperation is not optional, it is court-ordered." I knew I had overstretched my authority slightly, but someone had to stand up for Lydia.

"I see," Mrs. Ryan said, and made arrangements to meet me on Wednesday.

I arrived at exactly five-thirty, the appointed time. The one-story house was at the end of a rutted lane. Surrounded by an overgrown lawn and untrimmed bushes, the exterior paint was peeling and one of the shutters on the living room window was hanging askew. A girl with Lydia's pale coloring, but with a much more robust body, was sitting on the steps twirling the front wheel of her bike.

"Hi," I said. "I'm a friend of Lydia's. Are you Audrey?"

"How'd ya know?"

"You look like sisters," I said while silently musing that there was no way this pudgy kid—the victim of record—could have fit into a microwave oven.

"Well, Didi doesn't live here anymore."

"I know, but your parents are expecting me."

"My dad's not here." I looked at my watch. "And he won't be coming, either. He's bowling."

"Is your mother home?"

Audrey stood up and opened the door. "Mom! The lady's here!"

The Ryans' living room was furnished with a worn blue sofa, scarred coffee table, console television, and one chair. There were no knick-knacks or decorations on any of the surfaces, and the stained carpeting betrayed the track marks of a recent vacuuming. Catherine Ryan was sitting at the kitchen table. She did not get up but allowed Audrey to show me in. She ground out a cigarette and gave me a resigned look. Now I could see where Lydia got her dainty figure. Catherine's face was taut, and she had dark rings under her eyes. I took the seat opposite her and placed a stenography notebook on the table. Because I thought it made families nervous, I rarely took notes, preferring to scribble down quotes as fast as possible as soon as I got to my car. In this case, since I wanted the visit to seem "official," I had decided to be more businesslike. To continue the formalities, I had brought along an interview form which could be used in a home study. I began to ask the questions in order, beginning with the mother's name, address, educational, family, and marital history.

Lydia's brother, Mark, came out of his room to check out the visitor.

"You are supposed to stay in your room," Catherine admonished him. He darted back quickly. Audrey peered around another doorway. "And you, young lady, don't you have homework to do?" Audrey did not move. "You want to have pizza later, don't you?" Audrey continued to stare at me. Catherine looked at her sternly and began to count, "One, two . . ." Audrey shot outside again.

I noticed Catherine was wearing a bowling league shirt. "Is Mr. Ryan coming?"

"No. It is bad enough that I have to dredge this up again."

"I'm sorry about that, but I have an incomplete file. I don't even know exactly why Lydia was placed in juvenile detention."

"We had to do something. Didi's been in trouble with the police so many times."

I realized that the family called her Didi, and I wondered if Lydia would prefer me to use it as well. I made a note to ask her. "When was that?"

"First, she kept running away. She must have disappeared at least fifteen times in the last few years."

"And these were reported to the police?"

"Not most of them. I usually knew where she was, so I guess you could call it a 'stay away' more than a 'run away.' If she didn't like one of our rules, she would stay with friends until she felt like coming home again."

"Any other problems with the police?"

"She was caught shoplifting once, but they didn't prosecute her, although Stu thought it would have been better if she'd learned her lesson then."

"Is Stuart Ryan her natural father?"

"No. Her father was my first husband, Mitch Long, but he was always drunk or high and he abused me and Didi. Once, when he was in the yard with her, she started screaming. I looked outside and saw him shake her arm and it was dangling in a peculiar way. I had to take her to the hospital because it was dislocated. He claimed she fell, but I had seen him do it."

"Did you tell the doctor that?"

"I didn't dare because Mitch would have laid into me. Then, a few weeks later, Mitch came toward me and hit my butt in a friendly way, but Didi thought he was going to hurt me and she started screaming hysterically. That's when I realized she was afraid of him, so I moved in with my mother and we divorced a year later."

Catherine went on to tell me that she met and married Stuart Ryan when Lydia was six. "He had a child with his first wife, but she left the area and he never saw his son again. More than anything he wanted to have his own family, so I got pregnant right away with Audrey, and when she was born, he legally adopted Didi so we would all have the same name."

"Did they get along?"

"I think she always resented losing my full attention and took it out on him, but he was good to her."

Catherine went on to explain that until her third child was born, Lydia did well in school, then suddenly she stopped doing her schoolwork and it caught up with her in the seventh grade, so she had to repeat it.

"They tried a drop-out prevention program, gave her special tutoring, but nothing worked. Now the high school won't even take her back." Catherine swallowed hard. "I don't know what we did wrong. Stu and I both have high school diplomas and I am working on my college degree by taking night courses—one a semester—at the community college."

Catherine held her palms out in a gesture of hopelessness. "I guess I should have listened to Stu more, but by the time I realized I had spoiled Didi, she was already involved with boys." There was a long pause. "You know about Teddy Kirby?"

"Yes, Lydia, I mean, Didi, told me he was her boyfriend."

"We knew he was up to no good because of the way he never looked you in the eye. We warned Didi about him, but she wouldn't listen. After she came out of the hospital, we thought that would be the end of it, but it wasn't."

"Valley View Hospital," I filled in. "Why did she go there originally?" I was trying to piece together the timing of the love affair, the pregnancy with Teddy's baby, the abortion, and the murder.

"She was into drugs and drinking. We took her to a psychologist who saw her a few times and billed us over three hundred dollars before he said he couldn't help her. He claimed she was depressed and might commit suicide, and besides our insurance would cover it if we put her in Valley View. Stuart agreed, saying it would be better to get her away from Teddy, but we didn't do it soon enough. When they did her physical, they found out she was eight weeks along." Catherine scrutinized my face for some sign of either condemnation or approval.

"That must have been a rough time for all of you. Where did you go?"

"To a clinic near the university."

"Was that what Didi wanted?"

"Not at first, but we made her see how it wouldn't be healthy for her to have the baby."

"What happened when she was released?"

"The whole family went to counseling, and the doctor said she wished other families cooperated and made as much progress as we did. But Didi knew how to act and what to say to make everybody believe she was doing well, then two weeks later she was seeing Teddy behind our backs." Catherine shook her head. "I'm not sorry he died."

Mark came in because the zipper on his jeans was stuck. Catherine took him into the bedroom to fix it. While waiting, I realized that Mrs. Ryan loved Lydia, but for some reason she had been unable to manage her, and her daughter had spiraled out of control. Every fear had come true. She had abused illegal substances and had sexual encounters, become pregnant, and the boy she had chosen had been killed, probably because of his involvement with drugs. Mrs. Ryan had two younger children to raise, obviously not much money, and was trying to better herself at the same time.

Catherine returned and looked at the clock on the stove. I realized it was getting to be dinnertime and asked whether I should come back another day. "No, I want to get this over with and Stu won't be home until after you leave and then he'll bring pizza."

It was clear Mr. Ryan was avoiding me. Annoyed, I asked, "What happened next?"

"For a while things seemed to get better. Lydia stopped skipping school and met this other boy, Jason. We thought our mistake with Teddy had been forbidding him to see Didi, so we had Jason over for supper. Stu warned him that he wasn't permitted in the house when we were out, but if we were home he was welcome to visit, and he could phone anytime. He seemed polite and agreed to abide by Stu's rules, but he fooled us."

"Was Jason the one who threatened Audrey?"

Catherine's eyes narrowed. "I don't blame him as much as Didi. She was the one responsible."

"Tell me what happened."

"It was Easter vacation, but we had to work, so Didi was in charge. Jason came over for an hour on Monday, then stayed all morning on Tuesday, and when he returned on Wednesday, Audrey mentioned that Jason had been there while we weren't home, however I didn't tell Stu, because he would have gone ballistic on me. I did warn Didi that Jason couldn't come over again. Then, on Thursday, he came by with his friend Doug. Didi wouldn't let them in the house, but she didn't tell them to go away. Audrey started to call me at work, but Jason heard her through the open window and ran in and hung up the phone. Concerned, I called back, and Audrey rushed to the phone. Jason caught her by throwing a towel over her head and started choking her so she couldn't pick it up. Mark became frightened and ran out of the house. Doug caught him and used his bicycle chain and locked him to the fence, then went in to help control Audrey. She was screaming and Doug told her to shut up. He pulled out one of the knives from the dish drainer and said 'Shut up, or I'll cut you up in little pieces and put you in the microwave oven.' Audrey jumped at him. The knife sliced her finger and it started to bleed all over the place. While they were cleaning up the mess, Audrey ran out and got on her bike. She saw a man in his yard and asked to use his phone.'' Catherine shuddered. ''He could have been any sort of pervert.''

''What happened after that?''

''Audrey called me from this man's house and said the boys had knives and Mark was chained to the fence. I couldn't leave work so I called the police. By the time the police got there, Mark and Audrey were alone and Didi and the boys had hidden in the woods. When they caught them, they took them off to the police station and contacted the boys' parents. The charges against them were dropped, but Stu told them to press charges against Didi, since she was supposed to be taking care of her sister and brother.''

''And they did?'' Catherine nodded. ''That's when Didi was sent to JDC for aggravated battery, assault, and false imprisonment.''

''Yes.''

''But she wasn't the one who tied Mark to the fence or cut Audrey with the knife. She didn't even threaten them, the boys did.''

''Anyway, it was time she suffered the consequences of her actions.''

''What do you mean?''

''I mean everything: the drugs, the drinking, the lying and cheating, for screwing up her life with Teddy and getting pregnant, and costing us a fortune at Valley View, and sneaking out, and breaking all the rules.'' Catherine's nostrils flared. ''We had failed, the doctors had failed, so we wanted to give the police their chance.''

''Did you visit her in jail?''

''No. Stu said she had crossed the final line.''

''That's why you did not pick her up from JDC and HRS put her in a home near the university.'' Catherine stared out the window. I continued to clarify. "Then she ran right away and lived on the streets with Jason until he told her about the Tabernacle Home."

"It's our only choice."

"Do you think it is the right place for her to be?"

"We can't put any more money into her and she requires full-time supervision."

"Are you visiting her there?"

"When they tell me I can come, I will, but her father won't. His wound is too deep."

I realized that it was getting late and asked if I could phone if I had any more questions. Catherine said that would be fine. She stood up to go to the door and said she knew that I was the writer because one of her friends had worked in our office.

"Did you know that your daughter wants to be a writer?" I asked.

"Well, Didi wants a lot of things she will never have," she said with a deep sigh.

A few days later I called the Tabernacle Home and spoke to Marjorie Hoffman about visiting Lydia later in the day. She said the best time to arrive would be at three-fifteen. A long phone call kept me in the office later than I expected and I arrived at three-thirty. Alice Shaw was waiting for me, making it clear I was late.

"Well, what have you learned?" she asked.

"I met with Lydia's mother, who gave me some background on the situation."

Mrs. Shaw had not yet taken a seat nor offered me one. She crossed her arms stiffly and said, "I meant what did your superiors have to say about abiding by the Tabernacle Home rules?"

Once again I felt out of step with Mrs. Shaw and perceived how formidable the girls in her care must find her. Because I wanted to see Lydia, I had to avoid a confrontation, and yet I could not capitulate to her either. I spoke slowly, saying, "I did check with Lillian Elliott, who firmly believes that I have every right to see Lydia alone. However, I won't insist on that right now. Last time I was here I told Lydia I would visit once a week and the most important thing is to be consistent with her. If I can just say hello and see how she is doing, that will be fine with me."

"You have not clarified anything for me," Mrs. Shaw replied tartly.

"Since I am a volunteer court appointee, I not only have rules to follow, but have to answer to both Mrs. Elliott and the judge as well as file accurate and timely reports on this case.''

''I realize that,'' Mrs. Shaw said with a modicum of sympathy creeping into her tone. Here was a woman who at least understood responsibility to superiors.

''Mrs. Elliott said she would contact you to set up an appointment so she can explain the Guardian ad Litem program in more depth.''

''She hasn't called yet.''

''She is away today and tomorrow, but I am certain she will try first thing on Monday. In the meantime, may I see Lydia?''

''I don't think that would be wise. Not because I don't trust you, but I need to know what the rules will be up front. If we let you see her today, then tomorrow you might come back and want to take her off campus.''

''The regulations are very simple. The Guardian ad Litem visits an assigned child a minimum of once a month, usually more often at first, and then as frequently as required. At regular intervals, she conveys the child's status to the judge and confirms that the child's needs for medical care, counseling, clothing, shelter, food, and education are being met.''

''Are you insinuating that we aren't meeting those needs?''

''Not at all. I don't pry or check further unless I have a suspicion. For instance, when I go into a foster home, if the children seem healthy, I don't open the refrigerator to see if there is food in the house.''

''You already saw that Lydia is receiving excellent care.'' Realizing that I was unconvinced, Alice Shaw tried a more collegial approach. ''A disturbed girl like Lydia might say things that might put our program in jeopardy. If she lasts with us long enough, I know that our ministry will work on her, but we have to be vigilant not to allow one child's misbehavior to spoil it for the others.''

She turned and opened her desk drawer. ''Let me show you something.'' She handed me a copy of the Tabernacle Home daily schedule, which listed prayer meetings, Bible study, religious workshops, meals, an hour of personal time, and an hour of exercise broken up into thirty-minute segments between 5:30 A.M. and 9:30 P.M. ''As you can see, there is no time for visitors.''

I glanced at the wall clock. It was almost four. The schedule said that was an exercise period. ''I could take her for a walk.''

''No, she will come inside and see you in the place you were the other day.''

Realizing I had won a small victory, I merely nodded in acquiescence.

Mrs. Shaw gave me a crooked smile. "Just like you, my husband and I are volunteers, and so it is important for us to know that this investment of our time yields something that is spiritually rewarding. But now, in Lydia's case, we have an obstacle that may not be surmountable." Alice Shaw leaned toward me as though she were trying to break through our differences with reasoning. "I know you don't want to be part of the problem. In fact, you think you are part of the solution, but because Lydia is the only girl with a Guardian ad Litem she will be corrupted in a way the others will not."

I forced myself not to say something I might regret.

In any case, Alice Shaw barely paused. "Let's say we allowed you to take Lydia outside this facility," she said, walking toward the door. "Because we would not be able to monitor what she might hear or learn, her training could be compromised. You must remember these are truly cunning kids with appalling reputations. So we must reevaluate her placement here. Maybe we would serve the Lord better if we put our time, energy, and money into another needy girl." Then Mrs. Shaw waved for me to follow her to the same area where I had met with Lydia before. After pointing to where I should sit, she disappeared.

In a few minutes, Lydia, wearing Bermuda shorts and a flowery blouse, came inside. There was someone cleaning the floors on the other side of the partition.

"Hi, Lydia. How are you?" I asked, genuinely pleased to see her again.

She looked up with flashing eyes. "Why are you back so soon?"

"I told you I would come in a week."

"Well, I don't want to come to live with you, and there is no way you can make me."

Startled, I wasn't sure at first what she meant. "I'm sorry if I gave you the wrong impression. I am not even allowed to take you to my house. I will only visit you where you are living, Didi."

"I thought you said you were going to be my foster mother." Then she scowled. "And who told you to call me Didi?"

"Your mother and sister used that name so I thought you preferred it."

"I don't ever want to be called it again."

"I'm sorry for the mistake, Lydia."

"So you met my parents?"

"Your father was out, but your mother talked about how much she and your father care for you. I think there is a lot of love in your family. Also, she helped clear up some of the things that happened."

"Like what?"

"Like the fact that you never put anyone in a microwave oven, and that most of it was not your fault, but you were punished and nobody else was."

"It was my fault and I deserved my penalty."

"Surely you did not belong in juvenile detention."

"I took drugs and had sex and even fooled around with devil worship."

"But that's not why you went to detention."

"I was on the wrong path and if I hadn't gone there I wouldn't be here or have accepted Jesus as my savior. I know that this is the only right path, in fact, I have proof that my prayers are working."

"What's that?"

"I have been praying for a guitar, and then the day after you were here a guitar was donated to the center."

"I'd love to hear you play sometime."

"I need better picks. Would you ask my mom if she could bring me my old ones?"

"Sure, I'd be happy to help." I paused. "Last night I found my book of Robert Frost poems and was reading them. If you like, I could make copies of some of the poems and bring them next time."

"I'm not allowed to read anything unless they approve. You would have to show them to Mrs. Shaw."

"Sure, that's fine." I could hear someone coming down the corridor and thought our time might be up. "You have a birthday coming soon. Is there anything special you want?"

"No, I already got my birthday gift from God."

"What's that?"

"You know, my guitar. But I would also like a dress to wear to church. One girl prayed for a dress and got a brand-new Liz Claiborne."

Alice Shaw appeared from behind the partition and indicated that Lydia should resume her exercise class, then led me to the parking lot door.

"Lydia is interested in some poems. Is it all right if I bring them next time?"

"There's still the matter to settle with Mrs. Elliott, but if that works out satisfactorily, you may give her something to read so long as it is upbeat, and nothing negative.'' We walked past a picture of the crucifixion. ''Nothing about death.''

As soon as I returned home I called Mrs. Ryan. I told her how well Lydia looked and asked about the guitar picks.

''We threw those away with the guitar. Her sister broke it after she left. Anyway, why do they let you see her, but not me?''

''Actually, they don't want me to see her either, but I have a court order. How do you feel about their rules?''

''They are strict, which is fine so long as she doesn't get caught up in all the other nonsense.''

''Like what?''

''Didi told me on the phone that they are boycotting Betty Crocker products because '*she's* a devil worshipper.' I tried to explain that Betty Crocker is a corporation, not a person.''

Catherine Ryan went on to tell me every weekend the girls were taken in a van to various churches several hours away so they could raise money for the Tabernacle Home. ''They don't socialize with the members of the congregations; in fact, they aren't even allowed to speak to anyone unless they are spoken to. And there is something else that is bothering me . . . .''

''What's that?''

''At work someone brought me one of the Tabernacle Home's mailings about a pro-life rally. Along with the fund-raising information was a paper headed, 'My Testimony by Lydia.' Using her real first name, she confessed about her abortion and what happened with Teddy. Even my friend knew who it was. I don't like my daughter being exploited in that way.''

''They never should have published that with her real name or without your permission.''

''Could you do anything about that?''

''I'm not sure, but I'll check,'' I said, happy to have a reason to collaborate with Mrs. Ryan for her daughter's benefit.

My next stop was to Sawgrass High School to copy Lydia's school records. Since she had lived in the same county her whole life, the records continued from kindergarten. The summary for each year was accompanied by her school photo. I lined these up and stared as the five-year-old child's chubby face became narrower and thinner and her wide, excited eyes seemed to lose their luster. In some of the pictures she wore glasses, in others not, and I wondered if she had a vision problem that had been neglected. For the first few years in primary school her statewide scores indicated she was three-to-five years above grade level and her report cards were excellent. Then, after around third grade, the *A*'s and *B*'s were replaced by *D*'s and *F*'s. In fact, she had failed two full years and had been retained once. Why? Last April, after leaving Valley View, Lydia had dropped out of school entirely. Something had gone terribly wrong but had been ignored. The last page of her records was her most recent discharge from high school before going to juvenile detention. Attached to it was a bill for a book that had never been returned to the library: *The Complete Works of Robert Frost.*

Later that day Lillian called to say she had discussed my access to Lydia at the Tabernacle Home with the circuit director. "Nancy reviewed the documents and found a few unusual aspects to the situation. First of all, the Tabernacle Home is not a licensed HRS facility, although since Lydia was placed there by her parents voluntarily, it does not have to be. Also, the courts have never declared Lydia a dependent or a delinquent. Ironically, she has been given an interim status as a 'child in need of services,' with HRS providing some supervision, but as it turns out, no services."

Lillian then put Nancy Hastedt on the phone.

"Are you saying that there is nothing we can do?" I asked her.

Nancy gave a throaty laugh. "Don't forget, the court appointed you as her Guardian ad Litem, and there is an administrative order saying no agency may interfere with a Guardian ad Litem. According to the judge, Lydia must complete the one-year program there; thus in accepting her, the Tabernacle Home has contracted to keep her in accordance with the rules of the court. That means that the Tabernacle Home may not interfere with your duties."

"What if they threaten to throw her out if I demand to see her?"

"That would be a breach of contract and they might be in contempt of court."

"Is fighting them really in Lydia's best interests? Maybe the best thing would be to leave her alone and do the most minimal supervision."

"Do you feel comfortable with that, Gay?"

"No, but—"

"Why don't we wait until I've visited the place. Lillian and I have an appointment tomorrow. Mrs. Shaw insisted we come without you."

The next afternoon Nancy phoned me with her report. "Hi, we just met with Mrs. Shaw." I waited, expecting her to have a different take on the situation and somehow find me at fault. "It's far worse than you led us to assume," Nancy groaned.

On the other line Lillian chimed in. "I can't believe that woman! The first thing she wanted was our rules listed in writing so she could show them to her lawyer."

Nancy continued. "Mrs. Shaw said the Tabernacle Home was private and did not accept funding, and that their attorney advised that a lawsuit against them would not hold water. And this is before we had a chance to say anything or even take a seat in the room."

"We tried to defuse the situation," Lillian interjected. "I told Mrs. Shaw that you said that Lydia wants to stay at the Tabernacle Home, and that you reported that it was a very adequate facility. In a conceited manner, Mrs. Shaw replied that of course it was. Then she went on to say that Lydia could not go off premises for six months, as stated in their student handbook."

"Oh, and Mrs. Shaw gave us a typed list of instructions for you to follow," Nancy added. "My response was to tell Mrs. Shaw that I trusted the good sense and integrity of my volunteers and so I would not dictate to you, or anyone else."

"What did she say?" I asked, imagining Mrs. Shaw's pique at a structure that did not have workers blindly obeying their superiors.

"As you might gather, Mrs. Shaw was very defensive, and again, rather than respond to the point, she attacked. She said she was very unhappy that I had accompanied Lillian without making it clear that it was going to be 'two against one.' "

"I wouldn't want to have to be on the opposite side of the room against you two either!"

We all laughed.

Nancy then became more serious. "Unfortunately, Mona—Lydia's HRS caseworker—was there the day before and tried to clarify the Guardian ad Litem's role to the Shaws. She did us no favor, and probably hurt us by explaining that since there were so few guardians, in her opinion, they should be given to younger kids."

"What should we do about Lydia?" I asked, refocusing on my case.

"I am worried that the Tabernacle Home is not a suitable placement," Nancy responded curtly.

"However, she is comfortable there for now," Lillian interjected in her honey-sweet accent. "What do you think, Gay?"

"Do you sense we can work with Mrs. Shaw?" I asked.

"I hoped we could," Lillian replied, "but she is one of the most dominating women I have ever met. Her way is the only way. I don't think she'll compromise."

"Also," Nancy added, "she is smart and has done her homework. By now she probably knows the legal situation as well as I do."

"Lydia wouldn't be welcome at her parents' home," I said, thinking out loud. "We certainly don't want her back in detention. If she is forced to go somewhere she doesn't like, she'll run away, and then be at risk on the streets. Why don't we back off until we can find her an alternative placement?"

"I'm supposed to talk to Mrs. Shaw tomorrow with a list of our demands. My feeling is that they have to comply just like anyplace else," said Nancy emphatically, "or else the child needs to leave."

I could see that this might not be solved until Nancy and the Shaws dueled at dawn, but where did this leave Lydia?

Lillian offered a suggestion. "We need more backup for our position. I have the name and number of the doctor who cared for Lydia at Valley View. Why don't you contact him and discuss whether he thinks the Tabernacle Home is a good placement for Lydia?"

"Wonderful idea!" I said, anxious for an objective opinion. "She's been so unstable for so long, I feared moving her from even an inappropriate placement against her will."

Stability. I thought about a recent lecture I had heard on the importance of permanence that compared children's emotional security to a bucket. If a child's needs are met, if she receives the love and attention she craves, the sturdy bucket does not leak. But as soon as she is abused or neglected, tiny holes begin to puncture the bucket, and the vital fluids that maintain a child's stability start oozing out. If a child who enters the social service system isn't maintained with transfusions, the essential elements slowly drain away. Even worse, the system itself is capable of widening the holes, or even punching fresh ones. Moving children from place to place, treating them unfairly, not meeting their needs in a timely manner—all contribute to the leakage. Eventually it will not matter how fast you try to replenish the pail; like a sieve it empties itself instantly.

Fewer holes in the bucket. I had to keep that in mind and not unwittingly become another archer shooting arrows, even if my aim had been meant for a higher purpose. If the folks at the Tabernacle Home, with the help of Jesus, could mend Lydia's lacerated spirit, I did not want to be the one to reopen the wound.

And yet everyone, including the psychiatrist who had treated Lydia at Valley View, confirmed my sense that the Tabernacle Home was not in Lydia's best interests.

"She's too easily led and needs to learn to rely on herself, not another cult," the doctor told me.

"What are the chances for family reunification?" I asked her.

The doctor was extremely negative about Stuart Ryan, calling him "brittle, authoritarian, and mean." She also warned that if Lydia had to live with her family, she might be at risk for suicide. "Why doesn't HRS find her a supportive foster family?" she asked.

"Although her parents don't want her, Lydia is not yet a legal ward of the court," I explained.

"Aren't there any other alternatives in your community?" the doctor asked before hanging up.

From experience I knew that once HRS was in control of a child, they could move her without anyone's permission. My work with other guardian children had taught me that confused teenagers were the least likely to last long in one foster home. There were a million excuses for dumping them. A caseworker might determine that another child would do better in the home, and move the teen, or the foster parents could change their mind at any point. One call to the caseworker and the child was on the move again. So what other possibilities were there? Lydia was not a bad child. Maybe I could find an idealistic, affectionate family with a spare bedroom.

Barely containing my enthusiasm, I called Nancy. "Would it be permissible to place Lydia informally with another family?"

"As long as they did not expect state reimbursement, I don't see why not. Just remember Lydia has been adjudicated to the Tabernacle Home, so we have to deal with them first. I am supposed to call our friend, Mrs. Shaw, and tell her what rules we are going to stipulate. What should I say?"

"There's no reason to capitulate to them, is there?"

"Absolutely not. It would set a bad precedent."

I scribbled a list and recited it. "Initially I want to see Lydia two to three times a month, once outside of the facility, with arrangements beforehand about where and when it will be. The other times I want to see her alone either in a private office or outside on their grounds. I want to be able to call at an appropriate time to make these arrangements and I want her to be permitted to phone me whenever she wishes during her free time. She can call the guardian office collect so it won't cost them anything. Is that too much to ask?''

''Not at all. That's what any other guardian would want.''

However, despite Nancy's optimism, Alice Shaw's response was that she would get back to us with their counterproposal.

Nancy would not retreat. ''I told Mrs. Shaw that since this is court ordered, and not some privilege Lydia has to earn, our points are not negotiable.''

''How did she react?'' I asked.

''Mrs. Shaw's voice was icy and very formal, and she said, 'We'll have our decision by Wednesday, but I must ask that you warn your guardian to refrain from contacting Lydia before then, for the child's sake.' Since I didn't want Lydia to suffer because of our stance, I agreed.''

A few hours later the phone rang. ''Gay? Nancy. I just had a call from Mona Archibald at HRS. Pastor Shaw called her a few minutes ago and informed her that they will ask Lydia to leave unless we back off from our unreasonable demands.''

''What should we do?'' I asked.

''You can modify your requirements or . . .'' She drifted off. ''Just a moment, Calvin Reynolds from HRS is calling on the other line. You want to hold?''

''Sure.'' I closed my eyes and wished I had turned the case back to Lillian when the religious question was raised. Another guardian more acceptable to the Shaws might have protected Lydia better.

Nancy was back on the line. ''There's going to be an emergency hearing next Monday to allow the judge to determine whether Lydia will remain in the Tabernacle Home under their rules. That gives us a few more days to find an alternative for Lydia.''

Here was a challenge I relished. Producing films often brought the same rush, especially when something that had been set up for a long time fell apart at the last minute because of weather or a technical problem or an illness and I had to use all my wiles to save the day by lining up a completely different program. I called several former Guardians ad Litem, the heads of two neighboring programs, the director of a girls' school upstate, the district manager of several special HRS programs, a few wealthy women in a nearby city who might know someone who would take Lydia in. Then I started on my personal list of contacts. I picked two families, one in our community, one about fifty miles away.

"I would take her myself," I told my friends truthfully, "but it is a hard-and-fast rule that guardians may not even bring their clients to their homes."

Both families showed some interest but wanted to know more. My immediate concern was where Lydia would sleep Monday night if the judge ruled that she should leave the Tabernacle Home at once. Perhaps the Shaws would keep her a few more days, but based on their behavior, I thought that unlikely. I called Becky Morse, the foster mother of one of my other guardian children, and asked if she could act as an emergency shelter.

"Sure. Tell Mona Archibald that I will expect the group rate for her care, which is what I get for short-term kids."

"Becky, she's not in the system, so maybe they won't pay anything. If it turns out that way, couldn't you give her a few days without payment?"

"No, even if I would like to help you out this once, I don't dare, because then HRS would constantly be asking for freebies and favors."

"But if the judge orders her in shelter care, then HRS is obliged to pay you, isn't that right?"

"Yes."

"So, if that happens, would you take her in?"

"Yes, of course I will."

I awoke Monday morning dreading the shelter hearing. Before I went downstairs for breakfast, I pulled out the encyclopedia and looked up the Constitution of the United States. I opened to the preamble, something I had not read since the sixth grade.

The words "in order to form a more perfect Union, establish justice..." came alive for me. I turned to the amendments and scanned the Bill of Rights: Freedom of Religion, Speech, and the Press; Rights in Criminal Cases, Rights to a Fair Trial, Women Suffrage, and Civil Rights. What seemed to be missing, however, was children's rights. Even though you couldn't legislate love, why, at the very least, weren't children specifically given the right to safe, permanent, healthy homes? Just as women were no longer considered chattel, shouldn't there at least be an amendment listing the basic entitlements of every American, no matter the age?

At that moment, though, my immediate concern was a home for Lydia. I had no firm offers for Lydia, only a few ideas of places she might visit. Anyway, there was always the possibility that Judge Donovan, who had ordered her to the Tabernacle Home to begin with, would agree to the Shaws' demands, discharge his guardian—or suggest only the most minor supervision—and leave her where she was.

Nancy Hastedt and Lillian Elliott greeted me on the courthouse steps. "I didn't expect you both to come."

Nancy grinned. "I never turn down a ringside seat."

"We're waiting for Thorn," Lillian said, referring to Kit Thorndike, the lawyer who worked half-time for the Guardian ad Litem program, and whom we liked to think of as a "thorn in the side" of our opposition.

"Do you think the Shaws will bring their attorney?"

"Nothing would surprise me," Nancy said, her eyes gleaming.

I knew that Nancy relished this sort of challenge and that there were possible precedent-setting legal issues, but all I could think of was Lydia's reaction to having her life turned topsy-turvy once again. After Thorn arrived, I briefed them about the shelter bed at the Morses' and some of my possibilities, then we went upstairs to the courtrooms.

As we passed through the metal detector, we were greeted by Mona Archibald, who acknowledged Thorn and Nancy with a sardonic grin. "Why all the big guns for the microwave case?"

"Lydia Ryan never put anyone in a microwave oven!" I seethed.

Mona shrugged at Lillian. "That's what's in my file."

"I don't think you've ever read that file," I snapped, "or you would realize that a ten-year-old can't fit in a microwave and that Lydia wasn't even in the house when the incident occurred."

"I just don't understand why you are so hell-bent and determined to destroy this placement," Mona sputtered.

As Mona left to talk to the HRS attorney, Nancy rolled her eyes. "A bit hostile?" she asked rhetorically.

"Speaking of hostile, look over there." Lillian's eyes indicated the Shaws, who were standing at the far end of the corridor with Lydia in between them. She was dressed in a loose-fitting flowered dress, two sizes too large, with a soiled white collar. Her eyes were downcast and she was clasping a Bible.

"I should talk to her," I said.

Nancy pulled me back. "Not until the judge rules."

I smiled in Lydia's direction, but Alice Shaw blocked me, then took Lydia's hand, bowed her head, and said a prayer.

The bailiff called the Ryan case. We trooped into the judge's chambers. I was relieved that Judge Donovan preferred to hear juvenile cases privately. He also felt that black robes frightened children, so he wore cowboy shirts with pearl buttons and string ties with fanciful ornaments on the slide.

"Anyone else?" the bailiff called before closing the door. A short man, with a square frame, appeared from the waiting room. "Who are you?" the bailiff questioned.

"Stuart Ryan, the kid's father."

I looked around for Catherine Ryan, but she had not accompanied him. The guardian's chair was to the right of the judge, who sat at the end of a long conference table with the court reporter on his left. I deferred to Nancy, expecting—even hoping—she would take my place as spokesperson, but she gestured for me to be seated. Thorn pulled out the chair to my right, facing Calvin Reynolds, the HRS attorney, who had his paralegal at his side. Since there were not enough seats at the table, Nancy and Lillian stood behind me. Mona Archibald sat on the HRS side of the table, along with her supervisor. Stuart Ryan took the head of the table directly across from the judge. The Shaws, with Lydia between them, were given the bench behind Lydia's father.

Calvin Reynolds introduced the case while the judge thumbed through his papers.

"Who speaks for this child?" the judge asked. Calvin pointed to me. "Where's the guardian's report?"

Calvin indicated which document it was. Since this was an emergency hearing, the judge probably had not read my report ahead of time. Instead of skimming the introductory paragraphs, then skipping to the recommendations as he usually did, Judge Donovan leaned back and began reading the pages word for word. Those who had official copies read along.

My report first reviewed every court action and placement in chronological order, then was followed by a list of the people I had interviewed and the records I had in my possession. Next, I gave a factual account of the information I had received, the points of view of the people I had interviewed. In giving my impressions of the Tabernacle Home, I reported my observations in a flat, unemotional style. As to the educational program, I stated:

> A girl is not given any schooling until she has committed herself to changing her life and turning herself around. This takes a year. Only counseling and various therapies, combined with spiritual work, is undertaken during that time. Once a girl has been in residence for a year, she will be tested by the Accelerated Christian Education curriculum to determine where she is in

school. Then she will begin her studies with individual tutoring. Since no one has been in the program longer than nine months, no one has received any education yet.

Regarding the strict rules, I quoted from the Tabernacle Home manual and summarized Mrs. Shaw's explanations.

The girls have very limited contact with the outside world, see only their parents under supervised conditions, have no money, and are restricted in their fraternizing with members of the church communities they visit for worship. This isolation is considered important in having them give up their old, destructive ways and building a new positive future for themselves.

I factually described when and how I had been permitted to be in contact with Lydia, quoted from my discussions with her psychiatrist, and included copies of the clinical notes Valley View had sent in response to the court order. These medical files were not circulated to the others but were available for the judge to read and would become part of Lydia's sealed file.

Determined to set the record straight about the microwave oven, I retold that incident in some detail, quoting from police files, and went on to say:

Lydia Ryan was sent to the juvenile detention center and released 45 days later. The Ryans were very upset with Lydia. They did not visit her in JDC because they felt she allowed this situation to happen, even if she did not fully participate. "She crossed the line," reported Catherine Ryan. At the time of her release her parents refused to allow her back in the home and she was placed in shelter care. Lydia ran away from there, but then found the Tabernacle Home through a friend and her parents signed her in. Lydia Ryan was deemed a Child in Need of Services (CINS), was placed under Protective Services of HRS, and adjudicated to remain at the Tabernacle Home and complete their one-year program. She was also ordered not to run from that placement.

I recounted my visits to the Tabernacle Home and described its amenities and cleanliness, then noted the problems I had experienced in trying to see Lydia.

Alice Shaw explained that if the rules of the Tabernacle Home were violated, they would rather dismiss Lydia Ryan from the program than bend to the Guardian ad Litem's request. Since Lydia Ryan has been unable to speak freely to her Guardian ad Litem yet, her real wishes and desires are not known at this time.

Kit Thorndike had faxed me some legal points he wanted included in the report and I had been careful to use the language he proposed.

The Florida Supreme Court Administrative Order for the Guardian ad Litem program states in *Standard 5.3* Guardian ad Litem Right of Access to Child:

"The circuit director shall assure that the Guardian ad Litem's access to appointed children is not restricted by any agency or person. Visitation by the Guardian ad Litem, which includes transporting the child away from placement, should be arranged with the caretaker or supervising agency prior to the visit."

At this time, such access is being willfully withheld by the Tabernacle Home, which makes it impossible to continue oversight by a Guardian ad Litem. Lydia is thus denied protection of her civil rights. There is little or no supervision of this program by any outside licensing or unbiased authority. However, Lydia is involved in a rigorous conversion program that could have positive benefits for this fragile young woman.

Everyone in the room turned to the final page, my list of recommendations. I glanced at Lydia's father, whose beefy face had reddened from his neck to the top of his almost-bald head.

As Guardian ad Litem for Lydia Ryan, I make the following recommendations:

That, if she wishes, Lydia Ryan be allowed to remain at the Tabernacle Home temporarily until a better situation can be found. This desire to remain should be communicated, in private, to her Guardian ad Litem and another witness of the Court's choosing.

That Lydia Ryan remain, if possible, in Child in Need of Services status so that an appropriate placement outside the traditional foster care system can be found.

That if such a placement cannot be found within 30 days, that Lydia Ryan shall be adjudicated a dependent of HRS.

That if she is adjudicated dependent, HRS should endeavor to find her the least restrictive placement that meets her needs.

That she receive a psychological and educational assessment to help place her in the most appropriate program and environment.

That she be placed in a nonpunitive program that will help her prepare for independent living, while catching up on her high school education.

That the appointment of the Guardian ad Litem be continued in this matter.

Judge Donovan put down his papers. "I would like everyone to leave the room, with the exception of Lydia Ryan and the court reporter."

Calvin Reynolds started to say something, then thought the better of it, and stood.

We stood in predictable clumps in the judge's antechamber, a room too small to comfortably hold this divergent group. The Shaws took one corner while the HRS attorney, paralegal, Mona, and her supervisor conferred in the other. Stuart Ryan crossed his arms and stared at the ceiling while Nancy, Thorn, Lillian, and I formed our own tight circle.

"Is this usual?" I whispered.

"Never saw it happen before," Nancy replied.

"What do you think she will tell the judge?" Thorn asked me.

"That she wants to remain where she is."

"But do you think she can speak honestly?" Lillian wondered.

"It is all she knows right now."

Since we were the only ones talking, it was hard to be certain our words weren't overheard, so we fell silent too. After an interminable fifteen minutes, the court reporter opened the door to the inner office. Sitting where her father had been, Lydia looked shattered. As she clutched her Bible, tears streaked her face and her nose was running. I waited for the Shaws or her father to hand her a tissue, but nobody offered her one.

We were barely seated when the judge gave his ruling. "I have decided that the Tabernacle Home is too restrictive for an almost seventeen-year-old girl, and I am removing her from that facility. She is going to have to make her way in the real world soon enough and needs proper preparation for that challenge. Any comments?" He looked directly at me.

"I want to make it understood that I am not asking for her removal from the Tabernacle Home, and have only requested traditional access for her protection."

"Anyone else?" He raised his eyes toward the Shaws, but they didn't respond.

Stuart Ryan cleared his throat. "As her father, I do not understand what is going on. She is our daughter, and her mother and I want her home."

This came as a surprise, but perhaps he did not want to go on record as rejecting her again.

"Maybe that will be possible in the future, but not now," the judge said firmly.

"Then where will she be placed?" Calvin Reynolds asked.

Again Judge Donovan turned to me. "The Guardian ad Litem is to find Lydia a home where she would like to stay, and Lydia is to participate fully in the decision." He replaced his glasses, turned to the next file, effectively dismissing those present.

Stuart Ryan departed abruptly. Alice Shaw said, "I'm sorry it worked out this way, Lydia." Lydia handed her the Bible and the Shaws exited the room. Mona followed them, presumably to make arrangements for the transfer. The rest of the Guardian ad Litem staff passed behind me, while everyone else stayed in their seats in preparation for another hearing. Lydia seemed frozen in place. I guided her through the judge's outer office, into the hallway, and toward the elevator bank just in time for her to see her father getting on an elevator with the Shaws.

"Daddy!" she said so softly he could never have heard. She turned away, so I took the full force of Alice Shaw's glacial stare. In a paroxysm of pain Lydia gasped and I thought she might vomit. I pushed her into the rest room and rolled off a wad of toilet tissue in a futile attempt to assuage her cascade of tears.

"Lydia, I'm sorry. I know it is my fault that you are feeling like this, and if there had been anything I could have done to prevent it, I would have."

"What's going to happen to me now?" she sputtered.

"I have some ideas . . . ," I began lamely. After my trying to stop anyone from punching holes in her bucket, my very actions had opened this mighty cavity. Now, empty-handed, I stood before her with nothing to plug it.

"I want to go back to the Tabernacle Home. I liked it there! Why won't anyone listen to what I want?"

"What happened when you were alone with the judge?"

"He questioned me about the program, and then asked if I wanted to stay."

"And you told him you did."

"Yes, but he didn't care! He said he thought it was not healthy for me to be shut away. Everyone is always pushing me around and telling me what to do, and then when I finally am getting somewhere, they kick me out."

"I know that is how it seems, but the Shaws would not follow the rules of the court, rules that are in place to protect you and other children. Otherwise a lot of kids could be abused and we would never know about it."

"They didn't abuse me, they showed me how Jesus loves me and how to turn my life around."

I thought of Phil's words about what it meant to be saved. "You have accepted Jesus as your personal savior, right?"

"Yes," Lydia said with a hint of defiance creeping into her voice.

"Then he will always be there for you. Nothing that happens can ever take him away from you."

Lydia's sobs became muted. "Where will I go?"

"Tonight you will stay in a shelter home. I already spoke to a wonderful family, and if HRS agrees, they will look after you for a few days. Then, we'll do what the judge said. You and I will go around and visit lots of places and you will decide where you want to live."

"I want to go back with the Shaws."

"Maybe the Lord has other plans." I waited a few beats, then added, "You heard your father, he said he wants you to come home. Maybe that is where this is all leading. Would you like to go home?"

"More than anything . . . ," she said, followed by a fresh gush of tears.

"But that is not going to happen tonight."

"I have to go to a Christian home."

"The people I spoke to are Christians."

"Are they the right sort of Christians?"

"What would be the right sort?"

"Pentecostal Christians, who live God's word."

"I am not sure whether the people tonight will be exactly that, but we can make that our goal for the future," I said, thinking that a canvass of some fundamentalist churches might lead to a home for Lydia outside the social service system. I smoothed back Lydia's hair.

Mona opened the bathroom door. "There you are!" she said to Lydia.

"I've been on the phone trying to find you a bed tonight, but nothing is available yet. Why don't you come back to the office with me and we'll see what we can arrange?"

"I checked and Becky Morse said she would take her."

"It is hardly the guardian's responsibility to call up our licensed homes and try to place children there," Mona huffed.

"I realize that, but I was only trying for a home where I thought Lydia would be comfortable for a few days."

Mona glared at me.

Lydia turned to her. "I need to get my things from the Tabernacle Home," Lydia reminded. "And I want to say good-bye to everyone there."

Mona looked at her watch. "This is really going to screw up my afternoon. Could you take her there and—" She stopped herself. "Forget it, that would never work. All right, how about this? I'll go get her things and meet you back at our office here."

Thinking that this meant I would be taking Lydia to the Morses', only a few miles from the HRS office, I agreed.

"See you later, Lydia," I said in a friendly way, but she did not respond.

At the appointed time I arrived back at the HRS office, only to be told that Mona and Lydia had waited for me as long as they could but had gone to the shelter home.

"Is she at Becky Morse's?"

"No, she was placed at the Fowlers' in Orangeville," Mona's receptionist said. "Here's the number. You can call there tomorrow."

"But I told Lydia I would see her this afternoon." The receptionist shrugged. "Do you know how to find the Fowlers' house?" She shook her head, so I phoned for directions. June Fowler said she was expecting a new girl, but she wasn't there yet. Then she explained how to find them, more than twenty-five miles from where I had been waiting.

When I arrived at the small ranch home with bright green shutters and a driveway blocked with two tricycles, a man on a ladder was fixing a rain gutter. "Is this the Fowler home?"

"Sure is," the man said in a soft Georgia drawl.

"Are you Mr. Fowler?"

"Nope. I'm Pastor Sharp. Our church owns this house and the Fowlers live here because he's our youth pastor."

I explained who I was, then asked, "What's the name of your church, pastor?"

"The Orangeville House of God."

"Is that a Pentecostal church?"

"Most certainly is."

Relief must have flooded my face and the pastor returned a wide grin, as if glad to have made contact with another believer. "Lydia is a Pentecostal Christian and she was praying for this."

"Praise the Lord," he said with a winsome grin.

I went inside and found Lydia sitting at the dining room table having a snack with the family. I was introduced to the two identical Fowler twins, Melody and Steffie, who were five, and another foster daughter, Candace, who looked about twelve. Mona had left a few minutes before I arrived.

"What are you doing here?" Lydia asked with some annoyance.

"I told you I would come by this afternoon."

"Mona didn't need you to drive me, so why did you come?"

"Because I wanted to see you."

"You know, I saw that report of yours and I am really upset about it," Lydia said with a sniff. "Now everyone knows about my private life, even things that I was told nobody would ever find out."

"When did you read it?"

"Just now, in the car."

"Mona Archibald gave it to you?" She nodded. "I don't think that was a very smart idea, but you have every right to be angry. You've had a horrible day and everyone has been pushing you around for a long time." The family at the table was listening intently.

"You're the one who wrote the report," Lydia said accusingly.

"Yes, I did. But I am sworn to secrecy and those other people were not to divulge what was in it either. But that doesn't help the fact that it must hurt to have your life opened up in the courtroom, especially when you haven't done anything to deserve it."

Candace, who was sitting next to Lydia, reached over and touched her arm. "You're going to like it here, you'll see. It's the nicest home I have ever known."

I smiled at Candace. "This is a shelter home for Lydia. She'll only be here a few days."

Candace giggled. "That's what they said to me, and I've been here more than a year."

June Fowler nodded. "Yes, once we get a girl we never want her to leave. And that goes for Lydia. We were just telling her we would like her to stay with us as long as she wants.''

I muffled my annoyance. Foster parents were supposed to have been better educated in the psychology of these temporary situations. ''That may be a bit premature, and besides, Lydia's situation is different. She has not been adjudicated dependent by the court nor is she a foster child. We are trying to find her a home outside the system.''

''Why can't she go to her real mommy?'' Steffie asked.

''Maybe some day she will,'' June said to her daughter, then turned to me. ''I don't know what we will do with Lydia tomorrow, though. We weren't expecting a new kid today and Al and I both have to work. I don't think it is good for her to be alone on her first day.''

June and I shared a knowing glance. Lydia might run away.

''Why don't I come by and take her out to lunch?'' I glanced at Lydia. Her animosity had faded somewhat.

''You mean we could go to a restaurant?''

''Sure, anywhere you like.''

''And I would be allowed to go to a store?''

''I don't see why not.''

''Or other places I haven't been in a long time?''

Something in her tone made me suspicious. I knew she had a drug and alcohol problem, or maybe—like so many of these kids—she wanted to buy cigarettes, but that seemed to conflict with her fresh religious conversion. Mrs. Shaw's warnings about lying and manipulation also echoed in my mind.

I looked at my watch, then stood. ''I have a long ride back. Lydia, come out to the car with me and we'll make plans for tomorrow.''

When we were outside, I realized that except for the crying jag in the courthouse rest room, this was the very first time we ever had been alone.

''So, I'll see you about eleven, okay?'' Lydia was very still. ''Think about where you want to go to lunch and what else you might like to do.''

''I know what I'd like to do, but nobody will let me,'' she said in a singsong challenge.

''What's that?'' I braced myself.

''I want to go to the cemetery where Teddy is buried. I want to say good-bye to him.''

Foster parents are recruited, trained, licensed, supervised, paid by HRS and thus are employees of the state. Many seem to be motivated by religious conviction, others are dedicated to helping children, some find the financial supplement essential to their household income. While the extra few hundred dollars a month might not seem like much to feed, clothe, house, and supervise a troubled child, many of the foster families in this district house two or more children. One group home receiving $473 per month per child averaged six children for a while and used the $2,838 per month additional income to cover payments for a larger home and car. In regular foster homes children under twelve receive approximately $300 a month for their board rate, while those over twelve qualify for another $75 to $100 per month, depending on the severity of their problems. A few families spend the total funds on the needs of the children, but in my experience, most of the children receive hardly any garments over and above the yearly $200 clothing allowance, a few are served different food than the rest of the family, and some older children are expected to provide significant labor in maintaining homes and farms. One justification for using foster care funds for general family needs is that it is a puny "salary" for a round-the-clock "job." One family receiving $1,116 a month for three teenagers stated that it only came to $1.55 per hour on a twenty-four-hour-a-day basis for one person.

After the initial course to become foster parents, HRS provides no continuing education or foster care counseling services beyond visits from caseworkers. But these caseworkers are not well trained in parenting education or support services for complex families' situations or special needs children. Foster parents have complete control over who remains in their home. Children who misbehave can be threatened to be kicked out, and frequently foster children are moved at the whim of the foster parent. A great many of them are shuffled multiple times, and even though they are supposed not to remain in foster care more than eighteen months, more than half of Florida's foster children are there longer. Even more shocking is the fact that the youngest children in the system remain the longest.

However, the Fowlers were only providing Lydia with shelter care—a bed for a week or so until a permanent solution could be found. And Lydia was not officially a foster child. Because of the psychological risks of having her in that system, I hoped to keep her out of it entirely.

My goal for the day was simple: I wanted Lydia to begin to trust me. I vowed not to denigrate the Tabernacle Home or her parents.

Lydia was dressed in a shabby skirt and T-shirt. I assumed the Tabernacle Home had kept her plaid jumper uniform and the awful dress she had worn to court. Her sneakers had holes in them, sometimes the fashion, but the effect was pathetic, especially when her family could afford decent clothes. If she had been a foster child, at least she would have had a fifty-dollar initial clothing allowance, but in her present situation she had nothing.

She slipped beside me in the car and started chattering immediately. "The Fowlers are really *nice*! Candace and I stayed up for hours talking about everything, especially how we feel about the Lord. Best of all, they pray just like we did at the Tabernacle Home with everyone standing in a circle and holding hands."

"They are a Pentecostal home, aren't they?"

"Yes! Jesus did answer my prayers when he led me there. I don't ever want to leave!"

I didn't have the heart to try to explain the realities quite yet. "Let's go to lunch."

"I don't have any money."

"Don't worry, it's my treat. Anything else you'd like to do?"

"Visit Teddy's grave."

"I'll take you whenever you want, but are you sure you want to go today?"

She was quiet for almost a mile. "I don't think I am ready yet."

We had pizza and I was pleased that Lydia continued to be so talkative with me. We discussed Robert Frost's life in New England, what birch trees looked like, and that she hoped to live near mountains someday.

On the way back to the Fowlers', I asked if there was anything else she wanted or needed. "Yeah, but it isn't anything you can do."

"Try me, I like a challenge."

"First, I'd like to see my father on my birthday next week, but he won't even look at me."

"What about your mother?"

"She might call me."

"You want me to call her?"

"No, I can do that myself now. June said I could use the phone anytime I wanted."

"Let me know how it goes. Anything else?"

"I'm praying for a guitar. I had to leave the other one at the Tabernacle Home."

"Maybe your parents would get you another one for your birthday."

Lydia snorted at this impossibility, then a hard-to-read look darkened her face. "And there is something else . . ." Her voice seethed. "I am sick and tired of being called 'the girl who put the baby in the microwave oven.' ''

"Me too! I get furious when anyone says that and I am making it a point to let everyone know. You never did that and yet you keep getting blamed for it, even went to prison for it, which was totally unfair!"

"Maybe I didn't do what they said, but I was very bad and deserved my punishment."

"I don't understand what it is that you think you have done that is so terribly wrong."

"I've shoplifted and that was wrong. I even got caught for it, but they let me off, providing I never did it again." I recalled her mother mentioning this and realized that I was so vested in her innocence that I hadn't thought about her committing other crimes I did not know about. "And I never did it again!" she said emphatically, as though reading my mind. "I can learn a lesson, even though my father thinks I can't. He'll see! When I get another guitar, I am going to sing him a song that is a testimony of my Christian faith. It goes, 'I'm not the way I was, I'm on the other side.' Then he, and everyone else, will see how different I am."

"Listen, Lydia, everyone makes mistakes, but you have gotten an incredibly raw deal. I don't understand why your parents are still disciplining you for something that happened more than nine months ago. I'm not excusing the incident, but the truth is that nobody was seriously harmed and you actually played a much smaller role than the boys." I felt my face flushing with indignation as I said what was on my mind. "There is no way you deserved juvenile detention or what has happened to you since. You belong in a regular family, going to school like other girls your age, and having a good time. I'm glad you have found a religion you like and you are making changes in your life, but other people have to make some changes too. After all, they are the grown-ups and you are the child. You are entitled to more mistakes than they are. And you are also entitled to love and kindness and freedom and justice."

Lydia stared at me with flashing eyes. "You really care about this, don't you?"

I took a long breath. "Yes. I do. And do you want to know why?" She glowed in anticipation. "Because I care about you."

When I returned Lydia to the Fowlers', I promised to call her and we could make plans to look at other homes. Her face clouded momentarily.

The next day Mona Archibald phoned to say she had seen Lydia at the Fowlers' and wanted me to know that a problem was brewing.

"Are they going to throw her out?"

"On the contrary, they want her to stay permanently, which means she would have to become a foster child, and you and I both don't want that to happen."

"The families I had in mind won't be appropriate now because she only wants a Pentecostal family."

"There's always her parents."

"They won't accept her."

"That's not what he said in court."

"That was for the record," I replied. "Lydia wants to be reconciled, but her father won't even agree to see her for a few minutes on her birthday."

"She can't stay with the Fowlers. They both work and she would have no supervision."

"She could attend school like the other kids do."

"The high school won't take her because she is almost seventeen and still in ninth grade. And the vocational institute isn't accepting new students until January. You need to find her someplace else right away."

When I phoned Lydia, she said, "I have been waiting for you to call all day!" She bubbled on about going to the Wednesday evening church services and joining in the activities of the youth club. "Tomorrow Al is taking some time off to spend with me, but I could see you on Friday."

"What do you have in mind?"

"June and Al prayed with me about Teddy. So now I am ready to say good-bye to him."

That afternoon I phoned my literary agent, who is also an ordained Episcopal priest, and asked him for suggestions for what to do at the cemetery. He mentioned several Bible verses and suggested other readings that might have special meaning.

At breakfast the next morning I opened the paper and was startled by the headline: TEEN'S DEATH STILL A MYSTERY. The photo of Teddy Kirby's gravesite depicted an array of tokens and tributes left by his friends. The caption read: "On the first anniversary of his death, investigators, family and friends, are still searching for a suspect." Now I understood why Lydia had wanted to do this today.

Our first stop on Friday morning was to my parents' rose garden, where Lydia was given the shears and told she could pick anything she wanted. "Teddy loved yellow," she said as she snipped roses with golden-tipped petals and placed them in my basket. Then we drove to the memorial park.

It was not difficult to find the right spot among the plaques set into the monotonous lawn. From a distance the site appeared littered; up close there was a capricious array of mementos including a paper cross constructed from chewing gum wrappers, a collection of various brands of beer and soft drink cans. Unsmoked cigarettes were lined up like military guards surrounding a foil windmill on a stick, paper and silk flowers, a wilting birthday banner, a laminated yearbook picture of Teddy, and newspaper articles about his death encased in plastic, as well as several handwritten notes and poems. Lydia and I had both brought Bibles. We read several passages in unison, ending with the Twenty-third Psalm. Then I took out my *Complete Works of Robert Frost* and recited ''The Road Not Taken.''

I went back to the car to give her some time alone. Lydia kneeled and rearranged the roses, then came and sat in the car.

''Are you ready to go?''

''Almost.'' We both were quiet for a while. ''Sometimes you have to stop and think about what would have happened if everything had been different,'' she said solemnly. ''He could have lived, our baby could have lived, but then I might not have found Jesus. Do you think everything happens for a reason?'' she asked me with shining eyes.

''Some days,'' I answered truthfully, ''but other days, no.''

Over the weekend I stepped up my inquiries for a home. Knowing that there was no place for Lydia in the public school system, I started to concentrate on people connected with Christian schools, hoping I could find her someone who would accept her into an educational program. Monday morning, though, I was surprised by a phone call from Clyde Baxter, the drop-out prevention specialist at the county school board office. He said he had heard about the situation and had been asked why there was not a place for my guardian child in the public schools. At first I was irritated to have had my confidentiality breached, but since nobody knew Lydia's name, no harm had been done.

He said it would help to place her if he knew her identity. After giving it to him, he typed Lydia's student number into his computer and her record appeared on the screen. ''I know Miss Ryan. Had her in my middle school home room a few years ago. Nice kid. These scores show real potential.''

"She's been told that at seventeen she is too old to begin high school and there is nothing else available until next year."

"You can't get a kid back in school if you shut the door in her face." Mr. Baxter went on to list a variety of alternative programs. "If she will give it a try, we'll bend over backward to find a way to make her happy to be learning again."

I phoned Lydia. Al Fowler said she was out shopping with his wife. Before I could mention my discussion with Mr. Baxter, Al said they wanted to keep Lydia. "Could you come over and talk about it, because we need to know if you will support our position."

I said I could be there shortly. Lydia came out to greet me.

"Would you help me get something out of my trunk?" I asked. Lydia shrieked with delight when she saw the guitar case. "This belongs to my sister, who left it at our house several years ago. I asked her if you could borrow it for a while."

Lydia took the guitar out of the case and strummed it. "This is even better than the one at the Tabernacle Home. Can I restring it?"

"Sure, but why?"

"I'm left-handed."

Lydia busied herself with the task. I admired her dexterity as she undid the strings and moved them around. June came into the room and handed out plastic cups of iced tea, then took a seat next to her husband.

"We have a problem," I began. "I've told everyone we wanted to keep Lydia out of the foster care system, and HRS does not want to have to pay monthly fees for her. The only way I can see this working is if she enrolls in school and you would agree to keep her without subsidy."

June glanced nervously at Al. My guess was that she had become emotionally attached to Lydia, but he would have a more pragmatic approach. Still, they were living in a home owned by the church, so those expenses couldn't be too high, and they received payment for Candace. Also, Lydia had parents of her own who might take over her health costs, buy her some clothing, possibly give her an allowance, and Lydia could get a part-time job.

After a few hopeful seconds, Al Fowler shook his head. "We have contracted with HRS to provide two foster beds, and if we gave one away to Lydia, we would be violating that agreement."

"I am sorry if I may have misinterpreted what you said about your attachment to Lydia," I said dejectedly.

"Don't get Al wrong, we do care for her," June said, "we just have to play by their rules."

"Well then, let's talk about the school situation." I then told them about the possibilities. "What do you think, Lydia?"

"I'd love to go back to school if they would take me. If I stay here, I could go to Central with Candace."

"Look, Lydia," I began sternly, "you were placed here for a few days of shelter care until we could find a home for you. Frankly, we haven't made much progress in that direction, but we are going to have to come up with some options fast. Maybe Al knows a family in the church who might take you in. That way you could see the Fowlers often and maybe attend school with Candace. I know HRS is not going to take care of you unless the judge orders it, and he's already told us to seek an alternative."

"Nobody can make me stay somewhere I don't like unless they lock me up again!" Lydia began to tremble and June went over and hugged her close.

"Can't you ask the judge to change his mind?" June asked wistfully.

For a moment I thought about how foolish I would look after all my protestations to keep her out of the system, but then asked myself why I should care what the judge or Mona or Calvin thought about me. I had told Lydia she could choose her placement and now she had. If I tried to dissuade her, I would be another in a long string of people who had let her down.

How I wished I could have avoided the call to Mona! First I gave her the good news about the school possibilities, but she wasn't fooled.

"Isn't it a bit premature to be discussing this for Lydia when she might not be in this county next week?"

I tried to explain how the Fowlers and Lydia wanted to be together.

"My supervisor will be calling Al about that. It is one thing to have a bleeding-heart guardian trying to tell us how to do our job, but we expect more from our licensed foster parents."

I backpedaled and asked if I could request an official staffing conference to review the choices.

"Judge Donovan, in his wisdom, gave you placement authority here," Mona said facetiously. "Now you are finding out there aren't a lot of people waiting in line to take in someone who would put a baby in a microwave oven."

"Mona," I groaned, "you know she never did anything remotely like that!"

"All I know is that your interference blew a safe placement, where she was not only doing better than anywhere in the past, but cost the state nothing. Now we are shelling out for her every day. If you are going to drop the ball, I guess that means that I will have to pick it up and find her a home."

After I hung up, I phoned Lillian and poured out my heart. Lillian listened sympathetically. In the manner of a kindergarten teacher trying to prompt a child to take the right course, she said, "Now, Gay, what do you think is in Lydia's best interests?"

"To remain with the Fowlers and start school again."

"Most of the time the biggest hurdle is figuring out the solution. You know the goal, so now all you have to do is aim for it."

That night Calvin Reynolds called me at home. His voice sounded cordial, but since he was the HRS attorney, I was on guard. After a few pleasantries, he spoke as though confiding in a friend. "I wanted you to know what happened late this afternoon. Mona requested another hearing in front of Judge Donovan next week. She has found another religious facility about a hundred miles south of here. They have other children there who have guardians as well, so your access to her would not be a problem. Mona is going to take her there tomorrow or the next day, but I think it would be better if you went along."

"Why?"

"Lydia seems to trust you the most, at least that is what June Fowler says."

"Lydia is set on staying with the Fowlers and they want her too."

"They may not be as devoted as you think. Mona's supervisor had a long talk with Al about renewing his license. If something has to give, it is going to be Lydia."

"Is there any chance she could stay there?"

"May I tell you something completely off the record?"

"Yes."

"I agree that Lydia belongs where she is, but we cannot afford to put every runaway kid on the foster care rolls. When we get to court, I will do my job, which is to support the agency's position to place her in the other facility or return her to her family, however I will not oppose you vigorously. Also"—he lowered his voice—"Mona asked me to petition the judge to remove the guardian from this case, but I said I wouldn't because that would make me look foolish.''

''Why are you telling me this, Calvin?''

''Try to imagine what it is like to do my job. HRS has limited resources and manpower, so we have to ration our services. Every day I have to process a whole stream of children, each case more tragic than the next. In the big picture, a kid like Lydia is not so badly off. She has a family who could afford to support her. In another year she will be eighteen; and she is old enough to work. She doesn't have any obvious handicap. Now that is not a reason to ignore her, but she doesn't demand the attention that, say, an abused baby would get. Also, to be perfectly blunt, money spent on a smaller child might yield a greater reward. By seventeen, we figure there's not much you can do to change a bad kid.''

''She's not a *bad* kid!'' was my knee-jerk response, and I launched into a whirlwind defense.

''I know,'' Calvin answered softly, ''just remember what I said and also''—he gave a little self-deprecating laugh—''I think I'd rather be doing your job than mine.''

Due to Calvin's warning, the early morning phone call from Mona did not come as a complete surprise.

''Listen,'' she began in her most streetwise voice, ''I've found a possibility for Lydia.

''Tell me more,'' I replied evenly.

''I thought you would want to check it out yourself,'' she said cagily, and gave me the phone number. ''Just keep an open mind, that's all I ask.''

I called the Christian Farm Society and spoke to their director, Penny Eaton. She explained that the original Christian Farm Society began in Colorado in the 1960s, when their founders decided their mission would be to save America's troubled youth through Christian family living. I described Lydia's situation and her preference to be in a Pentecostal home.

''We are conservative, full gospel and fundamental, but not Pentecostal in nature. When the Bible speaks, we speak; when the Bible is silent, we are silent.''

I thought that this might be acceptable to Lydia and asked about their educational program.

''We don't have our own school, but we take them in vans to the

River Grove Baptist School, which has students from several Christian denominations. They have a place for Lydia and would like to meet her. When can you bring her down?''

"Didn't Mona Archibald, her caseworker, make an appointment?''

"No. She said you would be the one transporting her.''

I knew this was a trap. Since the judge had directed me to find her a home, I could not refuse. Also, Mona didn't want me claiming that she had coerced Lydia.

When I called Lydia, her reply was swift. "I'm not going! Why take me out of a program I like, just to put me in another? You asked me what I wanted and I told you. I want to stay here because they care about me, and I care about them. I like their fair rules. I like the way they support me spiritually. I like their kids and Candace. And besides, they treat me like nobody else ever has.''

"In what way?''

"With respect.''

Calmly, I asked Lydia to think about visiting the Christian Farm Society because there was no guarantee she could stay at the Fowlers'. "Just look at it with an open mind, that's all anyone can ask.''

The road to the Christian Farm Society was lined with live oak trees laden with pendulous Spanish moss. Horses frolicked behind tidy fencing, and here and there in shady groves were small playgrounds with swings and sandboxes.

Penny Eaton was warm and welcoming. Lydia was scrupulously polite but did not ask any questions as we toured the grounds. The facility consisted of six ten-child homes each staffed with a full-time married couple. They were well designed with large bedrooms and living spaces, a bright kitchen, and round dining tables with a built-in turntable in the center to make passing dishes easier. A study area contained reference books, an encyclopedia, and a computer. Each house had its own van for transporting the children to school and for family trips. Only the preschool children were at home, with both foster parents in attendance. Their work at the farm was considered their full-time job. Fathers were out in the pastures or repairing the dwellings while mothers were tending children and cooking. The atmosphere was far more open and cheerful than the Tabernacle Home, and it was made clear that the Guardian ad Litem, or anyone else, was welcome to visit Lydia at any convenient time.

"What do you think, Lydia? Would you like to apply to live with us?" Penny asked.

"I like the people I am with and I don't want to be so far from my real family. It took us more than two hours to get here. My parents will use that as an excuse not to visit me."

Penny looked to me for an opinion.

"I am impressed," I admitted candidly, "but I think Lydia needs more time to think this over, don't you?" I asked her. Lydia nodded and I could tell she was anxious to leave.

As soon as we were in the car, Lydia hurriedly said, "I prayed to have an open mind, but I could *never* live there." Then she methodically listed her reasons. "It's too far away from the county where I grew up and where my contacts are. What I said about my parents was true. They won't even come a few miles now. Do you think they'd drive two hours?"

"Maybe with some counseling . . ." Lydia scoffed at my optimism. "Look, Lydia, I agree with you. The main benefit of the Christian Farm Society is that it will not cost the state anything. But your explanation is very rational. That's what we'll tell the judge," I said.

Mona was just going to have to accept that placing a seventeen-year-old girl somewhere against her wishes would be a recipe for failure.

Despite the complexities of Lydia's case, there had been no effort to get any mental health counseling for her. Because she was not technically in foster care, she did not have a Medicaid card and her parents were refusing to pay any costs. There was a chance she might qualify for free services at the county clinic until she had a stable placement, but Mona and the Fowlers claimed they did not have the time to take care of this matter, so I agreed to make the appointment myself.

A few days later Lydia and I were sitting in the waiting room of the mental health clinic. Lydia asked my help filling out the intake questionnaires. She checked the box marked "sleep problems" saying she had insomnia, something that was new to me. When asked to express her feelings about her father, she wrote: "love."

"Is that all you want to say?"

"I do love my father."

"I know, but if my father refused to see me, I might have a few other feelings too."

"Can I put down more than one?"

"Sure, as many as you want."

In bolder letters next to "father" she wrote: "cold, unfair, temper."

When she went for the interview with Esther Kipper, the therapist, Lydia asked if I could remain with her. Dr. Kipper asked her why.

"Because there is some stuff I don't want to have to go over again and Gay knows about it."

I sat in a chair in the corner, but when Lydia prompted me I described her legal situation, the search for a home, as well as the facts regarding her delinquency and the false statements about her. Before the interview, Lydia told me that she was going to tell the truth. Keeping her word, she answered every question, even admitting she had tried LSD, uppers, downers, and marijuana, but not cocaine. She talked about how she found Jesus and that she would never use drugs again. "And I won't take any of those mind drugs, like they gave me at Valley View."

When Dr. Kipper asked Lydia if she had ever been raped, she said, "Yes, twice," which was a shock to me.

At the end of the session we talked about Lydia's options. I explained that unless Dr. Kipper saw any problems with our plan, Lydia and I were going to ask the judge to order Lydia into foster care and to keep her at the Fowlers'.

"Considering the difficult circumstances, I think that you have done very well, Lydia," the therapist said with a generous smile. "My opinion is that you should remain where you are, continue regular counseling, and start school as soon as possible."

"May I quote you for my report to the court?" I asked.

"Surely," the therapist said, winking at Lydia.

Two days later I picked up Lydia at the Fowlers' and took her to Central High School. Our instructions from the drop-out specialist were to ask to see the principal. He explained that although Lydia did not meet most requirements for admission, he would waive the rules because, "I hear you are a girl with real potential."

"Nobody ever told me I could do well before," Lydia said.

"You are very smart," I insisted, then looked to the principal for support.

"If you put in the effort, I know you can succeed," he said warmly. "We want to welcome you back to school."

"Do I have to take physical education?" Lydia asked.

"No. I don't think you would feel comfortable with a bunch of immature ninth graders."

Lydia's eyes sparkled. "What about guitar? I've been learning how to play on my own."

"We have two guitar classes in our music department. The goal is for you to get back into the routine and have a positive experience."

Soon Lydia was signed up for exactly what she wanted: courses in word processing, child development, ninth-grade math and tenth-grade English, guitar, geography, and experiential science. Since it was too late to start classes, she was told to come on the bus the following day.

"Your parents will be proud that you are back in school," I said as we headed home.

"I hope so. They never had much faith in me."

So often I had seen guardian children whose self-esteem had been eroded by years of criticism. I refused to go along with the pervasive belief that a child required more correction than praise. One of the most essential roles I could play was to keep reminding my guardian children how terrific they were.

"I've seen some of your ability test results. You can do very well if you want to."

"That's not what my parents believe."

"Have you talked to either of them lately?"

"Not my father!" Then she expressed her fury that every time Stuart answered the phone he either hung up or put her mother on without one word of greeting. "Mom tells me to write him and ask for forgiveness, and I have done it over and over, but he never answers. I say, 'Dad, please talk to me. Just tell me what I need to do to come home again.' "

"That must hurt your feelings."

"Nobody wants me . . . except Al and June." Lydia exhaled for so long she seemed to deflate. "Do you think there's any chance I can stay with them?" she asked plaintively.

We pulled up in front of the Fowlers' house. "I don't know. First you would have to be declared a dependent child by the court. Then you would be a foster child, a ward of the State of Florida. But, even then, the Fowlers could ask you to leave at any time or HRS could move you whenever they wanted."

"Couldn't you do anything to make them keep me?"

"I can protest the placement, but I can't insist they put you where you want to stay. They could send you to a group facility in another part of the state or to a foster home in another school district. I am sorry to say this happens all the time. I had one guardian child who was moved thirteen times in less than a year."

"Why can't I have a home?" she said tearfully. "The Fowlers are the only ones who want me."

"And someone else, remember?"

"You?" she asked tentatively. I was touched, but I shook my head.

"What can't anyone take away from you?"

"The Lord," she mumbled.

I nodded, hoping it was true, for right now the material world had bankrupted her.

"You know something, Gay?" Lydia said, brightening. "Everyone else always talks to me about what they are going to do to help me, but then time passes and nothing changes. You are the first person who ever did every single thing that you said you would."

"Well, I will continue to try for you, but even I can't promise the end result. Only the judge can make you a foster child, but that still doesn't guarantee you'll stay with the Fowlers."

"I know that, and I know that whatever happens it won't be your fault."

I began to see that trying to win might be a trap. Already I had won the right to place Lydia outside the system only to find myself crawling back to ask the judge to order the opposite. Would I be winning again if he now granted my request? And what if three months from now, Lydia changed her mind and wanted out? I could just imagine calling HRS and asking for another home!

If there is anything I had learned as a mother, it was never to say never. I could see that in this case the sole victory would be Lydia's progress and supposed that this would not be the first or last time I might have to reconsider my original premise, to admit I was wrong, or that the situation had changed. And no matter what happened with Lydia, I would have to return to the same judge and work with the same foster care personnel again and again.

As part of the preparation for the court date, I attended a formal meeting, called a "staffing," at HRS headquarters to determine whether Lydia qualified for foster care.

"Someone needs to chastise the Fowlers for becoming too emotionally involved with a child for whom they were only supposed to have temporary care," Mona's supervisor said at the start of the meeting.

"You're talking about a child like she's an ornamental clock loaned out to a home that is paid a fee to wind and polish it and keep it running, but not to care for it too much because they are going to have to pass it on,'' I complained.

But, in the end, the HRS supervisors decided not to approve Lydia for foster care.

While waiting for a court date, I checked to see how Lydia was adjusting to school.

"Everything is different when you are trying to do your best for the Lord,'' she explained. "They want me to learn secular songs in guitar class, but I have said I will only play spiritual ones.''

"Is there a problem with that?''

"No, the music teacher respects my beliefs.''

From an early age Lydia had demonstrated a spirited personality. Her stepfather in particular had tried to inhibit it, and she had defied him at every turn. Yet, properly harnessed, this same temperament gave her spunk and drive. If she used her religious differences to meet this need to define herself positively, that was fine with me, for the alternatives— from drugs to sex to running away—were self-destructive.

"When is the judge going to decide my case?''

"I haven't been given a date yet, but since there is no emergency, it will probably be sometime in the next few weeks.''

"May I be there?''

"I am certain Judge Donovan will want to hear how you feel.''

"He didn't listen to me last time.''

"I know but . . .'' I paused, then took a chance. "Who did he listen to?''

"You,'' she stated, then grinned. "Hope he does that again.''

The following Monday Lillian called at eight in the morning. "Lydia Ryan's on the docket for this afternoon.''

"How's that possible? I wasn't notified and Lydia probably went to school already. I don't even have a written report ready.''

Lillian told me to call Mona and insist she pick up Lydia from school. I was to write a report and read it to her over the phone, then fax the Guardian ad Litem office the final copy. Because HRS had come out against foster care for Lydia, the guardian office was preparing the legal documents necessary to state our case formally. After a hectic morning, I arrived at the courthouse shaken and unprepared.

Mr. and Mrs. Ryan were standing by the elevator, and I nodded to them. They ignored me. As I passed through the metal detector, I was asked to relinquish the Swiss army knife in my makeup bag.

Lillian greeted me with a conspiratorial grin. "Trying to sneak that in, were you?''

"Should've remembered and left it in the car," I said with some chagrin. I handed Lillian copies of my report. "Where's Lydia?"

"Mona has her in the waiting room at the end of the hall."

I rushed there and apologized to Lydia for not knowing about the court date.

"Are my parents here yet?" Lydia asked.

"Yes, in the hall."

"Would you ask my mother to come here? I want to talk to her without my father being around."

Antagonism seeped from the pores of the Ryans as I approached. "Lydia would like to see her mother," I said. Catherine gave a little jump, then looked to her husband for approval. He stared straight ahead at me, so she sidestepped him and went to her daughter.

As soon as his wife turned the corner, Stuart Ryan sneered at me. "What are you, some kind of nut?" He shook a copy of my court report in my face. "You've written lies about my family and I'm going to make sure you pay for what you've done."

"Do you have some specific objections?" I asked as I reached for my copy.

His eyes bulged. "What is this shit about having us pay for her care? We already owe thousands for her and I will be paying that off for the rest of my life." A violet blush spread from his neck to his chin like a barometer of his rising blood pressure. "I'm going to get you for this and put you out of business."

Just then Nancy stepped off the elevator and waved to me. Gratefully, I followed her. "Did you hear what he said?" Nancy shook her head, so I repeated it. "Can he sue me?"

"No. A guardian is protected under the law as a good Samaritan."

The bailiff guarding the door to the judge's chambers had overheard me. "Did you say someone threatened you?" he asked.

"In a way . . . ," I demurred.

"Who?" he demanded.

"Mr. Ryan," I said, gesturing in his direction.

The bailiff glanced from me to Nancy. "You want me to speak with him?"

"No," Nancy replied. "I'll mention it to the judge so it will be on the record."

"Everyone for the Ryan case," the bailiff called a few minutes later.

To avoid confronting Mr. Ryan again, I went to fetch Lydia.

Just before we went into the judge's chambers Lydia said, "I want you to know that I prayed for God to put me where he thinks is best. If it is not his will for me to stay at the Fowlers', I will go wherever the judge says, and make the best of it.''

"Oh, Lydia!" I said, "you put everyone else to shame. I don't know what the Lord's will is, but in my heart I believe you belong with the Fowlers and I will do everything in my power to make the judge see it that way. And while I am at it, I have some other business to attend to in there on your behalf.''

"What do you mean?''

"You'll see!''

The judge glanced at my report, which was mostly a description of the Christian Farm Society and Lydia's reasons for not wanting to go there.

At present Lydia Ryan is functioning at the highest level that she has in several years. She is attending school and doing well, working toward her goal of joining the vo-tech after Christmas. She is involved in church activities, including a drama group, is seeing her mother and siblings every few weeks. Her relationship with her foster family has grown even tighter, and she is particularly close to her foster sister/roommate. Breaking up this harmonious situation at this time is going to set Lydia back on the progress she has made.

The judge looked to the HRS attorney for his perspective. "In our opinion this child does not meet any of the qualifications for an abused or neglected child to be placed into state-supported foster care," Calvin Reynolds began in a flat tone. "We are recommending a private placement at the Christian Farm Society. Mr. and Mrs. Ryan have agreed to sign the papers for her admission there.''

This was news to me. Mr. Ryan nodded at the judge. The judge scrutinized my side of the table. Since Kit Thorndike, the Guardian ad Litem attorney, had not been able to come, Nancy was on my right, with Lillian behind her. "What does the guardian say?''

Nancy pushed forward a copy of the guardian office's motion for a change of placement pursuant to the Florida Rules of Juvenile Procedure and Florida Statutes 39.442. "We respectfully disagree with HRS's position and are asking for Lydia Ryan to be placed in temporary legal custody of the department in foster care so the child might remain on a permanent basis in the same home where she now resides," Nancy explained.

"Would you state your reasons?"

Nancy nudged me.

On the drive to the courthouse I had made an attempt to frame my argument but had not been able to do so. Something I had recently read resonated in my mind. At the risk of being late, I had turned my car around and returned to my office. For a film project I had been reading Lisbeth B. Schorr's *Within Our Reach, Breaking the Cycle of Disadvantage*. Now, in the judge's chambers, I reached for the book and opened to page 146.

"Your honor, I cannot dispute the facts of this case, and I must be accountable for changing my initial recommendations. I never would have suspected that Lydia and the Fowlers would develop a rapport so swiftly. But the fact is that they did." I paused to make eye contact with Judge Donovan. "Your honor, every day you have the formidable task of placing children outside their homes and you must hope that they somehow find the love and security absent in their natural families in these surrogate ones. Now, almost despite the court—not to mention your appointed guardian, and the other professionals assigned to this case—something wonderful and unexpected has happened. Lydia and her foster parents have become deeply attached." I quoted from the book. " 'The failure to develop strong early connections with someone, who in Professor Urie Bronfenbrenner's phrase, "is crazy about the kid" has been found to lead, with haunting frequency, to an adult personality "characterized by lack of guilt, an inability to keep rules, and an inability to form lasting relationships." ' Here we have a young woman on the brink of independence," I continued. I looked around the room, trying to win sympathy. "If we sever this fragile bond now, maybe she will never form another one, and the self-destructive path she started down will lead to her ruin. Lydia is a special girl and I am proud to have gotten to know her." My hands began to tremble. To steady them I pressed my palms to the table, and then without premeditation, I stood up. "Before I go any further I want to make a point for the record. For too long Lydia Ryan has been called 'the girl who put a baby in a microwave oven.' It has been acknowledged that she never did this, but still the label persists." I stared at a few of the offending parties. "From now on I want it noted that anyone using this term is deliberately slandering her and I will take legal steps to have her compensated for damages."

I slipped back into my seat and spoke more softly. "The Lydia Ryan I know sings and plays the guitar, is loving and funny. She likes poetry, especially Robert Frost. She knows all about 'the road not taken' and she is asking your honor to give her this chance to follow the road of her choice toward the happiness she seeks.''

''What are your other recommendations besides foster care placement?'' Judge Donovan asked with some impatience.

I listed my requests rapid-fire. ''That Lydia Ryan be permitted unsupervised and unrestricted visitation with her natural family as often as is mutually agreeable, that she be encouraged to continue her schooling to receive a high school diploma—and also receive ongoing assistance if she remains in school for higher education past her eighteenth birthday—that no change of placement be made without a court hearing, and that the appointment of the Guardian ad Litem be continued in this matter.''

''Any other comments?'' The judge stared at Calvin, but true to his word, the HRS attorney did not enter any further arguments.

However, Mona jumped into the fray. ''I know the guardian feels she has to safeguard Lydia, but she has to see it from our point of view. This girl has been charged with delinquency and is a certified risk to young children. What about the Fowler twins? Don't we have a responsibility to them?''

''What do you think is the risk?'' the judge asked her.

Mona hesitated, then awkwardly stated that Lydia had been in Valley View, and before that, had been the ''paramour of a boy who was murdered in a gangland-style slaying.'' She stopped to clear her throat. ''At the last court appearance your honor ordered the guardian to find an alternative placement, but because she was unsuccessful, she wants the department to support this person from our limited funds.''

The judge nodded for me to comment. ''I made several attempts to find her a private placement,'' I stated, ''but Lydia, as well as the Fowlers, believe that the Lord led her to them.''

Calvin suppressed a grin by pretending to scratch his nose.

''I would like to speak,'' Stuart Ryan said.

''Go ahead,'' said the judge.

''Why is everyone bending over backward to do what Lydia wants? After all, she is a known child abuser, she is listed in the HRS abuse registry computer and went to juvenile detention.'' The abuse data base lists every known record of child abuse that has been investigated and not discarded. It is checked by employers hiring people to work with children and in court cases involving child neglect and abuse.

Lillian leaned forward. ''Did you know she was in the computer registry?'' she whispered to me. I shook my head.

Stuart Ryan's voice deepened. "Lydia would do whatever she is told if she didn't have some busybody do-gooder telling her she can get her way all the time." He shot a nasty glance at me.

Nancy pushed her chair back and stood slightly. "I want it recorded that earlier Mr. Ryan made some threatening remarks to my guardian."

"We can't all be happy campers, Mr. Ryan, but I will not tolerate any inappropriate behavior in my court," the judge said gruffly. "Do you understand?"

"Yes, sir," Mr. Ryan answered, then flushed purple again.

"Now, do you or her mother have any reasons not to want her at the Fowlers?" the judge asked.

"I cannot pay child support there," Mr. Ryan replied.

The judge removed his glasses and stared across the table at Lydia. "And is this what you would like?"

"Yes, sir."

"And why is that?"

"Because I have prayed to stay with the Fowlers and I think that is where Jesus wants me to be."

I looked over at Judge Donovan, whose stony face did not betray his thoughts. "Anyone else?"

"Now you can see why I couldn't argue with her," I said, unable to control my smile. "Maybe you are willing to fight those beliefs, but I surrendered."

"I rule in favor of the motion for change of placement," Judge Donovan said resolutely, and dismissed us all.

Nancy tapped me on the shoulder to remind me to leave, but I still was trying to figure out what had happened. "What—?" I asked, and dropped the Schorr book.

"Our motion. He approved our motion," Lillian hissed as she handed me the book.

I caught Calvin's eyes, which crinkled slightly in covert approval.

Lydia waited for me by the door, her parents having disappeared in a blink. "We won," I said in case she was also confused.

"This is the first time I can leave the court with a smile," she said. "Thank you so much."

"Don't thank me," I said, turning her to face the judge.

"Thank you, sir," she said, then ducked out the door.

"But what about being named a child abuser on the computer?" Lydia asked in a tinny voice. "Does that mean that if I ever have a baby someday, they'll take it away from me?"

Nancy jumped in. "Absolutely not. Those records are wrong. Now that we know they exist, we'll file the papers to get them expunged."

"What does that mean?"

"Clearing your name from the computer," I explained. "And while we're at it, we'll get your delinquency files expunged too. Right, Nancy?"

Nancy nodded. "From today on, everything will be new and fresh, and the only way for you to get anything bad on your record will be if you really do something wrong."

Mona seemed impatient. "I have to stay for some other cases, and it's too late for Lydia to go back to school. You want to take her home?"

"Sure, I'd love to," I said.

As soon as we got in the car, Lydia asked, "Can I use your cellular phone to call June at work and tell her the news?" I showed her how to dial the number. "Hi, is Mrs. Fowler available?" She waited. "Hi, Mom, it's me, Lydia. I'm on my way home!"

I held my breath. Until I saw the signed order placing Lydia in foster care, I was uncertain what we had won, but the language in it was stronger than I expected, saying that Lydia's return to her parents would be "contrary to her health, safety, and welfare."

All through winter vacation I held my breath as I hoped that Lydia would behave herself, but she had nothing but good reports. The one low point was when Lydia was tormented by sadness because her father would not permit a Christmas Day visit with the family. "I had presents for them, but he won't let anyone accept them."

"Did he have a reason?"

"My mom says it's because HRS is trying to collect reimbursement for some of my foster care expenses."

I held my breath when the time came for her to enroll at the vocational school, but they kept their promise and accepted Lydia into their program, where she enjoyed more autonomy and being able to complete work at her own pace.

I held my breath as the Fowlers moved to another home, worried that this might be an excuse to ask Lydia to leave. Instead they took another teenage girl, and soon Candace, Lydia, and the third sister became "the three musketeers."

I held my breath when I went to see the assistant state attorney to clear Lydia's files. Neither her shoplifting arrest nor assault charge would remain on her records, she assured me. I held my breath as I filled out the forms to have Lydia expunged from the abuse registry. The process took two months and the paperwork that came from the district administrator of HRS did not exonerate Lydia; her name was expunged because of a loophole. But it served the purpose.

Based on the May 1991 amendments to Chapter 415 of the Florida statutes, the person held responsible for a child, and thus designated as a perpetrator of abuse/neglect or exploitation, must be an adult, 18 years old or older. Lydia Ryan, who is alleged as the perpetrator, was not legally an adult. Therefore the report will be expunged.

I brought Lydia two copies of the report, one for her and one she could send to her parents. She read it several times, then said, "Now that I have a clean slate I really am born again."

I held my breath as she began going with a boy who refused to attend her church. In a few weeks she decided in favor of the church. I held my breath when she started dating another boy she had known from her days with Teddy, one who had also taken drugs, but this time she would only date him at her church youth groups, and he joined willingly.

I held my breath when she confessed that she was falling in love with someone else, a boy in her vo-tech class. I held my breath when she phoned me to say she had an emergency, then deflated with relief when she only needed a ride to her therapist because June was sick. On the way we talked about her new love. "Now that I realize sexual relations are a sin, I won't have them again until I'm married."

"I know you feel that way right now, but when a boy and girl really care for each other, sometimes they find they cannot wait." I then launched into a presentation of birth control methods as well as AIDS, and told her I would never think less of her if she asked for more information about any of this. She promised she would.

I held my breath many months later when she reported she and the latest boy were engaged and things were "getting serious."

"What are you doing about contraception?" I inquired without missing a beat.

I held my breath during the pause until she said she had gone to the doctor and was on the pill.

I held my breath when she called because she had been in an accident on the way to school. The school bus had been hit, but everyone was all right. She had missed her shuttle to the vo-tech from the high school and was stranded. I was happy to come to her rescue and catch up on the latest news.

"Guess who I heard from last week?" she asked teasingly.

I made a few guesses, but all were wrong. Then she told me that she had received a call from one of her friends at the Tabernacle Home, who reported the facility had closed its doors.

"I guess you would have had to leave there anyway," I said.

"Yes, but they were good people and they did a lot for me," Lydia replied in their defense.

I did not comment further, but I no longer regretted any of my actions that brought the brief upheaval in Lydia's life.

On one occasion there was nobody to take Lydia to a doctor's appointment. She had been losing weight for no apparent reason and needed some testing. I held my breath while anorexia and bulimia, thyroid disease, pregnancy, and sexually-transmitted diseases were systematically eliminated. She was treated for mild anemia and a sensitive stomach.

I sighed with relief when an early morning call from June Fowler was only a glowing report about how well Lydia had adjusted to their family. "She's a teenager, of course, with highs and lows, but Lydia is really special to us."

On Lydia's eighteenth birthday we went to the best restaurant in the county together. "What's *escargots*?" she asked, mangling the word.

"Snails, but if you are daring and like garlic, go ahead. Tell the waiter you want 'ess-car-go.' "

She practiced a few times and giggled. "May I also have lobster tail?"

"Sure," I replied.

Immediately her eyes clouded with tears. I asked what was wrong.

"Last week I went to see the twins in a school play. Nobody told me that my brother also was appearing on stage, so I was surprised to see my parents sitting a few rows in front with my sister. At the end of the performance, I went up to my mother, who said a few words, and gave my sister a hug, but my dad turned his back to me and started to walk away. I followed him and said, 'Please talk to me, Dad. Please.' I told him, 'I still love you, why won't you even look at me?' I reached out and tried to tug on his arm, but he shoved me away and I fell back into the edge of a seat." She gulped, then continued, "Everybody saw me crying, but nobody even stopped—except my foster mother.'' Her face hardened. ''I've made a decision. I'm not going to try to see him anymore.''

Our drinks were served and I toasted her birthday by clinking my ginger ale glass against her cola. I then took out three gifts. ''You can open one with each course.''

The first was a tape she had wanted, Berlioz's *Symphonie Fantastique*.

''I heard it in music class and I'm going to play this at Halloween,'' she said, then told me the story behind the score, something even I had not known.

The snails were served and she fumbled with the unusual utensils. After a few tentative chews, she decided the snails were terrific. As I admired Lydia's shining hair and flushed cheeks and bright, luminous eyes, and the way she flung her arms expressively as she talked and tossed her head when she laughed, I recalled the withdrawn sprite in the plaid uniform and could see beyond that to the waxen waif who had hung out with unsavory characters and had taken drugs to assuage her inner anguish. How far she had come from those days!

After eating her lobster tail, Lydia opened her next present, an appointment book similar to my own, which she had admired. ''Wow! This is great!'' She studied it page by page, planning on how to enter her schoolwork, church work, job, and other categories.

I told her the date to mark for her next six-month judicial review. ''After that, I will no longer be your guardian, but while they might be able to get rid of me on paper, you'll always be in my heart, Lydia. And I'll be here to help you, no matter what.''

''I know that,'' she said, shaking her finger at me as though I were a silly child.

The waiter brought a small birthday cake. Lydia blew out the candle and I handed her the last gift.

''Robert Frost! My own copy!'' She thumbed through the index, then selected a particular poem. ''Would you read it to me?''

I did as she requested, although my voice faltered as I read the last few lines of ''Acceptance.''

> ''Now let the night be dark for all of me.
> Let the night be too dark for me to see
> Into the future. Let what will be, be.''

Writing fiction is so much more tidy than real life. If this had been one of my novels, this chapter would have ended on the high and hopeful note of Lydia's birthday celebration. Just a week after the lobster dinner, though, Lillian phoned me.

"Next week's court docket has Lydia Ryan down for a status conference on a criminal indictment of some sort."

"Lydia! Nobody told me!" My temple pounded painfully. "She's been perfect. I don't understand . . ."

"Better check on it."

"She's eighteen. Am I still her guardian?"

"Because she is still in school and remains in foster care, you haven't been officially discharged yet."

"Would she be tried as an adult?"

"Yes." Lillian sensed my anxiety. "Don't get all worked up until you find out what this is about."

I dialed the state prosecutor's office. "Yes, she is on the docket," the clerk said, "but it is an old case that is up for review."

"What was the offense?"

"Aggravated battery." The clerk read me the criminal case number. "You know, the microwave oven case."

"But that was to be expunged when she was eighteen. Why is it still active?"

"I don't know. You'll have to ask Mr. Harmon, the new assistant state attorney."

"Could you connect me?" I had met Merv Harmon once before when he had taken a deposition from a child who had been raped. He had been gentle and considerate, so I felt comfortable calling him.

"Hello, Mrs. Courter, what can I do for you?" I explained that I was Lydia Ryan's guardian and asked what was going on. "It's a status conference to determine the final disposition of her two counts of aggravated assault with a deadly weapon," he continued.

"Frankly, I don't understand why this is even coming to court," I began. "The last person I spoke to in your office assured me that this would be wiped from her files when she was eighteen."

"It might have been if the delinquency caseworker at HRS had filled out the required paperwork, but he didn't, so it has remained in the active file. This status conference will determine if probation should be continued or if the case should be disposed of in another way."

"Have you read the file?"

"Briefly."

"I know it is confusing, but the bottom line is that the entire charge is baloney. There never was any baby or any microwave oven."

"That's not what my papers say."

"The supposed 'baby' was her eighty-pound sister, and the only time a microwave was involved was in a verbal threat by her boyfriend."

"It says right here she pled nolo contendere, Latin for 'I do not wish to contest,' which essentially is a guilty plea," he said condescendingly.

"Lydia is a casualty of a misunderstanding."

"She was represented by an attorney and then served time in juvenile detention."

"If you will read further, you will realize those are not the correct facts of the case."

"What do you want to do, retry the case on the phone?" His voice had taken on a nasty edge.

"Look, this is a young girl who absolutely did not commit any crime. Since I was not her guardian at that time, I am not certain why she pled as she did, but I know she was set up for reasons that have nothing to do with this case. We've worked together before, Mr. Harmon, and we were both on the same side, the side of the victim. Lydia is the victim in this case, and if you want I can prove it to you."

"Are you a lawyer?"

I was taken aback. "No. I am a Guardian ad Litem."

"Well, you sure sound like a lawyer."

Was this a compliment or a complaint? I wondered.

Mr. Harmon continued, "Nevertheless, I suggest you talk to a lawyer because as far as I am concerned this case is going to remain on the books as a serious offense."

"Why aren't you willing to give a kid a break?"

"I have stated my position," he said, then hung up.

My next call was to the public defender's office. Jules Gervais had been assigned the case, but he was not in. His secretary explained that Lydia's original attorney at the time of the alleged offense had been someone else, who was now in private practice. She would give Mr. Gervais the file and my message.

Even though I had not heard anything by the end of the day, I drove to Lydia's house on my way home from my office to discuss the latest turn of events.

"You promised me it was over!" Lydia said, her face turning to chalk.

"I thought it was. I gave you copies of the HRS computer expungement and I took the former assistant state attorney's word that the files would automatically be sealed when you were eighteen. The problem seems to be that the delinquency officer at HRS didn't file the necessary paperwork to wipe the conviction from your records.''

"They keep lying to me," Lydia said with a strangled groan.

"In what way?" I asked.

"When it happened, my lawyer said I wouldn't have to go to jail, and I did."

"How much time did he spend with you?"

"Maybe fifteen minutes. He told me I could tell the judge I was guilty and then I would get some sort of probation and community service. He said it might be the easiest way, but I wouldn't give in. Why should I? I didn't do anything. So then he explained that I could say I was not guilty, but that would mean a trial. He warned me that they would dig up everything about my past, like what happened between me and Teddy. They'd even want to know with whom I had sex and when.''

"So you were afraid that by going to trial your personal life would be exposed."

Lydia nodded morosely. "Then the lawyer said there was a way out by not saying I either did it or didn't do it."

"By pleading no contest?"

"Yeah, but what he didn't tell me is that I could go to jail for that too." Lydia's body shuddered and she broke into sobs. "It will never be over. Never!"

"Oh yes it will!" I vowed. "Even if I have to chain myself to the judge's bench until this case is wiped clean."

"Would you really do that?" she asked, her head tilted toward me.

I watched the glistening tears roll down her cheeks and replied, "Absolutely!"

"Where can I get some handcuffs?" I asked Nancy Hastedt, then explained my predicament.

"What is it that you want to accomplish?" Nancy asked seriously.

"I want the charge to go away. It was wrong from the first and Lydia deserves a fresh start, but for some reason the state attorney refuses to cooperate.

"Who's the judge?"

"I assume it is Judge Donovan."

"He knows Lydia's story. Don't you think he'll be compassionate with her?"

"Yes, he should be. She's been a model citizen since he placed her in foster care."

"Then tell him that. He's the one with the power to clear her record."

This time I was not about to be sidelined by some missing paperwork. I contacted the caseworker who handled delinquency cases for HRS.

"Why wasn't Lydia's case closed when she was eighteen?" I asked him directly.

"Don't know. The file never made it to my desk."

"Weren't you assigned her case from the beginning?"

"Yes, but there hasn't been much follow-up since she's been in foster care," he admitted.

"That's because she's stayed out of trouble, right?"

"Yes, however, she used to run with a very degenerate crowd. You know about her and Teddy Kirby, don't you?"

The sneer in his voice set me on edge. "And you know that the microwave incident never happened, don't you?"

"That's over and done with," he responded flatly.

"If you had filed the correct papers, it might have been, but now Lydia has to go to court again."

"What do you want me to do?" the delinquency caseworker asked with a resigned sigh.

"Tell the judge that not only has she not committed any other offenses, but she's also been on the honor roll and add how terrific, bright, cooperative, helpful, agreeable, and delightful she has been. If you need corroboration, check with her foster family and her foster care caseworker."

"I'd be delighted," he said with a warm chuckle. "I'm tired of delivering bad news."

Jules Gervais finally returned my call. "Good timing, Mrs. Courter, I was just reviewing this case, and frankly, I couldn't make head nor tails of it. Would you mind filling me in?"

After I told him the microwave tale, he said, "But she pled no contest." I described the circumstances. "Poor kid, she's locked in."

"Can't the judge just dismiss the charges?"

"Are you a lawyer?"

I laughed. "That's what the prosecutor asked. Some guardians are lawyers, in fact in the Orlando area that's all the bar will allow, but I am ignorant of the law, so forgive me if I have said anything out of turn."

"I like your style. A lawyer wouldn't dare ask that question."

"Because a dismissal wouldn't be legal?"

"On the contrary. It can be done, it just never is."

"Are you saying that there is a loophole here that nobody uses?"

"Precisely. But there would be hell to pay if I tried it on Judge Donovan. How's about this? You're the kid's guardian and you know the case better than anyone. When we get to court, I'll introduce the facts, then I'll turn it over for you to argue."

"What do I say?"

"Whatever you want."

"May I ask for a dismissal?"

"You can ask," he chuckled. "However, it is highly improbable that the judge would agree. But he might offer to seal the file or make some other concession."

"Good. Judge Donovan knows Lydia well and I think he will be sympathetic."

"Didn't you know Judge Donovan is having knee surgery next week? Judge Piercy from Williamstown is taking over."

"Nancy, quick, what do you know about Judge Piercy?" I explained my reasons for needing to know.

"He's one of the good guys, but since he's only going to be in your county for one or two weeks, he's not going to overturn any of Judge Donovan's orders."

"May I ask for another hearing date?"

"Not without good cause," Nancy replied. "Don't worry, Judge Piercy has a soft spot for women, if you know what I mean. Use it."

"Phil," I asked my husband, "would you be upset if I went to jail for contempt of court?" We were watching the news of a local cocaine bust.

"Over clearing the girl's name?"

"I'm trying to figure out how to get the judge's attention in her case. If I make a big enough stink, he'll either grant what we want or put me in jail."

"I'll bail you out, darling. I always will."

The morning of the hearing Jules Gervais asked me to bring Lydia to the public defender's office so he could brief her. Lydia was wearing a lime green suit with a starched white collar. Her hair was brushed shiny and pulled back with a matching grosgrain ribbon. With her demure white stockings and flat leather shoes, she looked more ready for a church luncheon than for a criminal court appearance. Heeding Nancy's advice, I had taken pains with my makeup, selecting a bright lipstick. Not politically correct perhaps, but this was for Lydia's sake.

Mr. Gervais asked Lydia questions regarding her initial plea. Then, while thumbing through the court file, stumbled on something. "Hey, what do you know?" He grinned like he had found the Cracker Jack prize. "Look here! The most honorable Judge Piercy was also the replacement judge the day Miss Ryan was sent to juvenile detention."

"Oh, no," Lydia whimpered.

Confused by the contrasting reactions, I turned from Lydia to Jules. "What's good about that?"

"Visiting judges don't like to overturn each other's decisions. Out of respect, they either uphold them or defer the ruling until the original judge returns. But, if Judge Piercy could be moved to realize that he might have erred the first time, there's a possibility he'll give Lydia another chance."

We walked from the public defender's dingy offices in the basement of the old courthouse across the street to the new courthouse. Already the Florida sun was blazing down, but beside me Lydia was trembling like a palm frond in a gale.

"Whatever happens, Lydia, you are not going back to jail," I reminded her.

"But I'll be known as a criminal for the rest of my life," she said, her face stricken with shame.

When we took our seats on the bench, someone slipped beside us. "I got off from work," June Fowler said, and squeezed Lydia's hand.

Lydia sagged with relief. "Thank you for being here with me, both of you. I know whatever happens that you've tried your best. And I've prayed to Jesus and told him that I shall listen to his will. If the judge doesn't believe me, I won't ask for my record to be cleared. I know I have sinned, so if this is how I have to pay, I accept it."

June nodded approvingly, but my heart froze as I resolved not to leave the courtroom without winning her a victory, if only to prove to Lydia that she was a better person than she believed herself to be.

"Did you bring them?" Lydia asked me suddenly.

"What?"

"The handcuffs." She had taken me literally! I explained that I hadn't been serious, at least about the handcuffs.

"That's all right," Lydia said solemnly, "it wouldn't have worked anyway."

"Why?"

"Look around this place. Everything is real smooth wood. There isn't a single place to attach handcuffs."

After more than an hour Lydia Ryan's case was called. Together Lydia and I walked to the podium in front of the judge. Merv Harmon explained that Lydia Ryan was present for the final disposition on her two counts of aggravated assault with a deadly weapon. He said that she had served time in juvenile detention and was on probation. Something in his flat, condemning tone irritated me. Mr. Harmon knew the whole charge was phony, so why didn't he lighten up?

When he paused, I jumped in. "But she didn't do it to begin with."

Jules stepped in front of me, and said under his breath, "Not yet. I'll tell you when to speak."

I flushed with embarrassment. There was some discussion over days served and prior offenses. The delinquency caseworker explained that Lydia's probation record had been perfect, that she was a model student, and she hadn't been in any further trouble.

Surprising me, Jules Gervais then entered a creative argument. "When this incident occurred, Miss Ryan's parents were upset with her defiant behavior and were so angry that it was thought she might be abused by them. At that time she did not qualify for foster care or any HRS programs, so for her own safety juvenile detention was suggested as an alternative."

Huh? was my reaction. Since when had Lydia been sent to jail for her own protection?

"I think the person who knows this case best is her guardian, Mrs. Courter. I would like to ask her to speak *now*," he finished by emphasizing the last word.

I didn't dare contradict the defense's story about why she had been placed in jail, but this was my only chance to straighten the official record. "Your Honor, the point is that Lydia Ryan never put any baby in any microwave oven. There was no baby. There was no oven. There were no assaults with a deadly weapon."

"You can't retry this case now," said Merv Harmon, rising to his feet.

I pulled out a piece of paper from the top of my file and waved it at Judge Piercy. "This is an expungement from the child abuse registry written by the district administrator of HRS. Based on my petition, they completed a thorough investigation of the matter and have officially wiped their records clean of this incident.'' (The fact that they had done it on a technicality did not matter at the moment.)

The judge waited for anyone else to speak. There was no response, so I plunged on. ''It's true that in the past Lydia Ryan has had difficulties with school and other adjustments, but she is not a criminal. Given the support of loving foster parents and concerned teachers, she has blossomed. She is on the honor roll and will graduate next year, even though she had to make up several years of lost time. She has remained free from trouble, has a part-time job, has taken an active role in church activities, is a responsible baby-sitter for the younger children in her home. A few months ago she reached her eighteenth birthday. The former prosecutor had told her that her record would be clean, but because of a bureaucratic mistake, this turned out not to be true.'' I took a breath. ''If anyone ever deserved a chance to start a new life as an adult, it is Lydia Ryan.''

I took a quick breath and started to launch into another argument, but the judge interrupted me. ''Guardian, what is it that you want?''

''I want the charges to go away. She never did it, so it never happened. I want the case dismissed.''

Merv Harmon shot up. ''You can't do that! She pled guilty. She served her time. You cannot dismiss a case after the fact.''

''She never should have been talked into pleading no contest in the first place,'' I retorted. ''She was confused and upset and was led to believe the charges would be dropped if she did that.''

''You can't rewrite the law,'' Mr. Harmon retorted defiantly.

Why was he fighting so hard? Was it just a legal reflex or did he really want to see Lydia's punishment continue?

''Does HRS have any objection to what the guardian is proposing?'' the judge inquired.

''No, Your Honor,'' the delinquency caseworker answered. ''I wish every kid turned out as well as Lydia has.'' I stared hard at him. He received my nonverbal message and plowed on. ''She's a terrific kid, one of the best,'' he stated with some theatrical verve.

I sighed with relief and turned back to the judge, who was rubbing his chin.

''Guardian, are you a lawyer?''

''No, Your Honor.''

''That's why you don't realize what you are asking for is hardly ever done.''

"Does that mean that this is an irrefutable point of procedure or that it is very rarely invoked?"

"It's hardly ever used."

"Then, Your Honor," I said slowly and allowed a smile to fill my face, "please consider it now. Sometimes justice falls through the cracks." I was warmed up and on a roll. "Sometimes people in a busy court make mistakes. Sometimes anger and confusion camouflage the truth. If there ever was a time to invoke a special provision, that time is today."

"I don't like to overturn one of Judge Donovan's decisions," the judge muttered.

Jules Gervais lit up. "This may be a coincidence, Your Honor, but on the date Lydia Ryan was sentenced, you heard the case."

The judge glanced at his file, then peered over his reading glasses at Lydia. "I have never done this before, but I am going to take a chance on you. There are people in this courtroom who care about you and believe in you. Since HRS and your guardian agree, your case is dismissed. It never happened. You can begin again. Remember, this is a very special opportunity. I never want to see you in a courtroom again." He handed the file to his clerk.

Lydia's face was frozen in confusion.

"That's it," I whispered.

"What?" she mumbled.

"We won."

"Won?" she echoed.

I kicked her heel and leaned close to her ear. "Say, thank you."

"Thank you, Your Honor," she said under her breath.

With my hands still on her shoulders I marched her down the aisle. I glanced at Merv Harmon, who was shaking his head in disbelief. The delinquency caseworker grinned. June stood by the double oak doors and held them open. Outside Lillian was waiting. I hadn't seen her come in. As soon as I looked at her, I burst into tears. My emotional release surprised me and I fumbled for a tissue.

Before I could wipe my tears, Mr. Gervais pumped my hand. "Amazing. Never seen anyone do that before! A landmark decision. Will you argue all my cases for me?"

Lillian hugged me. "You were magnificent."

"No, Lydia was."

"What happened?" a perplexed Lydia asked her foster mother.

June shook her head. "I'm not sure, but I think it is terrific."

"Merv was furious," Jules commented slyly to Lillian.

"Why shouldn't he want to give a kid a break?" Lillian asked in her molasses-sweet voice.

"Just his style," Jules replied with a shrug. "Can't stand losing. He fights just as hard to put the abusers away."

"How did you come up with all that truth and justice and the American way stuff?" Jules asked me.

"Too much television, I guess."

"I didn't want you to stop," Lillian said proudly.

"Superb strategy," complimented Jules.

"What do you mean?" I asked.

"Not giving up until you won your case."

"You think the judge gave in just to shut me up?"

"Exactly. I couldn't have gotten away with it, just like I couldn't have asked for the dismissal." Jules shook Lydia's hand. "You are a lucky young lady today. From what I hear, you deserve it. I wish you good fortune in your life from now on." He slipped back in the courtroom.

Lillian followed him to the door. "I have another case too. But this has made my day—no, my year!"

"It's only the last day of January."

"Nothing will top this," she said, smiling like the pope blessing the crowd.

I felt so buoyant I could almost float out of the courthouse. "C'mon," I said to the others. "I'm taking everyone to lunch."

2

All the Possibilities

The Stevenson Family

Something turns over
in the heart, like the black
side of a mirror turned
to the light. I'm exhausted
by the thought of all
the possibilities that are lost.
—**WENDELL BERRY**

I HAD BEEN A GUARDIAN over a year by the time I met Lydia, and by
then I was accustomed to being in the courtroom. Without my prior
experience, I would never have the boldness to ask for her case to be
dismissed. When I received my very first assignment, however, I was
very much the novice, and by the luck of the draw had landed one of
the most complex cases in the circuit at the time. As the story unraveled,
I realized that while I had been trained to handle most of the circumstances, I had never expected to have so many problems in one family
as well as to have to participate in a criminal prosecution. I was a rookie,
and yet the first time I ever attended a trial I was there to advocate for
Alicia Stevenson, a fifteen-year-old girl who allegedly had been sexually
molested by her natural father for almost ten years. I had known Alicia
and her two brothers—whom I also represented because one guardian
usually handled all the children in a family—for many months, and although I was concerned with their feelings about testifying, I had not
considered my own emotional reaction as I took my place in the courtroom on the opening day of the trial. All the events leading to this
moment had not prepared me for the realization that a man's future was
at stake, and that my actions had the power to influence what happened
to him.

I almost expected to be exposed as an imposter. Everyone else—from
the bailiff to the court reporter to the judge—belonged here. I was an
outsider. In the weeks leading up to the trial, I had felt that nobody
would pay attention to my opinions, but on the contrary, I had been met

with respect. During the pretrial meetings, I had discussed one particular concern with Grace Chandler, the assistant state attorney, who was the prosecutor for the case.

"I don't want the defense questioning Alicia about her sexual experience with the boys she dates because it isn't relevant."

To my surprise, Grace Chandler not only agreed but thanked me for reminding her. She even photocopied the appropriate statutes to have them ready to quote.

Once over the hurdle of being rebuffed completely, I asked, "What about clearing the courtroom during the children's testimony?"

"As the Guardian ad Litem you can request that."

That sounded simple enough, but how would I do it when the time came? The time had come. The participants were filing into the courtroom. I watched as Alicia's father, Richard "Red" Stevenson, took his seat at the table with his defense attorney. I knew all about his dysfunctional upbringing and hard luck story, but I represented and supported his children. Everything I felt about him was based on how it affected Alicia and her brothers, Cory and Rich. So no matter what the father had suffered, I did not believe he had a right to inflict his perversities on anyone else, least of all his offspring.

As people milled around the courtroom waiting for the proceedings to begin, I felt as hollow as a dried gourd. This was not a dramatization. A man was charged with a heinous crime, and if judged guilty of sexually molesting his daughter before her twelfth birthday, he would be subjected to a minimum mandatory sentence of twenty-five years in prison. His accuser—his daughter—was a troubled child. She would have to take the stand, and with her father's eyes boring into her, reveal her humiliating story in public. Her younger brother, Cory, whom I also represented, did not believe her and was going to testify against his sister. Her older brother, Rich, sided with Alicia and was scheduled to describe his father's sexual molestation of him as well. There were other children, including Alicia's friends and a stepdaughter from a previous marriage, who were willing to testify that they had been raped by Alicia's father, but it was uncertain whether the judge would allow them to come forward.

In the preceding months I had gotten to know the three Stevenson children and care deeply for them, but now it was out of my hands. The trial had been set in motion. The complaint centered around the few times Alicia could recall dates and circumstances. Since having sex with a child under twelve brought a much stiffer sentence, her father's guilt hinged on pinpointing the exact dates that incidents took place as well as giving the precise locations of any crime that occurred within the boundaries of our county. This was complicated by the fact that until very recently Alicia had never told anyone of the abuse or tried to run away. Would a jury understand how a child could feel that these experiences were an expression—albeit a distorted one—of her father's love and not want to be separated from him?

Alicia and her brothers were not permitted in the courtroom because they were testifying. I was there for them, and the magnitude of the responsibility made me tremble as I saw the door from the judge's chambers open. I consciously had to release my fingers from gripping the edge of the maple bench so I could respond as the bailiff called out, "All rise!"

The afternoon I first met Alicia I was at least as apprehensive as she was. The file—the first I had ever received—revealed that she had confided her father's sexual molestation to a neighbor, who had contacted the child abuse hotline. Police had been summoned and she had been removed from the home. After a week in a shelter, she was placed in Ruth Levy's foster home.

"You'll love Alicia," Ruth said with conviction when I called to introduce myself and set up an appointment to visit Alicia.

Ruth mentioned that Alicia's younger brother, Cory, who had not wanted to leave his father, was in a foster home more than forty miles away, and her older brother, Rich, had become uncontrollable in the latest of his many foster homes, and nobody knew where he had been transferred.

"Why are the kids separated?" I asked naively.

"There's not a foster home in the system that will take three mixed-sex teen siblings," Ruth explained as if she were patiently teaching a child. "Long before Alicia's problem was discovered, I had Rich here for two nights. Never again. We must have had a hundred kids at one time or another, but he's the only one my husband won't allow back in the house. In fact, when he heard the name 'Stevenson,' he almost didn't give permission for Alicia."

"The file doesn't say much about Alicia's mother. Do you know anything about her?"

"She hasn't been around for at least ten years. Her father remarried four or five times since. The guy must have something, but when I saw him in court he looked pretty creepy to me."

"Are there any other relatives?"

"A grandfather, but he is siding with the father against Alicia."

The trip to Mrs. Levy's home took forty-five minutes. I didn't understand why Alicia had been placed so far from her residence, neighbors, friends, and school, not to mention her brothers. Her foster home was a U-shaped ranch house on a suburban cul-de-sac across the street from a pond.

Ruth Levy wore tight black knitted slacks and an oversized T-shirt handpainted with daisies. Her figure might be described as maternal and her voice had a decided Long Island honk. Ruth explained that she was an experienced foster parent, having cared for foster children in New York before moving to Florida, where her husband had taken a job in the electric power industry. Right now there were four other foster girls under her care, each of whom had a laundry list of serious problems.

Although nobody else was home yet, Ruth's voice dropped. "I don't know how to say this, but Alicia displays some inappropriate behaviors."

"What do you mean?"

"She kisses people full on the mouth, even her brothers. And some of the other girls have seen her showing her breasts off to boys in school."

Before I could respond, we heard the sound of the front door opening. When Alicia walked in the house her eyes were cast down. Ruth waved her over to meet me and she reluctantly took a seat.

"Hi, I'm Gay, your Guardian ad Litem. Do you know what that means?" Alicia shook her head. I told her that I would be there through the entire court process, including a trial if there was one, and that I would still be involved until she left foster care at eighteen.

"Are you going to tell me what to do?"

"No, in fact I will try to tell everyone what you think is best for you."

Alicia looked up for the first time and stared at me with her cobalt blue eyes. "What if you don't agree with what I want?" As she blinked her naturally thick lashes, her lower lip protruded with a Bardot-like pout. I was taken aback by her beguiling expression, first because it was so winsome, but also because it had such a smoky, sensual quality.

"We'd talk about it and I would try to understand your point of view."

Her lower lip receded slightly and her eyes widened. She gave Ruth a sidelong glance. "Let's say I didn't want to live here anymore." She sat back and crossed her arms.

Did Alicia want to leave Ruth's, or was this a test? "If you really don't want to live here, then you and I would talk about why you are unhappy, look at the possibilities, and ask HRS to move you to a situation you would prefer."

"And what if they refused?" asked Alicia, who already knew the system far better than I did.

"Then we would go to the judge and tell him what you wanted. Don't forget, though, he makes the final decision."

Alicia reached over and hugged Ruth. "You know I was kidding, don't you?"

Ruth made a playful fist and pummeled her cheek affectionately. "You had better have been, Ally-Oop, or I would have lost my best girl."

I decided to take Alicia out for a snack so we could talk privately. Alicia pranced down the walk, swinging her pocketbook and her rear in time to a song in her head. Her foster sisters looked on jealously.

"I'm the only one who has a guardian," she said, tossing her head in their direction as she slipped into my car. When I turned on the motor, the preselected classical music station blared a violin solo. Alicia made a sour face and pulled out a tape. "Mind if I put this in?"

Without waiting for a reply, she did. The beat was insistent, the vocalist screeching, but I made out the words: "Youth gone wild." I glanced over at Alicia, who said, "Sometimes that's how I feel." The next time we were together, Alicia brought another tape, already reeled down to a new song called "Here I Am," with another message for me. Soon I learned to expect the tapes, for they were Alicia's way of telegraphing what was happening with her. That first time, however, before I could follow the lyrics further, Alicia stopped singing and said, "I guess I should tell you that I have been doing something illegal."

We had turned onto the main highway from the Levys' subdivision. I kept my eyes on the road and steadied my voice. "What's that?"

"My boyfriend, Lou, and me, we're . . . you know . . . doing it."

"What's illegal about that?"

"He's nineteen."

"Then he's the one who is illegal, not you. And if you want it to happen, nobody's going to prosecute him."

"Oh, I want it all right. I love Lou."

"Tell me about him . . . ," I began, while my mind was spinning with concerns about birth control and AIDS as well as the implications for the court case. When we pulled into Hardee's parking lot, Alicia was gossiping about where they had gone, what they had done, when and how. Suddenly any preconceived notions of what I would do as Alicia's guardian dissolved and I was swept along in her chattering tide.

What had I expected? Someone more withdrawn, someone who seemed like a victim? Someone less overtly sexy? If I was struck by her blatant sensuality, how would a jury feel? Was she receiving counseling that would help her understand why she had affected this persona? I realized I didn't know very much about her at all. Even though she was the center of the abuse complaint, I did not have much about her history. The Stevenson file was mostly filled with papers relating to her older brother.

The case of Richard Leroy Stevenson, born September 2, 1972, had been opened officially in 1977 when he had been placed in a residential treatment facility for severely disturbed children. From that time he had undergone an exponentially multiplying series of examinations, programs, placements, and interventions.

There were hints that Rich was a troubled child from the moment he entered kindergarten at the Sawgrass Primary School. After a few months, he was taken out of the regular classroom and placed in a group for emotionally handicapped children. Notes in the file indicated that he arrived at school with multiple bruises. His parents had said he was an active, uncontrollable child. Soon he became so disruptive in school, the family agreed to allow the state to place him in the family cottage section of a psychiatric hospital, then he was switched to their high-risk treatment center. After two psychiatric evaluations, seven-year-old Rich was returned to his home and attended the Treetops School, a county facility for chronically emotionally and physically challenged children. When Rich became unmanageable there, it was decided that his home life was too unstable and he was placed into foster care. A year later, Rich's foster parents rejected him, so he was admitted to Wilson Hospital's inpatient psychiatric unit. When he improved after only a month, he was transferred to the state's most expensive residential psychiatric program: Panther Ridge.

Almost a year passed and he was returned to his family. Out-patient counseling was provided by the county mental health center, and Rich remained home until he started to attend Sawgrass Middle School. When his classroom work faltered in the middle of sixth grade, the school established an individual tutorial program for him, but his behavior became more disruptive both at school and at home so he was admitted to the Riverside Ranch for Boys, one hundred miles to the north, where he lasted the summer. To keep him closer to home, a space was found for him in a companion facility only five miles from his family. Amazingly, Rich remained there through the fall until the following Easter vacation, which he spent with his father, who then kept him at home. By August, though, he had been placed in an emergency shelter near the university, where he underwent a fresh series of tests. In the midst of these evaluations he attempted suicide by jumping out a third-floor window. After further therapy, a more "homelike" setting was recommended and he was sent to another foster family. But there was no mention of where he was presently living.

Once I had the raw chronology sketched out in my computer—the only way I could make sense of Rich's peripatetic placements—I read every narrative, looking for the genesis of this child's nightmarish journey through the world. Perusing the test scores over a ten-year period, I listed the IQ results next to the testing dates and noted that this measure of potential slid from a high of 103 to a recent score of 86. Every school, every hospital, every doctor, every teacher had rendered this boy's mind stupider and stupider, yet they never offered him what he needed most: a warm, loving, accepting, permanent family.

My confusion was compounded when I found two birth certificates with different last names. Was Rich adopted? It took a while to discover the answer, but here is the simplified version of his background. Tammy Stevenson was the maiden name of Rich, Alicia, and Cory's mother. When she became pregnant with Rich, she married the baby's father, Richard Leroy Hamburg, a few weeks before Rich was born. (Apparently she had been married to someone else at the time of the conception, with the affair contributing to the grounds for divorce.) "Red" Hamburg's first wife had died, the second disappeared. His marriage to Tammy Stevenson was his third. (Red claimed his mother had been a prostitute, and she had allowed him to observe her sexual alliances with customers, some of whom also abused him. He had never known who his father was.)

Tammy's father, Jeremiah Stevenson, had managed his family's boot factory in Vermont. When his father died, he sold the business, bought citrus groves in central Florida, and moved there with his adopted daughter, Tammy, but not his wife, who refused to leave her family in New England.

Tammy quit high school and ran off with the man who would become her first husband, but then she met Red Hamburg. Soon she was expecting their child. Jeremiah Stevenson welcomed Red Hamburg and even gave him money to invest in a boat repair business. Alicia followed Rich eighteen months later, and then Cory was born about a year after that. By this time little Rich was a hellion running barefoot through the groves, and Alicia had a digestive disorder that gave her the pervasive smell of vomit. Tammy's approach to her children's problems was to do the minimum possible, then run off to spend time with her friends.

Jeremiah began to think of what would happen if he died. Tammy was too flighty to ever manage the grove, and it would be twenty years before the grandkids could take over. There was Red, but he wasn't legal kin. Then Jeremiah Stevenson had an idea: he would adopt Red and make him, and his kids, equal heirs with Tammy. Red was thrilled. At last he would have a father. The adoption documents were prepared, and at age twenty-six, Richard Leroy Hamburg, Sr., changed his name to Richard Leroy Stevenson. The children's birth certificates were reissued to reflect the new name and Tammy Hamburg became Tammy Stevenson again.

Once I had this figured out, the various names on the paperwork made sense to me. More important, I had a sense of the family relationships as they had been in place during the crucial months when these children were very small, for this is the time that a child either learns to attach and trust or does not.

If there is a common microbe that festers in almost every household where abuse and neglect flourish, it is something that prevents caregivers from bonding to their children. But what is this ephemeral glue popularly called "bonding"? Bonding involves the emotional transaction from the parents to the child and actually it is nothing more than falling in love. Parental sensitivity to the child's wants and needs is what signifies effective bonding. If you really fall in love, the person whom you love comes first. When a parent ignores, or is unable to meet, a child's need for comfort and protection, bonding has not been successful. People who never made these attachments as small children have blanked out their feelings toward others as well as themselves. And they pass on the disconnection they suffered. If you have not been loved, you cannot love. Those denied empathy find themselves devoid of empathy and thus perpetuate the cycle of abuse.

Every child requires—and is entitled to—nothing less than the unqualified love and attention from someone who thinks she is the most important individual in the world. Only from this secure place can she function optimally in life. Unfortunately, many children have more tenuous attachments, which result in different degrees of maladjustment.

When a parent offers affection in small doses, or is inconsistent in providing for the needs of the child, the result is a child who is anxious about what to expect and resistant to people. The next level of disturbed attachment occurs with parents who are actually insensitive to a child's needs. This child may actually feel threatened by other people's approach. Her anxiety may be coupled with avoidant behavior, with the child cringing, or avoiding the caregiver and others. In the worst cases, when the child is abused by the caregiver, the child is not only insecure but also so disorganized emotionally that she cannot function or develop normally. Sometimes parents are so immature that they turn to their child to supply their needs and blame the child for not being loving or caring toward them.

Attachment disorders, and their subsequent effects on children, are standards of psychological literature, but for some reason the basics are often ignored by courts, which focus on the narrow rights of biological parents rather than the essential entitlements of the child to have a safe, secure place to be. After months of piecing together bits of the Stevensons' story, it became clear that these three small children had spent their first precarious years isolated in the groves with minimal parental love or attention. Tammy had given her babies only as much care as did not interfere with her social life. Her husband left home early in the morning and returned late at night to work at his marine repair shop, and his hobby, boat racing, often took him out of town on weekends. Jeremiah adored his grandchildren, but did not see himself as their primary caregiver. When I asked Jeremiah about these early years, he recalled stopping by to see his daughter only to find no adult in the house. Cory was in his crib and Alicia in her playpen, both with bottles of curdled milk and reeking with the smell of feces. Toddler Rich was locked in the house with some bread, juice, and a television to keep him company. When Rich could not tolerate the pestering sounds of his younger siblings, he would make feeble attempts to amuse or feed them. Sometimes, in confusion and frustration, he would whack them to shut them up.

Then, when Alicia was four and Cory was three, Tammy ran off with another man. They were gone for several weeks. When she returned and said she wanted to take the children away with her, Jeremiah stepped in. He warned Tammy that he didn't trust her with the children and forcibly would prevent her from removing them. He offered Tammy part of her inheritance immediately if she would sign over the children's custody to Red.

A few weeks before Rich was six, Tammy left Stevenson Groves for good. The date was 1977—precisely when the initial entry was made in Rich's official file. It was clear from Rich's history that he had never formed a secure attachment during the crucial period when children either learn trust or mistrust. From then on it was a slippery slope toward the wretched place where he was at the moment.

I reviewed the last eleven years of each of the children's lives since Tammy left. Starting with Rich, every time it had seemed as though something might work out, another disappointment or tragedy reared up to destroy any progress he had made. The last notation in Rich's file was perhaps the most pathetic. On the most recent Labor Day weekend, sixteen-year-old Rich and some friends went swimming in the creek. His best friend at the time was Sam, a boy who had been a success story at Rich's latest rehabilitation program, and someone he admired. There are slightly different versions of what happened that afternoon, but everyone agrees Sam was on a log, reaching to grab a turtle, when both slipped into the water. Everyone laughed. Sam went under. Sam liked to kid around. Then there was a moment when Rich began to wonder. Rich jumped in and swam to the log. He dove once and thought he touched something, but when he pulled, it was only a tree branch. He dove again, this time more frantic. Rich came up sputtering and crying. By the time assistance arrived at that remote spot almost an hour later, Sam had not yet resurfaced. Divers did not find the body for several days.

No wonder Rich attempted suicide shortly afterward.

I couldn't fathom how I could help Rich after so many crushing defeats, but before I faced that challenge, I first had to locate him. I called HRS and began to track him down. A clerk called me back and told me I wouldn't have to worry about him because he was in a locked psychiatric ward halfway across the state and wasn't ''going anywhere for a long time.''

Once I knew where Rich was, I quickly determined there was not a pressing need to see him right away. It was clear he was safe. Besides, psychiatric placements were usually very short term. They'd probably move him back to our area in a few weeks. Better to see him in a foster home than in a psycho ward, I decided, and soon convinced myself that there was no rush to see Rich.

I would concentrate on Cory next.

If you studied a map of the district served by our courts and social service agency and attempted to triangulate the three farthest points, you could have pinpointed the locations where the three Stevenson children were living. Rich had special needs, but I did not understand why Alicia and Cory were in different counties, area codes, and school districts. Not only was this an inconvenience for the children, who almost never could arrange either to see or speak to each other, but it created more work for their caseworker, Mitzi Zeller.

I first encountered Mitzi Zeller when I arrived to read and copy the massive files she had accumulated about the Stevenson family. She had a mop of curly auburn hair that she kept trimmed to a sensible cap close to her head. Except when she went to court, she wore jeans or western skirts, plaid blouses with pearl snaps, and always cowboy boots. Her voice had a trace of a western twang and she had an easy, rolling laugh.

"What do you know about Tammy Stevenson?" was my first question.

"Not much. She's been missing for about ten years. I understand she lived in this area for at least five of those, but never visited her children or her father. Eventually she married the guy she ran off with—or was it his brother? Anyway, they had a kid, a boy I think, then he went to jail for six years. Maybe you remember that case? The Jiffy Rapist, they called him.

"You mean Tammy managed to marry both a child molester and a rapist?"

"Looks that way to me."

"What's Rich like?"

"A Looney Tune, always was, always will be," Mitzi said with a grunt. "I can't count how many times I had to get up in the middle of the night to remove him from a foster care placement and sit it out with him until morning in this office." Mitzi lit a cigarette and puffed tense little bursts of smoke. "Then I'd have to beg and plead for hours to find someone—anyone—who'd try him for a few more days. We have shelter homes that pride themselves on being able to handle any kid, yet good ole Rich managed to do them in. One place didn't last until I drove back to the office."

"After Tammy left, did Red marry again?"

"Don't know what that guy has, but the women stand in line. There have been three wives since Tammy, and one or two before her. The last one didn't bail out until Red was jailed. The one before that— Denise—left when she learned that he had been messing with her daughter, Sunny."

"Sexually?"

"Yep. Kid was around nine. Red made Sunny sit on his lap with his bathrobe open and nothing on underneath and used his hand to move her up and down on him. She called her grandmother as soon as she could and said that 'Daddy hurt my bum.' Her grandmother brought Sunny into the hospital and the child was examined. There were some vaginal lacerations and bleeding, and they took a semen sample from her thigh, but for some reason Red wasn't prosecuted. I guess Denise decided to get the hell out of there and took her daughter with her."

"Did she leave Alicia and Cory behind?"

"They were *his* kids. Alicia was younger than the stepdaughter. From what I can tell that's about the time he started diddling with her."

"And there was no stepmother to walk in on him."

"Not for a few months. But then number five—or is it six?—showed up. Her name is Vicky, and the kids seemed pretty attached to her."

"Why aren't Alicia and Cory with her now?"

"Vicky claimed she didn't want any more to do with the Stevensons if she could help it, but Cory keeps asking for her." Mitzi took a long drag on her cigarette. "So far those two are managing okay, but I'm holding my breath because they are still Stevensons. Alicia might stick it out with the Levys. Cory is at the MacDougals on a probationary basis because they once had Rich for two weeks and are worried he's going to act like his brother."

Mitzi's adversarial attitude toward the Stevensons was beginning to irritate me. Rich was a disturbed child, probably due to years of neglect. Alicia was the alleged victim of an incestuous relationship. While there was no direct evidence that Cory had ever been abused, he had been in trouble with the law twice: for throwing watermelons at a barn and for driving a neighbor's tractor and leaving it a mile down the road when it ran out of gas. To me both were in the realm of pranks and hardly signified a criminal mind. If anything, his problems sounded like a distress signal.

"I've met Alicia and I think she's adorable," I said. "And I'm looking forward to visiting Cory tomorrow."

"I wish you luck with the whole tribe," Mitzi said as she fumbled for the last cigarette in her pack. "Maybe you can make a difference, but after what they've been through, I doubt it."

I was lost. Both sides of the road were marked as state forest lands. Ahead stretched a baby blue Florida sky unbroken by a single cloud. It was after three and I was late for my first appointment to see Cory at the MacDougals. According to my notes, I should have crossed a bridge by now. On a whim, at a new intersection I took a road, which wound around to a more populated area, and kept working my way to the left. In two more turns I was on the road I wanted.

The MacDougals lived at the end of a rural lane. Cattle grazed beside the fence. I rang the bell and waited. After several minutes Renata MacDougal came to the door and opened it a crack. "Didn't think you were going to make it."

"I missed the bridge."

"You don't cross the bridge if you're coming from the east."

For a second I wondered if she had purposely led me astray, then dismissed the notion. I must have given her the wrong idea of where I lived.

She opened the door a few inches farther. "In all my years as a foster parent, nobody ever came to check on me before."

"I'm only here to talk to Cory about his situation and let him know he won't be alone when he has to go to court."

"He thinks his sister made the whole thing up," she said as she led the way to a round table in the kitchen. Renata MacDougal was a formidable woman with muscular arms—I suspected she could wield a chain saw with one hand. In the center of the table was a basket lined with a quilted gingham pad where a fluffy gray Persian cat wearing a blue ribbon was surveying the room. As soon as Renata sat down, the cat pounced onto her lap.

"Cory can't accept the truth about his father. After a while, he'll learn the value of the structured life he has here compared with the disorganized one he had before."

I glanced around the house, which was spotlessly clean. Not a wrinkled cushion or errant sneaker betrayed teenagers in residence. "How's Cory adjusting?" I asked.

"He's been having trouble controlling himself," Renata said, grimacing. "We've had bedwetters before, but never this." I waited while she stroked the cat. "I find his soiled underwear hidden under his bed. It stinks so bad I have to throw it out."

"You mean he can't control his bowels?" She nodded. "I would think that would be terribly embarrassing to a boy his age."

"As it should be."

"He might have a physical problem, or maybe it has to do with some abuse he suffered."

Renata MacDougal shrugged. "It's part of his lack of discipline. Conrad—that's my husband—he says what these boys need is to be humiliated until they stop making mistakes.''

''I don't know if I would use that approach . . .''

''That's how we broke Rudy of his bedwetting. Once boys get with our program, everything improves: their behavior, their attitude, even their grades in school. Here at the farm we have plenty of chores to do. It keeps their minds from wandering, keeps their bodies busy. When their heads hit their pillows, they fall asleep.''

''Tell me about their routine responsibilities.''

''They have to feed the cattle and the chickens and clean out the stable. There are fences to paint and windows to wash. They keep their rooms tidy and wash the dishes. If they don't do something right the first time, they have to do it again.'' She stood up and went to the window. ''School bus is at the corner. Just because you are here, doesn't mean that Cory won't have to do his chores.''

I was about to protest but decided a direct confrontation would only antagonize Mrs. MacDougal, who seemed rather rigid. I asked to use the bathroom. She pointed to one between the children's bedrooms. The room was immaculate. Towels were folded precisely into thirds and triangles of washcloths draped on an angle. The toilet seat lid was down and fitted with an embroidered terry cloth cover. The sink counter was bare. There were no cosmetics or toothbrushes. Not a single droplet of water or slight residue of soap scum indicated human habitation. Even the most meticulous housekeeper would be challenged to meet this spit-and-polish standard.

I tried to comprehend how a terrified thirteen-year-old, who had been forcibly removed from a chaotic home and placed here against his will, would react to this hyperfastidious environment. Might Cory's discomfort and inability to understand the new, fairly harsh rules have something to do with soiling his pants? Or had he been sexually abused by his father to the point where his anal sphincter had been damaged? And was he so ashamed of this molestation that he had to hide his dirty underwear?

I walked into the living room and saw three gangling boys lined up waiting for me. ''This is the lady from HRS who is here for Cory,'' Renata MacDougal explained.

''I'm not from HRS. They call me a Guardian ad Litem. Do any of you other boys have one?''

''No, ma'am,'' said the tallest, bowing his head.

''Look at the lady when she's speaking to you, Rudy.'' He glanced up shyly. "Rudy's been with us almost two years and he's going to go into the coast guard. And, that's Chris," she said indicating a chubby boy wearing glasses.

"And I must be Cory," Cory responded with an impish smile that contrasted with the shy, defeated expressions of the other two. "What about Alicia? Does she have somebody like you?" he asked.

"I'm Alicia's guardian too. In fact, I saw her a few days ago."

"Yeah?" He grinned, revealing crooked, stained teeth and a serious overbite.

"Did you know that today is her birthday?"

"Sure, but I couldn't get her anything. I don't have any money."

"What she really wants is a phone call from you."

Cory looked soulfully at Mrs. MacDougal, then back at me. "It's long-distance."

"You can call her on my credit card."

"Could I?" His Prussian blue eyes lit up.

Mrs. MacDougal was speaking softly to her cat. "Juniper, Juniper . . ."

I asked which phone he might use and she pointed to one next to a reclining chair. "Are you on AT&T?" She nodded. I picked up the phone, dialed Alicia's number, and entered the Guardian ad Litem office's credit card number, then handed Cory the phone.

"Happy Birthday, Ally!" he chimed, then babbled in a jumble of private sibling syllables.

"Has Cory seen a doctor?" I asked Renata softly.

"Haven't had time yet."

"Considering the difficulty you told me about, I think you should make an appointment with one of the child protection team doctors for a general checkup as well as to learn whether it is the result of any abuse. They may have ideas about how to help him regain control."

Mrs. MacDougal was cleaning the edge of the cat's eye with a tissue. I looked over at Cory, who was nodding and giggling on the phone, and caught his attention. With my hand I signaled to wind up the call. "Love you, Sis," he said with more sincerity than was typical of a boy his age, then, before he hung up, concluded, "don't forget, we're engaged and we're gonna be married. Just you and me, forever."

When Renata heard those odd concluding remarks, she rolled her eyes at me.

Cory sat quietly in the chair for a short while longer. When he turned toward us, his lower lip quivered.

"You miss Alicia." He nodded. "You guys need to see each other more often. Maybe over Christmas vacation?" My query was directed to his foster mother.

"I don't think that is a good idea," she said slowly. "When Rudy came back from visits with his sister, he misbehaved. Eventually I put a stop to them, and he's been better ever since. Right, Rudy?"

"Yes, ma'am," said Rudy, who was sitting on the sofa with his hands tucked between his knees.

"I think the three Stevensons need to stay in touch. Maybe I could arrange something over the Christmas holiday."

"The last time Cory saw his sister in court he became so upset he couldn't get any work done the rest of the day."

"Maybe he was upset about what happened in court."

"I want him home with our family for Christmas," Renata said, then sniffed the air as though searching for some noxious odor. I stood up. "Guardians usually take their kids out for a treat so they can become better acquainted. Where might be a good place to go around here?"

"Cory's not going anywhere today."

"I'll bring him back in half an hour."

"I'll have to talk to Mitzi Keller about this."

"No problem. She knows guardians do it all the time. C'mon Cory, let's find us a cold drink."

"Cool car!" Cory said as he buckled himself into my gray Thunderbird and wiggled around in the seat.

He was a young thirteen with baby soft skin, apple cheeks, and not a hint of facial hair. His eyes were a startling shade of blue with a thick coil of Stevenson lashes. His head was covered by a mop of straight hair streaked with multiple shades of burnished blond. The back was trimmed to allow for a "tail" to grow, the latest fashion for boys his age. He wore cutoff jeans and a stained T-shirt with a big-wheeled truck and SMASHER emblazoned across it. He was the sort of boy who melted the hearts of grandmothers and had preteen girls gushing: "Oh, he *is soooo cute!*"

"Where's the nearest place to go?" I asked.

Cory mentioned a tavern and a convenience store across the bridge. I pulled into the Qwik-King and told him to select a drink. He brought over an RC Cola and stared at the candy bars near the cash register. "What's your favorite?" He pointed to a Snickers bar and I bought it. Before I had paid, he had devoured it. I added a package of peanuts, then handed it to him in the car. Between sips and crunches he responded to my questions.

"Do you like it at the MacDougals'?"

"Yeah, they're okay."

"Would you rather be someplace else?"

"With my dad."

"That's not possible now."

"He didn't ever do nothin' to me!" Cory finished his soda and began crushing the can between his knees.

"Do you think the MacDougals are fair?"

"I guess."

"How do they punish you?"

"They make me do windows. I wouldn't mind it, if I could do them right, but even when I think they're perfect, Renata finds a streak and I have to start over with the towels and rags and newspapers in a certain order, then she inspects them again."

"Does she do that with the other boys?"

"Yeah, but they don't mind cause they are just a bunch of retards."

"I thought Rudy was going into the coast guard."

"He can't even read. Renata just says that because he likes boats."

We were back in front of the house. I handed Cory a card with the guardian office phone number and told him he could always call me collect.

"Yeah, sure," he responded. Even when he spoke sarcastically, there was something so guileless about his expression that it was difficult to take offense.

"You don't believe I'm on your side."

"Nope. You can't be on my side and my sister's side at the same time. She's the one who broke up our family and put Dad in jail."

"If you could have a wish right now, what would it be?"

"To be back home with Dad." He jutted his chin.

"You won't be able to go back with him until after the trial, and then only if he isn't found guilty."

"He won't be." Cory paused and waited for me to challenge him. When I didn't, he asked, "When will the trial be?"

"Probably not until this spring."

"But he's supposed to get out of jail next month."

"Yes, but he's in jail now for a different reason."

"Yeah, I know. When the judge said he was putting me in foster care, Dad said 'bullshit.' "

"When you cuss in court, that's called contempt. Your father got a forty-five-day sentence." As I spoke, I saw Cory's eyes flash with anger. "I guess you miss your father."

"I don't want to see him in jail."

"How about when he gets out?"

"Dad has to be supervised and he hates that HRS lady."

"I could be the supervisor, if you'd prefer."

"Yeah, I would," he said, then glanced aside.

"For now I'll call you once in a while just to check in. How often would you like me to do that?"

"I dunno."

"Once a week?" He grinned. "Okay, I'll call you next week. I don't have to tell anyone what you say to me unless I think you might be harmed. Otherwise everything is private."

A light rain was falling when we returned to his home. Renata MacDougal stood by the front door. Cory jumped out into a muddy rut and told her he was going to feed the cows.

I received a call from Lillian Elliott the next afternoon. "Gay, I don't know how to tell you this, but we have had a serious complaint about you," she said in a tense voice.

"From whom?"

"Phyllis Cady."

"Who's that?"

"She's in charge of the foster care program. She said that Cory would be asked to leave the MacDougal home if you ever phoned or visited there again."

"What did I do?" I asked, quickly trying to recall what might have caused the disturbance.

"Mrs. MacDougal claims that you came to her house unannounced. Now while guardians sometimes do that, we always suggest an appointment for the first visit."

"Lillian, I certainly did have an appointment. I could never have found that place, which has a rural route box number, without detailed instructions. Actually Mrs. MacDougal gave me incorrect directions, and I only found the place by chance. What else?"

"She was upset that you allowed Cory to make a long-distance phone call, without her permission, and that he ran up her bill for a half hour."

I explained about Alicia's birthday and using the office credit card, which Lillian could confirm. "Mrs. MacDougal showed me which phone to use and watched while I dialed.'' My voice became tinny, betraying my indignation. ''In fact, I even asked which long-distance carrier they used to be certain I didn't need an access code for AT&T.''

''Gay, I'm not upset with you. Complaints like this are a signal that a problem is coming to a head. I don't think you necessarily created it, but one obviously exists.''

''How can I protect his interests if I have no access to him?''

''Do you think he is in any danger there?''

''No, from most signs—exterior ones, anyway—it is a model home. But, Lillian, there is something creepy about it. It is too clean, too perfect. There are no indications that children live there. And I do have some concerns about Cory's health.'' I explained about him soiling his pants. ''First thing this morning I called Dr. Goldberg on the child protection team and asked him if the problem—which he called 'encopresis'—might be a sign of sexual abuse. He said the symptoms were worrisome and recommended an exam by a member of their team as soon as possible. I was going to call Mrs. MacDougal today and ask her to make an appointment with a child protection team doctor.''

''I'll make that request through Phyllis Cady. Nancy already has set an appointment to discuss your behavior with her and Mitzi Keller. You are welcome to come, but if you feel uncomfortable, we'll handle it without you.''

''I'll be there.''

We met in Phyllis Cady's small office. When I arrived, Lillian was already seated with her hands folded in her lap. Nancy Hastedt came in just after me and took the seat opposite Phyllis.

Phyllis thanked us for coming, then directed her comments to Nancy. ''Our foster parent is very distressed at having a virtual stranger come into her home uninvited and dictate how she will manage children under her care. She cannot have someone filling the child's head with the idea he has rights and privileges he has not earned. Renata MacDougal has been an exemplary foster parent who accepts some of our most difficult cases. We cannot allow one of your guardians to disrupt not only Cory's placement but also two other hard-to-place emotionally and intellectually challenged boys.''

''Before you blindly accept Mrs. MacDougal's version,'' Nancy inserted, ''I think Gay should tell you what happened.''

As I retold my side from the first phone call to set up an appointment to the birthday call to Alicia, the facts seemed too ordinary to have caused such controversy. I was complimentary about the spacious MacDougal home and attractive rural setting. I said that Cory seemed comfortable there and that he only wanted to leave to return to his father.

"That's not the way I heard it," Mitzi Keller said to her supervisor.

Nancy handed Phyllis a receipt proving the phone call had been billed to their credit card. "Also, Gay has a copy of her handwritten directions and the time of their appointment," Nancy said.

Phyllis studied them a long time before speaking. "Perhaps there was some misunderstanding, since Mrs. MacDougal has never had a guardian in her home before. All I know is that most of the children placed there do exceptionally well. One of her boys is going to enlist in the coast guard this summer."

"Isn't he mentally handicapped?" I asked.

Phyllis turned to Mitzi for verification. "Rudy would like to join the coast guard," Mitzi replied hesitantly, "and the goal is good for his self-esteem."

"What about Cory's self-esteem?" I blurted. "This is a child who deserves compassion and support, not punitive treatment." Lillian's head bobbed, giving me courage to continue. "I believe that empowering Cory and letting him know that he has rights in the system is important to his long-term emotional development."

Before anyone could interrupt, Nancy spoke. "I am fully satisfied that our guardian has acted within the scope of the program."

"Then you are forcing us to find Cory another placement," Phyllis said dourly, "which means he'll probably spend Christmas in an emergency shelter."

"Are you certain the MacDougals will throw him out?" Nancy asked.

"Only if Gay stays involved with the case."

"I'll be happy to step down, if that would be best for Cory."

"No!" Nancy stated firmly. "We are convinced Gay did nothing wrong. If we capitulate, Renata MacDougal can pull the same nonsense with the next guardian. But I am willing to suggest a compromise. I'll assume that Mrs. MacDougal was ill-prepared for Gay's visit and I would like someone from HRS to educate her about the rights and responsibilities of the court-appointed guardians. Also, I will take steps to have guardians appointed immediately for Rudy and Chris. In the meantime, because Gay does not think it in Cory's best interests to be moved abruptly, I will ask Gay not to visit or call Mrs. MacDougal until you've helped her to understand the advocate's role."

"I don't want to let Cory down," I interjected. "I told him I would phone him in a few days."

"We'll be happy to explain to him that you were asked not to call," Phyllis said.

"He needs a medical exam as soon as possible," I added. "Will HRS arrange for it?"

Phyllis's mouth twisted like she was thinking hard. "Might be difficult right before the holidays."

"Might be even more difficult if there is no medical evidence for the prosecutor," Nancy snapped back.

The Monday after New Year's the box of Christmas presents that I had sent to Cory was returned as "refused by addressee." I phoned Lillian. "Anyone know how Cory is doing?" I asked.

"Have you tried Mitzi Keller?"

"No, I have been lying low, as per instructions."

"You've followed your part of the bargain. Now what do you want to do next?"

"I would like to have some time alone with Cory and hear from him how he's doing because there's a court appearance on the Stevenson case coming up next week and I don't know what to write about him in my report."

"That's a fair request. Does it have to be at the MacDougals?"

"I would rather it were somewhere else."

Lillian arranged for Mitzi to call me. "Mrs. MacDougal will bring Cory to my office at one tomorrow afternoon." Mitzi's voice was tense, but polite.

"That's fine, as long as I can spend some time with Cory alone."

"Renata MacDougal will drop him off and return in an hour."

My phone rang at 7:30 A.M. the next day. "Mitzi Keller calling, sorry it is so early but I am going to be visiting clients all morning and I wanted to catch you. Renata MacDougal has canceled the visit."

"Why?"

"She's worried that you might interfere in Cory's discipline program."

"That's hardly an excuse. What if her discipline program is inappropriate or abusive?" This time I did not bother to mask my annoyance. "Who's looking out for Cory's interests?"

"I make frequent visits to that home. You saw it yourself. I wish all my clients had such a clean, wholesome environment."

"Clean perhaps, but I am not convinced it is a wholesome environment."

"He's doing fine there."

"What about the bowel problem?"

"Mrs. MacDougal said that has passed."

"Did he have the medical exam?"

"I'm not sure," Mitzi replied defensively. "Look, Gay, I didn't cancel the visit, the foster mother did."

"I'll have to talk to Lillian or Nancy," I said in a slow, deliberate tone. "Maybe they would like me to ask the judge to order a visit."

"Isn't that a bit extreme?"

"What is extreme is that this child has a Guardian ad Litem who has been denied access to him for almost two months."

When I called Lillian, she reminded me that we would be in court in a few days to review Red Stevenson's performance agreement, the contract with HRS, which, if completed satisfactorily, would enable Cory to return home if his father was not incarcerated. The documents had been drawn up by HRS and agreed to by Mr. Stevenson, but the judge still had to approve the terms.

"You can use that opportunity to ask the judge what to do about Mrs. MacDougal."

On the appointed court date, I waited in the corridor for Mrs. Mac-Dougal to arrive with Cory. They never appeared. When his case was called, I went in alone.

Red Stevenson stood by his attorney while Judge Donovan reviewed the documents that stipulated Mr. Stevenson had to attend parenting classes, buy Cory an article of clothing each month, set up a bank account for him, and receive counseling. The judge put down the papers and then glared down from the bench at Mr. Stevenson. "I remember you and what revolting injuries you inflicted on your daughter." I had not been present at the initial hearings when Alicia had been taken into the state's custody but had heard that her testimony had been heart-rending.

The judge turned to Calvin Reynolds, the HRS attorney, and held the documents as though they smelled bad. "Can this performance agreement be waived so we can move directly to the termination of parental rights?" This was a startling turn of events, for it revealed the judge's prejudice against Mr. Stevenson as a parent even before his criminal trial. However, there were two separate legal cases: the criminal, which would determine whether Red was guilty of a felony, and the dependency, which would conclude whether he was a fit parent to raise his son. Obviously, if someone is found guilty of the criminal abuse of a child, he is unlikely to be considered a suitable caretaker, but not all child abusers are prosecuted criminally. The burden of proof is much weaker in a child abuse case, and if there is sufficient information that a child might be harmed by a parent, the state can place that child outside of the home for his protection.

Before replying, the attorney looked something up. "No, Your Honor, since we have already negotiated the performance agreement in good faith, and since the father has already taken some of the steps outlined in it, he has a right to continue to try meeting the terms under it."

Obviously annoyed, the judge reluctantly approved the document. He was moving the case file aside when I spoke up. "Your Honor, I am the Guardian ad Litem for Cory Stevenson as well as his sister, Alicia. Cory's foster parents have tried to prevent me from seeing him and they have also denied visitation between the siblings, even over Christmas."

A wave of irritation crossed Judge Donovan's face and his round cheeks flamed. "Is the foster family present?" he asked the caseworker.

"No, Your Honor," replied Mitzi Keller.

"I suggest that you speak to your foster parents and ask them seriously to reconsider their position in this matter. If they still will not cooperate, you are to take the appropriate steps to allow the children to visit." Mitzi Keller nodded.

"Is that all?" he asked me.

"Since the foster family has barred me from their home, it is impossible for me to serve as Cory's Guardian ad Litem. Since I was appointed by you, Your Honor, I would be happy to step down if you think it best."

"I want you to continue as the guardian," he said flatly, then turned to the next case.

Two weeks passed without further progress. Nancy insisted on another meeting at HRS. "Either Mrs. MacDougal permits you to see Cory today or we ask for an emergency hearing this afternoon for the judge to remove him from that placement."

The gathering was held in the HRS conference room. Lillian, Nancy, and I sat on one side of the table. Renata MacDougal was already there. Mitzi Keller came in with another HRS worker, Gloria Nyswander, the caseworker for the other two foster children in the MacDougal home.

While waiting for Phyllis Cady, Lillian told Gloria that the forms had been processed to appoint guardians for Rudy and Chris.

"They are no problem," Mrs. MacDougal said. "At least they know how to behave themselves."

"What sort of behaviors won't you tolerate?" Lillian wondered.

"Mouthing off, not doing chores, violence," she replied.

"What do you do to maintain your standards?" Lillian probed.

"I remove privileges one by one." She folded her hands on top of the table. "You see, these children have never had consistency in their lives. When they come to us they learn that we mean what we say. We don't bend our rules, so eventually they relent and give in. We don't care how long that takes." Renata MacDougal held up her hand in a thumbs-up. Then she rotated her hand and lowered her thumb to the polished wooden table and slowly pressed it into the surface, as though grinding the carapace of a hard-shelled insect. "We grind them down."

I was watching Nancy's expression. Her eyes widened and her jaw dropped. On my notepad I wrote: "Auschwitz guard?" then scribbled Mrs. MacDougal's precise words, underlining *grind*.

Gloria spoke enthusiastically. "Their system really works. When Rudy came to them, he was failing, and now he is an honor student."

"If you give them a chance, they could work wonders with Cory," Mitzi chimed in.

The rest of us sat in silence. Gloria broke it to ask Renata MacDougal, "Did you have a good Christmas?"

"We always do. We spent four hundred dollars on each of the boys."

"That's very generous," Lillian commented.

Phyllis Cady's appearance brought the meeting to order. She spoke directly at Nancy. "We're concerned that the interfering actions of a Guardian ad Litem have made it difficult for our foster parent to control this child."

"My guardian has not been permitted to see or talk to Cory since her initial visit." Nancy bristled. "The fact is that Cory has been denied access to his court-appointed guardian, he has not been able to communicate with or see his sister, nor has he been examined by a physician."

"Is that true?" Phyllis asked Mrs. MacDougal.

"I don't see why this woman is undermining me by attempting to contact Cory behind my back," Mrs. MacDougal said, pointing to me.

"I have met Cory only once, and never even spoken to him on the phone," I said defensively.

"What about the package you sent?"

"It contained Christmas gifts from me, but it was returned as not accepted."

"That's not true. When I received the delivery receipt, I went to the post office to pick it up, but it had already been sent back."

"Which post office?" I asked.

"Williamstown."

I opened my file until I found what I was looking for: the address label cut from the package. "I sent it UPS. Here is the original label."

Lillian kicked my leg under the table and suppressed a smile.

Nancy cleared her throat. "There is no point going on. I have heard enough to ask you to remove Cory from the MacDougal home this afternoon."

"Absolutely not!" Phyllis Cady's lips contorted in anger. "I will take the matter to court before I will allow your office to determine where our foster children will be placed."

"I already have the legal papers drawn for that possibility," Nancy said finally.

Phyllis Cady shifted in her chair. "Perhaps we can work out a compromise. If Gay wants to talk to Cory, she could schedule visits with him at HRS."

I waited a beat for Nancy or Lillian to jump in, but then could not restrain myself. "I am a volunteer Guardian ad Litem, not an abusing parent. If I am going to follow the judge's order that I continue as his guardian, I will meet him at his home or at his school whenever I feel it is appropriate."

"I can understand why you feel that way," Mitzi said, trying to be conciliatory. "Maybe it would be in Cory's best interests if you resigned and they appointed someone else, who Mrs. MacDougal could accept. That way Cory can stay with the MacDougals, where he is happy."

"I don't have an ego problem with this case. Nancy can use me however she prefers. If you like, I'll leave the room and you can make the decision without me." I reached for my purse.

Lillian placed her hand on my shoulder and kept me in my chair. "Gay, you are Cory's guardian. What would you like to do?"

"I don't have adequate information about this child's state of mind to make a decision." I thought quickly. "I would like to meet with Cory today and then I want him to have an appointment with a therapist within the next three days. Then I will make my recommendation."

Phyllis Cady shifted in her chair. "Let me talk to my staff and Mrs. MacDougal for a moment."

In the hallway Lillian shook her head admiringly. "What possessed you to bring that package receipt?"

"You did tell me to document *everything*."

Mitzi opened the door. "Would you be available to go to the Mac-Dougal home right away?" she asked.

"Yes," I replied.

"With Lillian along as your supervisor?" Phyllis Cady added.

"Sure," I said.

Lillian nodded that it was fine with her.

Phyllis Cady glanced at Renata MacDougal. "Will that be agreeable to you?"

Renata MacDougal looked directly at me and nodded. "I never had met a guardian before you came to my house, so I thought someone had singled me out to check on. Apparently I misunderstood."

The coolness and logic of her speech disarmed me. What had she been told when we left the room? "What about a visit with him and his sister?" I asked.

"That won't be a problem," Mitzi Keller filled in. "I'll make the arrangements for that as well as with a therapist."

Phyllis Cady stood up, as did Renata MacDougal. She lifted a tote bag that had been by her side during the meeting and unzipped it. Out popped the head of her cat, Juniper, who blinked his eyes in the bright light.

Forty minutes later I crossed the bridge and turned down the country road with Lillian following close behind. The sky ahead was blackened by an approaching thunderstorm.

Renata MacDougal came to the door. "I called the boys to come in from the barn. Don't want them to be out when this storms hits."

Hearing a scuffling sound, we turned. The three boys were wiping their feet on a mat by the back door.

Lillian pointed to the fifteen-foot Christmas tree under the highest point of the vaulted living room, and smiled. "Sounds like you boys had a wonderful Christmas."

"Cory, why don't you show these people your gifts?" his foster mother said.

Cory slipped off his shoes and came toward us silently. He lifted a radio-controlled truck off the shelf.

"Nice!" I said.

"Yeah." He nodded. "I got lots of cool stuff." There was a fragment of the twinkle I had noticed when we first met.

He held up a pair of brown cowboy boots, a Walkman, and then pointed out a sweater and some slacks.

"Don't forget the Disney season passes," his foster mother prompted. "Did you do your homework?"

"Yes, I finished the math assignment. Look." Cory turned to a short division page and showed it to me.

I checked the neat column of answers. "Looks perfect to me."

The sky rumbled. Lillian glanced at her watch. "Let's go out for a snack, okay, Cory?"

The boy gave his foster mother an inquiring look. She nodded and said it would be fine.

The three of us contorted ourselves into Lillian's racing green convertible. "Can you put the top down?" Cory asked.

Lillian looked at the tall trees, which were swaying against the charcoal sky. "That would guarantee rain." She put the car in gear. "Where shall we go?"

"There's only the convenience store and the tavern," I explained. Without blinking, Lillian pulled into the Sandy Lane Tavern. I loved Lillian's style. If I had done it, though, Mrs. MacDougal would probably have called Phyllis Cady to complain I had plied the kid with six rounds of beer and bought him a pack of cigarettes.

"Did you like your trip to Disney?" I asked Cory once our eyes adjusted to the dim interior.

"Yeah, once we got there, but we almost didn't go because of what Rudy did."

"What was that?" Lillian wondered.

"It's too personal to discuss."

The Cokes were served and I covered the hush by chatting about Alicia. After he drained his glass, Cory blinked his bright blue eyes. "Rudy, well . . . he wets his bed, then he doesn't tell anyone."

"That must have been embarrassing for him," I said, also thinking about Cory's similar problems.

"Yeah, it freaks him out when they find out, which they always do. You got to learn not to let them get to you. See, I always think of every day as a fresh place to start. Even if the past was dirty, the future can be clean."

Lillian gave me a sideways glance. "Where did you learn that?"

"Not from my father, I'll tell you that!" Cory chuckled. "Dad used to say, 'What's in your dirty little mind?' and I would reply, 'Dad, my mind is clean.' "

Silently, I tried to decipher what he might be trying to tell us about Alicia's sexual abuse, or possibly his own. Then Lillian asked, "If you could return to your Dad tomorrow, would you want to go?"

"Yes!" he replied unequivocally.

"Until that is a possibility, do you want to stay where you are?" Lillian continued.

"I'll stick with the MacDougals until I can go home because it's a cruel world out there on the streets." Just then a bolt of lightning splintered the silence.

After we stopped laughing, I said, "I guess that proves it, Cory. But sometimes it feels safer to remain somewhere you know because there always could be something worse, but there is a chance that there might be something better."

"I'm not taking any more chances."

"Okay, then do you have any other requests?" I asked.

"I still want to see Alicia. You know her and me, we're going to get married."

Lillian looked at me quizzically. "It's a joke they have," I explained.

Lillian handed Cory a business card with the Guardian ad Litem office number and told him how to make a collect call.

Cory put it in his shirt pocket. "I'll give it to Renata when I get home."

"No, Cory," Lillian said in a solemn tone, "you put this one in your pocket. I'll give her one later."

When we returned to the house, Conrad MacDougal came out to the car and opened the door on Cory's side. He was rail thin and way over six feet tall. I had never met him, nor had Lillian, but he ignored us. "Just the young man I needed to see."

Cory got out quickly and stood ramrod straight. Conrad MacDougal, towering above him, waved the math paper I had looked at earlier above Cory's head. The page was now covered with red X's beside every problem. "You'll have to do this disgraceful work over before supper."

"Excuse me," I interrupted, "but I checked the paper and the answers were correct."

"Oh, is that so? Didn't you notice that he copied every problem backward? See"—he showed me the book—"it's supposed to be eighty-one divided by nine, not nine into eighty-one." He crumpled the paper and threw it on the ground. "Now go in the house and do something the right way the first time for a change."

Without a glance backward, Cory hurried up the path. "Just a minute," I called. "I have something for you." Fumbling with my keys I opened my trunk and lifted out the UPS package with the label cut off. "Your Christmas present was returned to me by mistake."

Cory took it. "Better open it later," he said, then rushed to the porch as nickel-size circles of rain began to pelt the pavement. At the door, he turned, grinned, and said, "Hey, thanks a lot!"

"He doesn't deserve treats when he is doing so poorly in school," his foster father said. "That's why I came out and showed his mistakes to you. Humiliation goes a long way to burning something into the memory."

Lillian opened her mouth, then decided against making a comment. "I've got to be going. Gay, could you direct me back to the highway?"

We got back in our cars and started down the road. As soon as we were out of sight of the farm, Lillian sped up, passed me, then signaled she was pulling over by the convenience store.

"That man is worse than his wife!" Lillian seethed as we talked, windows open, sitting in our cars. The pouring rain formed a curtain between us.

"I don't understand why Cory defended them. We gave him lots of opportunities to raise a red flag, but he wouldn't do it."

"He can't allow himself to be truthful because he has no reason to trust us," Lillian said, shaking her head sadly. "Behind those gorgeous eyes is a wall of fear. If Cory hasn't been able to admit his father might be at fault, he certainly can't do it about the only other caregivers he knows."

"So, does that mean he has to stay in that"—I started to censor myself, then burst out—"that concentration camp! I think they take in those boys so they can have slave labor."

"It's definitely an unhappy home. But if Cory won't say anything, then all we can do is keep the pressure on the MacDougals to comply with the agreements we reached this afternoon so you can monitor the situation."

Alicia's foster mother, Ruth Levy, phoned the next day. Finally arrangements had been made for Cory to see Alicia on Sunday. "I'm going to pick up Cory and take him to a church picnic and a concert of religious music. Mrs. MacDougal said it was okay with her, but she wanted to check with her husband. I can't see anything in my plans he would object to, do you?''

An hour later Ruth called back. ''The visit is off. Mrs. MacDougal said that her husband did not want Cory to be rewarded with dinners and concerts when he was doing so poorly at school. Can you help?''

I sighed, and said I would call Lillian, but she was out. Since I had just been informed of the next date that Cory would have to go to court, I decided to call Mrs. MacDougal myself.

For once Renata MacDougal and I had an amicable conversation. She was pleased that the case was progressing against Mr. Stevenson. ''Cory won't settle down until he begins to accept his father is not the man he idolizes.''

''I was hoping he could work that out with a therapist.''

''He's going next week.''

''That's excellent. I understand Alicia might be seeing him this weekend.'' Mrs. MacDougal explained her convoluted reasoning about why Cory could not have special outings until his behavior improved. ''I realize that, but this is important to Alicia. Considering what that girl has been through . . .''

''We aren't trying to prevent them from visiting with each other, we just don't want Cory to have a fancy dinner or see a concert until he earns it as a reward.''

''But he could get together with Alicia?''

''Not at the Levy house, because they might go against my rules. But she can come here.''

I phoned Ruth Levy, who erupted. ''That woman! She makes me sound like a heathen.'' I dared not respond. ''Okay, let's call her bluff. The concert is on the way to Williamstown. I'll take Alicia there before the concert and pick her up afterward. It's a pain in the rear for me, but this time I won't let Renata weasel out of it.''

''Thanks,'' I said. ''You are wonderful to do this for the children.''

Monday morning I called Mrs. MacDougal to see if the visit had taken place. ''Oh, the little tramp was here all right. Alicia wore a sweater so tight Rudy's eyes were popping out of his head. Then Cory fought with Chris over their chores and I had to take away television from both of them for the rest of the month. Even worse, I caught Alicia and Cory using foul language in front of Rudy. He doesn't know better, but those Stevenson brats certainly do.'' Before I could respond, Renata continued, ''I'll tell you one thing, Alicia knows what a jerk her father is. She told Cory that he was never going back to their dad, so he should make the best of it. If the Levys were firmer with her, she'd turn out all right, but they're going to let her run wild.''

"Well, thanks for allowing them to visit, and let me know what the therapist says," I responded with every ounce of control I could muster.

Thursday of that week there was an urgent call from Mitzi Keller. "Mrs. MacDougal has thrown Cory out. Yesterday I moved him to the home of Birdie Rose and Patty Perez in Kensington Heights."

"What did he do?"

"He was caught smoking. Renata gave him some punishments, but he refused to do them, so she said she would contact me and Cory said, 'Go for it!' ''

"May I call Cory now?"

"Sure. Patty is a different type than Renata MacDougal." She told me the phone number.

When I put down the receiver, I found my hands were trembling. Poor kid! He hadn't wanted to leave, and now, probably because of my actions, he had lost one more parent figure in his life.

After I introduced myself on the phone, Patty said, "Why don't you come over? Cory would love to see you."

A few hours later I walked into a three-bedroom ranch house in a treeless new development. Cory came to the door, grinning. "Want to see my new pad?"

A slender woman was making ice tea in the kitchen, and without asking, poured a tall glass for me. "That's Patty," Cory said, then pointed out a stout woman on the couch, who had a baby in her arms. "And that's Birdie. They're my new mothers." He lifted a blanket on the floor. "That's Manuel. He's blind." My breath caught as I looked at a boy curled in the fetal position with his head on a plastic tape recorder. He was humming to the music accompanied by a gurgling noise that sounded like water running.

"Manuel needs suction," Birdie called, "and I don't want to put Sheila down."

"Be right there," Patty said as she rinsed her hands. Wheeling a medical suction pump over to Manuel, she stuck a tube into his tracheotomy opening and sucked mucus into a container. Then she gave him a kiss on the cheek and turned over the tape in the recorder.

"Cory," I began awkwardly, "I realize you didn't want to leave the MacDougals."

"It was my fault. I broke the rules and she threw me out."

Just then the baby startled and began to scream. Birdie altered the baby's position so she could rub her back. "Sheila's a cocaine baby and has fits like this every twenty minutes or so. My job is to sit here and cuddle her. Not bad, eh?" She gave me a broad smile that revealed tobacco-stained teeth. "We specialize in kids with medical problems."

"Cory doesn't have any that I know of."

"That's a matter of opinion. He just came from the MacDougals, right?" I nodded. "Well, this won't be the first time we've picked up the pieces from there, will it, Patty?"

"You've had other kids from that home?"

"Sure. They always come in like zombies, but in a few days they bounce right back, right, Birdie?"

Patty had her car keys in hand. "Gotta go get the kids at the bus stop. Be right back."

Realizing my car blocked the driveway, I reached for my purse, and took out my keys. Suddenly I had an idea. "Cory, would you mind moving my car out of the way?"

Cory's eyes almost popped out. "Me?"

"Do you mind?" All he would have to do was put the Thunderbird in reverse and back in into the next lot, a vacant field, then pull it up beside the garage. How much damage could he do? But my method was more deliberate. I wanted Cory to know that I trusted him.

When he was outside, Birdie said, "Don't worry, he'll be fine here. Tomorrow he has checkups at the medical and dental clinic and we've got him on the list for the county mental health center."

"But he's only been here one night."

"What's the big deal? I just sit here and make phone calls all day. Patty does the running around." Manuel made a choking sound. Birdie handed me the baby and turned on the suction.

"Nice car!" Cory came in and handed me the keys. "You know that I'm seeing Alicia this weekend, don't you?"

"You spoke to her?"

"Sure, Patty told me to call her as soon as I got here so she would know where I was. It's still long-distance, but I can call her anytime after six in the evening and talk for ten minutes."

A knot in my chest began to loosen. I looked around this home that was more cluttered and much less substantial than the MacDougal farm, down at the twitching baby in my arms, across at Manuel's erratic mewing, and for the first time, thought: Cory is going to be just fine.

* * *

One of my first forays to test the limits of a guardian's scope came with my next meeting with Alicia. We had planned to go out to dinner together and do some shopping with her Christmas money. As soon as we were seated in the Mexican restaurant at the mall munching corn chips and guacamole, Alicia began to unload her complaints. The Levy foster home was so far from her old school that she never saw her best friend, Dawn. Ruth wouldn't allow an overnight at Dawn's because it was against foster care rules. Then Alicia became more animated as she told me about a new boyfriend, who meant more to her than "anything in the world." They were making plans to give each other rings at Easter. As I watched her varied expressions, I tried to imagine what might become of her.

Just a few weeks past her fifteenth birthday, Alicia had her whole life in front of her. From her records I knew she had academic potential but was a mediocre student. Her fervor was reserved for attracting boys, but if she could learn to find satisfaction in accomplishing something through school or work, perhaps she would realize she didn't need a man to validate her self-worth. On the other hand, the more common scenario of using a sexual liaison to get out of foster care—either by dropping out of school or getting pregnant—seemed likely. Worse, Alicia easily could fall for any man who showed her any attention, one who might use her, abuse her, turn her onto drugs, infect her with AIDS, or otherwise ruin her chances for a future with more possibilities. I knew she liked animals and computers, music and movies, children and photography, old boats and cars. I could see her working in a veterinary hospital (her stated choice) or doing accounting on a computer (she did well in math) or singing in a church choir, or restoring automobiles. Rapidly her image metamorphosed from her schoolgirl blouse to a white lab coat to a smart business suit to a pair of overalls.

As she babbled on, though, I noticed that the thick coating of makeup made her skin into something older, harsher. Her blouse was unbuttoned to reveal the tops of her breasts overfilling a lacy bra. When a guy in tight pants swaggered by, Alicia tossed her head, batted her eyes, and thrust her shoulder forward provocatively. Though I tried to block them, Alicia's other possibilities loomed up in a series of images of her modeling for a sleazy photographer, hanging out in a seedy bar, selling her body on a street corner, wasting away in a hospice. I blinked back tears and tried to follow her patter without prejudice. Then Alicia asked a question that abruptly brought the present into focus.

"Do you think you could?"

"Could what?" I said, not certain I had heard her right.

"Could you find my missing mother?"

"I don't know . . . ," I began slowly. "It might not be something that guardians are supposed to do. Also, nobody has heard from her for at least ten years."

"That's not true."

"What do you mean?" I asked shakily.

"When I was in fifth grade, she drove up to the house. My father took the rifle from the wall and ran outside waving it. I heard her pleading to see us. My father called her a whore and warned her that if she ever came around again, she'd regret it. When she tried to get out of the car, he cocked the hammer. Rich was there then, he saw it too. He started to run out to stop Dad, but Dad pointed the gun at Rich and forced him back in the house. My mother gave up, got back in the car, and started to leave. When she passed by the front of the house, I saw her real close. She was crying so hard her face was shining." Alicia leaned forward, knocking her soda cup forward. We both ignored the spill. "That means she wanted to see us . . . and that she really loved us. Only Dad wouldn't let her and she was scared of him. Everyone was scared of him." Alicia trembled, not with sadness, but rage.

Where was Tammy? What if she were in jail, or worse, dead? What if she was a prostitute or an addict? Wasn't it better for Alicia to have some fond memories than to be slapped with the truth? No, I decided that only the truth would clear up her fantasies.

Alicia was waiting for my response, and when I did not answer at once, she lashed out at me. "You won't help me either! I asked Mitzi and she said she didn't have anything in the file and that was that. So what am I supposed to do? Forget I ever had a mother?"

"No, Alicia, no," I said in as soothing a voice as I could muster. "You need to know what happened to her. I just am not sure how to do it. I've never tried to find a missing person before, so I don't know how difficult it might be. Also, you might learn some things you'd rather not have known."

"Like what?" Alicia asked challengingly.

I stated my fears about her mother turning out to be a disappointment. "Okay, that's a possibility," she admitted. "It's also possible that Rich is right. He believes she died in an accident. I don't know where he got that from, but if it is true, I'd want to know. It must be in the records somewhere, don't you think?"

"I suppose so."

"But isn't there also a chance that she is alive and that she does still love me and wants me? I'm sure she doesn't know where I am. Maybe she doesn't know what happened with my father. Now that he's out of the picture, maybe she'll take me back."

My chest expanded with the same immense hopes. "Let's go home and talk to Ruth about this. I want her to know what we are doing because she might feel a little jealous."

"Why should she do that?"

"Because she loves you, Ally-Oop, that's why!"

Ruth was very quiet. She heard my explanation, then asked Alicia a few questions. Then she turned to me. "I was adopted by an aunt after my mother died, but I always wanted to find my father. When I was a little older than Alicia, I learned that they had known all along where he was. I became furious because I felt they had kept him from me all those years. My grandmother understood and took me to meet him." Ruth turned to the wall of photographic portraits in her living room and waited a few seconds to compose herself. "I met him, and I am not sorry I did, but he was—to say the least—a disappointment. A real loser."

"But you found some answers . . ." I said.

"Yes, so I understand why Alicia wants to do this."

"There's a good chance that we'll never find her," I added.

"But if nobody tries, I'll never find her anyway," Alicia said, her eyes staring off in the distance.

Nancy approved the plan to try to locate Tammy Stevenson. "As long as you think it is in the children's best interests" was her only caveat.

I asked Lillian the best way to proceed.

"Start with the police records on every member of the family," she suggested.

My court order gave me access to the criminal records of everyone connected with these children, but since I already had a substantial file on Red Stevenson I had not yet seen any reason to track any others down. I went to the sheriff's records department, handed over copies of my court orders on both the criminal and dependency cases, my identification card as a Guardian ad Litem, my driver's license as a picture ID, and asked for anything pertaining to Richard Leroy Stevenson, Sr., Red Stevenson, Richard Leroy Hamburg, Red Hamburg, Jeremiah Stevenson, Tammy Stevenson, and Tammy Hamburg. My court order had another name I had not noticed at first: Sunny Rhodes. The night before I had called Alicia and asked if she knew that person.

"Oh, that was my stepsister, the one that had to move out when my father messed with her."

So I added that name to my list, just in case there had been a complaint filed in that case.

The clerk mumbled something about it being a long list and it might "take some time." I agreed to wait. Ten minutes later she unlocked the door to her office. "Some of these files are marked confidential. I don't want you standing around reading them in the hallway. Come in, and I'll give you an empty desk and start bringing you files."

And bring them she did. Handwritten police reports, arrest sheets, investigative files, and more. The first pages referred to Red Stevenson's arrest for molesting his daughter, but a second set looked almost the same except that the name of the victim was Dawn Leigh Pruitt. Dawn! Alicia's best friend? There was a doctor's report on Dawn's gynecological examination that indicated penetration had taken place. Next there was also a report from a Mrs. Smiley about the suspected abuse of Alicia. I took down that name and phone number. I presumed that she was the person who had initially called the abuse hotline about Alicia's molestation. Since her name was supposedly off-the-record, I was surprised to uncover it in the police paperwork, but I wrote it down anyway, and later would be glad that I had.

Farther down in the paperwork there was a complaint from the previous summer accusing Red of the "sexual maltreatment of Cindy, Hallie, and Katie Curry." The report went on to describe how the girls traveled with Alicia Stevenson on the school bus and got off at the same stop. They were friends and sometimes they stayed overnight at the Stevensons' house. Cindy, the oldest, reported that Mr. Stevenson forced her into a room and she had to struggle to get away. Concerned he was going to do something "nasty" to her, she spent the rest of the night on the front seat of his pickup truck with the doors locked. A worker in the groves reported seeing Red Stevenson playing tag with Hallie, and when he caught her, "he slipped his hands under the waistband of her shorts." Another time Mr. Stevenson held Hallie upside down and wouldn't put her down until she agreed to something. When the grove worker heard her screams, he came into view, and Red let her go. The youngest, Katie, reported that Mr. Stevenson liked to rub her in "funny" places. Although an official abuse report was filed by Mr. Curry, with the HRS investigation concluding the allegations were "indicated," no legal action seemed to have been taken.

The next report was for a burglary by Richard Leroy Stevenson the previous January. After I read the summary, describing the perpetrator as "emotionally disturbed," I realized this was a charge against Rich Jr. and not his father, although the incident had not shown up in his HRS file. I asked the clerk to search under Cory's and Alicia's names and in a few minutes she located the charges against Cory for stealing a tractor and vandalizing a field of watermelons. He had been given a sentence of a hundred hours of community service but had not completed any of them. Thankfully, Alicia had no criminal file of her own.

The clerk kept reappearing with additional assault reports against Mr. Stevenson, some as much as fifteen years old. At the bottom of the pile were incidents filed under the name of Hamburg. I leafed through them rapidly and there she was: Tamara Felice Stevenson Hamburg. I copied down her date of birth and a Social Security number, then noted a box that listed an FBI number.

"What's this?" I asked the clerk.

"They get an FBI number when they've been charged with a felony," she explained. The clerk pointed out an arrest sheet from 1979. Tammy had been charged with defrauding an innkeeper by passing a bad check to pay a bar tab. Her last known address was a rural delivery box five miles from the groves. I looked at the signature of the officer who had arrested her: Glen Cunningham. I blinked and stared again. Glen was the father of one of my children's friends. No longer on the police force, he had started a landscaping business. All of a sudden I decided that I needed something to control the black spots on my rosebushes.

Not only did Glen Cunningham have the right chemical composition for my horticultural problem, he remembered Tammy Stevenson Hamburg very well.

"Not a bad kid, just immature. We were in middle school together, and even then she could drink the boys under the table. Cute little thing, good dancer, but she got messed up with that fellow who took her to Oklahoma and dumped her, then came back married to Red Stevenson. When he started running around on her, she took up with another guy who ended up in jail. Really knew how to pick 'em, didn't she?"

"What happened to Tammy?"

"I heard she moved away with the kid she had with the last guy."

I explained that I wanted to find Tammy for her daughter's sake. "Do you know where I would start?"

Glen shuffled his feet. "You have a court order, right?" I nodded. "You have her DOB and Social Security number?" I nodded again. "You give them to me and I'll see what I can do."

"But you're not still on the force?"

"You want me to try or not?"

"Thanks, Glen," I said, and paid for the bug spray.

On my way back from the nursery I made a slight detour and went by Cory Stevenson's foster home. I was amazed how both Birdie and Patty seem equally in touch with the mental, emotional, and physical needs of their diverse charges, and Cory was doing splendidly there. Within two weeks Cory had been placed in a special program at his new middle school, had seen Dr. Goldberg, and was on a waiting list for therapy at the county clinic, although he could not get a preliminary appointment for several months. Dr. Goldberg diagnosed Cory as being hyperactive and having a respiratory infection, but too much time had taken place since his bowel problems to diagnose any abuse.

Even though I was at peace about Cory, I still worried about Rudy and Chris languishing at the MacDougals. To clear my conscience, I had written Lillian a letter stating that I had serious concerns about the suitability of that home for any child and asked that she should pass on the letter to anyone she thought should see it.

> After your experiences at the two meetings with HRS, including the one with Mrs. MacDougal, as well as the visit to her home, you and Nancy might agree that there are indications that this family's style of child rearing leaves much to be desired. My notes document an authoritarian approach, threatening attitude, verbal abuse, humiliation, expectations far exceeding a child's emotional and developmental level, punishments with extreme time limits, work and chores above and beyond normal household patterns, and general lack of knowledge regarding contemporary parenting skills.
>
> Further, in her dealings with me, Renata MacDougal routinely told lies about me and others. She would not permit the siblings to visit and kept this Guardian ad Litem from the home for more than two months until a court and HRS ordered a visit. She never took Cory for medical or therapy appointments, despite frequent requests to do so.
>
> On the surface Renata MacDougal presents well and has complicated rea-

soning behind most of her actions. However, underneath lies a controlling aspect that might be more relevant in the management of a prison camp than a foster home. Since almost all my contacts with Mrs. MacDougal have been confrontational, I have documented this case carefully. These notes might be of use to some future investigator. Other persons who have been associated with this family have also voiced concerns about the destructive nature of that environment.

I understand that there is a scarcity of foster homes, and that the MacDougal family has been willing to take difficult cases, but my sense is that no child is well served by a placement there. At best, children in foster care need more emotional support than that family provides. At worst, serious psychological harm could come from putting children with fragile self-concepts there for any length of time. Perhaps this home meets all current HRS standards—at least on paper—but I believe a much more in-depth analysis of that home should be undertaken, with particular emphasis on the mental health of the parents.

Please understand that the spirit of this letter is not spiteful or vindictive. My only concern is to protect the children there now or in the future.

Lillian told me the letter had been forwarded to Phyllis Cady and that Rudy and Chris had been assigned guardians of their own. Satisfied, I concentrated on the Stevensons.

Cory ran out to meet me as I pulled in the driveway. Birdie Rose followed carrying the baby. "I once drove this car!" he said to Birdie and stroked the Thunderbird's hood.

Birdie chuckled. "I taught Cory to suction Manuel and he's great with the baby too. I think he likes being the oldest child and being responsible." She shifted the baby to her shoulder and went back in the house.

Leaning against my car, I brought Cory up-to-date on some of the issues that concerned him. His father was getting out of jail in two weeks and we set a date for his first supervised meeting.

"So how's it going here?" I asked.

"I love this place. Birdie and Patty are always fair, not like Mrs. MacDougal. She had a favorite, which was Rudy, and she would bust me for doing stuff, but never Rudy."

"What do you mean by 'bust'?"

"You know, get more chores to do. There was no dust allowed in that house, not a single speck, so we cleaned every day." He changed to a high-pitched voice. "Mrs. MacDougal was Little Miss Perfect. She always found something wrong with whatever you did."

"I remember that bathroom by the bedroom was really tidy. How did you keep it so clean?"

"Oh, that was the easiest one!" Cory giggled. "We weren't allowed in it."

"But it was the one between your bedrooms."

"The only toilet and shower we could use were the ones in the garage."

"Even in the middle of the night?"

He nodded. "I should have told you, but Mrs. MacDougal warned me not to trust the Guardian ad Litem."

"Have I ever lied to you about anything so far?" I asked.

"I don't think so."

"Was Mrs. MacDougal always truthful with you?"

"No, she lied all the time." He grinned. "Hey, don't worry, I trust you now."

Three days later I returned to my office from lunch and found a note on my desk that read: Cunningham Nursery called to say your order is in.

I dialed Glen Cunningham at once. While waiting for him to come to the phone, my pulse resounded in my temples.

Glen didn't waste any time with a greeting. "Her name now is Tammy Spate. Her address is post office box 9190, Mead, Washington."

"Where's that?"

"Outside of Spokane."

"That's about as far away from Florida as you can get."

"You said it. Want her phone number?"

"How'd you do it?"

"I have my sources." When I didn't respond, he added, "How are the roses?"

"Haven't killed them yet." Then I thanked him and hung up.

It was noon. Nine o'clock in the morning in Washington state. Should I just pick up the phone and say: Hi, your daughter—remember her, the one you abandoned ten years ago?—wants to know if you love her. I felt dizzy and put my head down on my desk. Here was a woman who had left her children, who had a police record, who probably had been—or still was—a substance abuser. She had married Red Stevenson, who not only had sexually abused his daughter, but may very well have done the same to several of her girlfriends and a stepdaughter. Now she had started a life with a new man and had tried to put her past far behind her. What did I think I was doing meddling in her life? On the other hand maybe she was so settled and so happy that she would welcome her other children. Maybe she had loved them all along but had literally been chased off by Red and his rifle.

I went to the office kitchen and made myself a cup of spice tea. After a few sips, I felt calmer. What was the worst thing that could happen? Tammy could hang up on me, reject her children through me. They would never have to know. I could handle the disappointment and move on from there. The tea was bitter in my mouth. I returned to the kitchen and added a large teaspoon of sugar.

After I finished the tea, I wondered what the Stevenson children might gain. Could this be their ticket out of foster care? If Rich Jr. had the love and support of his very own mother, even he might overcome his horrible predicament. Then I conjured up Tammy standing at an airport gate her arms outstretched welcoming her long-lost children into her life. I knew it was a long shot, but it was the only one I had.

I didn't contact Tammy that day, or the next.

I made guesses as to the best time to call, finally settling on Saturday at nine-thirty in the morning, a time her kids might be watching cartoons and she might not be too busy, yet too early for her to be out running errands. I wrote down a few lines and tried them out on my husband. (Although I kept the names and details of cases confidential and never let him see the files, Phil could not help overhearing some of my phone conversations or wanting to know where I was going and what I was doing, if only for safety reasons. I often discussed the theories of how to approach a case with him, and his advice and viewpoints have been invaluable.)

When I worried about disrupting Tammy's life, he asked, "Do you represent her or her children?" Then he said, "I think you should record the phone call."

"That's illegal!"

"Think of what you have to gain."

"The click of the phone if she hangs up on me."

"Exactly! The kid needs to hear it, otherwise she's going to continue with her fantasy forever." He came around and massaged my tense shoulder blades. "And what if the mother says something wonderful, like she wants to see her children? Wouldn't it be great for her daughter to hear those words in her mother's voice?"

"How would I do it?"

"I'll set it up for you. Which phone do you want to use?"

With great reluctance I allowed Phil to put the tape in place, figuring I'd deal with the consequences later. What follows is a transcript of that call, with some minor editing for clarity, confidentiality, and deletions of extraneous or overlapping comments.

TAMMY: Hello.

GAY: Hi, is this Tammy?

TAMMY: This is she.

GAY: Hi, my name is Gay, and I'm calling because your daughter, Alicia, asked me to help her find you.

TAMMY: Oh?

GAY: In Florida.

TAMMY: Yeah?

GAY: Is this a good time to talk or should I—

TAMMY: It's fine, it's fine.

GAY: I don't think you've been in touch with the family for many years and you probably don't know what's been going on.

TAMMY: No, I don't. The last I heard was more than ten years ago, and I was told they did not want me to have any contact with them.

GAY: Well, in the last six months—there's been some legal problems with Mr. Stevenson, their father. He was accused of sexually abusing Alicia, and some of Alicia's girlfriends, and also Rich—

TAMMY: Rich was accused of it too?

GAY: No, Mr. Stevenson, the father, was accused of abusing Rich. And so Alicia and Rich were taken away from Mr. Stevenson and put in foster homes. They left Cory there because there was no indication that he was abused. But Alicia and Rich were real worried about their brother and they went to court and stood up there and very bravely told the judge that they thought their brother was at risk and they got him removed from their father's home.

TAMMY: Okay, good.

GAY: The current situation is that Mr. Stevenson is going to have a criminal trial coming up. That's the way I got to know Alicia and all the children. I volunteered to be something called a Guardian ad Litem, where I represent the children's best interests and I make sure they are in good foster homes and they are getting their medical and psychological care and no lawyers are giving them a hard time. I stand there as the adult when they can't speak for themselves.

TAMMY: That's good.

GAY: And one of my jobs has been to get to know the kids real well, and I'm very fond of Alicia. We were out to eat and she said she always wondered what happened to her mom and could I help her find you. I didn't know if I was allowed to do that or how difficult it was to find somebody, but I asked the people in the office I work with if I was allowed to do that and they said yes. And so it wasn't very hard because it was just following the addresses. And I guess HRS—that's the foster care agency—they never even went looking for you.

TAMMY: There was a lot going on when Red, their father, and I divorced. He and my father didn't want me to see the children. However, I tried several times to see them.

GAY: That's what Alicia said. She remembers you coming to the house and she wonders if you wanted to see her or wondered what ever happened to her.

TAMMY: They made sure they had an unlisted phone number so I couldn't get it and I was never allowed to see them.

GAY: That must be hard.

TAMMY: The last pictures I have, gosh, they were just little guys.

GAY: Also, I don't want you to think I am calling because you have any legal or financial responsibility because you don't. That's not an issue.

TAMMY: I'm not worried about that a bit.

GAY: I haven't even told Alicia I got this phone number because you might have a life of your own or you might have reasons for not wanting to get involved. That would be very understandable.

TAMMY: No, I definitely will get involved, definitely. I always hoped that when they got old enough they would try and find me.

GAY: Good.

TAMMY: So, I'm open. I'm available.

GAY: Are you remarried?

TAMMY: Yeah, I'm remarried and I have a ten-year-old son, Billy, who knows that he has other brothers and a sister. And I have a little two-year-old daughter, Heather.

GAY: Unfortunately none of your children are living together. Rich has a lot of emotional problems. He has not done well and he's been in a lot of special camps and schools.

TAMMY: They started that when he was younger. His dad said that he was afraid Rich would end up killing Cory, so he had him to psychiatrists and all sorts of different people. He tried to tell me that I was the problem. I would very much like to have something to do with all three of them again.

GAY: Well, Rich is the worst off and, of course, he is at that difficult age when boys have all those hormones raging. Despite the things that have happened to Alicia, she's a tough cookie and has a lot going for her. She has a terrific foster mom.

TAMMY: Good, that's half the battle right there.

GAY: Cory is a bright bouncy kid who is very clever with his mouth. They're all very pretty children. They have these gorgeous blue eyes, especially Cory.

TAMMY: Oh, he always did!

GAY: And these big dark lashes. Cory's at the age right now where he's really sprouting. Alicia is about five foot two.

TAMMY: Like me. That's my height.

GAY: Apparently Alicia has been molested for a number of years.

TAMMY: No wonder Red didn't want me to have anything to do with them.

GAY: That may have something to do with it. But considering everything that has happened to Alicia, she's a terrific kid. Do you work these days?

TAMMY: No, I'm home all the time.

GAY: And your husband knows they exist?

TAMMY: Sure he does. We keep no secrets from each other.

GAY: What would you like to happen next?

TAMMY: Alicia can call me. Anything she wants to do. Please let them know, let Rich know, let any of them know, that I am here if they need me.

GAY: For some reason Rich believes you are dead.

TAMMY: His father probably told him that. What does Cory think?

GAY: He hasn't brought it up.

TAMMY: Cory was so young when I left. All he knows is what he has been told, and I'm sure it was not good.

GAY: Alicia really believes in her heart that you would like to be in touch with her.

TAMMY: I would.

GAY: Oh, that's so good! I didn't want her to be disappointed.

TAMMY: No, no, no! The only reason I haven't had contact with them is because of my father and their father.

GAY: Alicia told me they threw you out when you tried to get back there—

TAMMY: They did. See, when I left, Red was having an affair with another woman—my best friend, Denise. My dad knew about it too and didn't think I should leave over it. I told him I was not going to live that kind of a life and Dad said, "Honey, I'll give you whatever you want, any amount of money, if you can stick it out." I told him no amount of money was going to make a difference. When I left, my father told me that when I was able to I could come and get them. But then he got quite bitter about it and changed his mind. I knew back in those days that Red had sexual problems, but I had no idea that they were in that direction. None whatsoever, or I never would have left any of those children in that situation.

GAY: Well, probably it didn't come out until later, when they were a bit older. Is Denise the one Red later married?

TAMMY: Yes.

GAY: There are documents saying that her daughter, Sunny Rhodes, was removed from the home because Mr. Stevenson had abused her and she went to live with her real father, Mr. Rhodes. When little Sunny left, that's when he apparently started in on Alicia. Now none of this has been proven in court. I would bet, though, that the way things are going, Red will be in jail serving some time pretty soon.

TAMMY: Well, that's the place you put those sort of people. I hope in there he will get the help he needs.

GAY: Since he really wants to get Cory back, he has had to work with the courts even before any criminal problems in terms of getting therapy. Whether or not he completes the therapy and does all the things he has to do to get Cory back is unknown. It is hard to keep children away from their parents legally.

TAMMY: There should be something I can do to keep the kids away from him. I never gave up full custody.

GAY: There probably is. I'm not a lawyer, but I'm a mom too. To know this has happened to a child of yours has to be quite upsetting.

TAMMY: I think it would be best to get them totally away from this situation once all of this is over.

GAY: I don't know what's around in terms of money, but it might be easier if one person came to Florida rather than two or three of them going to Washington. You might want to tuck that away and think about it. They certainly would be available to be visited. And I'm a person who can act as an intermediary between the people involved—foster care, HRS, lawyers, and courts. I have a credit card I can use to make free calls, so I'd be happy to keep you informed.

TAMMY: That would be great. I'd really appreciate that.

GAY: Let me give the news to Alicia. This is going to flip her out. Fifteen-year-old girls . . . you know . . .

TAMMY: They're very emotional. Just pick the right time and do it the right way.

GAY: She's about forty-five minutes from here. I'm thinking of calling her to find out if she's home. I hate to tell her this on the phone. If I can get down there, I'll see her now, then I can make a credit card call for her if she is ready to speak to you.

TAMMY: I always hoped they'd contact me someday. I just don't like the fact that Rich thinks I'm dead.

GAY: That might be easier for him to believe than being deserted. But Alicia has this memory of seeing you in a car and you not being allowed to get to her. That gave her hope that you wanted her.

TAMMY: I do. I do! Every one of them! Cory has a birthday coming up.

GAY: Yes, he does.

TAMMY: I never forget. At least there will be some contact from now on. Now you tell Alicia I love her. Just tell her . . . I want her . . . she's always been loved.

GAY: I will.

TAMMY: Thanks for calling, Gay.

GAY: Thank you, Tammy.

I popped out the tape and called Ruth Levy, who said that Alicia was home. I told her I had something to give Alicia and would be there in about an hour. During the ride I replayed the tape, tears welling up as I listened to Tammy's warm, affectionate voice. "I definitely will get involved," she had said as though she really meant it. The tape was indeed a precious record and I was thankful Phil had persuaded me to make it.

Now, how was I going to break the news to Alicia? I practiced a few phrases before I remembered what she had said to me when we were alone the first time in my car. I smiled as I decided to echo her own words back to her.

"I guess I should tell you that I have been doing something illegal," I said to Alicia when she opened the front door. Her eyes widened. "It's illegal to tape a phone conversation without the person's permission." I held up the tape. "It's a call to your mother. I found her."

"No! No way!"

I beamed and nodded. "Really. That's why I recorded it. To bring you proof."

She staggered backward down the hallway. "She . . . doesn't . . . want . . ."

"No! No! She wants you! She loves you! She always has!"

Ruth Levy, who had been folding laundry, came to see what was going on. One of the other foster girls, who had overheard the conversation, filled her in.

"You found her? So soon? How is it possible?" Seeing Alicia's distraught expression, Ruth waved the other girls away. "Why don't you take Gay to your room?"

Alicia closed the door. I handed her the tape. She placed it in her pink plastic tape recorder and pressed Play.

There were the electronic beeps of me punching in the credit card number, then Tammy's first hello.

"Hi, is this Tammy?"

"This is she," Tammy said.

Listening to her mother's voice for the first time in more than ten years, Alicia clutched the tape player to her chest and sat down on the lower berth of her bunk bed.

"Hi, my name is Gay, and I'm calling because your daughter, Alicia, asked me to help her find you."

Tears splashed dark spots on Alicia's violet sweater. I handed her some tissues and kept one for myself. Together we listened and cried as I heard the same remarkable conversation for the third time.

After we had talked for a while, Ruth came in and I told her about the call. I asked Alicia if she wanted to speak with her mother. She shook her head.

"I guess she's not ready," Ruth said. "It's quite a shock."

I saw a shadow of rivalry in Ruth's expression that made me wince inside. Should I have warned her that I had located Tammy or at least have told her why I was coming over before I did? Then she might have broken the news to Alicia first. I had wanted to do it, but was that fair? Ruth was Alicia's emotional support person. Not only had I stolen something from their relationship, but I had ignored the fact that Tammy might supplant Ruth in Alicia's heart, even though legally it would be months or years before Tammy could regain custody of any of her children.

I apologized to Ruth for not including her sooner, which she deflected graciously. I decided it was time to leave them alone. Ruth saw me to the door.

"Give me Tammy's number and I'll have Alicia call her when she is ready," Ruth said.

I agreed, then admitted to myself that I didn't like being excluded either. Still, I knew it was best handled as a private matter between Alicia and her two mothers.

On the way home, though, I felt triumphant. For the first time I could see a shining light beyond the impending travails of the trial. I turned up the music on the radio to hear Bette Midler singing "Wind Beneath My Wings" and soared along toward home feeling just a little bit like a hero myself.

What I had accomplished so far had given me the strength I needed to face Rich Stevenson.

Monday morning I made the necessary phone calls and started out for the small city sixty miles to the north where Rich was. The Three Rivers Mental Health Facility looked like any other industrial building in an office park complex. I presented my identification at the glass window.

Dr. Corinne Newman motioned me through a door and locked it behind her. She took me into an office crowded with four desks and offered me a seat. She studied me for a long moment, then removed her glasses and slipped them into the breast pocket of her lab coat. "Before we begin, you did bring your credentials, didn't you?"

I handed over the packet I had shown the sheriff's office clerk. The doctor, however, made photocopies for her files.

"I'm sorry to report that Richard has had a bad morning. After breakfast he refused to replace his tray on the rack. An orderly asked him twice, then physically helped him comply because it's important to maintain routines. When he resisted, the orderly wrestled him to the carpet. Richard sustained a laceration to his right eye. After that we had to restrain him, and thought it best to medicate him."

"With what?"

"Ah, Thorazine, do you know what that is?"

"An antipsychotic," I replied, trying to suppress my rage as I thought about *my* kid being injured, shackled, and mollified with chemicals. "Does he take that drug regularly?"

"No. He was on medication for the first few days until our behavior modification program started to show results and he kept gaining levels of privileges. This is really not an appropriate placement for him because it is basically a seventy-two-hour evaluation facility."

"Where should he go next?"

"That's the problem. There's an HRS district case supervisor trying to find him something, but so far he hasn't been successful, and the news of this latest crisis isn't going to help."

"May I see Rich?"

"He's asleep. Thorazine does that." She checked her watch. "It might be wearing off enough to wake him." She hesitated a moment. "Or maybe you'd rather come back on a better day."

"It's over a hundred miles round-trip . . ."

"Yes, well . . ." She pulled out her ring of keys and led me down two corridors and asked me to wait by the nurses' station.

An anorexic waif of a teenager with wispy blonde hair drifted beside me. "You a doctor?"

"No, a visitor."

"Visitors aren't allowed back here."

"I'm a special case."

"Who are you here to see?"

"Rich Stevenson."

"Oh!" Her eyes brightened and she brushed back her hair. This maneuver allowed me to see her heavily bandaged wrist. "I'm Daphne, Rich's friend. I just *love* him. He's so cool! And his story made me cry and cry. I thought I had it tough! God! First his mother and brother are killed in a car wreck and then his dad goes to jail. No wonder he's acting crazy."

"What do you mean, Daphne?"

"I hate what happened this morning. It wasn't fair. He needs kindness, not bullying."

A nurse came in carrying a tray filled with paper cups of Jell-O. "Daphne, where do you belong?"

Daphne touched my arm. "Tell him I'll see him in group," she said, then disappeared as silently as she had appeared.

Dr. Newman beckoned me across the hall. She unlocked the door to a lounge. Plastic-covered sofa pillows from several divans had been laid on the floor as a makeshift bed. A boy in jeans was facing the wall. His arms were encased in a white canvas restraining device.

A beefy orderly knelt beside him, talking softly. "You got a visitor."

"Huh?" He turned his head and blinked in the bright light. "Who . . .?" His nose was dripping, but he couldn't wipe it, so he pressed it into the mattress. That gesture—of misery and helplessness— pierced me. I moved toward him.

"Take it off," Dr. Newman told the orderly.

More gently than expected, Rich was unbound. I noticed his back was covered by islands of infected acne. He rolled on his side, eyes still closed.

"Can you sit up?" the orderly asked.

Rich's eyes opened again, then shut. "Thirsty . . . ," he muttered.

The doctor left the room and returned with a paper cup of water and set it on the table. She pulled up a chair for me on one side, while the orderly helped Rich to his feet. He staggered toward the table on un- steady feet. The orderly arranged Rich in the chair and held the water cup up to his mouth. When he sipped, he did not center the cup in his mouth. Some water spilled down his chin. He turned away from me, embarrassed.

"It's okay," I said. "I didn't mean to wake you from your nap. I'm a friend of Alicia and Cory and I wanted to meet you too."

"You seen them?"

"Yes, both of them within the last few days. They're fine and they asked about you. I promised to call and tell them how you were."

With enormous effort Rich lifted his chin and focused on me with the familiar large marble blue Stevenson eyes. To me that moment is like a frozen drop of water in a strobe-lit Harold Edgerton photo. For in that split second Richard Leroy Stevenson, Jr.—the weird, the crazy, the violent, the sick, the reviled, the shunned, the holy terror—became Rich, my guardian child.

The upwelling of feeling, the sense of connection was utterly unex- pected. Any fears dissolved. "We're fine," I said to the doctor and the orderly. "We'll just talk for a while."

The doctor nodded to the orderly and they backed away, leaving the door wide open.

In the simplest terms I explained about being Rich's advocate and that of his siblings. I gave Rich a brochure and a card with my office phone number and went over how to place a collect phone call to me. The orderly brought Rich his tray so he wouldn't miss lunch.

Rich lifted his fork. "Do you mind?"

"Go ahead."

He pointed to a plastic tote bag on a table at the far end of the room. "That's mine. Could you bring it here?"

I went and retrieved it and he pulled out three notebooks filled with drawings. There were a variety of fine pencil sketches showing the Grim Reaper, skeletons, and other personifications of death. One cemetery scene depicted tombstones engraved with the names of dead rock stars including Elvis, Jim Morrison, John Lennon, Buddy Holly, Keith Moon, Jimi Hendrix, and Duane Allman. In the center was a very small, but elaborately embellished grave marked: Richard Stevenson, Jr., the year of his birth, and the current year.

"Where do you want to live?" I asked.

"With Ally. In our own apartment. I'd take care of her. They think I can't, but I can't do worse than our father. I've seen what he did, but nobody will listen to me."

"What do you mean?"

"This summer, when I was still home. You know there was only one bedroom, and my grandfather had that."

"I thought he had his own house."

"He rented it because he was having heart problems and didn't want to live alone anymore."

"So where did everyone else sleep?"

"I crashed on the couch and Ally and Cory had bunk beds on the porch."

"What about your father?"

"He had a twin bed in Gramps's bedroom."

"But he was married until recently."

"She slept on the porch in the cot most nights, or they'd open out the couch bed and I'd get the cot."

"What is it that you think you saw?"

"Hey, I know what I saw, okay?" he said belligerently. I nodded that I was listening. "So, Dad came out to the porch, picked Ally up like a baby, and took her into the dining room and laid her on the floor. It was dark, but there's this green light on the VCR. I could see the shadows and hear the noises."

"And . . . ?"

"And? And? And he was fucking her, that is what he was doing! Fucking her real good."

"Would you tell that to someone else, someone who could help prosecute your father?"

"Sure, I would."

"Do you think your father should go to jail?"

"He's there now, isn't he?"

"That was for cussing the judge. He'll be out next week. But I mean for a longer time because of what he did to your sister."

"Hey, he fooled around with me too."

"Like how?"

"You know, jerked me off, and made me do it to him."

"When was that?"

"I don't remember."

"We don't have to talk about that now. But let me ask you one thing. Do you think Cory should go back and live with him?"

"No, he'd be next, if he hasn't done it to him already."

I encouraged Rich to eat his lunch. He complained about the food and how boring it was at the hospital. There was nothing to do, no school, no activities. He wanted out as soon as possible. He also wanted a pizza.

When Dr. Newman returned, she smiled at us. "Looks like Richard might be ready to join the others at group."

"Too tired," he mumbled.

"I met a girl, Daphne, and she said she hoped you would come," I added.

"She did? You know why she's here? She tried to off herself this weekend. But she'll be out of here tomorrow and I'll still be locked up." He wagged his finger at Dr. Newman. "Right, Doc? You love me so much you won't let me go."

"That's not exactly the way I'd put it, Richard."

"See, they don't tell me nothin'! Like, it isn't important for me to know what's happening in my own life."

"I'll try to find out what is happening and call you," I said.

"Nobody can phone me here."

"They said I could call the nurses' station and they'd get you."

Rich brightened. "Okay."

"Okay, you'll come to group with me?" the doctor asked.

"Guess so . . ." Steadying himself with one hand on the table, Rich stood. I placed his notebooks in his bag, tucked the guardian information on top, and handed it to him.

"See you soon," I promised.

"Yeah," he said with the cocky Stevenson grin that Cory had per-
fected. "Soon."

Today, when I look back on my notes of the next few weeks of the Stevenson case, I wonder how I had time to conduct my normal life. I know that I
had a manuscript in the editing process and was in the early stages of re-
searching a new novel, but I also was working almost full-time in our documentary film company and busy with one child still at home. Our
fourteen-year-old son, Josh, required the usual chauffeuring to soccer practice and orthodontist appointments, encouragement, nourishment, and attention. On one occasion Josh and I had plans to buy soccer cleats, which he
wanted to break in before the first game of the season. Just as I was finding
the car keys, Patty Perez phoned to say that Cory was upset after a call from
his father in jail and he wanted to see me. I went out to the car, where Josh
was already waiting. After explaining that one of my guardian kids, whose
father was in jail, was very upset and needed me, I said that even if we went
shopping the next day he'd still have three days before the soccer meet to
wear his shoes. Josh shrugged and got out of the car.

"Maybe it's not fair for me to be a guardian for other children if it
means I have to break a promise to you."

"Oh, Mom, I don't mind," Josh said graciously.

"Really?"

He gave me one of his deep-dimple smiles. "I love what you are
doing."

"Because it helps other kids?"

"Nah, that's not it." With a flip of his foot, he picked up his soccer
ball, tossed it in the air, and bounced it off his forehead. "See, ever since
you've been a guardian, you've been off my case."

Laughing, I realized that this was true. Something that had once irritated me—like a wet towel on the carpet or a glass placed in the sink
instead of the dishwasher—now went without comment. How could I
"sweat the small stuff" when my kid was doing wonderfully in school,
coming home on time, was cheerful, helpful, funny, clever and . . . and
normal! He loved us and we loved him. There had never been a moment
of disruption in his life because there had always been a stable marriage,
a comfortable home, plenty of food, and access to medical care. He was
close to his brother, his grandparents, a nearby aunt and uncle, plus a
large extended family that would support him when we were not around.

Nobody had ever hurt, abused, or neglected him—and his father and I would make sure nobody ever would!

Yet, as I hurried to meet Cory, there was a tiny tingle that made me wonder whether I had better focus more on my own sons—just in case.

The following week Red Stevenson was to be released from jail after serving time for his cussing offense. Red had called Cory and told him he wanted to see him that same day. Patty Perez didn't want Cory to be pressured into anything, but I soon determined that this is what Cory wanted and agreed to facilitate the reunion for him. Red only was permitted supervised visits with his son on the grounds of an HRS facility. However, Mitzi Keller, who was not shy about her intense dislike for Mr. Stevenson, claimed that she had too much office work to travel to Cory's foster home, bring him to her office, and return him home. "Hey, but if you are willing to transport Cory, that's fine with me."

For the child's sake, I made the arrangements for the first visit even though I had no desire to meet Mr. Stevenson, who knew I also represented his other children, the children who wanted him behind bars.

When we arrived at the drab HRS facility in the county seat, Cory's father and grandfather were already waiting in the parking lot. Jeremiah Stevenson came forward first. His gray eyes flooded with tears and his scrawny arms quivered as he hugged his grandson. Cory patted his grandfather's corded hand gently and led him to a picnic table next to the social services building. A long line of food stamp recipients snaked around the yard, but Cory didn't notice. He climbed on the bench, snuggled close to his father, and tugged on his arm like a much younger child.

Red Stevenson was a husky man with the expected red hair dulled by a greasy patina. He wore a full beard that retained flames of the youthful color. His cobalt blue eyes proved the genetic link, although it was hard to see them at first because Red refused to make eye contact with me.

Cory prattled on about what cars he might drive when he turned fifteen.

After about ten minutes, Mitzi Keller came out and sat down on the far end of the picnic table, but said nothing.

"You know your mother called your grandfather and said she might be coming to Florida?" Red suddenly asked Cory.

"Yeah," Cory admitted, since I had told him about the call.

"She has a hell of a lot of nerve showing up after all these years.

Who raised you? Who fed you? Not her, me! And what do I get for it? Shit, that's what. Now she thinks she can waltz in here and interfere.''

"Mr. Stevenson, please change that subject or I will have to end this visit," Mitzi said.

"Dad . . . ," Cory pleaded.

Red saw Mitzi's frown and said, "Okay." He placed his arm around Cory and squeezed the boy to him. Cory's head leaned against his father's chest. "You know I don't want anyone to take you away from me, don't you?''

"Yeah, Dad."

"Everyone is out to get me. They are talking about a separate trial for what they claim I did to Dawn Leigh. Now you know I never touched that kid.''

"I know, Dad. She and Alicia just wanted to stay together and made the whole thing up.''

"If they ask you to swear to that in court, will you?''

"I only have to tell the truth, right?''

Red ruffled his son's hair. "Good guy," he muttered.

Mitzi's mouth twisted into a disgusted expression. "I have another appointment," she said, standing. "But you should know that Cory's been caught smoking and he needs to stop.''

"You smoking again?" Red chided with some annoyance.

"Once in a while . . .''

"If we're going to get back together you are going to have to behave better.''

Mitzi seemed satisfied and started for the door, but I was furious. After Mitzi had departed, I said, "Cory, none of this is your fault.''

Then Cory did something odd. He reached for his father's hand and used it to hit himself in the face. "See, I'm hitting myself this time, you're not hitting me," he said, then did it again, much harder.

As planned, Patty Rose drove up to fetch Cory. Jeremiah cried again as they said good-bye, then waited on the picnic bench for Red to walk Cory to the car. Mitzi came out and pulled Patty aside to give her some new Medicaid forms, and I followed Red and Cory.

Apparently Red did not realize I was behind him. One moment he was chatting about a new hydroplane engine, the next he balled his fist and punched Cory in the chest so hard both the child's feet lifted off the ground at the same time, yet Cory didn't utter a sound of complaint.

"Hey, Dad, how about some cash?" he said a few seconds after the blow.

Mr. Stevenson reached into his pocket and handed Cory a five-dollar bill. Still unaware of my presence, Red clutched a handful of hair on Cory's neck and yanked his head back as far as it would go. I could see the boy's expression: a forced smile that didn't ease up until his father let go and his head snapped back. I stepped protectively between Cory and Mr. Stevenson, opened the car door, and told Patty I would be by the next day.

After they drove off, Mitzi asked Mr. Stevenson and me to come into her office.

"I don't like the way that visit went," Mitzi said. "I think we should curtail any more for a while."

Red Stevenson's head was downcast, but I could tell he was looking at me out of the corner of his eye. "I don't agree," I said. "Cory has only seen his father a few times in the past six months."

"Whose decision was that?" Mitzi asked.

"Mr. Stevenson didn't want his son to see him in jail," I filled in.

"You don't know how hard this is for me," Red said, softly. His bulky shoulders were hunched over and his arms hung docilely between his legs. His coloring and posture reminded me of a gibbon, a primate with long arms and no tail.

"It's hard for Cory, too," I began. "I think he needs more reassurance than criticism."

Ignoring me, Mitzi opened a file. "Mr. Stevenson, in reviewing the performance agreement, I must point out that you have not substantially complied with any of the requirements. You have not completed psychological counseling for abuse, nor attended a series of parenting classes, have not opened the bank account and made deposits in his name. You have not provided one item of clothing each month or completed the readings on the list."

"That's not true," Red replied forcefully. "I've spent more than seven hundred bucks seeing Dr. Osterman."

"Is that your psychologist?" Mitzi asked. Red nodded.

"I am going to need a report from him too," I added.

"He told me our sessions were private," Mr. Stevenson said.

"Guardians can have any records they want," Mitzi said without disguising her annoyance.

"The reason I want it, Mr. Stevenson, is so I can advise the judge whether or not I feel Cory should be returned to you if you do not end up in jail."

"But Mrs. Courter doesn't have to share that report with me," Mitzi countered. "If you want it as part of the performance agreement, I'll need to see it as well. Otherwise you'll have to obtain additional counseling for your problems."

"You two are going to gang up on me so I never get my kid," he said, petulantly.

"Not necessarily," I replied. "In fact, the prosecutor and Mitzi Keller have both requested no visitation until after the trial, but I stepped in to defend your right to see your son. Isn't that true?"

Mitzi nodded.

"Why did you do that?"

"For Cory."

"What about Tammy? She's trying to steal him from me."

"Alicia wanted to find her, so I helped them make contact. What happens next remains up in the air. Cory is so unhappy and confused, I want you to think about how you can make your visits with Cory more pleasant and less stressful for him."

"It's so hard for me now. I'm depressed and have serious financial problems of my own."

"When are you going to pay some money toward Cory's care?" Mitzi asked.

"I've had to ask Pop for twenty-five grand for the attorney and that means he has to sell the house so we have something to live on."

"If Cory were at home, you'd be supporting him," Mitzi replied.

"I can't ask Pop for anything more now. We're broke. Those little bitches are going to pay for it in the end. My lawyer is going to sue the Pruitts for false arrest and anyone else who tells lies about me. And now they're digging up every piece of dirt they can find."

"By the way, I don't have a complete social history," Mitzi interjected. "When were you first married?"

"I was eighteen and she was sixteen. It was in Oklahoma."

"What was her name?" I asked.

"Annette. She died in an accident."

"Did you have any children?" Mitzi continued.

"Yes, a daughter."

Apparently, after Annette died, this daughter was taken from him by the court, who declared him an unfit father because Annette had another daughter, who had been hospitalized with a broken pelvis. Both parents had been suspected of child abuse.

"My own mother wanted Annette's kid and helped take her away from me."

After that, Red stopped communicating with his mother. He claimed she was a "whore" who had men "right in front of me." She also allowed customers to "screw me in the ass" when he was little and "she kept the money."

I could hardly believe these revelations were being made in an HRS office in the presence of a guardian and a caseworker, and I was certain Mitzi was equally astonished. Together we questioned Red Stevenson for more than an hour using polite, soft-spoken voices and acting sympathetic rather than accusatory. We even managed to discuss Sunny Rhodes.

"That was blown way out of proportion. I came out of the bathroom wearing a robe and Sunny was watching television. She jumped up and leapt into my arms. To catch her, I had to let go of the bathrobe, which didn't have a belt. So of course the robe opened and I was naked underneath. Sunny saw my privates and screamed. Next thing I knew she'd called her grandmother, who never liked me anyway, and she told the police. But, once they heard my side of the story, they never prosecuted me."

After Red left, I sat limply in Mitzi's office. "Had you known that he had a child removed from him in Oklahoma with his own mother siding against him?" I asked.

"No," Mitzi admitted. "You wouldn't really champion Cory's return to that pervert, would you?"

"After what he's just confessed in here, combined with the way he behaved with Cory, he's even worse than I expected. But whether we want to or not, we have to deal with the fact that Cory loves him."

At this point the trial preparations were in full swing. Whenever the attorneys wanted children to appear, they had to be made available. After I told Grace Chandler, the state's attorney who was prosecuting Red Stevenson, what Rich had witnessed and experienced, she was anxious to take his statement. Without telling me, she called Dr. Newman and made arrangements for Rich to be deposed. Fortunately, Mitzi alerted me because as his Guardian ad Litem, I was the only other person allowed in the room during the interview.

I contacted Grace Chandler and warned her that Rich might still be on mind-altering medications. Grace thanked me and phoned Dr. Newman to request that Rich not be given drugs a few days before the appointment if at all possible. When the therapist seemed doubtful about him handling the stress without tranquilization, Grace followed my suggestion. "Promise him the pizza of his choice for cooperating."

Apparently that worked. When I met Rich outside the state attorney's office, he was docile and affectionate, hugging me like a long lost pal. Mitzi seemed anxious to get back to her office and said she'd meet us at the pizza restaurant. While we waited, Rich and I debated whether pepperoni was better with green peppers or mushrooms and wondered what sort of person ordered anchovies.

"I hate fish, especially if you see their disgusting eyes," he said.

"Do you know the Dr. Demento version of 'Fish Heads'?" I asked.

He didn't, but he broke up laughing at the words to the silly song.

When I first was asked to take the Stevenson case, I had thought that since I was trying to survive the throes of adolescence with our sons, I might be better off with younger ones. Later I discovered that knowing the jargon was a decided advantage. Who would have thought that being able to quote the lyrics to "Dead Skunk in the Middle of the Road" or that all-time mother-cringer, "Dead Puppies," would come in handy? Perhaps Dr. Newman and her peers might analyze these songs in terms of Rich's disorder, tying them in with his morbid preoccupations, but I knew that most boys that age took delight in these verses during a macabre phase that fortunately passed.

When we were called into the state attorney's office, Rich went in humming the fish head song. Grace Chandler bantered with him for a few moments before she took out her tape recorder and had him swear he would tell the truth. After those formalities, Grace asked a few routine questions, then narrowed in on the night he had seen his father molesting his sister. Rich repeated what he had told me almost word for word.

"Now, describe what your father did to you," Grace asked.

"He played with my privates."

"When was that?"

"Last summer."

"What happened?"

"We were working late to get the boats ready for the Memorial Day races, so Dad decided we'd camp out at the store."

"What went on that night?" Grace coaxed.

"We were getting ready for bed, well, not really a bed, we were going to share a double sleeping bag. I was wearing my shirt and bathing suit, but Dad said to take off my suit. I didn't want to because I knew what he meant."

"Why is that?" Grace asked.

"He'd done it before."

"He'd masturbated you before?" Grace asked to clarify.

"Yeah."

"Do you know what an orgasm is?"

"It's when you come all over."

Grace nodded. "Is that what happened when you were at the marine shop in May?"

"Yeah, he came and . . ." Rich's head drooped. I saw his shoulders heaving. Nobody spoke. "He made me . . . he made me come too."

Grace took some notes. "Do you have the street address for your father's marine repair shop?"

"No, but you know the Camel Hump Bridge?" Rich replied in an unsteady voice. "Well, right after you cross it, you take the first left turn and go back behind the shrimp docks, and his place is the last one on the end before the gas pumps."

"Aren't the shrimp docks over the county line?" Grace asked me.

"I'm not sure," I replied.

"Yeah, they are," Rich added.

"Where's your house?"

Rich described the area known as Stevenson Groves. Grace nodded. "At least that's in our county, but the incident Rich can pinpoint by date took place in the marine shop out of my jurisdiction."

"Does that mean you can't charge him on this count?" I asked.

"Unfortunately." Grace cloaked her annoyance and spoke gently to Rich. "Don't be ashamed of what happened. It was not your fault." She thanked him for his time and me for my help, and asked that I call her to talk about the rest of the charges relating to Alicia and the other girls.

Then Mitzi and I took Rich out for his well-deserved pizza—well, make that two pizzas, extra cheese and everything but anchovies.

The months leading up to the trial were especially hard on Alicia. She was doing so poorly in her new school she was asked to repeat ninth grade. Her foster mother, Ruth Levy, reported that Alicia seemed too preoccupied to concentrate on her studies. Alicia was in group therapy for sexually abused teenagers, but Ruth didn't think it had made any difference.

"Does Alicia receive any individual counseling?" I asked Ruth.

"Not at this time because the only Medicaid provider in our district is the mental health clinic, and they have a waiting list for individual therapists. The best program around here is at Valley View, but that's private.''

''I have a friend in their community relations department. Maybe I can ask them to donate some services.''

''Sometimes it's easier to get something for free than to convince HRS to pay for it,'' Ruth replied.

After a few days of wrangling, the Valley View Foundation contributed ten sessions with the female therapist who specialized in sexual abuse problems. When we spoke a month later, the therapist said, ''Every time we touch on a tender topic, Alicia clams up. Mostly she nods off.''

I was annoyed that the precious hours of free counseling were being wasted, but I also knew that Alicia's behavior was a form of disengagement, a way to escape from the apprehension that comes with having to confront the past. When the free sessions were about to end, Valley View sent their recommendations to Mrs. Levy.

''Listen to this!'' Ruth said in an irate voice. ''The counselor indicates that very little progress has been made due to Alicia's refusal to confront the issues of her sexual abuse. Then there's some gobbledegook about disassociation, acute anxiety, and her identification with the aggressor. They suggest—get this!—an 'in-patient program to stabilize the situation with twice a week therapy after that.' Each session would be sixty dollars an hour and the hospital care is four hundred forty-two a day, plus extras. Now where are we supposed to come up with ten thousand dollars?''

I groaned. Valley View was a private, for-profit, mental health facility that actively recruited for its adolescent unit, even advertising on television. Many health insurance policies covered in-patient therapy, and I had heard of teens being admitted by parents fed up with oppositional behavior, drug or alcohol use. Miraculously, each child was released at the precise moment his family's insurance benefits were exhausted. While the hospital did have some excellent clinicians on staff, I was wary of these sales tactics, especially when I learned from their ''director of marketing'' that doctors were paid ''commissions'' for in-patient referrals.

''Just explain that Alicia is not covered by insurance, but you'd love her to receive treatment at their expense. That will put an end to that.''

''I don't want this in Alicia's file,'' Ruth said with much agitation. ''It makes it sound like she's crazy.''

''She does have serious problems, Ruth, but I doubt she needs to be hospitalized. Maybe we can use this diagnosis to continue to get therapy for her. She's going to need special support around the time of the trial.''

"That's what I am here for,'' Ruth replied softly.

In many ways Alicia typified the sexual abuse victim. Inferior school performance was one indicator, but her sexually oriented behaviors were more illustrative of what had happened to her. Alicia displayed inappropriate mannerisms for a child of any age, even a belligerent fifteen-year-old. Ruth described Alicia answering the door with her blouse opened, lifting her skirt and touching her vulva in public, as well as catching her fondling boys and allowing them to squeeze her breasts and buttocks. On Halloween Alicia had gone into a community group's haunted house but had not come out with the other girls. When Ruth went in after her, she found Alicia in a corner under an eerie skeleton that glowed in black light lifting her sweater and revealing her naked breasts as visitors came around the corner. Even I had observed Alicia lifting her skirt and scratching her genitals in the front hall of the house, where anyone in the living room could see her, and I had heard the stories of her sexual exploits firsthand. Her foster father, Milo Levy, had to be ever vigilant and never dared hug her without another adult in the room. He avoided being alone in the house with Alicia, or any of the other foster girls, because even an accusation of sexual abuse by an angry foster child could ruin his reputation.

Before being placed in the Levy home, Alicia had been in shelter care for several weeks. She and another girl had run away and hitched a ride to the beach, where they met two guys who were all too happy to share a hotel room with them. Alicia giggled as she recalled the "nonstop fucking'' and said she'd done it with a black man they had met at a bar while the others watched. When the boys started to bring their friends around, though, she had had enough and called HRS to report her whereabouts. Mitzi recalled finding her in a filthy room, wearing sexy, punk clothes, bleached hair, and heavy makeup that made her "look like a whore.'' She had sores on her legs and arms and some wounds cut into her ankles in an attempt at primitive tattoos. At the Levys', Alicia's hair had grown back into its natural wheat color and she had a small wardrobe of more modest clothing. Still, she had not altered her highly sexualized approach to life.

And why should she have? Here was a child whose mother had abandoned her. Alicia remembers that around the age of five there was an incident in a toolshed when Red sat on a mower-tractor seat and asked if she wanted to drive. She climbed on his lap and he kissed her neck and hair and told her how much he loved her. While she held on to the mower's wheel, he reached up and slipped his hand inside her panties. He explained that this was her secret place and only her daddy knew about it. She said it had felt peculiar, but not terrible, and he had patted her there for a long time until he squirmed around and made "a funny noise like he was feeling sick." After that, he would come to her when she was in bed at night and rub her the same way. Sometimes he stuck his finger in her "rear end," sometimes in her "front end." When she told him she didn't want him to do it, he promised to buy her something if she would let him. "It wasn't so bad," she said, "and besides, I got everything I wanted."

Over many years Alicia had been groomed by her father to be his sexual companion. After I had known Alicia for many months, the real horror of this incestuous relationship came into focus. Alicia's self-esteem was bundled with her sexuality. For years she had been rewarded with love, privileges, and material goods for allowing her father to molest her. Most of the time the sex had been gentle, and to his twisted mind, consensual. Alicia had found sex with her father to be pleasurable and something she may even have initiated once in a while. Eventually, as she matured and began to become interested in boys her age, she started to realize that her relationship with her father was taboo. Even so, she never tried to resist him, nor did she voluntarily confide in anyone because by then, she found a perverse pleasure in defying the rules of society, being some sort of a romantic outlaw.

Nevertheless, others in the community had noticed that Red Stevenson behaved oddly toward his daughter. In middle school, Alicia began to hang out at a convenience store close to the school bus stop, which was managed by Dee Smiley. Mrs. Smiley had told investigators that she had heard Red shouting at Alicia to get into the pickup truck by saying, "C'mon, you cunt." According to the report, a few weeks later, Red had a beer bottle in his hand when he came to fetch Alicia. As he prodded her outside the store, he shoved the bottle between her legs and kept poking her until she got into the truck. Then he told her to clasp it between her thighs.

"The odd thing about it," Dee Smiley explained, "was that Alicia took it as the normal way to act."

Not long after that, when Red didn't come for Alicia when expected, Dee Smiley gave Alicia a ride home from the store. "I made some comments about not liking the way her father treated her, and I guess the moment was right because she was angry at him for not coming on time. She said he was punishing her because she wanted to go out with a boy her father called a piece of trash. I told Alicia that if she ever wanted to talk to me about anything, I would be there. Before we got to the grove, she started crying and told me what her father had done.''

I realized that this must be the same Mrs. Smiley who turned up in the police files and was the person who probably reported Alicia's problem to the abuse hotline, which then led to her removal from the home.

Repulsion is a common reaction to incest, especially of the father-daughter variety, and yet I never had an intensely negative reaction to Alicia's situation, perhaps because my role was to understand the child's perceptions, as well as to figure out how she might overcome her past. To me, it wasn't the sexual act that was ugly, but rather the father's corruption of love and nurturing into sexual performance. Was it any wonder that Alicia had no self-worth other than her sexual prowess? Or that she had difficulty trusting anyone because the person who had been her sole emotional support had betrayed her? Although Alicia wanted the foundation of her existence to be formed from the concrete her father said it was, when she grew up she realized it was made of jelly.

Why didn't Alicia tell anyone sooner? Her father had not threatened to harm her if she didn't comply, and she was free to go to school and see friends. There were stepmothers in the house much of the time. Later I would learn that at least one of these women had strong suspicions and had tried to broach the subject with Alicia. Did Alicia keep silent because she was jealous of her stepmother's relationship with her father or was she angry at the woman for not offering to protect her? At some point, though, Alicia realized that what her father was doing was wrong, but to protect herself from feeling like a transgressor, she justified it in her mind. If nobody knew about it, it was all right. Much later, she would confide that one of her worst fears was that other people would not understand and would stigmatize her. As it turned out, her grandfather sided with her father, either denying it ever happened or blaming her for seducing her father.

Another grim consequence of this incestuous relationship was the long-term erosion of Alicia's power to grow and develop. Because she had subjected herself to her father's will, ignoring her own needs and wishes most of the time, she was suffused with feelings of powerlessness. Instead of believing she could function in the world on her own, she felt that she had to do whatever anyone—particularly any man—asked. As young people develop into functioning adults, they learn step-by-step mastery of skills, how to work toward goals, how to use choices responsibly, and to delay gratification. Alicia's growth had been stunted by her father, who usurped self-mastery by violating her body with deceit.

Even more distressing, the disclosure of this abuse further undermined Alicia's control over her life. Immediately she was yanked from her home and placed in shelter care. When she applied some measure of autonomy by running away, she became the criminal, was picked up by the police, and moved to a foster home without her consent. She lost her house, her possessions, her brothers, her friends in the neighborhood, even her school. From then on she became a "case," both in dependency and criminal court. She had to respond to the summons of attorneys, doctors, caseworkers, even her child advocate. No matter how hard I would try, I knew I continued to represent "them" to Alicia, who sometimes saw "us" as more the enemy than her father.

From our first encounter, Alicia had been open with me about her sexual activity. Because I never condemned her, she continued to confide in me. While I would listen, I usually didn't ask for details, unless to clarify what she meant. If she said, "I was doing it with him when I got my period," I might ask, "You mean having sex with him?" Then I would listen to the rest of the story. My comments always focused on her health. Suggestions about birth control or a frank discussion concerning AIDS were common threads in our ongoing dialogue. I brought her books, including the updated *Our Bodies, Ourselves* and *Learning About Sex: The Contemporary Guide for Young Adults,* which was used in the sex education program at our son's school. This book, by Gary F. Kelly, combined straightforward information with a discussion on ethics. While I showed these books to Ruth Levy, I did not ask her permission to give them to Alicia, because as her guardian, I felt the information was essential to her welfare.

One of my early discussions with Ruth centered around birth control and teenage girls. "Nobody in my house is going to be on the pill," she announced. "That's like writing a blank check for them to have sex."

"But some of them are probably going to be sexually active. Don't they need protection from disease and pregnancy?"

"I'm willing to give them the information, but not provide assistance. My job is to teach them to respect their bodies, learn how to say 'no,' and develop a sense of values."

Ruth's theory was lovely, but her values offered no immunity to Alicia, whom I knew to be at great risk. Soon Alicia told me she was using condoms and had tried foam. I brought her statistics about the effectiveness of combining two barrier methods to increase the chance of preventing pregnancy as well as disease. By the spring, when Alicia had a "serious" boyfriend she saw three or four times a week, Ruth faced the fact that they were sexually active. She called me to ask if I would object to Alicia taking the pill, if only to "regulate her periods." Without wondering why she had changed her mind, I said I thought it was a splendid idea. When Alicia began using an oral contraceptive, she and I discussed the side effects. Six months later Ruth informed me that she had made an appointment for Alicia to have Norplant inserted. Norplant is an implantation of slow-release hormone capsules under the skin of the upper arm that prevents pregnancy for five years, but which may be removed at any time.

"When she's eighteen, she won't qualify for free birth control," Ruth explained, "but Medicaid will pay for the Norplant now, which costs around eight hundred dollars."

"I think you made the right decision," I said. "This will give Alicia the freedom from pregnancy for several years after she is out of foster care so she can get her education and start on a career."

A few weeks after he settled into the Rose/Perez house Cory had a birthday. I decided to buy him a battery charging system for the radio-controlled truck he had received at Christmas from the MacDougals. When I arrived for the party, the living room resounded with a cacophony of children punctuated by Manuel's suction machine. Pizzas were served followed by a birthday cake with fourteen candles.

"Show Gay your birthday present to me," Birdie said coaxingly. Cory looked confused. She handed him an envelope and he passed it to me. I took out his latest report card. "All *A*'s and *B*'s," Cory boasted. "I'm on the honor roll for the first time in my life!"

When it came time to open the presents, Cory unwrapped the battery charger, then looked at it dubiously.

Birdie glanced from him to me. "He doesn't have that car anymore. Mrs. MacDougal didn't let him take it with him. In fact, she didn't give him anything that he acquired at her house, not even most of his clothing."

"But his Christmas gifts were his!" I put my arm around Cory. "We'll take the charger back together and you can pick something else out, okay?"

"Yeah, sure, but I'd like my old truck back, and some of my other stuff too."

How well I remembered Mrs. MacDougal bragging at the HRS meeting about the four hundred dollars she had spent on gifts for each child, then later showing me everything she had given Cory. No . . . not showing just me, showing *us*. Lillian had been there too.

"How can Renata MacDougal get away with this?" I railed on the phone to Lillian the next day. "First she tells lies about me, then she throws Cory out for nothing, and to top it off, she keeps his gifts and clothing. Here's a kid with nothing: no parents, no home, no sister, no brother, no money, and he is denied the few objects that belonged to him."

"It happens all the time," Lillian responded slowly. "A foster parent gives a kid a bike, but when he leaves to go to another foster home or to return to his natural parents, he is told that the bike was on loan. Then the foster family passes it down to the next one."

"How can HRS condone that?"

"The 'official' policy is that the children's possessions go with them, nevertheless you rarely can prove to whom something belongs."

"Maybe not in most cases, Lillian, but remember Renata bragging at the meeting? That was in front of her HRS supervisors as well as Nancy, you, and me. Then, later that day she showed off each item to both of us. Don't you remember the brown cowboy boots, the pass to Disney, the red radio-controlled car, the Walkman, and the baseball outfit?"

"Sure do. Call Cory and get as accurate a list as you can. Then you write two letters, one to Mrs. MacDougal requesting the items on Cory's behalf, and the other to Mitzi Keller."

The response was as unexpected as it was swift. Phyllis Cady phoned Nancy at the guardian office. "Our policy is to back the decision of our foster parents."

"Phyllis," Nancy said in her most conciliatory voice, "this is an unusual circumstance. Renata MacDougal listed the gifts to us at the meeting, then flaunted them in front of Gay and Lillian."

"Come on, Nancy," Phyllis urged, "don't you have some really dreadful cases to pursue? I know I do." She hung up.

Nancy phoned and told me what Phyllis had said.

"Where's Judge Wapner when you need him?" I asked.

"Exactly!" Nancy replied. "May I have permission to put your name on the civil case in Cory's behalf?"

"Absolutely!" I said, elated there finally might be an antidote to Renata MacDougal's venom.

* * *

"I haven't done one of these since law school," Kit Thorndike said as he described a Writ of Replevin, the method to recover possession of personal property.

A few weeks later the papers arrived in the mail. I felt a jolt as I read the first page of the documents.

IN RE: The Interest of:

CORY STEVENSON, a minor child.

Gay Courter, as Guardian ad Litem and next friend of Cory Stevenson, a minor child, petitioner,

vs.

THE FLORIDA DEPARTMENT OF HEALTH AND REHABILITATIVE SERVICES and CONRAD MACDOUGAL, and his wife, RENATA MAC-DOUGAL, Individually and as agents for THE FLORIDA DEPARTMENT OF HEALTH AND REHABILITATIVE SERVICES,

Respondents.

I had never before been involved in a lawsuit. I scanned the petition, which listed the property in exhibit A and explained that "the petitioner was entitled on behalf of Cory Stevenson, a minor child, to possession of the property based upon the fact that the property was gifts to the minor child and that the property was wrongfully detained by the MacDougals and HRS, who believed they could retain the property because they had a right to use the same for other children who came into their care."

I called Nancy and asked what would happen next. "You are not going to believe this, but I just got off the phone with Calvin Reynolds, HRS's attorney. He states he will fight us through any court because he can't let this become a precedent."

"Do you mean we're going to have a trial for the cowboy boots and the Walkman?"

"Yes, and I'm delighted. If we win, it will warn other foster parents not to do the same."

When I saw Nancy in court the following week, she pulled me aside. "Want an update on the 'Scrooge Suit'?"

"The what?"

"Have you forgotten Cory's cowboy boots?" she said in a mock-stern voice. "We're calling Mrs. MacDougal 'the mother who stole Christmas.' There's a hearing next Thursday to decide whether the case will be heard in civil or dependency court."

"Should I attend?"

"No, it's just a technical matter and will take five minutes."

Late Thursday, though, Nancy called me from her home. "Kit Thorndike has a decision on Mrs. Scrooge."

"Already?" I asked, disappointed that I had not been present.

"It was totally unexpected. After Calvin handed Judge Donovan the documents, he looked up and bellowed, 'Is this about a foster kid's cowboy boots?' Calvin started to argue the case right then and there, and Thorn didn't stop him. Calvin yammered on about not interfering in a foster parent's decision. Then Thorn explained how Mrs. MacDougal had listed the gifts at an HRS meeting and had shown them to two guardians. 'How far are you prepared to take this case?' the judge asked Calvin, who mumbled something about going to the highest court. 'Oh no you won't,' Judge Donovan retorted. 'I hereby order you to go to that foster home within twenty days and get every single item belonging to that child and to return it to him at once. If some of the articles are missing or broken, you are to get their value in cash from the foster parents. And I do not ever want to hear any mention of this matter in my court, or any other, again.'" Nancy paused and chuckled. "So, the Scrooge Suit is over."

"And Cory will get everything back?"

"Yes, and I'm very pleased," Nancy said, sighing contentedly for the first time I could recall.

Dr. Newman intercepted my phone call to Rich, who was in a group meeting. "Richard is doing much better. He made it to A-level status—that's the one with the most privileges—and has maintained it for several weeks. When he slips up, we ask, 'Is that your best A-level behavior?' That's usually enough to get him to comply. His caseworker is arranging something with a psychiatric facility that has an adolescent outpatient program called Garrison House."

Mitzi Zeller couldn't wait to tell me about the facility in Sarasota. Connected with Garrison Memorial Hospital's psychiatric department, Garrison House was a pilot project to prepare adolescent children for independent living. Residents in the program ranged from age sixteen to

twenty and lived in two-story duplexes. Placement was difficult to arrange, but they had tentatively agreed to take Rich, pending a report
from Dr. Newman.

"Will he continue to receive therapy?"

"Counseling by the live-in staff is ongoing, but not of a formalized
nature. If he needs individual sessions, he can make his own appointments at the Garrison Clinic and will get himself there using public
transportation. Buses pass right by the complex. He'll be using them to
get to his job and to school."

"But Rich hasn't even completed middle school."

"He'll be tested and placed appropriately, probably in night education
classes. This is a reality-based program. The residents do their own shopping, cook under supervision, have bank accounts that they must balance.
Everything is designed to prepare them for living independently while
offering them support if they make mistakes."

"Do you think Rich is ready for this?" I asked skeptically.

"We're under a mandate to select the least restrictive environment
for him."

"Does Garrison House know about his history of violence?"

"They have his file. Dr. Newman thinks he may do well with more
autonomy."

"Mitzi, I'm his advocate, but you don't hear me begging to have him
out on the streets, at least not until I see some evidence of self-control."

"The case manager for the special assessment team has decided on
Garrison House."

Maybe I had missed something in Rich's bulging file. I sorted the
papers by date, then pulling out a yellow highlighter, tried to find some
evidence of preparation for Garrison House.

Rich hated guidelines of any kind. Most of his placements had failed
due to his uncontrollable aggressions. One foster mother reported that
when he was given a list of their family's rules, he said, "You want me
to circle the ones I will follow?" Later that same day he ran off, taking
the foster father's machete. Another time, when Mitzi tried to calm Rich
on the phone, he threw the phone against the wall, cracking the hard
plastic shell. Worse, in recent weeks, he had become increasingly delu-
sional, telling everyone his father killed his wife and now had a contract
out on his life. His doctor reported that he complained of being dizzy
and fuzzy and his excuse for his behavior lapses was that he "couldn't
think straight."

There were more arrests in his HRS files than I had located in the police records. A joy ride with a friend in a neighbor's car had led to a charge of grand theft auto. He had at least three breaking and entering notations, had been picked up for bringing a .44 Magnum to the high school and threatening a student. The gun turned out to belong to his father, who, he told Mitzi, "sleeps with a gun."

Rich's file contained several references to his interest in firearms. He related an incident shortly after Christmas to a therapist. Rich and his father were quarreling when his father handed him a gun and said, "Why don't you shoot me if you hate me so much?" The report said that Rich had taken the gun and loaded it, then explained, "I couldn't do nothin', not even point it at my dad. Instead I pointed it at myself. But I couldn't even do that right."

Another therapist reported that Rich described watching his father have intercourse with his sister, saying he said he had felt "dizzy and sick, like I wanted to throw up." Rich had readily admitted drug and alcohol abuse, saying he preferred marijuana but that he had "done rock" (crack cocaine) and liked to "huff gasoline." The therapist suggested that this wasn't as much a thrill-seeking diversion as Rich's way of seeking consolation from his misery.

Rich's suicide attempt by jumping out of the window of one of his shelter homes—and his other discussions about ways to "off" himself—did not surprise me. What did this boy have to live for? There was not a single person in his life who was there unconditionally for him—not a parent, grandparent, teacher, neighbor. His yearning to blot out the terrifying past, ignore the suffocating present, and suspend concerns about the formidable obstacles of the future was utterly comprehensible.

I considered whether to tell Rich about finding Tammy. Did he really believe she was dead? When I mentioned this to Alicia, she explained that one of their stepmothers—Peggy, whom Rich had liked the best—had had an automobile accident when Rich was about fifteen. After she was released from the hospital, she never returned to their home. Perhaps he adjusted to that loss by pretending—or convincing himself—that she had died. I had heard that when a child was separated from an idealized parent, he had to work through the grieving process. Some children "killed off" the missing parent in their minds, which may have accounted for why Rich claimed his biological mother as well as Peggy was dead. Wasn't it far easier to think they had died rather than contemplate the possibility that they had not returned home because they had rejected him?

The truth was, of course, that Peggy and Tammy and the other mothers had forsaken Rich and his siblings emotionally. Otherwise they would not have allowed them to be abused by Red. I also knew that studies indicated that once a child suffered through three major separations, he might be considered unsalvageable. No reason to add another mother with the power to reject him quite yet. I decided to wait until Rich was more settled before I gave him the news about Tammy's reappearance.

Ruth Levy cared deeply for Alicia, of this I was certain, but Ruth ran a busy group home for as few as three or as many as seven adolescent girls. None of Alicia's foster sisters was the model of decorum or psychological health. They arrived physically battered, sexually abused, emotionally neglected. They had been pawns in custody cases, raised by mentally ill parents, or were victims of tragedies. A few came from inpatient psychiatric beds, some were on antipsychotic or antidepressive medications. Some were at high risk for suicide. By comparison, Alicia was remarkably stable. As Alicia's advocate, I beheld the parade of other children from her viewpoint and came to resent the drain on Ruth Levy's energy, emotions, health, and stamina. Whenever I visited Alicia, her major complaints centered around the latest in a long line of roommates. Invariably they stole her clothes, messed with her possessions, created problems for her at school. The longer she stayed with the Levys, the greater her resentment. And while Ruth juggled the needs of the girls skillfully, Alicia's requests were often set aside because of a more dramatic problem instigated by a newer, sicker child. More than anything else Alicia wanted a consistent family she could truly call her own.

Because Alicia lived in a world of negatives, I always tried to say "yes" to her. If she called me, I would be available if possible. If she needed something, I would attempt to procure it. When she inquired about her mother, I tried to locate her, surprising myself as much as anyone when Tammy was found. Even before that, Alicia had been searching for a way to be with her brothers and create a family among the three of them. She had asked me if I would allow her to move in with Rich when he was eighteen.

My knee-jerk reaction would have been to respond: "Are you crazy?" But I waited a few beats and instead said, "Sure, as long as I could justify it to the judge."

"What does that mean?" Alicia asked challengingly.

"You and Rich would have to prove you could behave in a responsible manner. You'd both need to have jobs, some savings in the bank—even if it was only a few hundred dollars, it would be a cushion for emergencies. You'd require transportation, a plan for your education, a safe place to live."

Alicia contemplated this and talked about how she might achieve these goals, but the idea was so unrealistic it faded away. If I had reacted adversely, however, the daydream might have persisted, and she might have begun to resent me for opposing her.

"I'm your voice, Alicia," I reminded her over and over. "When you can't be heard, I will speak for you. But I can't look foolish in what I say. We'll work together to come up with sensible, logical plans, but always ones that you want, because it is your life, not mine."

Guardians are always conscious that there is a fuzzy edge between the expressed wishes of a child and the mature perception of her best interests. My mandate was clear. I could listen to Alicia's feelings and wishes, but then I had to consider the whole picture and make recommendations based on my adult, unbiased opinion of what was best for her in the short as well as the long run. If Alicia had come to me saying she didn't like the food at the foster home because she wanted ice cream instead of salad, I could sympathize with her cravings, but I would have to explain that salad was better for her and I could not support her on the ice cream issue. In fact, in her brother Cory's case, this was not such a stretch because he wanted to smoke. I understood that he liked smoking, but there was no way I would defend in court his right to smoke.

As children's rights cases are debated in courtrooms around the United States, how children should be represented is a heated issue. When an adult hires an attorney, he enters into a fiduciary relationship. A fee is paid for the service of representing what a client wants. If he desires custody of a child, his lawyer will argue for him even if the attorney privately thinks the child's best interests might be better served by living with another family member. The Guardian ad Litem does not have a client-attorney relationship with the child, which means that she does not have to represent the child's wishes if she feels they are harmful. Also the Guardian ad Litem does not have the same professional immunity from having to testify. And because a Guardian ad Litem can be called as a witness, she may have to relinquish a child's secrets. As I explained to all my charges, the advocate is also legally bound to report any abuse the child might confide. Even so, there have been very few times when I ever found myself in a position of having to go against a child's wishes. Sure, they have had preposterous ideas sometimes, but by joining with them to arrive at a solution—instead of responding with an automatic "no"—we usually were able to form a united front, giving me the confidence that I was not only doing the right thing, but also speaking accurately for the child.

While Alicia had her dreams of being reunited with her mother and/or brothers, I had to deal with a more concrete problem: Rich's move to Garrison House. Within two days of his arrival in Sarasota I had made contact with his new counselor, T.J. Costa. Their duplex had two girls and three boys, all sixteen and seventeen. "Rich is a fast worker," T.J. reported. "He already has a girlfriend." She went on to explain that while they could not control sexual behavior twenty-four hours a day, a pregnancy was cause for both partners to be dismissed from the program.

"What about birth control?"

"We leave that to the individual families."

"Can't you put something in the water?" I joked, then told T.J. that Alicia had once bragged to me that Rich had fathered twins when he was fourteen. I did not know whether this was true but had other reasons to believe that he had been sexually active.

T.J. shrugged this off. "Garrison House was designed to simulate the real life they will face when they are eighteen and can live anywhere they want." T.J. went on to explain that the residents had their own keys but had to be back on the premises by 5:00 P.M. "We hold their paychecks at first, but after they demonstrate that they can manage their money, they get their own bank accounts. We charge fines for misbehavior, which seems to be more effective than other discipline methods."

"Has Rich been in any trouble yet?"

"He's needed reminders, of course, but what seems to be motivating him is his relationship with Janet, the girl I told you he liked."

"Why is she there?"

"Janet has had trouble with manic-depression, which resulted in a recent inpatient stabilization program."

Recalling pixieish Daphne with her bandaged wrists, I asked, "Was she suicidal?"

"Yes, but she's had a good result with medication."

"Are they both in therapy?"

"We will take them to their first appointments at Garrison Memorial; after that, they are on their own. You see, part of the training system is suffering the natural consequences of not meeting your commitments."

The next time I called I asked to speak directly with Rich. He seemed upbeat and interested in an Easter visit with his sister. All the residents were going to their families, and he was the only one without an invitation. T.J. got on the line and said that they would provide bus fare. She asked if Alicia's foster home would accept him for a few days.

"I don't think so. Mr. Levy once had a run-in with Rich and swore he'd never have him back in their house."

"Could you ask around in your district? Otherwise one of the staff here will have to take him home."

"Do you think he's stable enough to travel on his own?"

"We haven't had any problems with him that would indicate he couldn't manage as a guest for a few days."

I contacted his caseworker, Mitzi, and asked if she could find a family to take Rich for Easter. "Are you kidding?" Mitzi groaned. "He'll ruin my weekend for sure."

"He hasn't seen his sister or brother for months, except in court."

"Why can't they admit him to Garrison Memorial for a few days?"

"C'mon, Mitzi, it's a holiday."

"You want him at your house?"

"You know guardians can't bring kids to their homes."

"Isn't that convenient?" she said, facetiously imitating the "church lady" from "Saturday Night Live." Then her tone became more ominous. "Look, Gay, I know you mean well, but you've never seen Alicia and Rich together. They don't behave like normal brother and sister."

"In what way?"

"Once, when they met in court, they kissed each other full on the mouth, like lovers."

"Might he stay with another foster parent?"

"What worries me is the two of them running away."

"But that would blow his place at Garrison House, where he's happier than he has been in a long while. Also, Rich has a girlfriend there."

"Okay, okay," Mitzi said. "Let me see what I can do."

Rich was given a job bagging groceries in a supermarket. He worked for two days, then didn't show up for the rest of the week. He told T.J. that he didn't like anyone bossing him around. She warned that if he didn't hold down a job until Easter vacation, he would not be permitted to visit his sister. This seemed to do the trick and he stayed in the next position, as a biscuit maker at a diner, for more than a week.

On Good Friday Rich missed his first bus and didn't know how to contact his host family, but he did have Mitzi's emergency number. She ended up meeting him at the bus station at 11 P.M. and driving him to the foster home. Further confusion on Easter Sunday made it impossible for Alicia to see him where Rich was staying. Fortunately, Mr. Levy relented and allowed Rich to come by for a few hours that evening. Ruth reported that Alicia was thrilled and Rich had behaved himself.

"Did you know Rich is getting married to this girl, Janet?" Ruth asked.

"When?"

"She's almost eighteen, and he claims they're going to elope after her birthday."

"But he won't be eighteen for more than a year."

"I expected it was another of his tall tales, like the one about his dead mother."

"Did Alicia tell Rich about Tammy?" I wondered.

"Not directly, but she hinted that she was trying to find their mother, just to see how he'd react."

"And . . . ?"

"Rich told Alicia that he never wanted to have anything to do with her again. He said, 'She's a rabbit, screws everything in sight,' and 'If she ever came around here again, I'd beat her ass.' Nice, huh?"

There was nothing I could say to defend Tammy who, even by the most relaxed definition, could never qualify as an exemplary mother.

Yet from the moment Alicia had heard her mother's voice on the tape, her focus had changed. Suddenly she had a real biological mother, who said she loved her; a stepfather, who wanted her to live with them; and two unknown step-siblings. In suburban Spokane nobody would know about what her father had done. Still, she was torn by her ties to Rich, who was involved with Janet, but not yet married; to Cory, who insisted he would never leave his father or grandfather; as well as to Ruth, for whom she cared deeply. Also, she would not be free to move to Washington until after the trial, which was many months away.

Keeping this in mind, Alicia, Tammy, and I were trying to make arrangements for her to visit Florida. If that went well, we would send Alicia (and Cory and Rich tentatively) to Spokane to visit the Spates as soon as school was out. The trial would most likely take place later in the summer. Once that was over, Alicia would move to Washington and start school there in the fall. If Red was adjudicated guilty, Cory might be willing to go with his sister; if not, Cory was determined to return home. Nobody was willing to make any plans that included Rich, since his situation changed almost daily.

There was one minor problem: Tammy could not afford the plane fare to Florida. She had saved a little more than a hundred dollars, then her son had broken his arm and that sum had gone for medical care.

I asked Mitzi if there was any way for HRS to provide a plane ticket. "We don't have a family reunification fund," she replied with some annoyance

"Just think how much money HRS will save," I argued. My calculations indicated that it cost at least $5,600 a year for Alicia's family group home board rate, plus additional expenses for clothing and Medicaid. Foster care administration was estimated at another $2,000 a year per child, which was probably far too low. If she were in the system until she was eighteen, living with her mother would save at least $25,000, possibly considerably more. In comparison, a $500 ticket for a mother to make plans to regain custody of her children seemed a sound investment. Yet no matter how much I persisted, Mitzi said there was no chance of getting a plane ticket from the agency.

I asked the judge if he would order HRS to provide the plane fare, but he said while he would approve the visit, he could not demand the allocation. He suggested applying to private charities.

"This is a classic example of being penny-wise and pound-foolish," I grumbled to my husband.

"Who's being pound-foolish?" he asked. "Do you realize how much time away from your writing and the film business it will take for you to locate five hundred dollars? In the long run it will cost less to purchase the ticket yourself."

"Guardians are not supposed to contribute in that fashion."

"I'm sure you can find a way to do it," he said with a chuckle, knowing that I found a little subterfuge appealing.

Within a few hours I had contacted a friend, who was president of a local service club that did charitable works on a personal need basis. I made a deal with her to contribute the amount of the plane ticket to their latest fund-raising event, if they would then buy the ticket for Tammy. Nancy and Lillian approved the club's donation, but until they read this, they will not have known about my more direct participation, which was not illegal, just unorthodox.

Tammy was thrilled with the news and said she would start saving for a rental car and other expenses in Florida. She promised to repay the service club a portion of the money when she had some extra funds.

Two weeks after Easter T.J. called me. "I'm afraid that Rich can no longer remain at Garrison House."

"What's he done?"

"He's impregnated Janet. The residents know the rules. A pregnancy means dismissal for both of them."

"Maybe that is why she is pregnant."

"Possibly, but if they want to fail, there is nothing we can do to stop them." Her voice was resigned. "Besides, I don't think Rich ever had a chance to make it here."

"What about Janet?"

"She could have completed the program if she stayed on her medication. She's a very bright young woman with an IQ of 140, but a poor-judgment history."

"What are her options now?"

"There's an excellent facility for single mothers in Naples. She can live there and continue with a school program for pregnant teens."

"What about Rich?"

"He will be harder to place. Let's face it, Rich is immature. He lies, acts irresponsibly, doesn't seem to care about anyone, and walks all over people who are nice to him, even Janet. But even though he is horrid to her most of the time, she doesn't want to be separated from him. They claim they want to get married and keep the baby."

"Janet will be eighteen soon, right?"

"Yes, and Rich could get married legally if they drove to Georgia, but I am not volunteering that information. Rich already called his father and asked if he would sign for him to get married."

"His father can do that?"

"Yes, technically the parent—even an abusing parent— retains custody until his rights are terminated by the court."

"What did Mr. Stevenson reply?"

"Let's just say he wasn't interested in helping Rich out."

"That's his first good deed this year." I shivered at the thought of the suicidal mother and irresponsible, agitated young father trying to calm a colicky infant.

T.J. promised to alert me when she had news about Rich's transfer.

Through the turmoils with Rich, people asked me how I could represent this troubled, twisted young person with such fervor. In her autobiography, *Blackberry Winter*, anthropologist Margaret Mead refers to herself as a "baby carriage peeker," the sort of woman with such an intense adoration of babies she is apt to become an overprotective mother. Because I have a keen interest in obstetrics and parenting (having written novels about midwives and childbirth, as well as produced, with my husband, a popular series of parent education films), people assume I, like Margaret Mead, adore children as a group. Not true. I like individual children enormously, but not every one.

During my first pregnancy, I worried that I might not automatically love my child. Of course, the minute I saw Blake I knew he was the most astonishing child on the planet. Even more amazing was the fact that his brother, Joshua, managed to captivate me equally. I cannot say that any of my Guardian ad Litem children fall into the same unique category in my heart. The emotional transaction is different. Still, my connection with Rich, and all my guardian children, is intense. The court order appointing me their guardian seals a bond. From that moment on they are *mine*. No matter who they are or what they have done, I take care of my own.

I supposed T.J. Costa had used whatever resources she had to incorporate Rich into the program at Garrison House. It was not her fault that he had been unsuited to it. Now, though, he was out of her control and she could forget about him, while I could not. Nor could Mitzi Zeller.

I knew that Mitzi loathed this young man, who had put her through hell, blowing placement after placement, often in the middle of the night. She had spent numerous evenings in the HRS office with him, driven him hundreds of miles from foster home to foster home, carried his dirty laundry in her trunk trying to catch up with him. With an already formidable caseload, he was often the squeaky wheel that received every last ounce of grease so that other children—perhaps those Mitzi believed had more potential to lead useful lives—were not tended to. But even though I fully understood Mitzi's reasons, I took umbrage whenever she maligned Rich. I bristled when she proclaimed that he'd never improve, that it wasn't worth spending more money on him, that he'd be as well off on the streets as in state custody, and that it was only a matter of time before his final state-supported placement would be a secure jail cell. Maybe she was looking at the percentages. Maybe she knew from experience that there was only a minuscule chance that Rich could ever be "salvaged." New to the game—as well as attached through the umbilical of the court order—I refused to concede the match just because the odds were not in his favor.

Janet was sent to stay with her mother while they found a place for a mentally unstable pregnant teen. Rich was not moved because there was nowhere for him to go. His deadline to depart Garrison House stretched from one to three weeks. I began to think that Tammy might be Rich's only possibility, but so far he didn't know she existed. I called T.J. to see what was happening.

"Janet and Rich are back in the duplex and are going to continue with the program," she replied in a subdued voice.

"What happened?"

"Janet had a miscarriage while she was home. Since she is no longer pregnant, it has been decided that they can have another chance." I felt relieved. "Rich has been asking to talk to you. Is this a good time to put him on?"

"Sure."

"Hey, Gay! You still my guard?"

"Your guardian, Rich. Yes, I still am."

"Okay, cool. Now, I have a problem."

"What's that?"

"I want to see Ally again. I called that lady she lives with, but she said I would have to talk to you."

"I'll see what I can arrange. We'd have to find you somewhere to stay."

"The place I stayed at Easter said I could come back."

"That would be great. I want you to see your sister and your brother whenever possible. You need to be in touch with your family."

"Not my dad."

"No, not him . . . but what about your mother?"

"She died in an accident."

"Well, Rich, I know you've had several moms. There was one who had an accident, I think her name was Peggy, but she didn't die. She just divorced your father. Did you know that?"

"I guess . . ."

"Okay, and then there was Tammy, your real mother, the one who gave birth to you and moved away when you were about six, then there was someone else for a while, then Peggy, then Vicky, right?"

"I liked Vicky, but she doesn't want anything to do with us now."

"I know, but . . ." I quickly calculated the consequences to what I might say, then realized that Alicia would bring it up sooner or later. "Rich, Alicia has been wanting to find out what happened to Tammy. So I helped her and we found that your real mother lives in Washington state, that's far away, near California."

"That's not possible. She's dead."

"No, she isn't. I've spoken to her on the phone."

"Yeah? Did she tell you that she left our house because she was pregnant by some other man and even my grandfather didn't want her around anymore?"

"I'm not certain she was pregnant then, but she did marry again, and she has two more children."

"Well, she's not worth bothering with. She's just a piece of trash who trapped my father into marrying her."

"I understand how you feel, Rich, but I wanted you to know that Tammy has heard about you and she cares about you."

"I have a headache."

"You aren't feeling well?"

"No, I feel sick."

"Why don't you rest up and I'll check on your weekend with Alicia?"

The phone hung up before I finished the sentence.

For the next few days I worked on the visit, hoping that if Rich heard Alicia's side of the story, he might be more interested in at least communicating with Tammy. After we had a host home ready and a bus ticket purchased, T.J. called.

"I'm sorry, but the visit with Rich's sister has to be put on hold. We can't release him into the community."

"What's going on?"

"He threw a chair at someone and he's become increasingly more disorderly. We've set up an appointment for him to have a comprehensive evaluation through Garrison Hospital, but the way it looks now his only option may be the state hospital."

"You mean locking him up in Chattahoochee?"

"I'm afraid so."

"Ms. Costa, I don't understand how one month this child is placed in independent living and expected to hold a job, attend school, and care for himself, then the next he's ready to be committed. You accepted him in a program, and while I am sure you did your best to counsel him, you didn't provide him with a single hour of therapy even though you knew his last placement had been in a locked psycho ward."

"We wanted to give him a chance," she replied weakly.

We talked more about the testing Rich was going to have and agreed to confer after that.

Seething, I called Lillian and dumped my frustrations on her. "Chattahoochee! Isn't that the original snake pit?"

"There may be no other alternative."

"What about Tammy?"

"How could she handle him when a staff of professionals cannot? What do we really know about Rich? Do we have a diagnosis? Is he schizophrenic? Does he have a bipolar disorder? Can it be controlled with medication? If he really is a risk to himself or others . . ."

My mind was churning with conflicting thoughts. I was saddled with what amounted to a hopeless case. But still, he was *my* case. If he had not been assigned to me, I would have turned away, not wanting to face the nasty subject, just as I didn't have to deal with someone else's trash or traumas. Yet there had to be a humane solution for Rich. A boy of sixteen needed a chance to grow and develop. There might still be time for him to overcome his deficits. As I turned this over in my mind, I realized there was a dark side to Rich that I had to face. This was one very twisted, deeply disturbed, sexually active, dysfunctional—and un-tamed—little puppy.

I was anxious to hear from Rich's doctor. If there was no profound diagnosis, maybe I could interest Tammy in Rich. If he had a mother who cared, maybe he could find the security he craved and then become strong enough to recover.

For the moment Rich was going through a stable period. T.J. had told him that if he cooperated with the evaluations and did his chores around the du-plex that he could still have a weekend with Alicia. Within a few days, though, T.J. gave me the results of the tests. The psychiatrist at Garrison Hospital found him unsuitable for independent living but filled in an appli-cation for him to attend a program in Tampa called Horizons Unlimited.

"This is a group home for boys with round-the-clock supervision, intensive mental health counseling including group and individual ther-apy combined with behavior control, some school or vocational educa-tion, although the main thrust is stabilizing the behavior. It's expensive, though."

"Sounds good to me. What about Janet?"

"She's gotten wind that they might be separated and is threatening suicide. We're afraid they may be planning to run away together, so we're keeping close watch on them. After Rich visits with his sister for a few hours, he'll be taken to Tampa that night."

"You're going to deceive him?"

"We don't think it will work otherwise."

"When he finds out he might explode. And what are you planning to tell Janet?"

"I can't discuss her case with you," T.J. said officiously.

"When will I hear from you again?"

"I'm off the case when he's out of here. Try his regular HRS case-worker."

Mitzi Keller was not in. I phoned Ruth Levy to talk about the week-end plans.

"Alicia is very upset about what is happening with Rich. Mitzi told her about Chattahoochee, so last Saturday she called Tammy and asked her if Rich could go to live with her instead of being locked up in the state hospital."

"What did Tammy say?"

"She asked to speak to me and explained that she had spoken to her husband, and while they agreed they would welcome Alicia and Cory, they could not bring Rich into their home because it might put their other children at risk. What could I say? She's probably right." There were several long beats, then Ruth sighed. "The more Alicia talks to her mother, the more I have to realize that I am losing her."

"Do you think she wants to live with Tammy?"

"She's confused. But at least Alicia feels she has some options. She's afraid to tell Rich what Tammy said. She doesn't want him to be hurt again."

Before the call was finished, my secretary handed me a message that I had to take an emergency call from T.J. on the other line.

"We had a staff meeting this afternoon and decided against the de-ception," T.J. responded in a staccato voice. "First we brought Janet in and told her they were both leaving the program, with Janet going to her mother's custody and Rich to Horizons Unlimited. Janet ran out crying, and when Rich heard from her what was happening, he went berserk—literally. He pounded in a door, broke a window with a chair, smashed the porch light, put a broom through half the screens on the porch, ran out in the street and scratched our van and broke its mirrors. We called the police and had him arrested. We're going to press charges for criminal mischief."

"Did Rich hurt anyone?"

"No, but he threatened to burn us down and beat our brains in."

"Is he in jail?"

"No. He's being transported back to Mitzi Keller's office tonight."

"What about Janet?"

"For her own safety she's already been placed in the suicide unit at Garrison Hospital. I suggest you call Mitzi and take it from there."

Very reluctantly I dialed Mitzi. "I'm going to spend another night in the office with him," she said, not bothering to mask her annoyance.

"What about the family that was going to take him for the weekend?"

"Do you really think we are going to reward this behavior with a visit to his sister?"

I spoke as calmly as I could. "Maybe he needs the contact with someone who loves him."

"Hey, if you want to take him on for the weekend, lady, he's all yours."

"You know that I'm not allowed to do that."

"Well then, do you have Tammy Spate's phone number?" she asked in a subdued voice. I gave it to her. "Do you think she might change her mind about Rich?"

"I think she cares about her kids and has many regrets, but I don't know what she is really like."

"We've initiated the interstate compact investigation that allows for reciprocal home studies, but I haven't received the paperwork yet." Mitzi's voice cracked, revealing a panicky edge. "After what happened, Horizons Unlimited might not take him. What else can we do with him? He has to have someplace to go."

I had almost forgotten that our family was going away for the weekend. Once I ascertained that Rich was going to Tampa—without seeing Alicia—I informed Mitzi I would be out of town but to call Lillian in case of an emergency.

On Monday there was a message for me to call Horizons Unlimited. A few minutes later I was speaking to yet another in a long line of well-meaning counselors. Garth Clay had a thick Appalachian drawl. He reported that Rich was doing fairly well but was bragging to other boys about running away with Janet.

"I'm trying to get him to understand why that is unrealistic and how, if he loves Janet, he'll want her to get well first."

"May I visit Rich?" I asked politely, knowing full well I could not be denied access.

Garth encouraged me to come and I made arrangements to make the two-hour trek at the end of the week.

When I arrived, Garth took me to his office. "So far Rich only co-operates long enough to get what he wants. We've used phone calls to his girlfriend as a reward system, and this is so important to him that he has complied with our rules.''

''Makes sense to me, at least the part about his desire to stay in touch with Janet. She's the only person in the whole world, besides his sister, who says she loves him. Do you know how she is doing?''

''She's being moved to a private psychiatric hospital, which is what Rich really needs too. Because he does not have strong internal controls, he requires an acute setting with more structure and external controls.''

''Where might he go?''

''There's no money for private treatment and the two public programs we've contacted have rejected him.'' Garth rubbed his chin and looked down at his paperwork. ''You know about his marriage plans, don't you?''

''I know he and Janet have had fantasies . . .''

''Hey, this is no fantasy. He has asked his father to give him permission to marry Janet immediately.''

''But his father has disowned him and Janet is underage too.''

''She's already talked her mother into it.''

My mouth went dry. These kids . . . too sick to be safe in unlocked facilities . . . were going to be married? ''How could anyone—?'' I finally sputtered.

Garth explained that while HRS refused to sign the papers, they had allowed Rich to contact his father. At first Red Stevenson had no interest in helping his son, but then Rich promised not to testify against his father in court if he allowed him to marry Janet.

''How can the father, who already signed the consents to terminate his parental rights to Rich and Alicia, be allowed to give permission like this?''

''Unless HRS files the consents and the parental rights are terminated by a judge, the father remains the person with the final legal say.''

''This is crazy—''

Just then, Rich came by the office. ''Hey, I know you! You're my guardian. You came to see me!'' He gave me a hug. Garth told us we could use the television room.

''You look better than you did the last time,'' I said truthfully.

''Yeah, it's cool here. Lots of pizza, television. I can use the phone whenever I want.''

''Who do you call?''

''You know . . . Janet.''

''But she's in the hospital.''

"I have permission to speak to my wife."

"You aren't married yet."

"We think we are. She was going to have my baby. That makes her my wife. We talk every morning and every night, and we kiss before we hang up like we would if we were going to sleep together."

"Sounds like you miss her . . ."

"Yeah, but it won't be long. We need to be together and away from the court scene. That isn't good for us. Too much stress. Listen, when I get out of here, will you help me see my sister? I need to say good-bye to her."

"Where are you going?"

"Me and Janet are moving to Nevada. She has grandparents who live on a cattle ranch. They'll even pay our way if we are legally married."

"I heard you spoke to your dad."

"I made a deal with him not to tell what I saw him do to Alicia."

"I thought you wanted to protect Alicia and Cory."

"Sure I do! My father's lied to me my whole life, so what's wrong with me lying back to him now? Once I get that paper and get married, there's nothing he can do to stop me from testifying."

When I left, I spoke with Garth in the parking lot. "I don't understand how HRS can allow this to happen. Both Janet and Rich are under their jurisdiction. Can't they halt a marriage between minors?"

"They have a hands-off attitude. They won't help, but they won't physically stop it either. I'd call it 'enabling' them to get out of the system."

Despondent, I drove for more than an hour unable to concentrate on anything except what I could do to intervene. HRS wanted to be relieved of this burden as expediently as possible, but I knew that marriage was not in Rich's best interests, or even the best interests of the community.

Even though I had no rights in the matter, I called the therapist at Janet's psychiatric hospital. "Is Janet making any progress with you?"

"Actually, I can't say that she is. In fact, she's a destructive influence and we don't want her infecting others who have more potential to be helped."

"Where will she go next?"

"Don't know. She's burned almost every bridge."

"So has Rich." I thought rapidly. "Is she dangerous to herself or others?"

"At times, yes. That's why she was in the suicide unit."

"How can we permit two unstable kids to go off together with no money, no support, no therapy? Both have violent tendencies. One's smart, one's without empathy. It could be Bonnie and Clyde all over again.''

"Might I suggest you request an HRS staff consultation to consider those issues?" the doctor offered. "It's your only chance."

Lillian helped me organize everyone involved in Rich's case for a summit meeting. Present were Mitzi Keller, Rich's caseworker; Garth Clay from Horizons Unlimited; the directors of the regional children's and psychiatric programs; two mental health workers; the case manager for the special assessment team; as well as a few others, whom I never identified.

We met in the oak-paneled boardroom of the university hospital. The first discussion revolved around whether Horizons Unlimited could be an appropriate placement for Rich. Garth said that they would accept Rich if he would agree to sever his relationship with Janet, for only then will he be able to commit to treatment. The case manager from the special assessment team suggested that Rich required a more secure setting than Horizons Unlimited could provide.

"Is Rich a candidate for evaluation in a locked facility under the terms of the Baker Act?" I asked. The Baker Act is a 1970 Florida ruling that may be used to involuntarily place someone in a locked facility for psychiatric evaluation. In order to qualify, there must be reason to believe a person is mentally ill, and because of this he has refused voluntary examination and is unable to determine whether an examination is necessary. Also the person must show that without immediate care he poses a real and present threat of substantial harm to his well-being, or that he will cause serious bodily harm to himself or others in the near future as evidenced by recent behavior.

Mitzi spoke up. "I've already been told Rich does not meet the Baker Act's legal stipulations."

I read from a recent psychological report stating that Rich was at risk for aggressive behavior, and told about his rage and vandalism at Garrison House, but nobody seemed especially concerned.

One of the mental health specialists listed the costs for various beds from $55 a day for Garrison House, $120 a day at Horizons Unlimited, to psychiatric beds that ranged from $195 to $350 a day, and up. She felt a community-based program was more in the range of HRS resources.

After mentioning the programs that—depending on your point of view—either Rich had failed or had failed Rich, I argued for intensive therapy to give him one last chance.

The director of psychiatric services said, "Mrs. Courter, while I respect your advocacy for this child, the state has spent a great deal on Rich Stevenson to no avail. A cost-benefit analysis dictates that my limited budget must be spent on the youngest and sickest children in the system."

Finally everyone was asked to summarize his or her position. Mitzi wanted to allow Rich and Janet a chance to get married, which would free up two places in the system. Horizons Unlimited was pressured by several of the specialists to try to work with Rich a little longer, since he had been relatively compliant there and had formed a tentative bond with Garth.

I stated that Rich needed to be in a locked facility with intensive treatment. "To allow him to be released with Janet without any money, housing, or support, seems like a prescription for them to commit a crime."

The director removed his glasses and gave me a benevolent smile. "Mrs. Courter, wandering around the streets of this city today we have two hundred dysfunctional people exactly like Rich and Janet."

"Are they all potentially violent?" I asked challengingly. "Are they all a danger to themselves and the community?"

The director half closed his heavy-lidded eyes. "Unfortunately we have neither the funds nor the legal right to hold any of them."

Two hundred Richs! Myopia had allowed me to focus on my guardian child alone. Until that moment I had fought for him vigorously, but now I felt deflated. If they would allow hundreds of demented people loose, I had no hope of winning any services for Rich.

The meeting adjourned with the decision not to spend any more of the state's funds on Rich.

From the earliest months of his life Rich had suffered a classic syndrome that led from the deprivation of security in infancy to a low self-esteem and seriously diminished sense of himself as a person by the time he started school. His educational failures resulted in further feelings of worthlessness, and soon he was unable to make realistic judgments or good choices. The more he flopped in program after program, the more he turned inward and reproached himself for being unable to function normally, and this brought him into an early onset of depressions. Over and over he was rejected. His father did not want him, nor did most of the mothers who moved swiftly through his life. Overwhelmed by feelings of grief and loneliness, his unresolved anger seethed beneath the surface. Hence his self-destructive and suicidal tendencies. Studies on these syndromes were made part of ongoing guardian training courses. I turned to a chart titled Results of Failure to Mourn Successfully Following Separation and ticked off every stage as one Rich had suffered through. While the recipe to create an antisocial person capable of psychopathic behaviors was well known, the remedy was more elusive.

A few days later I sat on the screen porch of Horizons Unlimited with this product of an unattached childhood, this rejected, dejected person with sapphire eyes and a crooked grin trying to figure out what might happen next.

Rich couldn't remain still. He tapped his foot on the floor while patting his knee with his hand. His head jerked as he spoke and every noise sent him spinning around. "The way they want Janet and me to get together could be a trick. They say I can walk away from here and get on a bus, but I've been around long enough to know that puts me on runaway status, and the police can pick me up."

"How will you get a bus ticket?"

"Janet's Mom is sending me one, then once Janet gets out of the hospital, she'll take us to get married." He had the permission from his father, or so he claimed. "This is my one chance to get me a family."

"You mean have your own baby?"

"No, to have a mother again. You know, Janet's mother will be mine too. She told me to call her 'mom' and I will."

"You know you also have a real mother."

Rich ignored this. "They're jacking me around," he said in an angry tone.

"Who is?"

"Mitzi and Clay and everyone." Rich crossed his arms and sulked. "If they don't let me get on that bus, I'm not going to be around this time next week."

"Where would you go?"

"If they screw me about this, I'll put an end to my life, and anyone in my way is going where I'm going—even if it is straight to hell."

There it was! Rich had made a direct threat to kill himself and harm others. I had enough to Baker Act him on those words alone.

I went to Garth Clay's office to see if Red Stevenson had actually sent a form saying Rich could marry. The file was shown to me and the paperwork was there. With Rich lingering in the doorway, Garth confirmed that he had spoken to Janet's mother, who had stated that she was sending a bus ticket and would take the children to be married. I told Garth I would call him later about something important, then left and phoned Lillian.

I repeated Rich's threats. "May I break confidentiality on what Rich said to me?" I asked.

"You are required to report it."

"Whom shall I call?"

"You've spoken about it to me and you should call Mr. Clay."

"Gay, you know Rich runs off at the mouth all the time," Garth said when I told him.

I repeated Rich's exact words. Garth exhaled loudly and said he would observe Rich more carefully.

"Rich thinks that if he leaves, you'll call the cops."

"We're merely giving him this chance to do what he claims he wants to do."

"What about the Baker Act?"

"I don't think he's going to hurt himself or anyone else, so that isn't the answer."

"He'd get a new psychiatric evaluation and that might qualify him for some help."

As a last ditch effort I managed to get Janet's mother on the phone that night. When I questioned the wisdom of assisting in this scheme, she said, "Janet has always done whatever she wants anyway."

Monday I called Mr. Clay. He was out, but his assistant, Kurt, told me that Rich had left on Friday morning, and they had not heard from him since. I tried Janet's mother. The phone was answered by a male voice, who said he was a friend of the family. I explained who I was. "I suppose Janet married Rich this weekend," I said.

"Actually, it didn't work out. When they went to the courthouse, the clerk said Rich's form from his father was invalid."

"Where are they now?"

"They're in a foster home."

"Together?"

"Yes, but it is temporary. Janet lived there before entering Garrison House, and they agreed to take her back until the paperwork could be straightened out."

Cheered by this stroke of luck, I called Lillian. The next day there was a prescheduled six-month judicial review of both Rich's and Alicia's foster care status. We discussed strategies for getting Rich more help. Lillian was going to speak to Kit Thorndike, the Guardian ad Litem staff attorney, about sending me the Baker Act forms, which as a party with an interest in the case, I could submit. She also told me to give Rich's current address to the clerk of the courts because if Rich had not married, he was technically a runaway.

In preparation for the court appearance, I had written two separate reports for the judge on each of the children because their needs were so different. In Alicia's report, I explained the reappearance of the children's mother and recommended a home study and a trial visit to Spokane before Florida severed responsibility.

The next day, in the corridor of the courthouse, Mitzi Keller showed me a pickup order for Rich.

"Mitzi, this is precisely what Rich was afraid of. You set him up to be a runaway, and now he might make good on his threats."

"I've been hearing that crap from the kid for years. He's been in the system so long he knows how to push everybody's buttons, especially yours. Anyway, I spoke to Rich about fifteen minutes ago." She smiled smugly. "Here's the deal. Rich already has spoken to his father about the new form and supposedly Red sent it to him."

"So they're going to try to get married again?"

"That's plan A, but he also questioned me about Tammy and asked for her phone number."

"Do you realize what this means?" I said excitedly. "Until now Rich hasn't even acknowledged that Tammy exists. Maybe he's thinking that he doesn't have to rush to get married to find what he's looking for."

Mitzi tossed her curls and gave me one of her skeptical smiles. "Yeah, well, I am not going to lose my job over that little jerk, so I have the pickup order for the judge to sign to cover my rear."

After we were called into Judge Donovan's chambers, Mitzi quickly explained that Alicia was in a stable foster home and doing well. Then she brought the judge up-to-date on Rich's situation.

"Where will you put him when you find him?" the judge asked the caseworker.

"In a foster home," Mitzi replied.

"What would prevent him from running away the next day?"

When Mitzi didn't have a response to the judge's question, I made my plea for a locked facility. I mentioned the phone call to his mother, suggesting that this was a window of opportunity.

The judge asked what I knew about Tammy. I filled him in on her present circumstances. "In any case it will take several months to arrange a reunion and right now I have a duty to inform the court that Rich told me that 'If they screw me about this, I'll put an end to my life, and anyone in my way is going where I'm going—even if it is straight to hell.' "

"Are you willing to Baker Act him?" Judge Donovan asked me.

"Yes, Your Honor. I have the paperwork here."

"We need three signatures. Will you sign, Ms. Keller?" To my surprise Mitzi nodded. "Who else can you get?"

"I think his counselor at Horizons Unlimited would agree," I said.

"Okay, pick him up, then Baker Act him. I don't want to look like a fool if he does make good on those threats."

When I arrived at my office, there was a message from Tammy in Washington.

"Rich called me!" she said, elated. "I can't believe I actually talked to my boy. His voice sounds like a man's. And do you know what he asked me? He said, 'Mom, if I don't get married would you want me?' What was I going to say? I had to say yes to my son."

Tammy's voice choked up, then she continued. "He said he had an old birthday card I had sent him and he had hidden so his father wouldn't throw it out, which made me cry. Then he told me about how his father had beaten him since he was young and he finally couldn't take it anymore."

I reached Mitzi to say that Tammy might be more inclined to help out with Rich.

She groaned. "That won't do anything for his immediate situation."

"What about the Baker Act?"

"You know the Baker Act will only lock him up for twenty-four hours? Then what?"

I pulled out a copy of the relevant statutes and read from section 394.463. "Actually they have forty-eight hours to examine him to see if he meets the criteria for involuntary examination and then they have seventy-two hours from when the patient arrives at the hospital to when the physician documents that the person has an emergency condition. After that, there is an additional twelve hours when he either must be released or transferred for outpatient treatment or be talked into giving voluntary consent for inpatient care, or the administrator can petition for involuntary placement in the least restrictive treatment facility consistent with the optimum improvement of the patient's condition."

"One day or three days, what difference will it make in the long run?"

"I was hoping for a psychiatric referral. Even if it is outpatient it's still better than having him on the street. With a good therapist and the possibility of a real mother, he might respond this time."

Mitzi exhaled loudly. "It's not going to happen."

"But you're going to pick him up, aren't you?"

"Not me. That's police work. However, I don't think anyone is going to look too hard for him for a few days, just in case he gets married in the meantime."

"You want him to marry, don't you?"

"It takes him off my caseload once and for all."

"It will never work," I said in exasperation.

"Nothing else has either," Mitzi reminded me.

Two days later Mitzi's early call woke me. "Rich is on his way back to Horizons Unlimited. You ever meet a guy named Kurt there?"

"Spoke to him, I think," I muttered sleepily.

"He's been the foster parent for several boys transitioning from that program to regular foster homes and has had a lot of success with emotionally impaired teenagers. He takes them to counseling or school every day when he goes in for his shift at Horizons, then brings them home to a family setting at night. It's expensive, over five hundred a month, but it is cheaper than a residential program. Kurt seems to have made some inroads with Rich and is willing to try him out in his home."

"What about the marriage plans?"

"Rich got cold feet and said he needed time to think about it. Janet's going home with her mother for a while." There was a long pause. "What do you think? You still want to Baker Act him?"

I told her I would get back to her. Lillian took my call at her home on the first ring. She agreed that it might be wise to put the Baker Act on hold. "Why not see what happens? I have a good feeling about his mother's attitude and Kurt stepping in now. You can always use the Baker Act if this placement falls apart."

That evening I spoke to Rich at Kurt's house. He claimed he loved the location, which was hidden in the woods, and the other kids were "pretty cool." Then he said he hadn't wanted his sister or brother to see him in the hospital or at Horizons, but he hoped they could visit him there. Kurt confirmed that guests were welcome, so I set about making arrangements for the three Stevenson children to get together for the first time in over six months.

* * *

I traveled more than three hundred miles that afternoon. My home was at one corner of a diamond while the other three points were the whereabouts of the Stevenson siblings. First I picked up Alicia at the Levys', then drove to the Rose/Perez home for Cory, and continued ninety-two miles south where Kurt lived in an entirely different district. After several wrong turns, we finally found the lane to Kurt's house.

On the way Alicia and Cory made me stop twice so they could each have turns at the front seat, but otherwise bantered quietly about rock musicians. As soon as they saw Rich, though, they became more boisterous.

Rich greeted Cory with a hard pat on the shoulder, then grabbed his arm in a wrestling hold and twisted it behind his younger brother's back. Finally I shouted, "Hey!" and Rich broke his hold.

Once inside the house I met Kurt, his wife, Noreen, and five other foster kids, including a biracial boy of six, whom they were adopting. Kurt offered me a seat at the table of the double-wide trailer and together we observed the Stevensons horsing around in the living room. At one point Alicia shoved Rich and he stumbled back against the wall, knocking his arm on the fish tank so hard that water sloshed over the side. Kurt directed the kids outside.

"Rich is a good kid," Noreen said with surprising warmth in her voice. "He's just a big baby. If I treat him like one of the smaller children, he does fine. I even read him the Dr. Seuss story *Horton Hatches the Egg*, and he loved it."

She handed me the book. Thumbing though it, I recalled the story of the steadfast elephant who is asked to mind the egg of a bird named Mayzie while she flies off to have a good time. Despite taunting and storms and being transported to a circus, Horton stays with the egg because "an elephant's faithful one hundred percent." Then Mayzie shows up suddenly and wants the egg back just as it is hatching into a half-bird, half-elephant creature. It didn't take a Freudian scholar to figure out why this story appealed to Rich.

Outside there was a large crash. Kurt leapt up like an uncoiled spring and was out the door before I had even processed the sound. Following after, I saw that Alicia and Rich were dueling with sticks. Alicia had been backed into a shed and had knocked over an empty steel drum. Nobody was hurt, but Kurt took away the ersatz weapons. I suggested it was time to go out for lunch and the kids got into the car. Alicia handed me a new tape to play. As we rode into town we were serenaded by Skid Row singing "Piece of Me."

Pizza Hut might have been fun for the kids, but it was an ordeal for me. The Stevensons used foul language, elbowed one another, spilled a drink, and shot spitballs to the ceiling.They ate messily and argued over who got the largest slice of pizza. There was poking and joking and smoking, as Cory passed around cigarettes to the other two while I was in the rest room. When I returned, I asked them not to smoke in front of me, and they went outside.

While I drove back to Kurt's, Alicia sat in the back with Rich, her head resting on his shoulder. After we arrived, neither wanted to get out of the car. I went in the house to talk to Kurt, who said that while we had been at lunch Janet had called three times.

Back at the car Alicia and Rich were saying their good-byes. He pulled her hair back so hard that she was grimacing. To get released, she punched her fist into his chest, then handed him her dime store ring and told him to wear it always, and not to give it to Janet. He promised he wouldn't and placed it on his pinkie. Then she kissed him on the back of the neck and he spun around and kissed her hard on the side of her mouth. She pretended to be disgusted and made a raspberry sound, but all the while she was squeezing his hand. Annoyed at being left out, Cory kicked dirt in the driveway.

Rich ran around and opened my car door. "Could you lend me ten bucks?"

"Sorry, I can't."

"Hey, never hurts to ask. No hard feelings?"

"Of course not, Rich. Talk to you soon."

That was on Saturday. On Tuesday I called and spoke to Noreen, who said that if Janet continued interfering, she had some doubts about Rich lasting there, but that at the moment he was doing fine and she had no complaints. Two weeks later the situation had improved even more. Noreen informed me that Rich had met a girl in group therapy that he liked better than Janet. The next time Janet phoned, Rich told her he was breaking up, and Janet claimed that she had a new boyfriend as well. Kurt saw this as progress and was going to enroll Rich in the school program he had selected.

By the end of that week, though, Janet had spoken to Mitzi to tell her that she was marrying Rich in a few days. Mitzi wasn't concerned. "The girl is full of stories," she reported to me. "Now she's claiming that she might have a venereal disease, or even AIDS-related complex."

"They are not exactly in a low-risk group. I think Rich should have a screening for sexually transmitted diseases, don't you?"

"I am thrilled to add it to my list," Mitzi replied.

On Saturday Alicia called to ask if what she heard from another foster parent was true.

"What's that?"

"That Rich ran away from Kurt's house."

I called Noreen, who confirmed that the previous afternoon Janet had arrived with a friend to pick up Rich. "At first he said he wasn't going to go with her, then when she said she was leaving, he got his things, and jumped in the car with her." Noreen coughed a few times, then said, "Frankly, I wasn't sorry to see him go. That kid belongs in a locked facility."

The honor of the next trip to a locked facility, however, went to Janet. Rich and Janet had been staying in an apartment near Cocoa Beach that belonged to a friend of Janet's mother. When they had a fight, Rich threatened to return to Kurt's, so Janet went into the kitchen and slashed her wrists. Rich called 911 screaming, "There's blood everywhere!"

Police had Janet committed to a local psychiatric ward under the Baker Act and took Rich into custody. After they ran Rich's name through the computer and found he was a juvenile on runaway status, they contacted his caseworker. Mitzi had to drive across the state to pick him up. Kurt and Noreen agreed to take him back temporarily, and that added another two hundred miles to Mitzi's journey.

By the end of the following week Kurt had proposed that he would resign from Horizons Unlimited and work full-time with his foster children, including Rich, if HRS would pay his salary. Kurt explained that this would be cheaper than putting either one of two difficult boys in a residential facility, and HRS was considering the idea. He also felt that he could prepare Rich for a successful reunion with his mother. This sounded like a fine solution to me, and I said I would back it.

But Rich was always two steps ahead of everyone. The next Sunday afternoon, Mitzi's call took me away from repotting my orchid collection.

"Rich and Janet were married on Friday. That means you and I no longer have any responsibility toward him."

I could hear the ebullience in Mitzi's voice and understood why she felt as she did, but I could not share her glee. Maybe she wouldn't have to drive all over the state to retrieve him, but nothing good could come of this marriage.

A few days later I received a copy of the marriage certificate and a notice that my duties as Guardian ad Litem for Richard Leroy Stevenson, Jr., had been terminated. Included was the address where Janet and Rich were living. Although it was more than a hundred miles away, it was around the corner from a nursing home where we often went to visit elderly relatives.

I went to the store and purchased the largest, most florid wedding card I could find and sent it to Janet and Rich. The enclosed note explained that I visited in that area and hoped to see them soon. I told them that even though I was officially not Rich's guardian any longer, they could always telephone me collect for information about Alicia and Cory, and I wished them well.

Mitzi phoned me the next week and sounded irate. "Is it true?"

"What do you mean?"

"You've been in touch with Rich and Janet." I explained about the card, but she didn't believe me. "I heard that you and Nancy are trying to get Rich's marriage annulled on the grounds he is mentally incompetent."

"I don't know anything about that, but let me check with Nancy."

I phoned Nancy immediately. "Hey, great plan!" she said, laughing. "If I had thought of it, I might have suggested it."

"Where would Mitzi get such an idea?" I asked.

"HRS is filled with strange rumors, don't let it worry you."

"Is there anything else I can do for Rich?"

"No, Gay. I'm sorry, but there isn't. The idea of an annulment might have some merit in another case, but I cannot see how it could help Rich. Do you?"

"I guess not. May I visit him when I am in the area?"

"Sure, you can do anything you want." Nancy went on to explain how hard it was to let go of a kid like Rich and sympathized with me for feeling as though I had not done enough. She pointed out that he had been not only victimized by his parents but also by the system. "We all should have done more for him, but considering what you had to work with, you did the best that you could."

My distress had not abated. "Why can't I agree with you?" I asked.

"Because of you, now Rich at least knows he has a mother he can contact. Do you realize what that means? He finally has at least one parent."

I tried to imagine Rich's future, but no matter how hard I tried, I could not match him with Tammy. Horizons Unlimited! Ha! I wondered how long it would be before he came back into the system. Only which system would it be: mental health, social welfare, or criminal justice?

As if she were reading my mind, Nancy added, "Don't forget about Alicia and Cory. They need you now more than ever."

3

The Unfound Door

Who Will Be Our Mother?

...A stone, a leaf, an unfound door. And all the forgotten faces

*Which of us has known his brother? Which of us has
looked into his father's heart? Which of us has not remained
forever prison-pent? Which of us is not forever
a stranger and alone?*
—**THOMAS WOLFE**

As THE DATE FOR TAMMY'S arrival approached, she and I spoke often about her children. For the most part Rich had avoided any discussions about his mother, but Cory was openly hostile. He insisted his father was innocent and that he would return to live with him after the trial. With no memory of his mother, Cory saw her reappearance as a threat because it meant that Alicia, and possibly even Rich, might move across the continent to be with her. Alicia had been writing her mother letters. They had exchanged photographs and a few phone calls. As the time grew nearer, though, Alicia admitted she was afraid that her mother might not like her or want her. Also she was uncertain she wanted to leave Ruth Levy.

I tried to reassure her—not that I could promise it would work out. "No matter what happens you will always know who your mother is. If you want, you can visit her, live with her or stay in touch."

Arrangements and permissions had to be approved by Mitzi Keller, who was in charge of the movements of the Stevenson children. Mitzi was worried about unsupervised visits with Tammy before the home study was complete. I could not imagine any serious problems. They were old enough to get away from her if she became abusive and there was no history of her ever hurting the children. At last Mitzi reluctantly agreed that Tammy could see her children, as well as take them to visit each other, but they each would have to sleep in their foster homes at night.

More than anyone, I realized that I had a vested interest in this working. But I could not shake some of my concerns. Tammy had talked a good game, but I reminded myself that this was a woman who had neglected her children in the past and had a dismal record in selecting husbands.

At last the final plans were set. Tammy was going to be met at the airport by an old friend, who was loaning Tammy her car. The plane wouldn't arrive until 11 P.M., so she would spend the night with her friends and drive to Alicia's house the following day. I would have lunch with her the day after that.

On the appointed afternoon of Tammy's reunion with her daughter, I phoned Ruth Levy. ''Tammy's here!'' Ruth announced. ''And Mitzi too. We're waiting for Alicia to come home from school. Oh, I hear the school bus!'' she said. ''I'll call you back.''

Less than an hour later the phone rang. It was Ruth. ''Alicia wanted me to call you, then she'll get on.''

''Is Tammy still there?''

''No, she didn't stay long, which surprised me to say the least, but she said she had to get the car back to her friend, who needed it this evening. I thought you said she was renting a car.''

''She was going to, but her friend offered hers.''

''You'd think that since she got a free ticket, she'd be able to contribute something,'' Ruth said with some vexation creeping in her tone.

''How did Alicia react?''

''Not like I would have expected. When she came in, she saw the three of us sitting in the living room. She said hello to Mitzi, then gave me a big hug and kiss—much more eagerly than usual—then she plunked herself down on the seat on the far side of the room and didn't even speak to Tammy. I finally had to introduce them like strangers, and even then Alicia barely looked at her mother. It was like she was giving her the cold shoulder.''

''I suppose she has reasons to be hostile toward her.''

''Well, I didn't appreciate her attitude one bit. She wasn't just aloof, she acted like a brat.''

''How did Tammy handle it?''

''She talked a little about her husband and other children, then she up and left.''

''Maybe when she sensed Alicia's animosity, she felt uncomfortable.''

''If she had stayed longer, maybe she could have broken through Alicia's wall. Tomorrow Tammy has a meeting with Mitzi in the morning to go over the home study paperwork, then is having lunch with you, and has to get the car back again, so she might not even see her daughter," Ruth snapped. "You want me to put Alicia on?"

"Sure."

While I waited, I tried not to feel annoyed at how critical Ruth was of Tammy, because I sensed she was having trouble letting go.

"Hey!" said Alicia.

"How'd it go?"

"Okay . . ."

"What's your mother like?"

"She's older than I imagined. One of the other girls here called her 'prune face'." Alicia began to cry. "I don't want to leave Ruth and go someplace I've never seen and live with people I don't even know."

"You don't have to go anywhere you don't want to."

"Mitzi said that if the home study is approved, they are going to ship me out there after the trial because I have to live with any relative that will take me in."

Placements with relatives were considered preferable, but I could not imagine forcing a fifteen-year-old to live with a parent she hardly knew. "Even if HRS orders it, I will represent what you want in court."

"What if nobody listens to me or you?"

Tammy's poor choices of husbands leapt into my mind. "Don't worry, Alicia, I have enough information in my file to convince the judge to keep you with the Levys, if it turns out that is what you want. Why not give your mother a break? At least use this time to get to know her better. You'll want to stay friends, no matter what, right?"

Alicia agreed reluctantly, then was eager to hang up the phone.

The next day I met Tammy for lunch. We hugged in the parking lot of the Waterside Inn like long-lost friends. She commented on how pretty Alicia was and understood that she was "shy," especially in front of Ruth and Mitzi. "I think she was worried about hurting Ruth's feelings," Tammy said astutely.

"It is going to take time . . ."

"I know that. I'm not going to rush her."

"Cory might be even more withdrawn. You know how he feels about his father."

After we placed our orders for omelettes, I purposely cut the small talk. I began by asking about the children from the time they were born. During her pregnancy with Rich, Tammy had been nauseated for many months and recalled spending much of that time in bed, which "annoyed the hell out of Red." After a difficult, heavily medicated breech birth, during which the doctor had manually attempted to turn the baby into a head-down vertex presentation, Rich required several days in intensive care. Tammy said she had a complicated recovery due to the side effects of the drugs as well as the pain from lacerated vaginal tissues. Labor with Alicia had been easier, but Tammy had hemorrhaged afterward and was so weak she could barely handle both babies. When Cory was born after they moved from Oklahoma to Florida, it was easier because her father was nearby, and he had a girlfriend living with him who helped her out with three babies in diapers at the same time.

Next I reviewed the history of her marriages, in reverse order. Tammy talked affectionately about Kirk Spate, her current husband, saying how much he loved children and the husky dogs they raised. As Tammy spoke, I observed her carefully. Her fingers clutched the iced tea glass tensely, but her eyes were focused on me and her voice had the same resonant warmth I had heard over the phone. But Alicia had been right. This was not an attractive woman. Her features were coarse, and her thin lips drew into a tight line between sentences that made her seem disapproving. Her words made her seem genuinely motivated to find a way to construct a bridge to her natural children, but her expressions were more negative.

"I should tell you where I was this morning," Tammy whispered after the meal was served. "I went to see my father. I called him from my friend's house and he said he wanted me to come by." She looked at her plate but did not lift her fork. "He gave me some old photographs of me as a child and of him and my mother. I didn't know whether she was alive or not, but he told me that she's still in New England. He hasn't been in contact with her for twenty years, but he hears about her from an uncle."

"So you know what it is like to grow up without a mother."

Tammy's eyes brimmed with tears. "I would never have left my babies if I didn't think I was getting them back. When I tried to see the kids, Red chased me off the property with a rifle. I was afraid of him, and I had good reason to be. You know about his first wife, don't you? The one he killed."

"Killed! How?"

"He shot her while she was sleeping on the couch. He claimed he was cleaning the gun and it went off. They tried him for murder but couldn't prove anything because there were no witnesses. He used to brag that she had bad-mouthed him once too often and he'd do the same to me if I crossed him.''

"Where did that happen?"

"Tulsa, Oklahoma.'' Then Tammy presented me with another bombshell. "What hurt most was that when I left, my father sided with Red against me. I never understood that . . . until now.'' She stared out at the parking lot as she continued. "He loved Red in a way he could never love me. Do you know what I mean?''

"You think they were . . . lovers?''

"I do now. I can't explain it, but my father seems so . . . feminine. I didn't remember him that way.'' She glanced at her watch. "Oh, it's later than I thought.'' She had volunteered to take her daughter to her new therapist at the county mental health clinic.

"You hurry on, and I'll pay the check.''

Tammy stood and started for the door, then she turned on her heel and waved back at me, and as she did so, there was something poignant about the gesture—something reminiscent of Alicia.

The next day was a Saturday. Tammy was planning to spend the whole day with Alicia.

When I returned from running some errands at six, Ruth called, frantic. "Where's Tammy?'' she demanded.

"Isn't she with Alicia?'' I asked, thinking that maybe Tammy had been late returning Alicia to the Levys'.

"The hell she is! That child has been waiting all day for her mother, who never showed up. We didn't have Tammy's phone number and she sure didn't try to call us, because Alicia's been sitting by the phone and grabbing it on the first ring.''

"I can't believe it. Maybe she had an accident.''

"Do you have the number where she's staying?''

I said I did and would get right back to her.

"Tammy?'' I asked when I recognized her voice on the other end of the line. "Are you all right? We were afraid you might have had an accident.''

"I'm fine. My friend's husband took the car to get the brakes fixed, so we've been hanging around here catching up on old times.''

"But Alicia's been waiting for you all day.''

"Oh, no! I told her I couldn't get the car today, but that I'd call and make arrangements to take her to see Cory tomorrow. She must have misunderstood.''

"Alicia's been so worried. Do you want to call her or shall I?"

"Would you? Everything is long-distance from here. Tell her I'll pick her up at ten tomorrow morning to go see her brother."

"May I give her this number?"

"Sure, of course you can. Tell her to call me if she wants."

Trying to control my irritation, I dialed Ruth and explained the miscommunication. "Tammy claims she was only going to call, not visit."

"That's not the way I heard it," Ruth retorted adamantly. "You would think that since she is only going to be here a week, she would want to spend every available minute with her children."

"Apparently she didn't have a car . . ."

"Hey, Gay, if it was your daughter, wouldn't you rent, beg, borrow, or steal a car?"

"Yes, but . . ." My mind churned with the revelations of Tammy seeing her father, her telling me about Red killing his first wife, as well as her suspicion that her father and ex-husband might have been lovers. Tammy had fears about greeting her eldest son, who so recently had been in psychiatric institutions; she had been snubbed initially by Alicia; and was going to visit Cory, even though he claimed that he didn't want to see her. "Don't you think this is stressful for Tammy? Perhaps she needs a day to reflect on everything."

"And perhaps Alicia needs a parent who does what she says," Ruth responded emphatically, then hung up the phone.

On Sunday Tammy picked up Alicia and drove her to Cory's foster home, where they stayed about an hour, then she took Alicia back to the Levys'. Birdie Rose, Cory's foster mother, told me that he was chilly but polite to Tammy. After she left, Cory said he was looking forward to seeing her again when she and I would visit him on Tuesday. On Monday Tammy was up early for the long drive to Cocoa Beach to meet Rich and Janet. The next day I was due to meet her at Cory's house.

Because I felt I had lost my objectivity about Tammy, I asked Lillian if she would accompany me on that visit. "I want so much for this to work, I'm afraid that instead of thinking about the children, I am rationalizing Tammy's behavior." I then explained how I had defended Tammy when she had not shown up on Saturday.

"Have you considered that Ruth Levy might have heard Tammy's intentions wrong? Don't forget she has a vested interest in retaining Alicia's affection and perhaps—even subconsciously—undermined that situation."

"I've thought of that," I admitted to my supervisor, "but I can't give Tammy my unqualified support, not when I scrutinize the men she has married and had children with."

"I'd be happy to put my two cents in," Lillian said and wrote down directions to Cory's foster home.

Cory was more subdued than usual. Patty was taking care of a neighbor's Yorkshire terrier and Cory sat on the floor beside the dog, leaning against the flowered divan where I was sitting. Tammy and Lillian took the rocking chairs next to each other and Patty came in and out of the kitchen, where she was preparing a bottle for baby Sheila, and handed it to Birdie. I started the conversation about a truck I had seen with huge wheels, then Tammy described her husband's pickup truck, which was outfitted in the winter with a snowplow. Suddenly Cory perked up and soon was smiling and joking with Lillian and his mother. When the dog pestered to go out, Cory said it was his turn and went for the leash.

Taking advantage of the time alone with Tammy, Lillian shifted her body to face her directly. "Is there anything that might stand in the way of your taking custody of your children?"

"No, I want them both with me, and even Rich if he wasn't married."

"Do either you or your husband have arrests or complications in your background that might be revealed in a thorough investigation?" Lillian inquired.

"Kirk had a DUI last year."

"Just one?" Lillian asked like a mother coaxing a child to show what she was holding in the hand behind her back.

"Well, two weeks ago he was stopped again, but he joined a voluntary treatment program at the VA hospital."

"What about drugs?"

"Not a problem."

"Not even in the past?" Lillian coaxed.

"I think Kirk used to smoke marijuana, but that was before I met him."

"Did you?"

"No, well, I tried it when I was a kid, but it never appealed to me."

"Would the DUI's preclude the Spates from getting custody?" I asked Lillian.

"The interstate home study will cover most of this, but I wanted to hear the worst to prevent the kids from getting their hopes up, only to find a skeleton in the closet at the last moment." Lillian smiled winsomely at Tammy, as if to indicate she hadn't meant anything personal by the scrutiny. "Anything else we should know first?" Lillian probed without a hint of accusation in her syrupy voice.

"Well, some years ago Kirk spent time in jail for a rape that took place near his army base. A few others were eventually charged, but he wasn't."

Rape! First there had been Red, then the guy in jail in Florida, and now Kirk. How could Tammy have managed—not only to meet, but to marry—three rapists?

The patio door opened and the dog bounded in followed by a sweaty Cory. "He's full of beans today!" Cory rolled around on the carpet with the dog, allowing him to chew on his arm and tug on his clothes.

When Cory was a little quieter, but still cheerful, I spoke seriously. "You know why Alicia wanted to find your mother, don't you?"

"She doesn't want to go home to Dad."

"Right. But you do."

Cory nodded. "And I will!"

"I know you want to, but you have to face the fact that one of three things will happen. If your father is found guilty, he'll be in prison for several years, probably until after you are eighteen." I took a long breath. "If he is found not guilty, HRS might determine he is not a fit father and still decide to keep you in foster care, or they might permit you to go back home. However, if they don't, would you agree to live with your mother and sister instead of staying in foster care?"

Cory looked up at Birdie and gave her a lopsided grin. "I'd rather stay here, wouldn't I?"

Birdie smiled back. "That's my kiddo! But, Cory, you hardly know your mother and you've never met her husband or her other children. How would you like to go for a visit, just to see what it is like?"

"Well, maybe for a weekend."

Lillian laughed and explained it was too far for a weekend.

"It would be a vacation," I added.

"Then, if you wanted to come back to me someday, you could," Tammy said softly. "Even if you didn't, you would be able to remember what it was like and we could stay in touch."

He glanced from his mother to Birdie, then grinned so wide he revealed his crooked teeth. "Cool! I've never had a real vacation."

Tammy had made tentative plans to take Cory out for a hamburger if he was willing. When she mentioned it again, he jumped at the idea. After he left, Lillian and I talked with Birdie and asked how he had been reacting to his mother's visit.

"He bragged that Tammy was spending more time with him than his sister. I don't know if that is true, but he wants to believe it is."

"Which means he's already forming a very slender bond with her," Lillian suggested.

"He needs a family of his own," Birdie said. "No matter how hard Patty and I try, we will never be able to give him that."

Altogether Tammy spent a week in Florida. This included the first visit to meet Alicia, an initial encounter with Cory, driving Alicia to one therapy session, a half day with Alicia and Cory, the journey to see Rich and Janet, and the meeting with Lillian and me before her dinner with Cory. She was supposed to try to see Alicia again before leaving, but it did not work out because Ruth did not want Alicia to miss school and Tammy didn't have transportation later that day.

In the next few weeks Alicia didn't say much about her mother's visit, but I noticed Alicia's attachment to Ruth had intensified. Before Alicia could accept what the Levys had to offer, she may have had to face the reality of her mother fantasy. On the other hand, I understood that Ruth was having some problems with lower back pain and had been advised to have surgery, and if that happened, the Levys might give up being foster parents for a year. Then where would Alicia go? Wasn't it useful to have a mother who was willing to take her . . . just in case?

Mitzi Keller was negative about the children visiting their mother during the summer. "We're not going to allow it unless we get a completely approved home study."

"What about one that authorizes a visit, not custody?"

"The department only sends kids on one-way plane tickets. They have to commit to staying there."

"Would you accept a job or pick a home without a trial visit?"

"We don't have funds for transcontinental vacations."

Furious, I phoned Lillian. "Don't worry," Lillian said soothingly, "you can ask the judge to send them for the summer."

"Can he order HRS to purchase the plane tickets?"

"Possibly, but I wouldn't count on it. What about that service club that bought the mother's ticket?"

"I don't feel comfortable going back to them quite so soon."

"There's a charity in my town that does that sort of thing and my sister is on the committee. We can check with them. How much would it cost?''

''Here's the crazy part, Lillian. I phoned my travel agent and he said that a one-way ticket is six hundred dollars, but the round-trip discount fare is only three-fifty. Mitzi still claims that HRS won't buy the cheaper fare because once they send the kids, they do not want them back, and thus won't give them the ability to return.''

Many varied fibers of rope were woven through Alicia's life and they often became hopelessly knotted. Sometimes I thought I spent half my time untangling loose ends until they lay flat again, if only for a short while. First there was the mother strand as Alicia worked with her feelings toward this person she had actively wanted to know, but about whom she had complex and conflicting emotions. Then there were the fibers representing the various boys to whom Alicia was attracted. I may have lost track of their names and faces, but the one constant was that there would always be someone to offer her the solace of sex. There were also her conflicted relationships with her foster sisters, which created complicated flyaway strands that kept the surface rough. But Ruth was the thickest umbilical fiber, the one person she could not function without. Thinner yarns represented Cory and Rich. Alicia wanted to grasp these, but they were often too jumbled to be there for her. School matters, counseling, and other interests—including a job—spiraled off into frayed edges that were not an integral part of the design but had to be dealt with. And winding through everything, often messing up any attempt at organization, was the one yarn with an elastic center thread that squeezed the others: the criminal court proceedings.

A few weeks after Tammy's departure, Alicia was scheduled to give a deposition, which is testimony under oath in the presence of the prosecutor and the defense attorney. On the phone Grace Chandler, the prosecuting attorney, confided that Alicia's friend, Dawn Leigh Pruitt, had given her deposition the previous week. Originally Red Stevenson had been charged with two counts of sexual battery, one for Alicia when she was nine, and one more recent for Dawn. Although both were criminal offenses, conviction on the charge of sexual battery before the age of twelve would result in a much harsher sentence.

''I'm uncertain about the Pruitt kid,'' Grace admitted. ''She confuses several incidents, which might discredit her as a witness, and the report I received from her psychologist suggests she has a worrisome score for lying.''

"What did Alicia's evaluation look like?"

"Much better. Her story is solid. Still, I'm thinking it might be in everyone's interest to come up with a plea bargain. If we nail him for molesting Alicia at age nine, under Florida law he'll have to serve a minimum mandatory sentence of twenty-five years in jail. A plea bargain for half that time would protect his children and give him a chance to get out eventually."

Before the proceedings, I talked to Lillian about how to handle the plea bargain discussions. "Shouldn't Alicia be asked how she feels about it?"

"Yes, of course, and you are the best one to explain everything to her and then communicate her wishes to the prosecutor. Also, during the deposition, if you don't like a question the defense attorney asks Alicia, you can say that you want the judge to certify the question."

"What does that mean?"

"The judge will decide whether the question should be allowed or not."

"So the proceedings stop and wait until someone can find the judge?"

"Sometimes, but usually they ask the judge later and get back to it. At least you've objected and it gives the kid a break. Also, if you think she is being badgered or if she gets emotional and needs a rest, you can request a recess."

"How will Grace feel about my interference?"

"She's not your concern. You are the guardian and you are there to represent what is best for Alicia, not what is best for the state's case."

Assembled around a rectangular table at nine-thirty on the appointed morning were Red Stevenson's defense attorney, Walt Hilliard, the person who had scheduled this proceeding; Grace Chandler; the court reporter; Alicia, and me. The formal deposition began with Mr. Hilliard asking questions. This was the third occasion I had heard Alicia tell the story. The first time had been with an assistant prosecutor who had been assigned the case initially. When he resigned and Grace took over, his notes had been too incomplete for her to use, so Alicia had been forced to suffer through the questions again. Since I was the only person who had heard the testimony twice, I was the only one who knew that there had been discrepancies between the versions. Now I feared Mr. Hilliard, who did not have a reputation as a nice guy, would be brutal if he also uncovered the holes in her story.

I had reviewed my entire file the night before. The moment Walt Hilliard opened his briefcase, I recognized the documents he took out and laid on the table. I was pleased that I had photocopies from the sheriff's department files and pulled out my matching papers.

When the police first asked Alicia the date sexual activity began with her father, she said that she had been five years old, which is also what she wrote in the police report the night she was removed from her home. In subsequent testimony, however, she had claimed she had been nine. In preparation for this deposition, Grace and I had worked with Alicia to see if we could pin down the dates. Several years earlier an incest case in Arizona had been lost because, while the victim had stated her father had intercourse with her several times a week for many years, she could not specify the dates and locations of each alleged occurrence. Thus the charges were considered defective, and the Arizona supreme court ordered the dismissal of the indictment even though the father had acknowledged that he had intercourse with his daughter at least a dozen times, had impregnated her, and forced her to have an abortion. No matter that few people can accurately state the dates they have had sex, this burden of proof was expected of a molested child. Grace believed that such precision was not required in this case, but the more unequivocal Alicia could be, the better.

After Mr. Hilliard recorded Alicia's name, age, and the details about where she lived and attended school, he asked, "When did you first have sex?"

"When I was nine."

"Where did this take place?"

"At my father's marine shop."

"Where was this?"

"The first property he had, the one before the underpass after you cross the railroad bridge on North Main."

"When was it?"

"The summer before Dad moved to the marina. I was going into fifth grade, my last year at Sawgrass Primary, but I wasn't ten till after school started."

"So this was sometime in the summer. When in the summer?"

"A few days after the Fourth of July, probably sometime that next week because my grandfather always had a barbecue on the Fourth and there was some leftover rolls and salads that were in the fridge at the shop that day."

So far so good. Next Alicia handled the detailed questions about having sex with her father with equal aplomb. She described how he followed her into the bathroom, showed her different positions for intercourse in a pornographic magazine, then made her pull down her panties, and bend over the toilet. Then she claimed he penetrated her. Alicia's voice was muted, but she had remained calm.

Then Walt Hilliard abruptly changed the subject. "Who is your best friend?"

"Dawn Leigh Pruitt."

"Where does she live?"

"She moved to Clearwater."

"Do you see her very often?"

"No."

"Why not?"

"My dad wouldn't let us get together anymore."

"How did you feel about that?"

"Mad. He did it to punish me and her."

"For what?"

"We ran away once."

"You hitched a ride with some boys, didn't you? Where did you go?"

"To the beach."

"How old were you?"

"Fourteen."

"How old were the boys?"

"Twenty, I think."

"Do you think it was safe for girls that age to go off with strange men?"

"We knew them."

"Did you have sex with them?"

I started to speak, but Grace beat me to it. "Objection."

Walt Hilliard didn't skip a beat. "Did you and Dawn stay in contact after she moved?"

"We tried, but my father didn't like me making long-distance calls."

"Isn't it true that you ran up a phone bill of over fifty dollars in one month?"

"I dunno," she said in a childish voice.

"Did he punish you for that?"

"Yes."

"That's when you ran away to be with her and the boys?"

"I guess . . ."

"You guess? Is that what happened or not?"

"It's what happened."

"Isn't it time for a break?" I asked.

Grace called a recess. Alicia and I hurried to the rest room and she went into the stall, while I waited. After five minutes, she came out and splashed water on her face.

"That guy's a pig."

"Yes, well, that's his job." I made a snuffling porcine noise in my throat and Alicia burst out laughing.

We went out and bought Cokes from the machine while we waited for Mr. Hilliard to reappear.

After we were seated, Mr. Hilliard pulled out a yellow legal pad and pointed to a name. "Who is Hank Edwards?"

"A friend of mine."

"Where does he live?"

"At the Marina Motel."

"Is that near your father's shop?"

"Yes."

"Is he the same race as you?"

"No, he's black. So what?"

"Does he work at the motel?"

"Yeah, he's the night manager."

"Did you ever go to his room?"

"I guess I went in there once in a while."

"At two in the morning?"

"No, like in the middle of the day."

"A witness told me that she has seen you coming out of his room at all hours of the night."

"That's a girl who hates me and wants to start trouble."

"Do lots of people hate you?"

"Yes."

"How do you know they do?"

"They call me names."

"Like what?"

"Slut and Mrs. Goodfuck."

"Why would they call you that?"

"They have grudges against me."

Walt Hilliard turned away from Alicia and began sifting through pages while Grace and I sent signals of dismay to each other. All we needed was for this kid to come off like a paranoid, sexually active teenager!

Until that moment I had been confident Alicia would win her case. She had told her story consistently and behaved well. The court-ordered psychological profile had pronounced her competent to testify and said she would "be an effective witness." She understood the difference between a lie and the truth and would do well on the stand as long as she had appropriate reassurance, which I knew Ruth and I could supply in liberal doses. Although Alicia was usually compliant and passive, Mr. Hilliard had been able to provoke her on several occasions that morning, and he was probably going to build on these vulnerabilities to destroy her credibility.

Taking advantage of the moment, Walt Hilliard homed in on the inconsistencies in the initial statement that Alicia had handwritten for the police the night they took her from her father's home. "Did you write this?" He passed the paper to me to hand to Alicia. "Yes, I did."

Before I handed it back to Walt Hilliard, though, I showed it to Grace. My finger tapped the box with the time of day marked.

"Here you state that 'I was five when my father started to have sex with me.' A short while ago you said you were nine," Mr. Hilliard said more belligerently. "Which was it?"

"Both."

"How could that be?"

Alicia's eyes brimmed with tears.

I handed her tissues and said, "Let her calm down first."

Walt Hilliard looked at the ceiling, as if he were praying for deliverance from do-gooder guardians.

"What happened when you were five?" Mr. Hilliard asked.

"My father started touching me."

"Where was this?"

Alicia misconstrued the question and began to describe the location rather than the part of her body. Mr. Hilliard started to interrupt, then permitted her to proceed. "There was a toolshed in the groves. My father was working on the mower-tractor and he told me I could drive it if I sat on his lap. I climbed up and he ordered me to take off my panties so they wouldn't get dirty. I did, and he hung them on the shifter, then sat me between his legs, and showed me how to steer it."

"Was the mower moving?" Mr. Hilliard asked.

"No, it was pretend," she said, her voice rising so that it sounded like a much younger child's.

"What else happened?"

"He told me he loved me and that we could do special things together when we were alone, but they had to be a secret or everyone else would get jealous."

"What were those things?"

"I don't remember."

"No further questions," Walt Hilliard said, surprising me.

Now it was Grace's turn to clarify Alicia's testimony and demonstrate the strength of the case.

"You were telling us about what happened when you were five," Grace said, her voice warm and reassuring. "How do you know how old you actually were then?"

"Well, it's funny, but my panties were brand-new because my other ones had holes and my stepmother bought new pink ones for kindergarten. I was only allowed to wear them on school days. It had to be a school day because those panties were pink."

Grace and I glanced at each other smugly.

"What did your father do when you were on the mower?" Grace asked.

"He patted my bottom."

"Hard, like a spanking?"

"No, it was nice, except—" Alicia closed her eyes and I noticed her head roll to one side, as if she were falling asleep.

"Alicia? Are you all right?" Grace asked.

Alicia snapped to alertness. "I'm fine."

"Did you tell anyone?"

"No, I promised I wouldn't."

"Why?"

"Everyone would have gotten mad at me."

"So that is what started when you were five. Is that why you wrote that age on your statement?"

"Yes."

"What time of day did you write that statement?"

"It was the middle of the night."

Grace took out her copy of the document and pointed to the time. "Was it at two-forty-five in the morning?"

"Around then."

"Do you usually stay up that late?"

"No."

"Why were you up so late that night?"

"The police came to my house and asked me questions, then Deputy Moline took me to the police station and told me I had to write this paper before I could leave."

"Then what happened?"

"Somebody from HRS came and took me to the shelter home."

"What time did you get there?"

"They were having breakfast."

"Did you sleep at all that night?"

"No."

"How were you feeling?"

"Terrible. I was crying and upset. I didn't want to tell everything over and over. I didn't want to leave home. I thought my father should have had to leave, not me."

"Did you take anything with you?"

"No."

"When did you get your things?"

"A week or so later the HRS lady brought me some clothes, but nothing else. About a month later the policeman took me to get what I wanted."

"What was that?"

"My private stuff, like perfume and brushes and the rest of my clothes."

"Anything else?"

"We couldn't find my stuffed animals or the glass unicorn or my books, pictures, or my diary."

"You kept a diary?"

"Yes."

"What did you write about?"

"My friends, school . . ."

"Did you write about what happened between you and your father?"

"In a way. I made little notes."

I knew that, much to our regret, the diary had never been found. Probably Mr. Stevenson had destroyed it, but Grace wanted to place some doubt in Mr. Hilliard's mind about this crucial piece of evidence.

Mr. Hilliard shuffled through his notes.

"You stated that the first time you had sexual intercourse with your father was at his old marine shop, the one he had in town," he said.

"Yes," Alicia replied.

"And you stated that the incident occurred in the bathroom."

"Yes."

"Could you describe it?"

"It was a regular bathroom."

"What color?"

"The walls were green and the toilet, sink, and bathtub were beige."

"There was a bathtub in the marine shop? Are you sure you aren't getting that bathroom confused with one at home?"

"No, it was really big. It has a woodstove and little table and everything."

"Where was this?"

Alicia's jaw tensed. "I told you, in the marine shop." Her voice was on the edge of breaking.

Fortunately the ordeal was over.

When I took Alicia home, Ruth Levy pulled me aside and had me come into her small office behind the kitchen. "How'd it go?"

"She got upset a few times, otherwise she did very well."

"There's something I have to tell you," Ruth whispered and closed the door. "Today I was at a foster parent group meeting. One of the other mothers asked about Alicia and I mentioned that she was being interviewed today. Then that mother told me that she had been in court the day Alicia and Dawn were brought in to give testimony in her foster care hearing. They were outside in the hall waiting for their case to be called and this woman was around the corner, but she could hear them speaking. She claims she heard Dawn whispering, 'Let's keep our story straight,' and 'Don't forget that part' and then, 'If we do it right, they'll let us live together.' To her, it sounded like they were making up a story so they wouldn't be separated."

"What do you think?" I asked Ruth.

"Alicia has told me that she assumed the police were going to allow her to live with Dawn because Dawn's parents invited her. She never thought she'd wind up in foster care."

"Are you suggesting that Alicia invented the entire incest story so she could go live with Dawn after she moved away?"

"No, well . . . Honestly, I'm not sure."

"But Ruth, does it make sense for her to have created a story that began ten years ago? Wouldn't it be more logical for her to say that her father started molesting her recently? And she has so many details about a shed and a bathroom. Grace Chandler says that people remember these first sexual encounters vividly. I can't describe an average experience with my husband three months ago, but I could give you a long description of my first time with him." I paused to think this through. "Also, Alicia has never had a great imagination. I can't believe she'd make up something like him showing her dirty magazines and her father holding her elbows when he had her lean over the toilet to have sex with her."

"Alicia told me about that." Ruth rocked from one foot to the other. "Milo is about the same size as Mr. Stevenson. The other night he was standing by the sink helping dry the dishes that Mandy was washing. Mandy is ten, but she is probably around the same size Alicia was at nine. Mandy's back was to him and she was bending over slightly . . . and let me tell you, there is no way in hell that a man that tall could have done it to a girl her size in the position Alicia describes."

Because the trial date was temporarily scheduled for June, we began making plans for Cory and Alicia to visit Tammy as soon as it was over. The more we discussed it, though, the more negative Alicia became.

"What is worrying you?" I asked.

"If I live with my mother, I'll go back to drugs and partying."

"Do you feel that if you don't have Ruth around to depend on, you might not be able to depend on yourself?"

"I guess . . ."

"You're a different person than you were when you were living with your father. You know that you can control yourself if you want to."

"I don't want to go to Washington."

"Hey, nobody is going to force you," I said, then changed the subject.

The next day, when Alicia was in school, I called Ruth to discuss the trip. "She's very negative. What might have changed her mind?"

"Look, Gay, I know you found her mother and all that, but after the way Tammy has behaved, I can't push Alicia in her direction. You know how little time she spent with Alicia when she was here, and since then she has called only three times and sent two letters. If it were my child, and I wanted her to come and live with me, I'd do something at least every week."

"I see your point, but what does Alicia say about this?"

"You know she was disappointed and didn't warm to her mother the way she thought she might. Yesterday one of the other girls said something about her mother and she replied, 'You mean Ruth or the old hag?' ''

"Okay, Ruth, I will not push Tammy on Alicia. Just knowing that she has a mother might be enough."

"If she doesn't want to see her, what will you do about Cory?"

"He might want to travel without her, or maybe not, we'll see. Also, even if Red is acquitted, Mitzi says HRS is not going to permit him to have custody of Cory. Maybe if he forms a bond with his mother and her family, that will be his solution, although I know he'd prefer to live either with Alicia, or somewhere nearby."

"I'd take him as a foster child too, but I only have girls here."

"I know, Ruth, so unless they live with their mother it is unlikely they'll ever be together again."

Cory had healed under the ministrations of Birdie Rose and Patty Perez, but then Patty was offered a part-time job outside the district, which was also nearer to specialized medical care for Manuel and Sheila, whom they were going to adopt, and everyone moved but him. Cory hid his disappointment well, but HRS handled the transition abominably.

As soon as I had heard that Patty had accepted the job, I asked where Cory might go. Mitzi mentioned that there were two possibilities: one nearer his sister, another in his original school district where he had many friends.

"Does that mean he'll have to change schools with less than a month of the semester to complete?"

"He's not lighting any fires, so what difference does it make?" Mitzi snapped.

"Couldn't you find him a temporary bed in his school district? There are a lot of end-of-year activities he's looking forward to."

"Listen, Gay, I'll be happy if I can get one of these families to take him."

"Have you thought about introducing them to Cory ahead of time? Maybe he'd accept a new family better if he felt part of the selection process."

"Puhleeeze! Do you know the trouble we'd have if we let kids pick their placements?"

"Yes, I see your point," I said, even though I didn't, "but this is a special case. Unlike Cory, most kids have been abused and are afraid to return home, while Cory thinks home is paradise. If he were included, he might feel ownership of the decision and he might make more of an effort to fit in.''

''Well, it ain't gonna happen anytime soon,'' Mitzi said with finality in her voice.

Cory was moved to the Hornsbys, who also had a seriously asthmatic small boy, two children of their own, and a teenage boy they were in the process of adopting. Cory was so dejected he stopped working in the new school and would sleep through classes. When Mrs. Hornsby caught him smoking after warning him twice that it wasn't permitted, he was transferred to the Sheldons. They had a retarded daughter of their own, were raising their infant grandchild, and were already the foster parents of the most notorious children in our district: two- and three-year-old siblings who killed animals for kicks.

I complained to Lillian. ''They're treating this kid like a Ping-Pong ball.''

''And he's learning the system,'' Lillian agreed sadly.

''Marvelous system, isn't it? You don't like where you are living, so you figure out how to get thrown out, and thus find that rebellion brings more concern than compliance.''

''You're right. Kids would rather have the negative attention than be ignored.''

''Then how can we halt the cycle?''

''If he wants out, there will always be a rule he'll figure out how to break or a line he'll be willing to cross,'' Lillian added.

''Yes, but no matter what rule one of my sons breaks, I don't get to throw him out, do I? Eventually my son learns to comply or suffer the consequences. The consequence for Cory is getting what he wants—or thinks he wants.''

Mrs. Sheldon was cooperative in arranging visits between Cory and his father but told me that Cory acted much worse in the days after the visit. ''Maybe he shouldn't see him until the trial, otherwise I'll never get him to settle down.''

''I understand why you feel that way,'' I said, ''but there is no definite date. I think that a long, undetermined delay might make Cory even more angry.''

Mrs. Sheldon said she'd go along with my recommendations, but a few days after the most recent visit with his father, Cory called me.

''They arrested me!'' he shouted in a combination of rage and fear. ''I didn't even do nothing and this guy phoned the police!''

"Calm down, Cory," I said. "What happened?"

He explained that he had been on his way to catch the school bus when he looked into a neighbor's car and saw a pack of cigarettes lying on the front seat. "I was just going to take one or two," he explained in a whiny voice, "but the guy saw me from his window and called 911 before I had the car door open."

"You didn't take anything?" I asked.

"No, I swear I didn't, so how could they arrest me?"

"You did open the door and intended to steal cigarettes."

"Just a couple of smokes," he responded belligerently.

"But, Cory, they did not belong to you. Do you understand that?"

"Is that a reason to fingerprint me and everything?"

"Is the neighbor pressing charges?"

"I dunno, but I got another HRS worker on top of Mitzi and she's even more of a pain in the butt."

I took the name of his delinquency caseworker and called her. She said that they were trying to work out a deal with the neighbor. The Sheldons were throwing him out anyway, so Cory wouldn't be in the area much longer. I suggested that Cory be placed in a facility where he would receive the counseling he desperately needed. The worker reminded me that they were under orders to select the "least restrictive" environment.

"I like the theory," I told her, "but after so many failures, these foster homes are not the solution. What Cory needs are some successes." I hung up the phone angry at everyone, especially myself.

I realized that I should have seen this coming. Cory had been a time bomb waiting to explode. He had been furious when the court removed him from the home of his father and grandfather, enraged when they placed him in a shelter home, then moved him to another group facility. His first foster care placement with the authoritarian MacDougals had been the most destructive situation yet, and when they threw him out, he felt like a failure. Then just when he made his first real attachment, to Patty and Birdie, they had to move.

A few days later Mitzi announced that the Palomino Ranch had some temporary beds available. I despised substituting the term "bed" for a home for a child. To HRS, foster children were trouble units to be "placed" in "beds." Beds had to be in approved homes that contained the requisite number of bathrooms, smoke detectors, and fire extinguishers. There was never any mention of the family's personality, the style of parenting, the psychological match of child to parent. *Attachment* and *caring* and *love* were words that were never uttered, and certainly nobody seemed to speculate about what the child might have wanted.

To complicate matters, this was the highly emotionally charged period when we were trying to arrange a visit to Tammy in Washington and when Red Stevenson's case was being prepared for trial. As plea bargains and prosecution strategies were discussed, I soon realized that any situation that would make Alicia happy had Cory despondent and vice versa. Even I became confused as to what was bad news and what was good news, and wondered if it might not have been better for the Stevenson children to have been appointed separate guardians.

Lillian dismissed my concerns. "First of all, we don't have enough volunteers to cover all the cases as it is, so a family is handled by one advocate. I know it is unusual to have the children turn against each other, but I know you treat each of them as individuals. And if you need to talk about anything, I'm always here."

The next day I stopped by to take Alicia to a meeting with the prosecutor to go over some details of her testimony. While I waited for Alicia to finish dressing, Ruth came outside and stood by my car. "Mitzi talked me into taking a new kid yesterday." With her head she indicated a boy raking leaves. "Yeah, I know I said I wouldn't take boys, but they didn't have a place for that one and I had a twin bedroom empty with a separate bathroom, so I said okay. I'm not keeping Larry unless they give me another boy to keep him company." She rolled her eyes. "Don't even say it! I can't consider taking Cory because of how Milo feels about Rich."

"Cory's more like Alicia than Rich."

"I know . . . let's see if this kid lasts through the weekend."

"Please, think about it, Ruth," I begged just as Alicia appeared in a skirt so short I could see the lace edge of her panties. "I'd love those kids to have each other again."

On the way to the courthouse, we stopped for lunch at a deli. Alicia was in a foul mood.

"What's wrong?"

"I am sick and tired of everybody telling me and Cory what to do."

"Hey, kiddo, who are you talking to?" I put down my onion bagel and pulled out my notebook. "Now, what do you, Alicia Stevenson, want?"

"I don't want Cory to ever live with my dad again. That's more important than Dad going to prison."

"I'm glad you mentioned that because there is a chance your father might plead guilty if he is offered a less harsh sentence than he would get after a trial.'' I looked down at what I had written. ''So you'd like to have a plea bargain that protects Cory, right?''

''Yeah, and if they can't arrange that, then I'll go in front of a jury and do my best to convince them I am telling the whole damn truth!'' Alicia took a bite of her bagel like she was a starving predator and it was her prey.

Once we were in Grace's office, she went over Alicia's ages during the first sexual encounters with her father and had her describe the marine shop bathroom. Alicia again confused the ages when she was in the toolshed and the marine shop.

Grace held up two pieces of paper and spoke firmly. ''Alicia, are these statements you wrote?'' Alicia acknowledged that they were. ''I want you to take them home and go over them until you remember what happened, okay?''

''Yes, ma'am,'' Alicia said, more snidely than I might have preferred.

In the large outer office Alicia began chatting with one of the secretaries. Grace touched my shoulder and pulled me aside. ''If she makes a joke out of this, it will blow the case.''

''Grace, I don't know if it is proper to do this, but if I have information on Mr. Stevenson's past, should I give it to you?''

''Sure. We're on the same side, aren't we?''

''I'm on Alicia's side,'' I stated firmly. ''I hope it isn't too late to mention this—and you probably know it already—but when her mother was here she told me that Red's first wife was killed by him. He was acquitted of manslaughter.''

Grace paled. ''Where was that?''

''Tulsa, Oklahoma. Didn't you run a background check on his criminal record?''

''It might not have ranged far enough, but it is probably inadmissible evidence.'' She went on to explain the legal ramifications, and while I could see they protected a man's rights, I felt they were essentially unfair to the victim.

''What else do you know?'' she asked with a tired sigh.

I listed all of Red's wives. ''Maybe some of them would be willing to talk to you. Especially Denise Rhodes.''

''Sunny's mother?''

I nodded.

''Now she might be useful.''

* * *

A few days after Cory moved to the ranch, Grace Chandler called me. "Mr. Stevenson has accepted a plea bargain. He will plead guilty to a second-degree felony for sexual battery of Alicia and in exchange the state will drop the charge on Dawn Leigh Pruitt. He'll be adjudicated guilty and receive two years of house arrest, which means he has to be either at work or home, and ten years' probation, a total of a consecutive twelve years. That will make him fifty-seven when he gets done. Also, he'll be classified a certified sexual offender on his natural daughter and won't ever be permitted to have children in his home again, including custody of Cory. He may have supervised visits with Cory, only, but no contact with Alicia or Dawn. He must attend mental health counseling for sex offenders, pay court costs, the fees for Alicia's counseling, and will be responsible for some of Cory's medical and other expenses. What do you think?"

"Alicia was most worried about protecting Cory, and she really doesn't want to have to tell her story in a courtroom. But don't you think that is a very liberal deal for a man who is looking at a minimum mandatory of twenty-five years?"

"Yes, but this does protect the children from the ordeal of trial and further contact with their father."

"Then it is over?" I asked.

"No. The plea offer will be shown to Judge Donovan Monday morning for his acceptance."

Immediately I phoned Alicia, but since she was out, I spoke to Ruth first. "Now that he has admitted his guilt, Alicia's story is validated without her having to undergo the trauma of a trial," she said enthusiastically.

Later that evening Alicia called. She did not want to attend the plea bargain hearing. "I just want it to be over."

My next call was to Mitzi Keller. She had not been told the news and said she was bitterly disappointed that Red Stevenson might avoid any time in prison.

"I think this may be the best result, at least from the kids' point of view," I replied. "Alicia can get on with her life without having to testify in public, and once Cory understands he will not be going home again, he might look at his options more realistically and make a better adjustment."

"Cory will also have to realize that a man does not plead guilty if he is innocent," Mitzi added astutely.

Cory, though, had a different take on the news. "Dad did that to make it easier on us. It doesn't mean he's guilty."

"However, this does mean you can't live with him again."

"What about me living with Gramps?"

"I don't know about that. The authorities might think he has too many health problems."

"He'd have me to help him, and in another year I'll be able to drive!"

"There's also your mother . . ."

"I'm not living with that bitch," he replied in a fierce voice that dissolved into tears.

"Cory . . . I'm sorry." His crying increased. "Cory . . ."

"Just . . . don't"—he said between sobs—"don't hang up."

I stayed on for a long time. Unfortunately I was traveling to Boston for the weekend, but I promised to visit him on Tuesday.

Monday, though, brought another surprise. The judge rejected the plea bargain because the sentence was too light. He was insisting on a trial in two weeks. Grace Chandler hurriedly scheduled a pretrial meeting for that Friday.

I reached Alicia first with the news. She responded passively. "Whatever . . ."

Cory, though, took it harder. "What else can go wrong in my life?"

I reminded him that I would visit the next day.

Imagining a rustic retreat set on rolling acres of green pastureland, I was bitterly disappointed by the "ranch." Cory had not been settled into one of the family-style cottages, but was being kept for evaluation in the shelter dormitory section, which contained several dozen tough and formidable boys, many of whom were in transition either into or out of the juvenile justice system.

The unpainted concrete block dwelling was clean, and spacious, but depressingly bland. The boys either did chores, slept, lounged around the television, or sprawled in the dirt outside the front door. There were no supervised activities and the counselors were merely standing guard. Way off in the distance there were horses, but these did not belong to the ranch.

Stan Milton, the ranch supervisor, had met Cory almost a year earlier when he had entered his first shelter placement and was shocked at the change in the boy, who had metamorphosed from a cheerful downy-cheeked child to this much taller young person with a cracking voice and a defiant manner. "He has learned well what we have offered him," Stan admitted ruefully. "He's mastered the system."

"Is there any hope?" I asked.

"Sure. I knew his brother, Rich, but, thankfully, he's not like him. Cory thinks of himself as the 'good brother,' and I can work with that. When I called him on some of the behaviors that have gotten him to this place, he acted shocked, then denied he ever did anything wrong—blaming everyone else for his problems. After I talked him through this denial, he became angry at me. He cussed me out and threw a tantrum. In the end, though, he cried like a baby. That sadness is a breakthrough, for at last he is demonstrating appropriate emotions. It is not going to be pleasant for him or for the staff, but it is what he needs to do."

I couldn't believe what I was hearing! Finally someone was dealing with the real child with deep feelings—the Cory I represented—not some creature who required food, shelter, and training like an unruly pet.

"When will he move into a cottage?" I asked.

"He's going to have to demonstrate that he can follow the rules better, especially regarding his foul language, which we won't tolerate in our homelike settings."

"How is he getting along with the other boys in the shelter?"

"They're pretty rough and we're overcrowded, so it's not the best situation for him. But he's pretty much a follower, so my job is to convince him to follow the right path."

Stan showed me a handout he used with his staff: Nine Stages of Helping Emotionally Disturbed Clients.

"The problem with Cory, and lots of the boys, is that they move through predictable levels of adjustment, but because of inadequate management, often get stuck in a stage that blows their placement. Then they start over again at step one but never progress into a healthy phase."

Stan guided me through the process of how children adjust to new programs. He explained that the first period of time in a new home is known as the "honeymoon," when the child checks it out and tries to understand the family structure, personalities of the caregivers, and evaluates the rules to see how much deviancy is tolerated. During this time, the child merely watches and conforms. When he is comfortable, he enters the "limit testing" stage. Declaring he is no longer "Mr. Nice Guy," he allows his true nature to surface and begins to see how much he can get away with. If his defiant behavior is checked, he enters the "active resistance" stage in which he becomes even more insubordinate and dares others to "get outta my face."

"This precisely is where many foster placements collapse," Stan explained. "When the poorly trained caregiver gets involved in a power struggle with the child, it is impossible to break the cycle of conflict. Eventually the foster parent decides to give up trying and asks for the rebellious child to be removed from his home.''

I saw how Cory's smoking was classic limit testing. When the Sheldons didn't punish him for smoking, Cory escalated to stealing cigarettes to provoke the Sheldons into proving whether they were in it for the long haul or not. From Cory's point of view, they had failed the test. If Cory had been handled properly, he might have had a chance to move to the fourth level of ''beginning trust and achievement.''

''On the other side of defiance,'' Stan continued, ''the child is able to make a decision for himself about whether he should go or stay. Caregivers who respond by enabling the child to make responsible decisions for himself help him into the crucial fifth stage we call 'acceptance and progress.' ''

Now at last the child is actively able to join a family and enjoy the benefits of what they have to offer. ''However, this is a time when foster parents often relax their guard and focus their attentions on a more needy individual, which can lead directly to the next phase of 'negative personal demands and intense jealousy.' ''

I told Stan that I had seen this dynamic at play with Alicia, who had weathered most of the stages already in the Levy home. But she was always making claims on Ruth's time and sulking if her needs were not met instantly. ''What will happen to her?''

Stan explained that once someone like Alicia had achieved ''clear social improvement'' she might be ready to go out on her own. ''But she still has to clear the hurdle of separation and regression. At that point her fears of the unfamiliar might actually cause deterioration in behavior.''

''What might she do?''

''Sometimes when these children expect they might be leaving, they act worse than when they arrived,'' Stan explained. ''They're like wounded bears until they can express sadness about saying good-bye to one phase of life and moving on to another one.''

''I've seen some of this in Alicia,'' I sighed. ''But it's a long way off for Cory.''

''Nothing can be rushed. We'll take it step by step.''

I had left the Palomino Ranch with a renewed hope that Cory was in sensitive hands, but a week later Mitzi surprised me with some upsetting news. ''Stan Milton called to report that Cory had a sexual incident with another boy. Apparently Cory was found naked in the other boy's bed.''

"Did Stan say what happened?"

"No, the kids wouldn't confess, but I know the other one, and he's been in treatment for sexual offenses."

"What are they doing about it?"

"They're moving the other kid to a different cottage, but Stan is going to keep working with Cory."

"What does Cory want?"

"He said that since things in court weren't going his way—referring to the delays, I guess—he would stick it out at the ranch. That's a good sign, don't you think?" Mitzi asked hopefully.

"I like Stan Milton's attitude. Since Cory's always been abandoned by his many mothers, he might attach better to a man."

"Gay, Cory's back in town," Mitzi reported two weeks later.

"What!" I responded in genuine shock.

"After midnight last night, Cory and a bunch of other thugs went on a rampage and broke the hinges on the doors."

"Stan predicted something like that would happen. Why doesn't he stand by him and see him through this phase?"

"He tried to," Mitzi continued. "The rest of the boys are being charged with vandalism, but Stan wanted to give Cory a break because he may just have been part of the pack. In any case, the officials at the ranch won't keep him."

Mitzi gave me Cory's phone number at one of the temporary shelters for kids in transition, the same place he had been taken the night he left his father's house.

"Cory, how are you?" I asked after I had convinced the shelter worker to put him on the line.

"Okay, I guess. Time for a change anyway."

"What happened?"

"You know the stress with the trial coming up . . ."

Sensing that Cory was using words that would manipulate me, I hardened slightly. "Cory, we're running out of options for you."

"Stan will take me back at the ranch, I know he will. If I can stay cool until Wednesday, he'll take me back."

"I didn't hear that, but I'll check it out."

"If they won't, will you see if I can go home to my father?" he asked morosely.

"That's impossible right now."

"How about my mom?"

"Cory, that's off in the future. I'm worried about where you will sleep tonight and tomorrow."

"Gotta go," he said, and hung up.

Two days later Mitzi reported Cory was in trouble at the shelter for smoking. "They found his butts in a trash can, and the cook caught him lighting a cigarette at a gas stove. He's on probation. One more incident and I'll have to move him."

"Mitzi, have you ever seen Stan's list of stages?"

"No, what do you mean?"

I explained how Cory was right in the middle of the "get outta my face" phase and wondered if someone couldn't intervene to help him through it.

"Not when he knows the list better than we do. After I picked him up at the ranch, he actually seemed pleased with himself and said, 'Hey, I got what I wanted, I got out of there.' "

"Don't you see, no placement is going to work out until Cory lands where he wants to be: back home with Dad."

"That is never going to happen."

"Maybe he'd be better off there."

"With that pervert? Are you out of your mind?"

"I don't see the difference in being molested by a kid at the ranch or his father at home."

"Did I hear you say that?"

"Look, Mitzi, you know I don't want anyone to hurt Cory. However, you and HRS are not protecting him right now, so don't fool yourself into believing that you are."

"And I was going to ask you to go to the shelter and talk some sense into him," Mitzi said with much annoyance. "Now I have to find someone to talk some sense into you."

"I'll try to calm him down, but I want you to get him some big-time psychological help and fast!"

"There's no money for that."

"Grace Chandler paid for Alicia's evaluation out of her court budget. Ask if she'll do the same for Cory."

With a long sigh, Mitzi agreed.

"Lillian, what can I do for Cory?" My tinny voice betrayed my anxiety.

"Your idea of a complete psychological exam is excellent. We'd have to have something like that in place before we could recommend a more intensive placement like Horizons Unlimited."

"Frankly, until this trial issue is settled, I don't think he's going to cooperate anywhere," I continued.

"Keep talking to him, let him know he still has you," Lillian said consolingly.

With a heavy heart, I phoned the shelter. "Didn't anyone tell you?" the shelter director inquired. "Mitzi took Cory Stevenson yesterday after he destroyed some property when we caught him smoking."

"Let me ask you something. If you were Cory Stevenson's guardian, what would you do for him?"

"He's a sweet kid and I tried to cut him some slack, but he went down the list of our rules breaking the large ones and the small ones alike. I think he is having major trouble with his impulse control, so he either needs a program that is highly structured or a foster home that can give him plenty of attention."

Later that day Mitzi informed me that she had moved Cory to another shelter in a nearby district. "They have never had any of the Stevensons, so I talked them into it, but it is only a matter time. He's cussing just like Rich."

"Cory told me he wanted to go back to the ranch."

"They won't accept him. He's getting sicker and out of control. I have an appointment with the court psychologist. Not much we can do until then." Before Mitzi hung up, she told me that Alicia wanted to speak with me.

"Is it true?" Alicia said, sniffling. Mitzi had told Ruth to tell her that Cory had been moved again. "How many times is that?" she snapped.

"A lot, Alicia. The first two shelters, the MacDougals, the Hornsbys, the Sheldons, then the ranch, and now two more shelters." I counted on my fingers. "That's eight moves in about eight months."

"It's not right! They did this to Rich and you see what happened to him."

"I'm trying to find something better, Alicia," I insisted, but my voice sounded hollow.

"Promise me you'll always tell me where he is?" she asked, more distraught than ever.

"Yes, I promise."

The next day I was on the phone to Cory's new shelter counselor, who reported Cory had lice, probably from someone at the ranch. "He's so needy he even liked having his head checked for nits."

The counselor said he was playing one-on-one ball games with Cory and was receiving a positive response. "I don't recommend another group placement," he said. "What this kid needs is a small foster home, individual care, routine therapy at least twice a week, and a trust that someone will stick with him through the bad times as well as the good."

"When you find the place, call me," I replied sarcastically.

An hour later Mitzi had more bad news. "Cory has run away."

In a more subdued voice than usual, she explained how some of the boys who had rioted at Palomino Ranch had been shipped to the same shelter where Cory was staying. "Your darling Cory ran off with the biggest, loudest, foulest of the bunch: Marco Roundtree, the second worst kid in the system, after Rich Stevenson, that is." Mitzi continued her litany. "Marco is off his antipsychotic medication, so anything could happen."

"Are you going to look for him?"

"The shelter reported them on runaway status to the local police."

"But—"

"Gay, there is nothing more I can do with that kid." She groaned. "We would've had that psychological done by the end of the week. Do you have any idea how many strings I had to pull to get that appointment?"

"Where do you think he'll end up?" I asked.

"Who knows?"

"Don't you think he'll go where he has wanted to be all along?"

"What do you mean?" Mitzi asked.

"There's only one place he wants to live, and that is with his father. What would happen if he went there?"

"His father would be in more trouble than he would."

"Well, Mitzi, I won't tell, if you won't."

She didn't reply so I felt she and I had finally agreed on something: see no evil, hear no evil, speak no evil.

Keeping my promise to Alicia, I called to tell her I did not know where Cory was.

"What do you mean?" she said. "He's here!"

"Put him on the phone!" I said, furious and delighted at the same time. "How'd you get to the Levys'?" I demanded.

"We were at a gas station and this man asked where we wanted to go. He was delivering Bibles to a church only a few miles from the Levys'. Isn't that amazing?"

"And the other kid? Marco?"

"He got dropped off at his girlfriend's house."

"Cory, my boy, you lucked out, did you know that?" I spoke emphatically, not mincing words. The kid had frightened me and I wanted him to know it. "There are only two types of people who pick up hitchhikers: folks who are so religious they feel they are doing God's work so they don't worry about their own safety; and perverts, who are planning to hurt you. The chances of you ever finding the first type again are very rare. Do you understand me?"

"Yeah, Gay, I'm sorry."

"Good. Because you had me really scared. And I only get scared when I care about someone. I care about you, kiddo, you know that?"

"Sure, but in another way I'm not sorry, because the Levys say I can stay here."

Ruth got on the line and told me more of the story. "I guess it was meant to be. You know I've felt that Cory belonged here for a long time. When we got Larry, I thought immediately of Cory, but I didn't want to push Milo, but now even he says we can't throw him out. You should have seen the man who drove up with him. He was dressed in a suit and a tie and was delivering gospel tracts in our neighborhood. If that isn't a sign, I don't know what is, especially when you realize he also took the creepy kid, Marco. I shiver to think what might have happened if they'd been on the loose even another day."

"Have you called Mitzi?"

"No, she's not available, but I talked to her supervisor. I said that Cory can stay a few more days to get his psychological evaluation finished. After that, we'll see. I can't have him smoking in the house or upsetting Milo, but I think Alicia will help out with that. She's behaving like a little mother to him, and Larry seems relieved to finally have a roommate."

At last Cory had some respite from his sojourns. I took a breather from following his fiery trail and tried to analyze the situation. After almost a year of turmoil, Cory was living once again with his sister with no thanks to the authorities, who, in their wisdom, had removed him from an "unsafe" home and "protected" him from a pedophile. In the care of the state, Cory had already had one incident of sexual misconduct with a seriously disturbed older boy. He had had the opportunity to meet delinquents who had taught him the art of mayhem. He had made friends with a psychotic, who had helped him run away. And where had he run? To the person he cared for the most: his sister.

Why hadn't HRS placed these children together initially? is the question rational, though naive, people might ask. Whenever I'd broached the question, heads would shake, eyes would roll, and fingers would wag. That was not how it was done. There were no homes for teenage sibling groups. Boys and girls had to be separated. Nobody would take two Stevensons. From the beginning, the caseworkers had looked at Cory with distaste because he was from a tainted family. While I saw him as a victim of an abandoning mother and an abusive father, the "experts" viewed him as a problem unit who needed reforming. Where I had sympathy for the fourteen-year-old boy who had been forced by the court to leave a home where he believed he was happy and had been sent, without warning, to a shelter with hard beds and strict rules, the state saw him as a disobedient griper who didn't appreciate what was being done for him. Instead of evaluating Cory's requirements and trying to match him with foster parents with whom he might have attached, they put him in an authoritarian home with military-style rules that were in direct opposition to the laissez-faire environment of his childhood. Yes, structure might have benefited him, but not before he felt accepted and trusted. The next few foster homes were not that objectionable on the surface, but they were so overcrowded with needy children that no adult had the time or energy to focus on Cory.

If Cory had docilely conformed to the patterns of a new household and moved zombielike through his days without making waves, HRS would have been delighted. Yet any clinician would have seen that as a dysfunctional response and have diagnosed a depressed child. If Cory asserted himself by trying to attract attention to his urgent needs, he was seen to be acting out and misbehaving, which was reason to move him to a different place, renewing the cycle of maladjustment and failure. By now Cory had been labeled a troublemaker and was despised by the workers managing his file. To me, he was the victim of their stupidity, shortsightedness, and inattention. It was as if they had taken a child out of his bed and left him in the street to be run over by a truck, then had put Band-Aids on his massive wounds, and ended up surprised that, six months later, they had to deal with bones that didn't heal and a fulminating infection. If they had taken the time in the beginning to place Cory in intensive care, he might still have a few scars but would have healed better and been able to walk again.

Cory had not been offered any therapy to deal with the upheavals in his life. He was supposed to shut up and accept the loss of his father, his grandfather, his siblings, his school, his friends, his bed, his bike, his pets, the groves, the fishing pond, and everything that formed the sphere of life as he knew it. He was expected to absorb a new family and new set of values instantly, without any professional assistance. And none of this took into consideration the incredible conflicts about his sister and brother's accusations of their father, his father's jail sentence, the terror of the impending trial, or the reappearance of his biological mother. The bottom line was that Cory had no one who loved him and no home of his own.

I blamed myself. As Cory was moved from place to place, I followed behind in the wake, mopping up blood stains, but I had done nothing to get treatment for the wounds either. Lillian tried to convince me that, considering the circumstances, I had done my best, but I refused to accept this.

"I've tried being nice, Lillian, and that failed. So, I'm changing my tactics. Do you mind?" I asked if she would cosign a letter with me that listed everything that had not been done for Cory and set out a plan to make improvements in his life.

She agreed wholeheartedly. "Hey, you know my motto: whatever it takes."

I called Mitzi Keller and discussed how long Cory might remain with the Levys. She was noncommittal. Then I told her to expect a letter from me to her with copies to her supervisor.

"Oh, no! Are you going to accuse me of doing the absolute minimum for this kid?"

Precisely . . . I wanted to reply, but answered, "No. I am just going to formally request a staff conference to develop a long-range plan."

To try to stay on top of the situation, I talked with Ruth Levy almost daily and went to her home twice a week. During one visit, Ruth complained that Cory and Larry were doing a lot of wrestling. She explained that Larry had been severely sexually abused and she couldn't trust him not to "hit on" Cory.

I said I thought that Cory, who was the same age and size as Larry, should be able to handle himself.

"I mean that Larry has been known to act out sexually with other boys."

"Great," I muttered, then reiterated the need for therapy.

When I was alone with Cory, I asked him to call me if he was uncomfortable rooming with Larry.

"Yeah, okay . . . ," he replied dejectedly. For the first time, I saw that the mischievous glint had faded from his eyes. His face was pale and drawn and his once robust appetite was gone. He told me that everything felt "hopeless" and that he would never get home again. When I asked what he wanted, he said, "I don't care anymore."

Since it was summertime, he spent his days playing video games or sleeping. He did routine chores sloppily, but without protest, and spent very little time with his sister or the others in the family.

Ruth said she was thrilled that Cory wasn't making any disturbances and that Milo had been surprised that a Stevenson boy could be so "little trouble." She said, "If this keeps up, I'll be happy to have him here permanently."

"Ruth, if this keeps up, the kid might end up dead." She seemed startled when I told her I thought Cory was seriously depressed and asked her to report any suicidal notions at once.

As part of my more active role in heading off a crisis, I took Cory and Alicia out to dinner at the steak house that evening. I handed each cards with my home and business phone numbers.

"You're supposed to get in touch with me through the Guardian ad Litem office, but that can take time. I want you to promise to call me first if either of you leave the Levys'. You can always call me collect. I'm not suggesting you should run away, but Cory already put himself in an unsafe position once. And, Alicia, if you leave this home for any reason, I won't tell on you. I won't report you, but I will say you are safe and try to see that you don't get arrested."

"Can you do that?" Alicia asked.

"To me, being your guardian means making sure you are not harmed. After that, everything else is a big second. If I knew exactly where you were, I would have to tell HRS, but you wouldn't have to give me a phone number or the location. However, if I know what is going on, I can offer safe solutions." I put my arm around Cory. "I was so worried about you. I thought maybe you'd go to your father's."

"I did call him first," Cory admitted, "but he told me not to come to him because then he'd be in even more trouble."

Alicia gave Cory a weary look. "You forget how horrible it was with Dad."

"You think it is going to be better with Tammy? She left us for another man and never gave a shit what happened to us."

Alicia's eyes filled with tears. "Everything would be perfect if Cory could stay at the Levys' with me . . ."

I nodded, and squeezed her hand and her brother's at the same time.

* * *

I knew from Ruth's frazzled voice what had transpired. Right on schedule Cory had bounded out of the honeymoon and limit-testing phases into a big-time all-out demonstration of: GET OUTTA MY FACE!

"He's driving me crazy!" Ruth said. "I mean *BAD* with a capital *B*. Last night we got into a shouting match. When I asked, 'What do you want?' he screamed 'I want to leave.' This was ten o'clock at night, so I said no way, it was after hours and I wasn't calling HRS unless it was an emergency."

"That's what he needed to hear. Of course you know he was just testing you."

"Well, he's darn good at it!" she said with a sarcastic laugh.

"What are you going to do with him?" I asked, holding my breath.

"He says he was happier at Palomino Ranch, but I know they won't take him back. Mitzi's on vacation. I promised her that no matter what happened with Cory, I'd stick it out until she returned." She groaned. "I guess I'm not cut out for boys."

The next afternoon I called Ruth. "How is he today?" I asked, holding the phone away from my ear slightly to mute the expected negative response.

"Better. Like nothing ever happened. Interesting point, though, today was the day he was scheduled for his court psychological. On the way to the doctor I asked if he still wanted to leave my home, and he said he didn't. Then he cried. When we stopped at a light, I said, 'You need a hug.' I leaned over to give it and he came right toward me and hugged me right back. That calmed him down, and by the time we got to the appointment, he was almost normal. Later I told him that I really liked him, but not his outbursts. Then I explained that I wanted him to stay with us, but I knew he could control himself better."

"That's just what he needed to hear, Ruth."

"I'll be interested in what the psychologist has to say," she replied.

"Me too," I said, then praised Ruth again for handling a difficult situation with such aplomb.

For a few days everything was calm and then Ruth phoned about his latest outbursts. "I pulled Cory off Larry, whom he had on the floor crying, then he exploded with language that is unrepeatable. I didn't stop him. I told him he could say anything he wanted, but he couldn't hit anyone. He claimed he 'had to hit' Larry, and I asked him why he thought he could hurt someone. He said, 'because I'm better than they are.' What do you think of that?"

"Ruth, you know the cycle of abuse better than I do. Already Cory's trying to move from powerless victim to powerful victimizer, which makes me think he received much more abuse than he admits."

"I know, but when he gets so mouthy and defiant I almost lose control. God help me, but I wanted to slap him across the face. I lifted my hand, however instead of touching him I pointed to a sign in my kitchen that says: people who are the most unlovable need the most love. He said, 'Do you mean Larry?' Well, I really meant Cory, but that was even better. He went in and apologized for upsetting Larry."

"Great," I said, exhaling loudly. "Hey, thanks for hanging in there."

In a few days we had Cory's psychological diagnosis: attention deficit disorder mixed with some specific learning disabilities. His ability and performance tests indicated that he might have difficulty completing high school and alternative educational opportunities should be sought. He was expected to be a credible witness for his father's defense.

"I've argued all along that he needed professional help," I said to Ruth. "Can you try to schedule some therapy at the county clinic?"

Ruth agreed to ask Mitzi to sign Cory up when she returned from her vacation. In the next few weeks, Ruth called me frequently about Cory's tantrums. After one fight over the last scoop of ice cream, Ruth had to grab Cory's shirt and tell him to settle down.

"It isn't until after I get really fed up with him that he backs off, like he's waiting for me to provide external control. Then he becomes very obedient and docile. Why do you think he does that?"

"Maybe this is a pattern that developed with his father, or maybe he really can't restrain himself. That's why he needs to be seen regularly at the clinic and possibly given the appropriate medication for his condition."

"I've already made dental and doctor appointments, and I'm waiting until Mitzi gets back to get him to mental health. Also, he's interested in music," Ruth said. "I showed him Milo's electric guitar and said that if he got through one week without a tantrum, it was his to play. After that, he can use it any day he is in control of himself. He told me that our home is the best place he's ever been and that he plans to stay no matter what it takes."

"What does Milo think?"

"So far Milo is getting along great with Cory and is looking forward to giving him guitar lessons."

My next call to Ruth was to inform her that the trial date had been postponed again, this time until mid-August. She reported that Cory was "an angel." When he steamed up, she reminded him about the guitar and he simmered right down. "He's very affectionate and hungry for big bear hugs. There hasn't been a single tantrum lately and even Larry is doing better."

"All that peace and quiet can be addictive," I warned.

"One thing . . . ," Ruth added cautiously, "my suspicions about some sexual acting out between the boys have increased."

"Who's Larry's therapist?"

"He doesn't have one yet either."

"With his background!" I shouted. "What is HRS waiting for?" I seethed. "Call Mitzi's office and make certain it is the first thing on her list when she gets back."

"Yo, Gay!" It was Cory's voice on the phone, bright and chipper.

"What's up?"

"Do you have my mother's number in Washington?"

"Sure. But Alicia has it, doesn't she?"

"Ruth told me to call you first."

"What's going on?"

From across the room I heard Ruth's voice: "Tell her about the smoking."

"I was caught smoking in the house."

"Tell her you can only stay if you follow the rules," prompted Ruth.

"I heard that. Do you think you might smoke outdoors? Remember Ruth has allergies."

"I want to go to Washington."

"Listen, Cory, I'm going to be in your neck of the woods after lunch. I'll stop by and talk about it with you then."

An hour later Ruth Levy was on the phone herself. "Don't bother to come later because Cory won't be here. He smoked again in the bathroom and I have had it. I'm taking both him and Larry to HRS."

"But Ruth—" I started.

"Gotta run," she said, and then she hung up.

By the end of the day I had caught up with Cory at a new foster home less than a mile from my office. The Castillo family had two grown sons, one of whom was in the military. Living with them also was their daughter-in-law and small baby. Cory was happy to be back in the Sawgrass school district.

When Cory first came into foster care early in the fall, he was transferred from Sawgrass Middle School, where he had been attending eighth grade. In his four shelter stays he had missed at least six weeks of classes. In between he had attended three other schools that year but never satisfied the requirements for eighth grade, which would have to be repeated.

"In the fall Cory will be in the same place he started, so maybe he can just disregard his horrible year," Marta Castillo suggested. Also, she pointed out that Cory was closer to Stevenson Groves than he had been before. "I don't care what the father has done, he still is the natural parent, so if Cory wants to see him, it is fine with me," Marta said, then watched for my reaction.

"Cory is very attached to his father. He needs to be permitted to have contact with him." I filled Marta Castillo in on the plans for the trial.

"We'll be there for him," she said firmly.

"Mrs. Castillo, you've only had Cory a few hours, and lots of people have made promises they haven't kept."

Cory came into the room flipping a pack of cigarettes. "They said I could smoke here," he said, baiting me.

I shrugged. "Guess you'll have to think of some other way of getting thrown out." Cory's jaw dropped. "What are you doing tomorrow?" I asked. Cory looked at Mrs. Castillo, who said she didn't have any plans. "I'll pick you up at one. Be here."

"Where we going?"

"You and I are going to sign up for counseling at the mental health clinic."

That evening Ruth Levy phoned. She sounded guilty for not keeping Cory. "It was Alicia who tattled on her brother for smoking. You'd think those kids would have protected each other, but they were always on each other's case."

I had no response. Ruth, my last hope for Cory, had let him down in the end, and over what? Smoking! Cory's classic test.

"In the last week Milo and I had some heart-to-heart talks about the kids, especially Larry and Cory. We realized that we resented the fact that HRS tricked me into taking Larry for a few days, and months later he was still here. Then Cory landed on my doorstep and I thought that it was a sign that I should have him, if only for Alicia's sake, but now I see that was wrong. I should have wanted him for himself." Ruth sighed. "Even so, I tried. You know I did! The last straw was the way he treated Alicia, always teasing her and then hurting her feelings. She's getting panicky about the trial and I heard Cory calling her a liar and asking her to recant so they both could go home, which is the last thing Alicia wants. Now she is afraid that if her father is acquitted, she'll have to return to him.''

"I can assure her that won't happen.''

"She'll be hard to convince. Anyway, Milo and I got to thinking that it would be a big mistake having both kids here during the trial, what with one of them testifying against the other. We are committed to supporting Alicia's side, so we wouldn't be there for Cory anyway. Do you see what we mean?''

"I suppose . . .''

"You know, when Cory left, Alicia didn't even say good-bye to him. Later she said she was happy to see him go, so for her sake, we made the right decision.''

"I hope so,'' I said, but I could not agree with Ruth any further than that.

The next afternoon I drove Cory to the county clinic, filled out the required paperwork, and handed over copies of his other psychological reports and relevant papers. When his turn was called, I went with Cory to meet the therapist, Dr. Herb Farrington. When Cory walked in his office, Dr. Farrington tossed Cory a foam basketball, then pulled out another and aimed for the net centered over his wastepaper basket. The psychologist made an easy basket. Cory tried, but missed.

"Keep at it while I talk with your mom,'' he said.

I rapidly explained my role, then gave him a rundown on Cory's situation. "He's just made his ninth move in less than a year, and other than his court-ordered psychological tests, he has not had a single hour of therapy.''

Since I wanted Cory's therapy to be fruitful, I thought it would be helpful for Dr. Farrington to know about Tammy's reappearance, the home study in Washington state, Rich's checkered history, Alicia's situation, Cory's smoking, profanity, and tantrums. Every few minutes I would stop and ask Cory if my explanations were accurate. He would nod, but rarely added anything.

Then Dr. Farrington began to ask Cory some questions. "What do you think of your father?''

"He's a cool dude,'' Cory said, and finally made a basket. "Yes!''

"Do you love him?''

"Yeah, sure.''

"Who else do you love?''

"Gramps, and my sister, I guess.''

"What about your older brother?"

"He's a cool dude too, when he isn't being an asshole."

"He's been in trouble a lot." Cory juggled the ball from one hand to the other. "What about you?"

"I've done some stuff, but not as much. I'm the good one."

"But sometimes you like to be the bad one too."

Cory startled. The ball fell from his hands and he did not retrieve it.

"Do you drink alcohol?"

"A few beers only."

"Do you take drugs?"

"I've smoked a joint now and then, that's all, except for sniffing gas and glue."

"Do you feel that life is worthwhile?"

"Not most of the time."

"Ever think about killing yourself?"

"Sometimes."

"Do you have a plan?"

"No, but I could find a gun, I guess."

Then Dr. Farrington gave Cory a questionnaire to complete in another room.

When we were alone, Dr. Farrington asked, "Do you think Cory was sexually abused by his father?"

"Cory denies it vigorously, but he has a lot at stake in keeping his father out of jail."

After that, I left the room and Cory spent the rest of the time in private with the doctor. Before we left, we booked the next month of sessions. In the car Cory showed me a baseball card Dr. Farrington had given him. "I'll bring him a really sharp one next time," he said, smiling brightly for the first time that day.

After I returned Cory to the Castillos, I phoned Mitzi Keller to tell her I had signed the papers for the initial visit, but that she needed to get to mental health in the next three days to sign the consent forms for the ongoing therapy. "I'm leaving for a two-week vacation tomorrow," I said sternly, "and I don't want him to miss a single session while I am gone."

Lillian swore to me that she would monitor Cory's situation. I had insisted that the appointment clerk at mental health put a sticky note on her calendar with Lillian's phone number and to call her if Cory missed an appointment. I also informed Dr. Farrington of my trip and told him whom to contact if Cory had difficulties or was moved. Perhaps the mental health folks thought I was obsessive, but I didn't care. Somebody had to be there for Cory while I was away and I wanted backups in place, just in case.

My first call after I opened up the house after our trip was to Marta Castillo. "Hi, is Cory still there?" I asked, betraying my anxiety.

"Sure. He's doing very well. He's calling me 'Mom' and I call him 'son,' which he really likes. However, I do have one complaint and it is not about Cory, it's with Mitzi Keller. I am sick and tired of her putting down my kid. It's like she's waiting to prove that we're going to fail like everyone else." Marta gave a throaty chuckle. "My plan is to have her eating her words by Christmas."

I asked about school, which began at the end of the week. Cory was registered, but Marta didn't know if they were putting him in the remedial program the therapist had recommended.

"Since I am acquainted with the counselors at Sawgrass, I'll check up on it for you," I said.

When I discussed this with Lillian, she reminded me that this was not a Guardian ad Litem's obligation.

"What else can I do? I've called, written letters to Mitzi Keller—with copies to her supervisor—even put my recommendations in the court reports. Nothing has happened, not even one hour of therapy until I marched him to the clinic."

"Okay," Lillian said with a mock resignation to her tone.

Since this was my first case, I had innocently believed that the caseworkers and foster parents who were paid to care for foster children would be diligent and compassionate. I could never have anticipated the numerous excuses the authorities might invent for neglecting their charges. Soon I learned that it was far more expedient to do it myself than to try to flog someone else, and my experience with Cory proved the point for me.

I made myself available to drive him to therapy if it didn't fit into anyone else's schedule (though this was frowned on, because HRS is not supposed to rely on guardians to perform their transportation duties). I went to see his guidance counselor, checked with his teachers, and then got busy on his teeth. After Cory finally was taken to a dentist by Ruth, I asked about two extra teeth overlapping his lateral incisors. The dentist stated this was "a cosmetic" problem, one that would not be covered by Medicaid. I disagreed, because even my untrained eye saw that this was a structural problem that would worsen if the teeth continued to grow downward on top of the others.

The next time I took my son to the orthodontist I asked his doctor if he would examine Cory for free, then if he felt the problem would have a long-term effect on his oral health, give me a written evaluation for Medicaid.

"No," the orthodontist said, grinning mischievously. "If it is as bad as you suggest, and you think he is needy, I'll do the correction myself at no cost."

Two weeks later Cory and I were in the orthodontist's consulting room looking at molds of his teeth and a panoramic X ray. Indeed he had a serious condition that required extractions and several years of orthodontic correction. The doctor talked to Cory about his poor dental hygiene and the need for his cooperation if this was going to work. Cory agreed to do his part and the two shook hands.

Next I concentrated on school. The guidance counselor had never heard of the Guardian ad Litem program but was intrigued. "The more help the Stevensons can get, the better." She made certain Cory was in the appropriate classes for the emotionally handicapped.

After explaining that the trial would be coming up shortly, I said, "I expect Cory might misbehave in school if he gets upset, but I would appreciate it if you would not discipline him in the usual way."

"You mean paddling?"

I nodded. Florida permits corporal punishment in schools at every grade level at the discretion of the local school board. Our "progressive" educators reviewed the issue often but always voted to retain the right to paddle children as a discipline alternative. I have never been able to comprehend the schizophrenic thinking that makes it illegal for a foster parent (state employee) to spank a child but recommends a teacher (also a public employee) hit. "Because of the abuse in that family, paddling Cory might have extremely adverse results. Also, he shouldn't be suspended or punished too severely until he finds out what is happening to his father."

"What do you think he would most likely do?"

"Smoke probably."

"How should we handle it?"

"If he is caught, could he be sent to guidance and then could you contact me? My office is only three blocks from this school and I'll come and discuss it with him."

"That would be fine with me," she said. "Do you think he could end up with his father?"

"That's up to the jury."

I knew that Grace Chandler had been lining up her witnesses for the prosecution, and her case was stronger than we had thought. She had convinced one of Red's ex-wives to testify and was going to attempt to get the judge to permit Sunny Rhodes to take the stand as well. Rich and Janet were married and seemed more stable than ever before, so Grace felt Rich would be a credible witness. Grace was satisfied with Alicia's grasp of the facts and not particularly worried about Cory's testimony. So it appeared as though Red Stevenson would be spending most of the rest of his life in prison, which would simplify Cory's options. But first Cory, Alicia, Rich, and I would have to survive the ordeal of the trial. For over six months we had been expecting it to be scheduled. First it had been postponed from April to June, then every time we planned the trip to Washington state, the trial was rescheduled to conflict with the visit. There were two switches in July, a last-minute postponement to August, and finally, a date had been set for mid-September.

Tammy had been bitterly disappointed. "If we'd known this ahead of time, they could have spent the whole summer with me."

I had commiserated with Tammy, and told her that we would work something out as soon as possible. I made no promises though. The new school year was in full swing and the trial was definitely going to begin the following week. I felt as if we were drifting in a hot-air balloon. The wind seemed to be blowing constant in the direction of Red Stevenson's guilt, but until the verdict was in, we would have no idea of our final destination.

4

Shampooman and Lollipop

The Stevenson Trial

But the hearts of small children are delicate organs.
A cruel beginning in this world can twist them into curious shapes.
—CARSON MCCULLERS

WHAT DO YOU THINK is going to happen?'' Ruth Levy had asked me
as we looked over the clothes she had bought for Alicia to wear in court.

"I don't know," I said. "I've never attended a criminal trial before,
but Grace Chandler thinks she has a strong case. However, she warned
me that the only thing that is predictable is that everything is unpredictable."

"What worries her the most?" Ruth wondered.

"She isn't certain how the children will react during testimony and
cross-examination, whether Red Stevenson will take the stand in his own
defense, and especially how the jury will perceive a teenage girl accusing
her father of incest."

"She doesn't think Alicia will be credible?"

"She's mainly concerned about the first time Alicia had intercourse
with her father in the bathroom of the marine shop."

"That worries me too," Ruth said.

"Grace has a different concern. She thinks that bathroom sounds like
one in a home, not a mechanic's shop. She's afraid Walt Hilliard is going
to make it seem as if Alicia were confusing the location of the rape, or
worse, that she has made up the whole incident."

"Do you agree with her, Gay?"

"Every time Alicia's told that story all the details have been consistent," I said, but I was worried because Grace and Ruth were not persuaded.

Then there was a curious coincidence.

One of my son's friends, Shane, needed a ride home from an after-
school activity. I was going in that direction and volunteered. I phoned

223

his mother, who asked if I could drop him at his stepfather's upholstery shop, which specialized in boat cushions, canvas awnings, and sails. As Shane gave me directions, I felt as though I had heard them before. "It's behind North Main. After you cross the railroad bridge, you make the first left turn before the underpass."

When I saw the building with garage doors on both ends and a boat on a trailer in the yard, I asked, "How long has your father had this shop?"

"About a year."

I pulled into the parking lot. "What occupied it before?"

"Red's Marine was here before they moved behind the shrimp docks."

I braked hard. "Do you mind if I use your bathroom?"

I closed the door and faced the beige toilet. The walls in the large room were apple green. Above the toilet were shelves holding cleaning supplies and a floral deodorizing spray. Feeling dizzy, I sat on the toilet and looked around. There was a bathtub with a shower. Across from it was a woodstove with a bouquet of dried flowers in a teapot.

I stood up, turned around, and faced the walls and placed my hands on top of the toilet tank. My legs had to straddle the widest part of the toilet bowl. To keep my balance I had to stretch my back. A child of nine would have been at least four inches shorter, but if she were supple, she could have done it. Her butt would have stuck out at a very accessible angle. A tall man would have had to bend his knees, but that would make him unstable. To maintain his balance he could reach forward and grasp something—something like the braced elbows of the girl beneath him.

Here was the scene that Ruth had been unable to imagine: the child with her head facing the toilet, her back flat like a table, her arms pinned down by her father, her legs spread wide to bridge the toilet, her vulva pointed in the right direction. Also, if you saw the room, you could see that everything matched Alicia's description.

Shaking, I splashed cold water on my face and started for the door. With my hand on the knob, I stopped. I turned around again and this time I could conjure Red's hairy back and legs and arms and Alicia's soft baby skin and her curls drooped in front of her face as she was being taken by the man she loved most: her father.

First thing the next morning, I told Grace Chandler where I had been, and that afternoon the prosecutor drove out to the upholstery shop to take photographs.

* * *

After all the delays, the trial was set for the second Thursday in September. In criminal court there are only two parties to a case: the prosecution and the defense—which excludes the victim. Only fifteen states, including Florida, currently provide for children, who are victims, to be represented in criminal court, in this case by a Guardian ad Litem. However, because the child had no real status in the proceedings, the guardian, who speaks for the child, is odd person out, with little say in how the events will proceed.

The goal of the prosecution is usually punishment, but the guardian representing a child victim may realize that the child's needs may be in opposition to those of the state. In Alicia's case, Grace and I had been in agreement, and she had gone out of her way to insure that I was included in every stage.

On the Monday of the week of the trial, I brought Alicia to the courthouse so she could become familiar with the surroundings. To break the ice, Grace walked Alicia around the courtroom and had her sit in the witness's seat, then in the jury box, and even in the judge's place.

Alicia giggled as she pounded her hand on the judge's desk and bellowed, "Order in the court!"

Thinking I would be interested, Grace handed me the list of evidence that would be submitted by the defense. I didn't know what to look for, so Grace helped me. "Notice that something is missing?" When I shook my head, she explained that Walt Hilliard had not had Alicia's deposition transcribed. "Now he can't use Alicia's conflicting statements about her ages against her."

"Why wouldn't he get the transcription?" I asked.

"It's very costly, and now it's too late."

"Does that mean he won't be able to introduce any of the testimony from his interview with Alicia into evidence during the trial?"

Grace winked at Alicia, who was all ears. "A lucky break for us."

Grace's secretary called her to the phone. She hurried out. When Alicia was done playing judge, I steered her back to the state attorney's office. Grace was still on the phone. She waved for us to take a seat on her sofa, then said a few clipped words, hung up, and swiveled to face Alicia. "Just before you arrived, your father's attorney and I met in Judge Donovan's chambers to discuss another plea bargain. The judge said he would consider a plea that included a prison term." As she stared at Alicia, Grace's fig-colored eyes seemed to absorb all the light from the room. "What do you want to do?"

"How am I supposed to know?" She turned to me.

As Guardian ad Litem my main responsibility was to be the child's voice in court, but I refused to stretch this to include second-guessing Alicia's true feelings. She would live with the consequences far longer than I would. But even at that crucial moment, Alicia's eyes were partially closing as she made her somnolent escape from reality.

"Alicia!" I said loudly enough to rouse her. "Remember you told me your goals and I wrote them down?" Opening my accordion file, I found the "bagel memo." I showed Alicia my notes. "Your number one request was you didn't want Cory ever to live with your dad again. You said that was more important than your father going to prison. Do you still believe that?"

"I guess."

"How will you feel when you know your father is locked in prison and your decision helped put him there?"

"It's okay."

I took a deep breath. "Do you still love your father in some small corner of your mind?"

"Yes," she whispered.

"You don't want the responsibility of this decision, do you?"

She twisted her hands and her knees were trembling. "No."

"Let's take a break," I said, and led her out of the office.

Alicia backed into the corner of the farthest wall of the bathroom.

"Alicia, whatever you decide is fine with me." She hugged her arms to her chest. "Now, shut your eyes and listen to yourself. Only you know what's right for you, but you are hearing conflicting voices telling you what to do. One voice wants to go to trial and see what happens. It wants to give you the chance to tell your story and be heard by a jury. Another voice wants to run away and for this all to be over, no matter what. You might have another one reminding you of your promise to protect Cory."

I paused for almost a minute. "Now think, Alicia, and listen. And when you are ready, tell me which voice is the loudest."

As I watched, a transformation took place. Alicia's crossed arms fell to her sides. Her back straightened. Her chin lifted. Alicia opened her eyes. "Safe . . . safe and over."

"You've decided that you want Cory safe and the whole business over with?"

"Yes."

"Will you tell Grace that?"

"Yes. Yes, I will."

Alicia strode past me, out the bathroom door, and straight across the hall into the state attorney's office. She did not pause at reception but put her hand on the inside door like she had seen Grace do and waited expectantly for the buzzer to sound to let her through. I followed her past the maze of desks to the corner office, where Grace was going through a file cabinet beside her desk. Alicia marched in, sat in Grace's executive chair, and leaned back.

Grace looked over Alicia's shoulder at me, as though waiting for an explanation.

"I guess Alicia is taking charge," I said, smiling.

Grace understood at once. "She's the boss," she said, then came around and sat on the sofa in the spot Alicia usually took.

Alicia tapped one of Grace's pens on her blotter. "My father will have to remain in prison until Cory is eighteen."

"That's four years from now," I said to Grace.

"After that, I don't care what happens," Alicia finished.

"A ten-year sentence would work out to about that much time behind bars," Grace responded. "Is that all right with you, Gay?"

"I'm not in charge, Alicia is."

"Excuse me," she said without sounding facetious. "Is that what you had in mind, Ms. Stevenson?"

Alicia leaned way back in her chair. "Yes, it is."

Grace reached for the extension telephone on a side table and dialed Mr. Hilliard. She made the offer, then waited on hold. "Your father's there now. Hilliard is discussing the plea with him."

A short while later, Walt Hilliard was back on the line.

"Are you sure?" Grace asked, surprised. "My deal gets him out while he's young enough to do something with his life. Any guilty verdict is a mandatory twenty-five years. You want to take that risk?" She hung up and faced Alicia. "He wants to roll the dice. We're going to trial day after tomorrow."

The next morning my husband brought me the two local newspapers. One was a metropolitan daily; one was the county paper. Each carried a headline about the case.

The county paper said:

Jury Chosen in Trial of Man Accused of Raping Daughter

Attorneys selected a jury Tuesday for the trial of a local business man accused of having sex with his 9-year-old daughter. The man, whose name is being withheld to protect the victim, is charged with sexual battery on a child less than 12. The girl is now 15 years old.

The regional section of the city paper reported it differently:

A jury has been picked for the trial of Richard Leroy Stevenson, Sr., 43, charged with sexual battery on a 9-year-old child.

Stevenson was sentenced in county courts in the last year for saying "bull———" in the courtroom.

"Oh, no!" I shouted, then phoned Lillian and read her the stories. "One paper says *incest*, the other says *Stevenson*. Most people read both papers."

"Then everyone will figure it out," Lillian said. "Poor kid."

"When this is over she'll have classmates asking her how it was to screw your father. Can't we do something to protect her?"

"There's no way to muzzle the press," Lillian said, "but you could ask very nicely."

The editor of the regional section was a man I had met many times. He returned my call promptly and listened politely as I pleaded for him not to mention the defendant's name in future editions.

"Sorry, we've made an editorial policy on this case. All we do is report the news," he said in a world-weary voice.

"I am shocked and appalled by your callous attitude," I said before I hung up.

The jury was made up of five men, one woman, and one alternate, who was also a woman. Because they were going to be on the witness stand, Alicia, Rich, and Cory were not permitted inside the courtroom to hear other people's testimony. Lillian decided that I would remain in the courtroom so I could request a closed hearing for the children's testimony. I'd already asked Grace if the press could also be removed, but she handed me 918.16, the same statute that gave guardians access to the courtroom, which read:

When any person under the age of 16 is testifying concerning any sex offense, the court shall clear the courtroom of all persons except parties to the cause and their immediate families or *guardians*, attorneys and their secretaries, officers of the court, jurors, newspaper reporters or broadcasters, and court reporters.

Alicia was given Grace's office, and she used the prosecutor's chair and desk as if they were her own. Rich remained with Mitzi, who promised not to let him out of her sight. Marta Castillo supported Cory in an anteroom.

Lillian sat beside me on the right side of the courtroom. Behind us was a group of HRS workers with an interest in the case, some of Walt Hilliard's staff and family, and Ruth Levy. Fortunately there were not too many members of the general public. Grace Chandler, wearing a black suit and white satin blouse with a black-and-white striped bow tie, took her place at the table in front of me with another assistant prosecutor beside her.

On the left side of the room, Red Stevenson was flanked by Walt Hilliard and his partner. This was the first time I had seen Red Stevenson in a suit.

Before the formal trial began, the prosecutor had submitted a motion to allow the use of the Williams Rule. This would permit her to offer evidence regarding Red's past history of sexually assaulting other children in order to demonstrate that his crimes against his daughter were not isolated incidents, but rather one of many examples of his propensity to commit the same offense repeatedly. Grace had warned me that employing the Williams Rule was a controversial point of law, but without the judge's approval nobody could testify that Red Stevenson had committed crimes—for which he had not been charged—against the other children.

(Two years after the Stevenson trial, I watched the sensational Florida rape trial in which William Kennedy Smith was the defendant, and heard Smith's attorney, Roy Black, successfully argue against the application of the Williams Rule. Testimony from other women who had been allegedly attacked by William Kennedy Smith in a similar manner as the victim in the case was not permitted to be given.)

Grace had warned me that if the Williams Rule evidence was not allowed in the Stevenson case, everything would hinge on Alicia's account of what happened to her, plus Rich's version of the time he saw his father having sex with his sister. Everyone was worried how Rich would do on the stand, and even if he answered the questions adequately, his mental health history could discredit him. Alicia had discrepancies in her story, and she also could revert from being sweet and cooperative to pouty and mouthy, thus coming off as an incorrigible teenager. Then, if Cory testified against his brother and sister, a jury might have sincere doubts about Red's actions.

While the Williams Rule was debated, the jury was asked to leave the courtroom so they would not be prejudiced by pretrial testimony that might not be admissible in the regular proceedings. Then Grace Chandler told the judge that she would offer evidence of prior acts similar to those alleged in the Stevenson case as circumstantial proof of motive, intent, preparation, and method of operation, as the Williams Rule insisted.

Walt Hilliard objected, saying the rule could not be used merely to prove bad character or even a propensity to commit a particular crime. "Just because someone has done something before does not prove he has done it again." Also Hilliard called the rule a violation of the defendant's civil liberties because "he has to defend himself against more crimes when he has only been charged in the indictment with one."

After listening to sample testimony from two of the children as well as one of Red's ex-wives, the judge determined there were several similar methods of preparation and intent, and thus agreed to allow Williams Rule evidence. This was a blow to Walt Hilliard, who returned to his seat obviously disgruntled.

There was a brief break to reconvene the jury and gather the witnesses. I wasn't sure how long it would take, so I didn't leave the room. Some of the reporters milled around in the aisle. Casually I asked who was representing the paper that was printing the Stevenson name. The reporter introduced himself as Sterling Bailey.

"As Guardian ad Litem for Mr. Stevenson's daughter, I spoke to your editor," I said loudly, "but he refuses to change his stance and will continue to use this defendant's name, even though the victim just started high school in this town."

Mr. Bailey shrugged.

Out of the corner of my eye I could see the disapproval on the face of the woman reporter with the county paper. "Thanks for not mentioning the names," I said to her. Then, while I had her full attention, I turned back slightly in the other reporter's direction. "Mr. Bailey, later today you are going to hear shocking testimony from the defendant's daughter. As her Guardian ad Litem I speak for this child. So one last time, I beg you to ask your editor to reconsider his position and hold the family name confidential.'' My next move was unplanned, but I was determined to make my point. I fell to my knees in the aisle of the courtroom. ''Please, on my knees, I ask you to change your mind.''

The mouth of the female reporter gaped. Another member of the press jabbed Bailey in the back until he offered me a hand to help me to my feet. Without another word I went back to the seat, hearing the buzz of the reporters in my wake.

Grace Chandler crossed to the podium and moved it so that it was centered in front of the jury box. With her back to Judge Donovan and her profile to my side of the room, the prosecutor commenced her opening statements. As soon as she began speaking, I heard a loud ringing in my ears and my stomach heaved. Until that moment I had approached every phase of the case in a logical, and I hoped, compassionate manner. I had listened to intimate depositions from the children, heard Alicia describe having sex with her father, watched deviant interactions between the Stevenson children, as well as Cory and his father. I had read reams of files and had helped uncover information on the death of Mr. Stevenson's first wife and had accidentally visited the crime scene. But suddenly I was overwhelmed—and shocked—by my emotional response to the import of the moment.

''You okay?'' Lillian whispered, squeezing my hand. Later she told me I had turned so white, she thought the blood had drained into my shoes.

I nodded, even though I was unable to control my rapid pulse or racing thoughts. What if . . . what if Alicia had made it up? What if I had been drawn into her fantasy? I observed Red Stevenson's hunched back and tried to imagine what it must be like to have your children turn against you. Don't forget, I reminded myself, this was a man who had six wives, one dead by his hand, a few others abused. There had been other children who claimed to have been hurt by him. Many aspects of his life fit the profile of a pedophile and yet even with everything I knew, it was hard to believe.

Grace Chandler was saying ''look at the cold hard facts.'' To keep me focused on the unfolding events, I pulled out my steno pad and began to take notes. ''Today you will meet a child, for that is what she is, even though she is maturing into a young lady. This is a child, who because of her father's heinous crimes, has lost her home, her family, and any hope at a normal life.'' Grace's voice choked. ''Nobody wants to confront what happens when the person charged with the care of a child abuses that fragile trust in the service of his twisted cravings, but we must do our duty and examine the details of this depraved crime.''

When Walt Hilliard's turn came, he dispensed with the podium and strolled confidently in front of the jury, asking them to consider ''the standard of proof and to follow the road map of the evidence.'' He explained that there was but one crime of sexual battery being considered, and while other alleged crimes may be mentioned, Mr. Stevenson had never been charged with them. Then his voice dropped as he described Alicia as a ''very troubled girl,'' using the tone of someone who regretted the necessity of having to speak ill of the dead.

Turning on his heel as if he were about to leave, Walt Hilliard then spun around to renew their attention. ''Why didn't this young girl, who claims she was the victim of multiple years of abuse, tell anyone? There were stepmothers in her home. She had teachers and close friends. Why, all of a sudden, did she pick Mrs. Smiley, a virtual stranger? Pay attention to that witness and see if you believe what she tells you, then listen carefully to Dr. Leif, the state's expert witness, and rely on your common sense to decide if this man, Richard Leroy Stevenson, could have done the terrible things that are alleged by his young, confused daughter.''

Grace Chandler told the judge her next witness would be the victim. Looking at me, she said, ''Her Guardian ad Litem has requested a closed courtroom.'' During the brief break, I went into Grace's office to locate Alicia. Her head was lying on Grace's desk blotter, but she was not asleep.

''Ready?'' I asked. I went behind her and massaged her neck. ''This is the worst part, then it will be over.''

''I'm okay,'' she said as she straightened the folds on her new dress.

I walked Alicia into the courtroom and as we passed the reporters on the back benches stared sharply at Sterling Bailey, who looked away.

As soon as the bailiff shut the doors, Alicia took the stand. She was carrying the Bible covered in white leather and stamped with her name that Ruth had given her the previous Christmas. The pink flowers on her calico dress flattered her tawny complexion. A lacy collar framed her face. Her hair was pinned back with a matching bow. Without purple eye shadow, bright lipstick, or trendy clothing, Alicia looked younger than fifteen.

Grace Chandler adjusted the podium so that it was close enough to be personal, but not ''in her face.'' Then she began with gentle questions about Alicia's age, where she was living, and attending school. Next, she took Alicia back to when her father first molested her.

In a quiet voice, but without hesitation, Alicia described the toolshed. "It was kind of spooky, with lots of cobwebs. Dad knew I didn't like to be in there alone."

Just as she had during the deposition, Alicia told how she climbed on her father's lap and how he had touched her genitals.

I watched the jury. There were two retired men in their early seventies, one portly, one thin. One had been in accounting, one in sales. The mustached man was a recent navy veteran with a personable face. The fourth man, who was a local supermarket butcher, wore a brown suit, and had a bulldog's chin. The lone woman was over fifty and had cotton white hair and wore purple-framed glasses. I liked the alternate best. She was a schoolteacher in her forties who seemed the most alert and most likely to empathize with Alicia. The others behaved as if they had taken a pretrial course in blinking as infrequently as possible.

"When did your father change the way he touched you sexually?" Grace asked.

"When I was nine."

After clarifying how she knew how old she had been, Alicia explained that she used to help her father at his marine shop.

"What do you remember happened there the summer when you were nine?"

"One time I had to use the bathroom and my father came in while I was sitting on the toilet. He reached above my head and took down some magazines and showed me pictures of people having sex in different ways. My father pointed to the pictures of men's things, and then he unzipped his pants and showed me his, and made me touch it."

"Touch what?" Grace asked gently.

"His penis," Alicia said, then looked away.

"What happened next?"

"He jerked me off the seat and pulled my shorts down around my ankles. He turned me around so my butt was facing him and placed my hands on the tank of the toilet. He held onto my elbows and he jammed his thing inside of me."

"How did it feel?"

"It hurt," she replied flatly.

"Did this ever happen again?" Alicia nodded. Grace prompted Alicia to tell of a typical situation.

"If nobody was around the house my father would take off his clothes, put on his bathrobe, and walk around with it partially open so I could see he was interested. Then he'd have me lie down on the couch and he'd do it to me."

As soon as the particulars of the crime were patently stated, Grace turned the floor over to the defense attorney.

Walt Hilliard moved the podium into position for the cross-examination. Grace had warned Alicia that Mr. Hilliard would try to intimidate her, not only with his words, but also with his body language. As predicted, he loomed close to the witness stand and tried to cut off Alicia's eye contact with Grace.

I had stationed myself at a different angle from the prosecutor, and Alicia had been told that whichever direction she would look she would see someone who cared about her. Instead of taking notes, I lifted my chin and set my mouth into what I hoped was a supportive expression.

Walt Hilliard was smart enough not to badger Alicia, for no jury would want to see this former college linebacker bullying a tender teen. "Why didn't you tell anyone sooner?" he asked, as if he genuinely did not understand how someone could have suffered so long in silence.

Following instructions, Alicia did not respond at once. Grace had warned her to leave a few seconds in case she needed to object to an improper question. "There was nobody to tell."

"Wasn't there a stepmother in the house at the time?"

"I didn't think she would believe me."

"Why didn't you tell a teacher or a friend?"

"I was afraid to."

"Were you afraid your father would hurt you if you told?"

"No, I wasn't."

"Then why?"

She waited the requisite beat. "I was scared."

"You just said you didn't think your father would hurt you, so what were you scared of?"

Beat. "Ah . . ." Beat. ". . . being moved. Like my older brother. When my father didn't want him around anymore, he sent him away."

I couldn't control my involuntary grin.

"Did it ever happen again?" Alicia nodded. "Where?"

"Usually somewhere in the house."

"Anywhere else?"

"He took me on trips with him when he had to deliver a boat or some parts. Last summer we drove all the way to Mobile, Alabama, where we shared the same bed and did it every night.''

''When in the summer was it?''

''I remember *The Thorn Birds* was on television because he'd let me watch it if I'd do it.''

''There were a lot of people living in your house. When were you ever alone?''

''In the middle of the night.''

''Didn't anyone wake up?''

''Rich and Cory are very sound sleepers. Dad has to use the squirt gun to get them up in the morning.''

''It is hard to wake you up too?'' She nodded. ''But he could get you up for sex?''

''Yeah, like you can really sleep when someone is doing it to you,'' she responded with a nasty edge.

''Didn't anyone in your family suspect anything?'' Walt Hilliard questioned.

''My brother, Rich, did, but I told him nothing happened because if he knew the truth he would have killed my father.''

Walt Hilliard took a few steps backward, then consulted his notes. ''Do you like boys?''

Beat. ''I guess . . .''

''Do you like having sex with boys?''

''Objection!'' Grace said with a tinge of disgust.

''Sustained,'' ruled Judge Donovan.

Then Walt Hilliard asked when she first had sex with her father and she indicated it was that afternoon at the marine shop. ''What about when you were in the toolshed?'' She said that was different. He began a series of questions relating to discrepancies in her testimony from the early written statements and cleverly tried to confuse her, but she had done her homework. He did, however, annoy her enough so her polite responses took on an edginess.

Mr. Hilliard began reading quotes from Alicia's deposition. Grace Chandler objected to bringing in this evidence, which wasn't in the file.

''It was filed June twenty-eighth,'' Mr. Hilliard stated and showed her the date stamped on the paper.

I sagged. Grace's ''lucky break'' had been a clerical oversight.

Grace's cheeks flamed. She asked to approach the bench to explain she had never received a copy. The judge gave her a short recess to read the transcribed deposition over. I took Alicia back to Grace's office for a Coke. We watched Grace pace back and forth flipping the pages and reading worrisome passages aloud. Normally unperturbable, the prosecutor seemed genuinely shaken.

When the trial resumed, Walt Hilliard read from Alicia's conflicting written statements. "In this one you said that you had sex with your father 'about once a week from the age of five through nine' and after that as often as three times a week."

"I meant he touched me once a week."

"But that is not what you reported under oath," Walt Hilliard said, waving the transcribed deposition in front of her, "is it?"

Grace Chandler objected to this needling but the judge allowed it.

Walt Hilliard came back at her even more aggressively. "And when you were nine? What happened then?"

"He had sex with me."

"So what you wrote in your statement was not what you meant?"

"No."

"Then it was a lie, wasn't it?"

Walt Hilliard backed away so the jury could see Alicia's distraught face. In a studied gesture of kindness, he gave her a moment to catch herself, while he pretended to look at his notes.

"You explained how your father had sex with you for the first time in the bathroom at his place of business, is that right?"

"Yes."

"Can you describe the bathroom?" Alicia mentioned the bathtub and the woodstove. "Isn't that the bathroom at your house?"

"No, it is the one at the old marine shop in town."

Walt shrugged, then continued. "You testified that 'my father pulled my pants down around my ankles,' is that right?"

"Yes."

"Did you step out of your panties or did they stay around your ankles?"

"I'm not sure."

"Oh, now you're not sure! Do you remember what you said he did to you?" He looked at his notes. "You said, 'he jammed his thing inside of me.' Then you told us that 'thing' meant his penis. Now I want you to tell me about his penis. How did it feel to you? Was it hard or was it soft?"

"Soft."

"How could he penetrate you with a soft penis?"

"First it was soft, then it got harder."

"Oh, so now it got harder? Which was it?"

"Both, but it was from the rear, so I couldn't see and I was too young to know exactly."

"But now you know more about these things?"

"I should by now." The painful knowledge wrought by that familiarity was etched on Alicia's face.

"You say that your father had routine sex with you as often as once or twice a week, is that right?"

"Yes."

"Tell me exactly what you allege your father did to you."

"He would go in and out until he came. You know what that means?" Alicia finished with her Bardot pout.

"Did he try forceful, hard, pounding sex with you?"

"Yes."

"And nobody heard what was going on in that small house with so many people sleeping nearby?"

"I guess not."

"Didn't you know that all you had to do was say the magic words 'sexual abuse' and HRS would come and remove you from your father?"

"I wasn't sure what would happen."

"But you said that your brother had been taken away before, so you must have known you could get out of your house if you claimed abuse. Were you angry with your father the day you decided to tell someone?"

"No."

"Who is your best friend?"

"Dawn Leigh Pruitt."

"Where is she living now?"

"Clearwater."

"Where did Dawn Leigh Pruitt live before she moved?"

Alicia described a section of the county not far from Stevenson Groves. After some more rapid-fire questioning she admitted that she had been upset because her father had not facilitated a visit between the girls.

Then, unexpectedly, Walt Hilliard excused the witness.

Grace Chandler returned and entered an exhibit into evidence. It was the picture of the bathroom in the marine shop. She had Alicia verify that this was where the rape had occurred. Then she asked, "Were you ever afraid of your father hurting you physically?"

"Yes. He has hit me with a belt and with his hand."

"Do you still love your father?"

"Yes."

Out of the corner of my eye I noticed Red Stevenson straightening from his hunched-over position. He was shaking his head from side to side, as though he could not believe what had just happened.

The proceedings adjourned for lunch. Alicia's testimony had taken almost two hours, but she had held up beautifully. Ruth brought Alicia, Rich, and me sandwiches to Grace's office. At one point Rich asked Alicia to pass him a drink and called her "Janet." She teased him about it, but he didn't seem to realize his mistake. Cory, who didn't want to talk to his brother and sister, ate in another room with Marta Castillo and Mitzi Keller, and I spent the second half of the break with him.

As I walked back into the courtroom, Sterling Bailey touched my arm. "I called my editor. We won't be printing the family name in future editions."

I scribbled Lillian a note announcing the little victory. She squeezed my hand.

The prosecution called Dr. Colette Boggs, the court-appointed psychologist who had evaluated the three Stevenson children. Dr. Boggs discussed incest in general, some of the syndromes that victims present, including self-mutilation and low self-esteem, and how she diagnosed these characteristics in Alicia.

"Why don't girls like Alicia Stevenson tell anyone of the abuse?" Grace Chandler asked the expert.

"One reason is the fear of being stigmatized. Although we try to assure the victim that she has done nothing wrong, she may feel that because she participated she was somehow at fault. Also, as soon as the disclosure is made, the victim will be blamed for the subsequent trauma to the family. She also feels responsible for the fate of the offender, which is why some never reveal the secret. Other times children who have been violated for many years don't realize that something is terribly wrong until they are teenagers developing outside relationships and their own moral position."

Dr. Boggs answered questions about what she knew about the women who served in the capacity of Alicia's stepmother and pointed out that the history of transience gave Alicia the feeling that nobody could be trusted. Next the psychologist's testimony turned to defining posttraumatic stress disorder and Alicia's presentation of some of these symptoms. "We describe the victim's response in terms of freeze, flight, and fight. Initially, when a sexual attack occurs, the victim's brain pumps adrenal hormones, and these act like an anesthetic so that the incident can be endured without an overwhelming sensation of pain.''

"Would this result in someone not recalling an initial sexual penetration as excruciatingly painful?" Grace asked.

"Yes."

"Does that mean she did not experience pain at the time?"

"No, although her sensations may have been muted as a coping response. However. later, even a small amount of pain associated with a similar event can set off a traumatic response far more intense than is warranted by the actual situation.''

Colette Boggs went on to describe the flight response as one used to minimize anxiety.

"How does Alicia exhibit this response?"

"When she is asked to recall unpleasant memories, she seems to fall asleep or dissociates from the discussion at hand."

Dr. Boggs testified that the fight response ranges from temper tantrums to more aggressive acting out. When asked why Alicia permitted so many years of abuse, she explained that Alicia's passivity was "a form of accommodation.''

"Is this common?"

"Very much so. Some children either deny the abuse occurred at all or, even after it is out in public, recant the confession if pressured to do so.''

Watching the impassive jury, I suspected that Dr. Boggs's technical explanation was not hitting its mark.

After Mr. Hilliard's brief cross-examination of the psychologist, Deputy Moline from the sex crimes division was called to the stand. He answered the prosecutor's questions about the night he responded to a report of sexual battery.

"How were you notified?"

"By an abuse report that had been phoned into the child abuse hotline.''

"What time was that?"

"After eleven P.M.''

"Did you arrest anyone that evening?"

"No, but we did take the child into protective custody."

"What time did you arrive at the police station?" Grace asked.

"After midnight."

"What was Alicia Stevenson's emotional state?"

"She was trembling and crying."

"Did you have her write a statement describing the abuse?"

"Yes."

Grace handed the officer the statement and confirmed that it was the same document. "What time was it written?"

"At two-forty-five A.M."

In the cross-examination Walt Hilliard asked the deputy, "How would you describe Alicia's state of mind?"

"Tired, upset."

"Was she confused?"

"Not that I could tell."

"Did she want to leave her father's house?"

"Not at first."

"How did you convince her?"

"We told her that we had orders to remove her for her own safety."

"Did she think she needed that protection?"

"Not at that time."

The next witness was Richard Leroy Stevenson, Jr.

He came in the room escorted by Mitzi, and because he was technically another child-victim witness, the courtroom was cleared again.

"He needs lots of reassurance, or he's going to lose it," Mitzi said. "He's been a basket case in the hall. I told him to watch you, and you would nod that he was doing fine."

Under Grace Chandler's gentle questioning, Rich did fairly well. He explained that his father had often been violent toward him, which is why HRS had placed him out of the home when he was very young. He described being slapped in the face so hard it left a "handprint mark." He then admitted that he had seen his father having sex with his sister.

"Tell us what you saw?" Grace asked.

"I was in the living room sleeping on the couch and my father went out to the porch where my sister was sleeping, carried her into the dining room, and made her lie down on the floor."

"What did you see your father do to your sister, Alicia?"

"He—you know—had sex with her."

"Did you hear any words?"

"Just groans from them both."

"What did you do?"

"I closed my eyes and lay very still, cause I thought I was going to be sick."

"Did your father ever do anything like that to your brother?"

"I didn't see it if he did."

"Did he ever do it to you?"

"Yes."

"Can you tell me when that was?"

Walt Hilliard tried to object, but the judge let Rich respond. He told the story of his father masturbating him in the marine shop and said there had been other times before that.

"Has he done it since?"

"No!" Rich said so loudly I flinched.

Grace Chandler turned the witness over to the defense.

"You love your sister, don't you?" Walt Hilliard began. Rich agreed. "Have you ever taken any drugs?"

"I had crack once, and cocaine twice, some LSD. I was with someone who did needles, but I didn't want to."

"Anything else?"

"I did roaches twice, you know, marijuana."

"How old are you, Rich?"

"Seventeen."

"Are you married?"

"Yes, I got myself married in the summer."

"How did you get permission to get married?"

"My father helped me."

"Didn't you make a deal with him?"

"No."

"May I remind you that you are under oath to tell the truth. What did you promise your father?"

"I can't say. I want to take five."

"You want to stop for five minutes?"

"No, you know, not five, the Fifth."

Lillian and I glanced at each other, surprised at what the boy knew to say.

"You don't want to incriminate yourself by answering my question, is that it?" Walt Hilliard retorted facetiously.

"Yes."

"What is your wife's name?" Walt asked, without hiding the smirk on his face.

"Janet Stevenson."

"Where did you meet her?"

"We were in the same program."

"Was that program for the treatment of mental and drug problems?"

"Yes."

"Where were you before that?"

"In the hospital."

"Was that for emotional problems?"

"Uh, yes."

"During the few times you have lived at home during the last few years, did you see your father ever abuse your sister?"

"He'd hit her to wake her up. Like slap her face if the cold pistols didn't work."

"What are the cold pistols?"

"He kept these water guns in the fridge and he'd squirt everyone with cold water if they didn't get up with the alarm."

"Did he squirt you?"

"Yes."

"Did he squirt Alicia?"

"No."

"I thought you said you saw him squirt her. Did he squirt her or not?"

"Yes, he did, but she told me about it. I wasn't around or I was still asleep."

"What about Cory?"

"Sometimes he's hard to wake up too."

"When you described seeing your father lifting your sister out of her bed, what time of night was it?"

"Late, after midnight."

"Were you asleep?"

"Yes."

"I thought you said you were a heavy sleeper, so heavy in fact your father had to wake you with a squirt gun."

"I heard some noise and got up. I don't know why," Rich said, his voice rising with anxiety.

I stared at him resolutely, willing him not to lose it, but he didn't catch my gaze because he was looking off in the distance somewhere far above my head.

"Was it dark in the house?"

"Yes."

"Then how could you see what was happening?"

"There was a clock on the VCR in the living room and it made a green light. I could see in the shadow of that light."

"Who was living in your house at that time?"

"Me, my sister and brother, my grandfather, and I guess Vicky, my stepmother, was there too."

"Where did she sleep?"

"Sometimes in the room with my father, sometimes on the cot on the porch."

"Where was she that night?"

"I don't think she was there. Sometimes she'd stay away from the house."

"But that night was special. You remember what you think your father did to your sister. Wouldn't you have wondered where his wife was?"

"I guess she wasn't there."

"So tell me what you saw your father do."

"He picked her up and put her down then he made her legs go in the air and he got on top of her and fucked her."

"Who did he get on top of?"

"My wife."

"Who?"

"Janet, my wife."

I gasped. Rich had confused Janet with Alicia again!

"Your father was doing something to your wife?"

"No, my sister."

"Who is your sister?"

"Alicia."

"I thought you said it was your wife. Did you mean his wife?"

"No, my sister, his daughter."

"You got confused, didn't you?"

"I guess."

"Couldn't your previous drug problems have something to do with you getting confused?"

Before Rich could reply, Grace objected.

Walt Hilliard changed his line of questioning. "Where was the VCR?"

"In the living room."

"So there was enough light from this little VCR display to allow you to see all the way from the living room into the dining room and for you to realize who it was and know exactly what they were doing?"

"Yes."

"Now who did you see in those shadows?"

"My father and my wife—I mean my sister." Rich tossed his head like a dog shaking off water.

Walt Hilliard strolled by the jury making a sad face, as though he joined them in pitying the pathetic, bewildered boy on the stand. "No more questions," he said and went to his table and sat down.

Grace Chandler walked up casually. "Rich," she said in a hushed voice, "how do you feel about your father?"

"I hate him."

"Why?"

"For what he did to me my whole life and now what he did to my sister."

Grace Chandler called Margaret (Peggy) Elaine Abbott, Red Stevenson's next-to-the-last wife, to the stand. She wore tortoiseshell glasses and a fluffy haircut that made her look like a librarian in a fifties movie.

When questioned by Grace Chandler, Peggy said she had married Mr. Stevenson in August of 1979 and had remained with him, on and off, for almost six years. Peggy was asked about the relationship, which she admitted had been rocky the last two years, during which time they stopped having marital relations.

"Did you sleep at the Stevenson Groves house every night?"

"No, we used to swap turns sleeping at the marine shop for security reasons. There had been a burglary at the shop."

"Where would the children sleep?"

"Usually at home, but sometimes Red took one of the boys to the marine shop when it was his turn."

"Was Mr. Stevenson a good parent?"

"No. He didn't treat the children fairly and he disciplined them harshly." She went on to describe how he woke them up with the icy squirt guns, hit them with a strap, and once put soap in Rich's mouth for lying.

"Did Richard Jr. live with you most of the time?"

"No, he was in special programs so he was home only for vacations."

"Did your husband spend time with his children equally?"

"No, he preferred Alicia."

"What about Cory?"

"He was his grandfather's pet. He'd be over at his house much of the time."

"Were there many opportunities for Mr. Stevenson to be alone with his daughter?"

"Yes, she'd go to work with him when she wasn't at school. They got along unusually well. Not like a father and daughter."

"What do you mean?"

"They were very close, always touching."

"What did you think of that?"

"I didn't like it, but when I said anything, Red accused me of being jealous."

"Were you jealous?"

"In a way. Alicia knew she didn't have to mind me because he'd step in."

"Did you ever see anything improper between them?"

"Many nights he would lie down in bed with her. When I asked him about it, he said he did it to relax her and had been doing it since she was a small girl."

"Did you see what happened when he'd be in bed with her?"

"No, he kept the door closed, but he'd stay a long time."

"Anything else?"

"Yes." Peggy swallowed hard. "When he washed her hair—" Peggy started crying. "I didn't think it was right . . ."

"Can you describe what you saw?"

"Sometimes he'd run his fingers through her hair and say it had to be washed, and other times she'd be in the shower and shout for him."

"What would she say?"

" 'Shampooman, I'm ready, Shampooman.' Or he'd call into the bathroom and say, 'Are you ready for the Shampooman?' "

"Who was Shampooman?"

"Her father."

"Did you ever see what went on in the bathroom?"

"Once I didn't realize who was in there, so I opened the door, and I saw him reaching into the shower and washing her hair."

"What was he wearing?"

"Nothing."

"What did she wear in the shower?"

"She was nude."

"When was this?"

"About a year before I left him."

"How old was Alicia when you left?"

"Thirteen. She was grown up, with breasts and pubic hair and I thought she was too old for him to go into the shower with her."

"Did you ever see anything else?"

"A few months later I came into the house from work early and the bathroom door was open. This time he was washing her hair over the sink, and he was behind her in his underwear and moving back and forth, you know, like sex movements."

"Was she protesting?"

"No, it was like . . . she liked it. I got freaked out and didn't say anything. I just went to sit at the table and I watched them when they came out, and he was drying her hair and being really nice to her and calling her that name I hated."

"What name was that?"

"My little lollipop."

"Have you heard that before?" Lillian whispered to me.

"Never! I've never heard anything about Shampooman or Lollipop. Nobody ever said anything about the shower either!"

"He's a dead man," Lillian scribbled on my pad.

All through the cross-examination I stared at Red Stevenson's back, trying to imagine him in the bathroom with Alicia, his hairy arms soapy with shampoo and his slippery hands moving from her scalp to her neck and down to her breasts and maybe getting under the shower with her, rubbing up and down on her, and possibly penetrating her.

Walt Hilliard could not shake Peggy's insistence that she had observed perversions between father and daughter. He asked why she didn't report him and she sobbed and said she didn't know where to turn and was afraid nobody would believe her. She had tried to talk to Alicia about it, but her stepdaughter had "clammed up." Peggy admitted being resentful of the relationship, but also said it "made her sick" and was one reason the marriage had failed.

Although Grace had determined that at least five other girls had been molested in some fashion by Mr. Stevenson, she could not use them to testify. Dawn Leigh Pruitt's psychological had indicated she might do more harm than good, the three Curry sisters had moved away, and Grace had not tracked them down. The only child who had been subpoenaed was Sunny Rhodes, the stepdaughter who claimed Red had molested her shortly before he started up with Alicia.

The first surprise was Sunny Rhodes's maturity. Because she was tall, had a womanly figure, as well as a knowing, intelligent look about her, Sunny seemed more like a college student than a sixteen-year-old.

Sunny testified that she had been about eight or nine when she had lived at the Stevenson house. Alicia was six months younger and they had shared a room. Sunny recalled several occasions when Mr. Stevenson pulled down Sunny's panties and rubbed her bottom, but she never told anyone. Then Grace asked her to describe the incident she recalled the best.

"Red came out of the bathroom wearing an open bathrobe. I turned away and tried to watch television, but he made me sit on his lap, said I had to do what he wanted or he would hurt my grandmother.''

Sunny said Red made her spread her legs, and hold them out while he pressed his penis to her vagina. ''I screamed and screamed and said it hurt. He slapped my face and told me to shut up.''

''What happened next?''

''I pretended I was going to the bathroom, but really went to the phone in the bedroom and called my grandmother.'' Sunny took a few gulps for air. ''She came over and took me to the hospital to be checked.''

Shortly after that Sunny stated she went to live with her biological father, who has had custody of her ever since.

Walt Hilliard asked a few clarifying questions, and then Dr. Mort Diller testified that at that time he was the medical examiner at Sawgrass Memorial Hospital. Dr. Diller had examined Sunny Rhodes, and he said that she sustained lacerations consistent with attempted vaginal penetration. He also found semen on her inner thigh.

During his cross-examination Walt Hilliard asked the doctor whether formal charges had been made against anyone during that incident, and the doctor admitted that none had. After further questioning, Dr. Diller could not explain why nobody had prosecuted anyone in that case.

''Do you have any physical evidence that links Mr. Stevenson as the person who allegedly molested Sunny?''

The doctor said that there was none.

For her final witness, Grace Chandler called Dr. Rudolph Leif, who gave a long list of his credentials, including the fact that he had been the primary physician on the child protection team since 1957. He had examined Alicia after she had been removed from her home. Dr. Leif testified that Alicia Stevenson had reported that she had been having sex with her biological father every week or so since the age of nine, the last time being four days before the examination.

Grace Chandler led him through a detailed discussion of Alicia's physical situation. He described her having reached her menarche at age twelve, and as a Tanner V, ''which is a way to describe the highest level sexual maturity based on pubic hair and breast development, with full estrogen effect.'' The doctor noted that Alicia had carved several sets of initials on her ankles with a needle. Then he launched into his gynecological exam, which thankfully Alicia was not in the room to hear. ''The hymenal opening is central, and six millimeters wide and four millimeters vertically, even with labial traction. It was thick and pink with no visible scars. The inlet easily admitted two fingers with no discomfort for the patient.''

Grace Chandler asked whether these findings suggested that Alicia could have been sexually abused and he said yes, but estrogen in sexually mature women creates vascular changes in the vaginal area, thus making it difficult to ascertain whether or not a girl had been sexually active.

When it was his turn, Walt Hilliard moved very close to the doctor and came to the point. ''You described Miss Stevenson's hymen. Isn't this the structure that usually disappears after a woman has sexual intercourse?''

''Hymens vary widely,'' the doctor replied curtly, then launched into the differences in shape and elasticity.

''Is it possible that Alicia Stevenson is, as we say, a virgin, and that she may never have had sexual intercourse with a man?''

''Yes, that is possible,'' the doctor replied, causing an audible gasp to resound in the courtroom.

Lillian drew a big question mark on my pad. I scribbled back: ''No way! She's had sex with numerous boyfriends.''

Walt Hilliard persisted in trying to clarify what the doctor meant. ''Are there any physical findings that would prove the charges against Mr. Stevenson?''

''Even if we could prove she had had sexual intercourse with someone, there is no evidence it was with her father.''

''Can you prove that she either did or did not ever have sex with anyone?''

''No.''

''How could she have had sex and still have a hymen that indicates she could be a virgin?''

''If she had been fondled over a long period of time, this might have stretched her hymen and prepared her to accept a mature male penis without additional tearing of the hymen,'' the doctor replied.

Grace returned with a copy of the doctor's medical report and asked if it was the one he had submitted. He certified that it was. She asked him to read his conclusions, and he did, by saying that Alicia presented history of prolonged sexual abuse, and a record of sexual activity.

''Now you are claiming that Alicia may not have had any sexual activity at all. Doesn't that contradict what you wrote?''

''My writings refer to a history of abuse and sex as described to me by the patient. However, my physical findings are inconclusive as to whether she has ever been sexually penetrated by a man.''

With that alarming summation by the doctor, who had been an unfortunate choice as a witness for the prosecution, Grace Chandler rested
the state's case. Judge Donovan adjourned the proceedings until the next
morning.

The doctor's testimony confused me. Even if Alicia never had sexual
relations with her father, she had told me enough about her affairs
with boys for me to be almost certain she had been sexually penetrated. The medical examination had come early in the case, so I was
not certain which of the boys she had been with before or after, but
she had indicated that her father had not been the only one for several
years. So how could she not have shown physical evidence after this
level of experience? Later, when I discussed this with other specialists,
I concluded that Dr. Leif's examination had been less thorough than
he indicated. Of course there were always possible anomalies, but I
felt the doubt cast by the doctor had canceled out the "Shampooman"
disclosures.

The testimony that concerned me most was Cory's. His sea foam eyes
and long droopy lashes were so winsome he was more likely to be believed than his less fetching, more disturbed brother, or even his alluring
sister. I realized that I might have information about Cory that Grace
Chandler might not have gleaned from official files. But would giving
her help with her case mean I wasn't properly protecting Cory? I wrestled with that quandary for a while, then decided that it was more important for Grace to have all the ammunition she needed to use against
Red Stevenson.

Friday morning I had been asked to pick up Cory at his home because
Mrs. Castillo couldn't come to court until she dropped another child at
school. Cory had been warned he might have to testify that day and was
touchy. Since I had prepared the list of questions to discredit him, I felt
like a traitor, and once again I wondered whether or not he should have
been appointed a separate guardian.

Noticing him tapping his foot erratically, I asked him if he was
nervous.

"Nope. I'm saying the truth."

"Good for you."

"Last night Dad said it would be over in a few hours and then I could
go home with him."

I explained that even if the trial was concluded that afternoon, we'd
still have to hear what the jury had to say, and that might take until

Monday. "Also, even if your father is free, it might take time for HRS to do the paperwork before you can go home."

I didn't have the heart to tell him that no matter what the verdict HRS might never return him to his father. But I did need to prepare him. "Even if your father had never hurt your brother or sister, I don't think he has been a very good father in the past and I am not convinced he will make a suitable father in the future."

"Why do you say that?" Cory challenged.

I listed many ways his father had neglected him, including not paying for medical and dental treatments, not keeping up with his part of the performance agreement, and I reminded him of his father's violent temper.

"I thought you were supposed to be my voice and say what I wanted. What if I told you I wouldn't live anywhere else?" he said, choking back tears. "Then would you help me?"

As we turned in the courthouse parking lot, I watched his anguished face. Then I made my decision. "Cory, if your father is not found guilty, and if you still want to live with him, I will do my best to make that possible for you."

There was a whole new cast of characters sitting in a cluster in the rear of the courtroom: a bevy of heavyset, hard-looking women who looked like a gang of biker gals on a marshmallow diet.

One of them was Dee Smiley. She was called to the stand. Her name had been on the defense's witness list, but I had thought that since she was the one to whom Alicia had confessed, she would have been sympathetic to the daughter and not the father.

The convenience store manager was wearing an oversize black T-shirt with a lightning bolt across her breasts, a tight, short shirt that barely covered her industrial-size chassis. Her backless heels made a slapping sound as she mounted the witness box. When she turned around after taking the oath, it was obvious she was chewing gum. Then she rotated to face the jury, waved, and said, "Hi, guys!"

The jury members, though, must have had their coffee laced with sedatives because their faces remained poker-faced.

After Dee Smiley identified herself as the manager of the convenience store closest to Stevenson Groves, Walt Hilliard asked her how she knew the Stevenson children.

"They hung out at my place. I like having kids around. I talk to them, listen to their problems," she said in a soothing voice, one that might appeal to a child.

"Did you know all the Stevensons?"

"I got close to the oldest boy, Rich, first."

"How did that happen?"

"I met him because of a tragedy." Dee Smiley told of being at the creek when Rich's friend, Sam, had drowned. She had been nearby with some smaller children, and when she heard the screams, she tried to help. After that, Rich would come by her store all hours of the day or night and talk. When asked what she thought about Rich, Dee replied, "You could tell he was a troubled youngster."

"When was the drowning in relation to the night Alicia told you her problems?" the defense attorney asked.

"About six weeks before."

"How did you meet Alicia Stevenson?"

"She'd come by with Rich, and then when I was friendly to her, she really lapped it up."

"Do you recall what she told you about her father?"

"That he messed with her and she didn't like it."

"Did she explain what she meant by 'messing with her'?"

"No, she just asked if I knew what that meant. I said that I did and it wasn't right, and she said she knew that but he would continue as long as she lived in that house."

"When did you see her again?"

"After she left the groves."

"Where was that?"

"In the parking lot of the HRS building. I'd come to see her after the court hearing that placed her in foster care."

"Was she alone?" Walt Hilliard asked.

"No, she was talking with her friend, Dawn."

"Did you hear what they were saying?"

"Yes. Alicia said if she had known what would've happened, she wouldn't have made up the story to get her father in trouble."

"Did you question her about this?"

"I asked if her father had really messed with her and she said no, he hadn't, and if her father had let her go out with a guy she liked, she never would have said anything to me."

"Who was this person?"

"A man who worked at the motel behind the marina."

"Was he the sort of man a father would want seeing his daughter?"

"No. He was much older, in his twenties, did drugs, didn't have a job, and he was of a different race."

When it was her turn, Grace Chandler confronted Dee Smiley harshly. "Have you ever been arrested in this county?"

"Yes, once."

"What were the charges?"

She gave the prosecutor a nasty stare. "Grand theft."

Grace then asked Dee questions about her relationship to the various children who hung out at the store. "Were you related to any of them?"

"One was my son, and one was my nephew, but the rest were kids who didn't have anyone who cared enough to do things with them."

Grace pursued why she would want to take on other people's problem children. "I know how hard it is out there. I didn't want any of them to turn into Adam Walsh's next victim."

I realized Mrs. Smiley had meant to say a victim like Adam Walsh, because Adam was a Florida boy who had been kidnapped, murdered, and found decapitated a few years earlier, but nobody challenged her syntax and she was asked to step down.

While the next witness was being called, I heard a flurry of voices behind me. I turned around and saw a woman speaking animatedly with Mitzi Keller. She quieted when Cory Stevenson was put under oath.

Cory was wearing a suit that Mrs. Castillo had borrowed, a blue shirt that had belonged to one of my sons, and a red-and-blue striped tie. Like a parent at a recital, I held my breath and hoped he would handle himself well.

During the initial questions, Walt Hilliard treated Cory respectfully, and he soon relaxed enough to loosen his grip on the side of the railing. The defense attorney asked him to describe the sleeping arrangements at the Stevenson house.

"There were bunk beds. I was on top most of the time and Alicia was underneath."

"What were they like?"

"They were old and rusty in the springs."

"Did they make any noise when you sat on them or got up?"

"Yes, they made a crinkly noise. Kind of like old steps."

"Are you easily awoken in the night?"

"Yes, I'm a light sleeper. I always hear the screen door open when my grandfather goes out to smoke."

"Do you think your father could come and get Alicia out of her bed and take her into the dining room without you hearing it?"

"No."

"Have you lived in the same household with your sister most of your life?"

"Yes, always."

"Have you ever heard anyone called 'Shampooman'?"

"No."

"How do you feel about your father?"

"I love him. He treated us great until Alicia and Rich started this stuff. Then Dad got, I guess what you call, frustrated, by what they said about him."

"How do you feel about your sister?"

"I don't understand why she would accuse Dad of doing that to her so I kind of hate her inside, but's she's my sister so I gotta love her too."

"How do you feel about your brother?"

"I guess I love him, but I also kind of hate him too because he's lying about what Dad did to him and my sister."

"Where are you living?"

"In a foster home."

"Why are you there?"

"Because of what Alicia said my father did to her."

"Do you think she is telling the truth?"

"No."

"Did your father ever hurt or abuse you in any way?"

"No."

"Are you afraid of your father?"

"No. I want to go home and live with him."

When her turn came, Grace Chandler used her rougher no-nonsense tone. "Where did your sister shampoo her hair?"

"In the shower."

"Did your father help her?"

"Sometimes."

"Why would she need his help?"

"She covered her face with a washcloth so soap wouldn't burn her eyes when her hair was being rinsed out."

Grace moved her podium slightly, and as she did so, I noticed that she had the two typewritten pages of questions I had prepared for Cory on top of her notes. After each question, I had written in parentheses the answer I believed was correct. I have put my comments in the same manner after the questions.

"Cory, have you ever been arrested?" (He was arrested for vandalism to a truck and crops worth $1,500 and received a sentence involving community service, which he has not fulfilled.)

"Yes, I messed with a tractor."

"Did you receive a sentence?"

"No."

"Weren't you supposed to do some community service?"

"Yes."

"Did you fulfill that?"

"No, HRS moved me before I could."

"With whom were you arrested?" (Dennis Smiley, the son of Dee Smiley. The date was only two days before Alicia supposedly reported the abuse to Dennis's mother.)

"Denny Smiley."

"When did this happen?"

"Last summer."

"Was that around the time Alicia left home?"

"Yes, the same week."

"Who is Dennis's mother and what does she do?"

"Mrs. Smiley runs the convenience store near our house."

"You are living in a foster home now, is that right?"

"Yes."

"How many places have you lived since you were taken from your home?" (Five foster homes and six shelters.)

"A couple of places."

"Would eleven homes in less than a year seem about right?"

"Yes."

"How did you feel about leaving home?" (He says it was the worst day of his life.)

"It was the worst day of my life."

"Do you want to go back to your father?"

"Yes."

"Did your father promise you anything for cooperating with him?" (He promised him a 1932 classic-model truck, which he had to sell to pay his attorney.)

"He said things would be better when I got home again."

Until the moment came, we were unsure whether Red Stevenson was going to take the stand to defend himself. I had met him several times while supervising visits with Cory and found him coarse and unpredictable. He had not hesitated to denigrate Alicia in front of me, pummel Cory inappropriately, and even badger Cory to testify on his behalf. He also had a volatile temper when he was challenged, which I hoped he would reveal during cross-examination.

Richard Leroy Stevenson, Sr., took the oath in a loud, resonant voice. He stated his name, age, residence, and other pertinent facts without hesitation. He told about owning a marine engine repair shop first in town and then at the marina, but that he had sold it to pay for his defense.

"How was your business doing before that?" Walt Hilliard asked.

"Not so good. Just after I moved to the more expensive shop at the marina, there was a recession and people weren't spending as much to buy and maintain racing boats, which was most of my business."

"How did this affect your life?"

"I was under a lot of stress, so I didn't pay as much attention to my family. If I had been, Alicia might not have gotten in with that crowd of boys. When I figured out what was going on, I put my foot down, made some rules about dating, and she became upset."

"What did you notice that she was doing?" Walt Hilliard asked in a friendly manner.

"She was hanging out at the motel behind the marina with older guys and was seen going into the room of a black man and coming out in the middle of the night."

"Did she have any friends with her?"

"Yes, there was one girl, Dawn, whose parents didn't care what she did. Finally I told Alicia I didn't want her seeing Dawn, and she defied me. Then, when Dawn's family moved away, she was always after me to let her go visit Dawn. But knowing the trouble Dawn could get into, I said no."

"How did Alicia accept that?"

"She said she'd get back at me and go live with Dawn."

"You've had HRS involved in your life for many years, is that right?"

"Yes, because of my son Rich's problems. When he was a baby, his mother abandoned the family and he never got over it. As soon as I knew I couldn't handle him, I asked HRS for help and they placed him in special schools."

"Was Alicia familiar with how HRS works?"

"Yes, she thought if they took her away from me, they'd let her live with Dawn, which was her mistake, because she hasn't seen her friend since."

"How did your financial problems affect your marriage?"

"I was distracted and had no urge to make love."

"You didn't want to make love or you couldn't?"

"I couldn't. I was impotent."

"Did you ever go into the toolshed with your daughter?"

"All the children followed me around the groves."

"Did she climb up on your lap and sit with you on the mower-tractor?"

"Sometimes I'd put her on the mower seat with me and take her around when I cleaned up between the trees."

"Did she ever come to work with you at the marine shop?"

"I didn't like to leave the kids alone in the house because they could get into trouble, so if they weren't somewhere being supervised, I'd keep them with me."

Walt Hilliard stepped backward. "Did you ever shampoo your daughter's hair?"

"Mostly she would shampoo it, but I would help her rinse it out so she wouldn't get soap in her eyes."

"What were you wearing when you did this?"

"My shorts and a shirt, but sometimes I would take off my shirt so it wouldn't get splashed."

"Was your daughter naked?"

"No, she covered herself. I'd hand her a towel over the rod."

"Have you ever molested or sexually abused your daughter?"

"No. As God is my witness"—Red raised his hand, then swiveled to face the jury—"I never touched Alicia."

Walt lowered his voice. "Do you love your children?"

"Yes," Red whispered. "I love my daughter and both boys, even after what they've said about me."

"Thank you, Mr. Stevenson," Walt Hilliard said somberly.

Grace Chandler moved her podium so it was facing Red. Even though she was much shorter than he was, she seemed to loom over him as her voice lowered and slowed. "How many times have you been married?"

"Five."

No matter how many lists of dates and names I made, I was never able to derive a logical series of Red's marriages or relationships because the information from the children, documents, and legal sources conflicted. Some said he had been married five times, others six.

"What was your name before it became Stevenson?"

"Hamburg." Red explained how he was later adopted by his ex-wife's father.

"Have you ever been arrested for a felony?"

Before his attorney could object, Red responded that he had been arrested once for making a false statement, but Walt Hilliard wouldn't allow this to be clarified.

Under questioning, Red explained that the children's mother was Tammy, who had been abusive to Rich, neglectful of the other children, and then ran away with another man.

"Who is Dawn Leigh Pruitt?"

"A friend of Alicia's."

"Where is she living now?"

"In the Clearwater area."

"Do you know why she moved?"

"No."

"Didn't her father tell you it was to protect her from you?"

"No."

"You admit you often helped your daughter wash her hair. Did she call you 'Shampooman'?"

"It was something we started when she was little, and it stuck."

"Did you ever call her your little lollipop?"

"We had lots of silly names, like most families."

"How old was she when you stopped helping her wash her hair?"

"Thirteen or fourteen."

"Don't you think that it is a bit odd for a father to be entering the bathroom with his sexually mature daughter and helping shampoo her hair?"

"I didn't see anything wrong with it, besides I gave her a towel."

"Do you expect the jury to believe that you went in there and handed her a towel, which she put around herself with the shower fully running, and then you shampooed her hair?"

"I keep several towels in the house."

"You heard your daughter describe an incident when she was nine and you came into the bathroom at the marine shop and sexually attacked her. Did you ever go into that bathroom when she was there?"

"I might have handed her toilet paper or something."

"Do you know how it feels to be raped by a man?" Again Hilliard objected. "Did you ever sleep overnight at the marina with your son Rich?"

"Yes."

"Why?"

"There had been some thefts of outboard motors and we were trying to prevent that."

"Was there a bed for either of you to sleep in?"

"No, we used sleeping bags."

"Did you get into the same sleeping bag with your son?"

"We only had a two-man bag."

"Did you touch his genitals or ask him to touch yours?" Grace asked.

"No, I wouldn't do that to anyone after what was done to me."

"What was done to you?"

"When I was seven I was raped in an orphanage."

"You lived in an orphanage?"

"Yes, my mother put me there when she couldn't take care of me. My father left me when I was a toddler."

"What happened when you were raped?"

"Four men gang raped me, so I could never inflict that kind of punishment—that pain—on someone else."

"How do you discipline your children?"

"I try to use the reward system for good behavior."

"Where did you learn that?"

"I took a parenting class when Rich was in grade school."

"Why were you taking that class?"

"It was recommended when I had a hard time controlling Rich."

"Before that, did you ever spank Rich?"

"Yes, before taking the class, I thought that was what you were supposed to do."

"Did it help?"

"Rich had so many problems I never could control him."

"Is that why you abused him?"

"I never touched my daughter or my son or Sunny either. I don't know why they would say those things about me." Red looked out at the audience. "Anyone who would do something like that belongs in a jail."

This was the end of the defense's list of witnesses. Grace Chandler said that she wanted to have a rebuttal witness, so there was a brief adjournment. While this was happening, Mitzi Keller came forward and introduced me to Cynthia Schenker.

"Dee Smiley's a liar," Cynthia said excitedly. "I was working for HRS then and my job was to transport Alicia back to the shelter. It was getting late, so I went over to where she was standing with Dawn and I heard what she said to Mrs. Smiley."

Grace Chandler, her arms filled with file folders, was in the aisle. I tapped her shoulder. "This woman claims she was a witness in the HRS parking lot."

Cynthia told the prosecutor her version of the incident.

"Would you be willing to testify?" Grace asked.

When Cynthia agreed, Grace told her to come to her office at once.

Lillian was amazed. "I don't believe this. How did that woman just happen to be in the courtroom?"

"In 'Perry Mason' every trial has a surprise witness," I said.

"Well, I've never seen one in real life before."

When the court resumed, the jury was removed and a procedure called a Richardson hearing was held to determine whether or not the prosecution could call someone who had not been placed on the official witness list. Grace had to explain that until a few moments earlier she had not known, nor could have known, of the existence of Cynthia Schenker, who insisted she had been present when Alicia supposedly recanted.

Then the surprise witness took the stand to explain why she had been in the courtroom. "I had been working for HRS at the time and had been involved with Alicia. I cared about the kid, and when I heard that this might be the last day of the trial, decided to come to see how it turned out for her." She said she never expected that something she had overheard in the parking lot might be of use in the trial.

The judge decided to allow the new witness to testify but wanted to give the defense time to take her deposition. Because it was so late, he adjourned the proceedings until Monday afternoon.

Mitzi met me on the courthouse steps on Monday carrying a paper cup of coffee. She pointed to the delicatessen across the street. "Guess who's having a cozy breakfast over there?" She made a disgusted face as she described seeing Jeremiah and Red Stevenson fawning over Dee Smiley and some other lady in tight pants.

When court reconvened, the former caseworker, Cynthia Schenker, described how she had been in the HRS parking lot with Dee Smiley and had overheard Alicia tell Dawn that she was sorry for the mess and wished that they were not going their separate ways.

"Did she indicate the story about her father's molestation was not true?" Grace asked.

"No, she was apologizing to Dawn because her friend had to be interviewed by the police."

Walt Hilliard challenged Cynthia's version. "Isn't it possible that Alicia told Mrs. Smiley something that you might not have heard?"

"No. I was tailing Alicia so she could not get in anyone else's car, and I was especially vigilant with Mrs. Smiley. That woman has a rescue fantasy about these kids."

Walt Hilliard then questioned Cynthia about her past. "Is it true that you left your job at HRS because you were under the care of a psychiatrist?"

"Yes, but it had nothing to do with the job. I was raped on a visit to California."

"Is that why you are especially protective of girls like Alicia?"

"I care about them, but I was a caseworker long before I was attacked."

Next the prosecutor called Stan Milton from the Palomino Ranch as a witness to rebut Cory's testimony about being a light sleeper to prove that he could have slept through his father's molestation of Alicia.

Under oath, Mr. Milton explained that the shelter portion of the ranch housed difficult children who were considered at high risk for running away, so they had personnel on awake duty around the clock. Those on the night shift were required to keep a written log of every time a child woke up for any reason, including trips to the bathroom, walking around, or nightmares.

"Are there any references in the log to Cory Stevenson getting up at night?"

"None."

"Was he easy to wake in the morning?"

"Not the hardest I have ever seen, but certainly not the easiest either."

"Would you characterize Cory Stevenson as a 'light sleeper' in comparison with other boys his age?"

"No, I would not."

There was a break before the closing arguments. Grace was pleased the way the order of the trial ended because that meant she would give the first closing argument as well as the last rebuttal. "There is always some psychological value in having the last word."

At the moment I didn't see that she needed that, for her side had, to my mind at least, been far more persuasive. The Shampooman revelations had been devastating. Nobody on the jury could think it proper for a father to be helping a daughter in the shower after she reached puberty. Sunny Rhodes's testimony had been backed with solid medical evidence. Cory had appeared young, sweet, yet naive. Just because he had not seen something did not mean it did not happen. The most damaging evidence against Grace's case were Dr. Leif's unsatisfactory gynecological examination and Red Stevenson's portrayal of himself as a frustrated father trying to discipline a wayward daughter. Several times people had mentioned that Alicia had wanted to hang out with an older Afro-American boy. In this southern town, with a retirement-age jury, prejudice about little white girls and big black men had to have an effect.

Grace Chandler moved her podium in front of the jury. Like a diver about to attempt a forward dive with a half twist she closed her eyes in preparation, then began to speak. First she thanked the jury for their patience and their wisdom, then suggested they rely on the collective memories of what they had heard to put together a complicated case of children molested by the person they should have trusted the most to protect them: their father.

Reviewing the charges, Grace stated that the real issue was to determine whether or not Mr. Stevenson, an adult male over the age of eighteen, did, in fact, place his penis in his daughter's vagina before she was twelve years of age at a location in this county.

"Whether or not you like Alicia Stevenson or Richard Leroy Stevenson, Sr., is not the issue. Your only concern should be: did Mr. Stevenson commit this crime against his daughter or not. The judge has ruled that you may consider the evidence that he may have committed the same type of crime on Sunny Rhodes and Rich Stevenson, Jr., which demonstrates a clear pattern of criminality. In each incident with Alicia, Sunny, and Rich look at the similarities: a child was available, and because of Richard Leroy Stevenson's propensity, he did perform a sexual act with them. You heard Mr. Stevenson testify that he himself had been the victim of a sexual crime when he was a child. This is not surprising. We have long known that a victimized child often grows up to continue the cycle of abuse, reproducing the same vile acts generation after generation."

Grace stepped back and stared in Red's direction. "The defendant admitted he was abused as a boy. The defendant admitted he had his daughter on the seat of his mower, but he left out the fondling, which his daughter so poignantly described. In fact, he left out a great deal while still being forced to confess that he did share a sleeping bag with his son in the marine shop and routinely shampooed his adolescent daughter's hair when she was undressed in the shower.

"The defense attorney will probably point out the inconsistency in Alicia's statement as to what age she was when various sexual acts occurred. But use your common sense. Imagine what it was like to be a fifteen-year-old girl who finally was prodded to admit what had been happening in her home for many years. Imagine how you would feel when that whispered confession is broadcast through the HRS abuse registry and filters down to the local police. The sheriff comes to your door and asks if it is true. You are taken from your home in the middle of the night, and immediately are asked to put your most intimate secrets on paper. You are alone. It is almost three in the morning. You are upset and sleepy. In your mind sexual molestation began when someone touched your private parts. To you, that was at the age of five and continued from then on, escalating to full penetration at the age of nine. Suddenly these ages and dates are crucial, but if you are the victim they blend together as part of the same crime: father-daughter incest.''

Grace leaned on the rail in front of the jury. ''Mr. Hilliard will try to put doubts in your mind. He will ask you to consider whether Mr. Stevenson could have penetrated his daughter in a flaccid state. But please recall that Alicia was able to explain that her father became hard. Remember, this happened when Alicia was only a nine-year-old girl, someone far too young to have familiarity with specific sexual details. She only knows what she felt, that it was happening—and happening to her.

''You have heard about the crowded sleeping arrangements in the Stevenson household, and yet Peggy Abbott, who was the stepmother in that house for the longest period of time, admitted she and her husband sometimes took turns sleeping at their shop, leaving the perfect opportunity for abuse. Also, Mrs. Abbott reported that in the last few years of the marriage, sex dropped off, and Alicia testified that around the same time, the rate she had sex with her father increased. For all intents and purposes Alicia was Mr. Stevenson's wife. A man may shampoo the hair of his wife in the shower, but his teenage daughter?'' There was a long pause as the question lingered in the air. ''And yet we have had multiple reports, including one from the defendant, that they played the Shampooman game until long after Alicia was a fully developed young woman.''

The prosecutor went back to her notes. ''Dr. Boggs, the psychological expert, reviewed the many symptoms Alicia presented that showed a troubled child crying out for help. Another signal is self-mutilation, and you heard Dr. Leif say she carved initials into her ankles. In fact, there were so many indicators that a concerned neighbor picked up on the clues. But the defense will dwell on the fact that in some areas this child's memories are vague. Dr. Boggs explained that frequently abused children block painful memories. Even normal adults tend to remember the highs and lows of a relationship more than the average daily incidents, so it is not surprising that Alicia was able to have excellent recall of the crucial moments when she was first fondled in the toolshed and when she was first penetrated in the marine shop bathroom.

"Another question is why Alicia delayed reporting the incest for so long. Dr. Boggs said that disclosures often are not made until the abused child confides in a trusted adult during adolescence. Isn't that what happened here? Mrs. Smiley was someone Alicia saw almost every day, someone who had shown concern for other children, someone who had been there when her brother's friend drowned.

"Dr. Boggs mentioned that disclosure often comes after a traumatic event. If you look at the dates, you will notice that there were two disturbing incidents in the Stevenson household a few weeks before Alicia revealed her secret: Rich Jr.'s best friend drowned and Cory was arrested. Also, note that both of these events involved Mrs. Smiley, since she helped out at the creek and it was her son who was arrested with Cory.

"And speaking of young Cory Stevenson, remember Dr. Boggs's mention of the accommodation syndrome and denial of abuse? You may find it difficult to believe that another child in this home, young Cory Stevenson, could be there during years of abuse to several children and not know it. But this was the only home, only security he knew. He understood what happened to children who made trouble because his older brother had been sent away at the age of five. While we don't know if he was ever abused, we do know that he had a vested interest in denying abuse because if he admitted it, he would lose his home just the way his brother did.

"Now let us look at the similarities between Alicia's story and Sunny's. Very often there is a pattern to these crimes, and one can easily be observed here. Mr. Stevenson starts with fondling, then leads to penetration. Both Sunny and Alicia reported the open bathrobe, being violated on the couch. The only difference is that Sunny had a grandmother she trusted with the secret. When Sunny told, she was protected. Alicia had nobody to tell.

"You cannot overlook the fact that Sunny Rhodes was immediately taken to the hospital and underwent treatment for sexual assault. At the time Sunny said her stepfather had been the perpetrator and there were no other likely suspects. Dr. Diller described the actual injuries she sustained due to an attack in her genital region. Unfortunately, there was never a similar examination performed on Alicia Stevenson prior to the onset of sexual maturity, and the estrogen effect may have masked the evidence of penetration of an immature female. Yet, while there may not be absolute physical evidence of sexual abuse, the doctor has testified that two fingers could be easily inserted in Alicia Stevenson's vagina during an examination, more than enough to permit the entrance of a mature male penis.''

Grace's voice took on a new fervor. ''As adults we may see this differently than the children. But look at it from their point of view. Alicia may have told people she was 'sorry for the mess.' Of course she was. She had no concept of what telling would mean. Isn't it ironic that the perpetrator continues to sleep in his same bed at night while all three of his children have lost their home, been separated, and placed into HRS custody?'' Grace said, pointing to Red. ''That man remains in his home, and it is his children who are punished. It is the children who are bounced from one foster home to another. It is the children who have to get on the stand and be humiliated, embarrassed, scrutinized, and punished.''

Grace Chandler closed her notebook and stepped back from her stand. She walked slowly in front of the jury members, trying to make eye contact with each of them. ''These children have suffered. Two of them have testified to abhorrent acts done to them by their biological father.'' Her voice choked with emotion. ''The time has come to speak out and say that you believe the children, children who had nothing to gain and everything to lose by coming forward. I urge you to put an end to what has happened to these young people, an end to their abuse, as well as the abuse of others. For, if you choose to believe Mr. Stevenson, you are giving him the capacity to perform the same crime again and again.'' Tears filled her eyes. ''Thank you.''

The courtroom was silent. Walt Hilliard was the only one moving. As he stood up, his face seemed pained, as though Grace's summation had touched him as well. In a measured voice he also thanked the jury for their time and attention, then spoke in a deep, confident tone. ''A serious crime has been charged in this case. If Richard Leroy Stevenson, Sr., is found guilty of a felony in the first degree—sexual battery upon a person less than twelve years of age—the State of Florida requires a minimum mandatory sentence of twenty-five years, and yet a mere seventeen percent of the time in this trial was spent on evidence related to this actual charge, while eighty-three percent dealt with other matters only peripheral to the case.

''To keep your attention focused away from the fact that there is not a single piece of proof to substantiate the charges, the prosecutor had to lean on the emotional aspects of a confused young woman's description of events. You have heard words distorted to sound sensational, but is being called 'Shampooman' a crime? Of course not! Nor is calling your daughter a nickname like 'Lollipop.' Members of the jury, don't be confused by these diversions. The only issue is whether or not you think this man is guilty of a heinous crime.

"At first this may seem a daunting task. Concentrate on the issues and refuse to be misled by the extraneous matters that have been brought up to confuse you. Above all remember that as a jury in the State of Florida you must feel that the prosecution has proven beyond all reasonable doubt that Mr. Stevenson is guilty as charged."

Walt Hilliard paused. He took a few steps backward and began again, this time in the more didactic voice of a professor from Civics 101. "How will you sort out sentiment from the fact?" Walt Hilliard held his arms out to the jury in supplication. "When it comes time to make your decision, read the rules of deliberation, study the laws of evidence, and you will see that before you can pronounce this man, this father of three abandoned children, who has done his best under difficult circumstances to raise his family, you must have a conviction which does not waver." His arms fell to his sides.

"When you examine the evidence, you will find it flimsy at best," he said as though the conclusion was obvious. "When pressed to tell what really happened, Alicia becomes muddled about touching and fondling. She said her father felt her breasts when she was five, but an affectionate father might brush up against a child's chest or pat her bottom without it being dirty or sexual." He shook his head sadly. "I feel sorry for Alicia because she is mixed up and alone. And I feel pity for her older brother, Richard Jr., whose mental problems have been so severe he has required extensive psychiatric treatment. Even in this court he demonstrated his obvious disturbance when he used his wife's name when he meant his sister.

"And his sister has serious problems as well. Abandoned at a crucial age by her mother, this lonely child escaped into a fantasy world. This is a young lady with a vivid imagination. She said she had sex regularly with her father but couldn't describe it accurately. She claimed they sometimes had gentle sex, sometimes forceful, violent sex. However, Dr. Leif, a medical expert with more than thirty years experience in examining abused children, could not state that this girl ever had sexual intercourse in her life, let alone forceful, violent sex with a mature male on a regular weekly basis for more than five years. Yes, Dr. Leif allowed that in hypothetical cases the estrogen effect hides some of the evidence of sexual penetration, but not everything. Wouldn't you think that Dr. Leif, the state's expert witness, would see evidence of sexual trauma? But he did not say that. In fact, he agreed it was possible that she may never have had sexual intercourse in her life.''

There were no windows in the courtroom, but a late afternoon storm was lashing the courthouse and the rumblings permeated the walls. Again Walt Hilliard changed his voice, sounding more like the sensitive social worker than the abrasive lawyer. ''Alicia Stevenson is a very troubled teenager. There were financial problems in the family so she couldn't have a closet filled with pretty clothes or a car to drive. When the boat business declined, she was stuck in a one-bedroom house with two siblings—one of whom was mentally ill—a stepmother, who was not getting along with her father, and an ailing grandfather. She wanted out of there in the worst way. Then she remembered how her stepsister Sunny Rhodes got out.'' Walt's voice modulated to a husky stage whisper. ''And do you know what? It worked. The trouble is she didn't have another home to go to the way Sunny did. She dreamed she could live with her best friend, but by the time she realized this was not going to happen, it was too late. Alicia was forced to tell her story over and over again and guess what happened? Her explanations began to change and the truth began to unravel. She became trapped by her web of lies.''

Mr. Hilliard turned toward the audience and waved his arm to indicate the section where I was sitting with Lillian and the HRS workers. ''How could Alicia retreat from those stories? How could she let down these well-meaning women who have so much invested in prosecuting perpetrators in order to protect our community's children from evil? No, it was too late. Even if Alicia wanted to, she could not recant. She tried. In the HRS parking lot, with some of these good women nearby, she attempted to apologize for 'the mess' she made, but nobody was listening then.''

Walt Hilliard strolled back toward the jury. He put his hands on the podium and leaned forward. ''I have pity for this child. I have compassion for her pain, and that of poor, confused Richard Jr.'' Then he raised his voice. ''You, the jury, are the ones who must weigh what they have claimed with the more balanced testimony of the other adults. In each case you must ask yourself where each person was coming from. Look at the ex-wife who testified. Peggy Abbott had a failed marriage and admitted resenting the time this father spent with his children, so she made the worst, most egregious interpretation of innocent events. Yes, perhaps Mr. Stevenson woke up his children with squirt guns or washed out his son's mouth with soap. Perhaps you might not approve of these discipline techniques, but are they a crime? If they are, why was he not charged with them? If, as it is alleged, he molested another child, why was he not charged with that crime either? Do not forget that Mr. Stevenson is charged with only one count against his daughter. One count. One story she made up to get out of the house about when she was nine years old. Not when she was fifteen. Oh, no, not when there could have been physical evidence to link him with her.''

Now Walt was shouting and the storm outside was thundering. ''Why, there is not one shred of physical evidence in a young woman who claimed to have regular violent, pounding sex.'' Pelting rain could be heard reverberating in the distance. ''How is that possible? How could an experienced physician testify that Alicia Stevenson might be a virgin?''

Walt Hilliard's passion far surpassed anything that Grace Chandler had been able to muster, and for a moment I thought I had walked into an audition for ''L. A. Law.'' His hands slid down the sides of the podium until they fell limply at his side. ''I ask you not to look at the facts in the case and decide if they are mostly true. I ask you not to decide if there is clear and convincing evidence for you to believe that something probably happened.''

The attorney stepped forward like a preacher about to anoint the congregation. ''Mr. Stevenson is presumed innocent unless his guilt is so clearly proven that you, the jury, can see that no reasonable doubt remains as to the guilt of the person charged. I ask you to do your duty and decide whether the evidence in this case makes you fully convinced and satisfied as to a moral certainty—*a moral certainty*—that Richard Leroy Stevenson, Sr., is guilty of sexual battery on his minor child beyond a reasonable doubt.'' His tone lowered again to sound as paternal as possible. ''For, if after you deliberate, you have reason to question any or all of the testimony, you must not send this man to prison for what will certainly be close to the balance of the rest of his natural life.''

The defense attorney hung his head. ''Please go and deliberate with guidance of God, and with honest appreciation of all of us here. Thank you.''

I wanted Walt Hilliard's business card in case anyone I knew ever needed a criminal lawyer. Jeremiah Stevenson had mortgaged his house and used the last of his savings to pay the retainer, but for them it had been worth it. After that summation, it would be difficult to convict this man.

Clearly at a disadvantage, Grace Chandler came forward to give her rebuttal closing. She gazed at the jury at eye level, then turned to indicate Mr. Hilliard seated at the table with his client. "You have just been entertained by great theatrics, but do not be deceived that they were anything but that. Mr. Hilliard is manipulating your emotions and ignoring that there are hard, cold facts that Mr. Stevenson has sexually molested at least three children over many years duration. I can't feel sorry for Mr. Stevenson, and I can't concern myself about how he might fare in prison when he did not concern himself how his natural born children would suffer for the rest of their lives from the deep psychological wounds he inflicted on them to satisfy his own lust.

"Yes, you must find him guilty beyond a reasonable doubt, but that does not have to be an abiding conviction of guilt. As you deliberate whether the state has proved that this father did to his daughter what is charged, you, the jury, are permitted to take into consideration what he also did to his son as well as to Sunny Rhodes."

Grace lifted her chin righteously. "Defense attorneys use many tactics to deflect your concerns. Notice that Mr. Hilliard became the most upset when talking about Sunny Rhodes. Her testimony was the strongest, most corroborating evidence. She was molested when she was almost the same age that Alicia was when her first penetrations began. Sunny Rhodes was examined by a doctor, who has verified the physical findings of sexual abuse. I do not know why Mr. Stevenson was not charged for that crime, but he did abuse her, just as he abused his natural daughter, Alicia, in the same manner."

Grace was not speaking from notes, so she hesitated now and then. "You see in front of you a pleasant-looking man dressed in a suit and tie. It is difficult for good people to comprehend that a man could have sexual intercourse with his own children. But it does happen. Pedophiles are people with serious mental problems. There is no logic to what pedophiles do. And they are clever. They must get the object of their desire through subterfuge. Alicia was groomed by her father with little kindnesses and gifts, even money. He conspired with her and made her feel she was doing something special. He boxed her in, made her keep the secret, until she finally felt strong enough to reveal it.

"Remember the words 'violent, forceful, hard, pounding sex'? These were not Alicia's words. These were the attorney's phrases. The truth is even more difficult to grasp. Alicia's father was kind and loving to her. This father taught his daughter that loving a parent meant having sex with him. And, you have heard her say, that despite everything, she still loves her father, proving that what happened between them had a loving, if perverted, aspect to it.''

There was a long pause as the prosecutor allowed this awful truth to permeate the room. Grace turned to the audience, then back to the jury. ''We have heard four children testify in this courtroom. Either three are lying and one is telling the truth, or three are telling the truth and one is lying. To evaluate whether Cory Stevenson might be the solitary one telling the truth, you must consider his underlying interest. He has been utterly miserable in foster care. Home is the haven to which he wants to return. Now let's look at another of the defense's star witnesses. Dee Smiley is the one person who has testified that Alicia may have lied. Yet Mrs. Smiley is the only person who has recanted her story. For some reason she has ignored Alicia's cry for help and has befriended the abuser.'' Grace shook her head sadly. ''You saw Mrs. Smiley. You decide if she made a credible witness or not.''

Grace Chandler stiffened her spine. ''This case has shattered the childhood of at least four young people. The Stevenson children will never be the same. Even if Cory has not admitted abuse, he will have to live with himself and his problems. Isn't it pathetic to realize that Mr. Stevenson, who admits that he was horribly abused as a child, may have passed on the same legacy to his children? But these insidious violations can be stopped. They must be stopped. Molestation is a common result of being abused as a child. Please, help put an end to the cycle of abuse now!''

While the jury deliberated, the different parties in the case formed into islands on the first floor of the courthouse and spilled out on the steps. Red Stevenson was surrounded by Walt Hilliard, the attorney's partner, Cory, and his grandfather. Dee Smiley was outside smoking with another woman, who was wearing tight black stirrup slacks, a black satin blouse with a rose embroidered across the chest. I saw Red Stevenson come up behind the other woman, slip his hand around her waist, and give her an intimate squeeze.

Rich had been returned to Janet's mother's home Friday afternoon and had not been recalled on Monday, so Mitzi Keller joined Ruth Levy and Alicia while the other HRS employees, including Cynthia, formed a flank of support nearby. Lillian left to call the Guardian ad Litem office. Not knowing what else to do, I circulated between Cory's camp and Alicia's followers like a hostess for the cast party of ''Family Feud.''

When I was standing beside Cory, his grandfather pleaded with me.

"Please, no matter what happens, may Cory come home with me to-night?"

"I don't think so," I replied sympathetically.

"I don't want to be alone," the grandfather said, his body trembling like a cornered coon.

Cory had pasted on a chipper expression. "Don't worry, Gramps. I know it is going to turn out just like it is supposed to be."

I didn't have the heart to prepare Cory to have his balloon burst. What would it matter? If it burst, it burst, and I would deal with the fallout.

I noticed that Alicia had drifted away from Ruth. I eased away from Cory and over to her. I put my arm around her shoulder. "Almost over."

Alicia wasn't paying attention to me. She was watching her father.

"You want to talk to him?" I dared ask.

"Uh-huh," she muttered under her breath.

I looked around the corridor. The attorneys were talking elsewhere and Jeremiah was sitting on a bench with Cory. Steering her slightly with the pressure of my arm, I led Alicia to her father.

"Dad . . . ," she said in a whisper.

Red looked at her, his eyes shining with tears. "I never meant to hurt you with anything I did."

"I know. Me too."

Suddenly self-conscious, Alicia headed for the water fountain, pre-tending that is where she had been going the whole time.

Then Lillian was by my side. "How are you doing, Gay?"

"Numb. You know, no matter what happens, nothing is solved for any of these children."

In less than an hour and a half we were called back into the courtroom. Walt Hilliard took this as a fortuitous sign. In the elevator he was patting his client on the back. "They couldn't have had much to deliberate over. You'll see."

Red was not so confident. He was trembling. As the door opened he spoke to me. "You're planning to keep my boy from me no matter what happens?"

I looked him in the eye. "No. I'll do what is best for Cory, even if it means fighting HRS."

For the first time the children were allowed in the audience of the courtroom. Cory sat to my left, flanked by Marta Castillo on his other side. Alicia was to my right, sitting beside Ruth Levy. I stared straight ahead as the jury foreman handed the verdict to the bailiff, who gave it to the judge, who passed it back.

Then it was read aloud.

"Not guilty."

Cory jumped out of his seat. "Told you!" I held him down until the judge dismissed the jury, then I allowed Cory to pull me along with him to see his grandfather. Jeremiah was clutching his chest and breathing erratically.

I started back to Alicia, who was crying against Ruth's bosom, but the reporters circling Grace Chandler made it impossible for me to get to her. I watched as Ruth led her out the door.

Grace was ashen. "This typifies the difficulty in getting a conviction in sexual battery cases in this county," she said to the reporters. "Now you see why victims fear pressing charges."

Red Stevenson was being interviewed by another reporter. "I just knew the truth would be told, but I was scared like anyone would be."

"What are your plans for the future?" Red was asked.

"I'm going to try to get a job, get my son back, and my life together."

"Will you remain in the area?"

"I've been here for sixteen years, and I now have no reason to leave."

Extricating myself from Cory, I eventually made my way to Grace Chandler's office. The prosecutor was sitting beside Alicia on the couch. Tears streaked Grace's cheeks as she told a story of something that had happened to her grandmother. I had missed the first part but heard the ending.

"She told me, 'Don't worry, they'll get theirs in the end.' And your father will get his too."

"Nobody believed me," Alicia said, her voice more furious than sad.

"I believed you," Grace said sincerely.

"Guess I can't sit at your desk anymore," Alicia said dejectedly.

"Sure you can. You can come to see me anytime."

Ruth had to be home for the other girls and asked me to join them as soon as I could. I said I would and then spent a few moments alone with Grace. I thanked her for everything and she generously acknowledged my assistance.

I ran my hand along the mahogany rim of her desk. "The most important thing you did was to give Alicia control of your office. It was therapeutic somehow."

"I noticed that," Grace replied simply. "And I meant it when I said I wanted her to come to visit. Tell her I care, okay?"

* * *

I spent the next hour sitting around the table at the Levy household trying to deflect questions from Alicia's furious foster sisters. "It just goes to show you," one of them said, "adults can abuse kids as much as they want and get away with it."

"Yeah," another one chimed in, "nobody has ever listened to us and nobody ever will."

My next stop was to the Castillos'. Marta had bought Cory's favorite coffee ice cream and they offered me a bowl. "When can he go home?" Marta asked.

"I don't know."

"May he call his father?"

"Yes, of course. Call him now if you want."

There was only one course of action for Cory. He had to go home, otherwise he would never accept a placement in a foster home or be willing to visit his mother.

As soon as Mitzi heard my viewpoint, she became irate and said she would never be party to "offering up a child to a pedophile on a platter."

"Cory can resist sexual advances from his father," I argued. "Also, do you think after Red's recent experiences in jail and court, he would try anything with his son?"

"He's free to molest anyone he wants."

"That's true. He's a free man, and there is nothing you or I can do about that."

"Oh, no?" Mitzi said. "I can hold Cory in foster care."

"Why? To prove a point or keep him safe? You know Cory had some sort of sexual escapade at the ranch and another at the Levys' with Larry, so what are you protecting him from when you keep him away from the one place he wants to be?"

I started to build a case for sending Cory home.

Red had finished the parenting class required by the performance agreement. Cory's therapist, Dr. Farrington, said he would write a report suggesting that Cory be allowed to have a trial visit home again, but only if he continued in therapy and remained under the court's protection as a child in need of services.

Next the guidance counselor reported that Cory had been suspended from school because a friend of the Castillos had come by claiming to be his brother and had signed him out. When Mitzi heard this, she claimed it was proof that "Cory is like his father and brother, and to send him home would be to insure he would become a criminal."

I reminded Mitzi that HRS did not have a sterling record for parenting him either and that this latest incident involved a friend of the foster parents and not anyone in his family. "I think Cory is trying to tell us that he is going to continue to act out until he gets his way and goes home."

"So, you think we should reward that behavior?" Mitzi asked as a challenge.

"I believe he will never accept the rules of HRS, or society, because he feels he and his father have been wronged. Now his father has been cleared by a jury of his peers, further justifying Cory's position."

"But, Gay," Mitzi pleaded, "you believe Red is a pedophile, don't you?"

"I think Red molested Alicia, Sunny, Dawn, and all the other girls, and I think he murdered his first wife. I think he is a creep and a lousy father. And I believe that Cory will figure this out after he lives there again. When he does, he can decide whether to return to foster care, this time with a positive attitude, or go to his mother in Washington state."

"That's probably where we are going to send him anyway."

"Not without his agreement, Mitzi. I won't have him transported like luggage."

"That's where we differ."

"There's a judicial review coming up in a month with Judge Donovan, who presided over the trial. He heard the evidence," I said. "You and I will both present the facts to him and he can decide."

Lillian Elliott had agreed to accompany me on my first visit to the Stevenson home. I had borrowed my husband's pickup truck for the drive to the groves because I felt it would be more inconspicuous. Even though we had been expected, Jeremiah greeted us in his bathrobe and explained that Red Stevenson had to see someone at the marina about a temporary job and would be back soon. The kitchen counters were covered with soiled pots and dishes, and roaches moved around with impunity. There were cigarette butts shoved into beer and soda cans and a smoky residue in the air.

The phone rang. It was Red apologizing for not being there. He asked if we could meet him at a fish restaurant near the marina instead.

"Please let me have my Cory back," Jeremiah begged as we left.

When Lillian and I arrived at the restaurant, we found Red sitting at the table with the woman he had hugged in the courthouse. Red introduced us to his "fiancée," Bernadette Gonzales. Bernadette couldn't have been more than twenty-five. She had creamy skin and wore a black velvet choker around her neck with a dangling heart pinned in the center. Her lips were painted a purplish red and she had a thick layer of violet eye shadow. She reminded me of a cheap imitation of Liz Taylor.

Bernadette explained that she was a dental hygienist who had recently completed formal training and was finally "making good money."

In her inimitable way, Lillian didn't flinch from the direct approach. "Are you currently living with Mr. Stevenson?" Bernadette nodded. "Will you continue to cohabit with him if Cory comes home?" Again she agreed.

"Do you have any children of your own?" I asked, then was relieved to learn she had none, especially no young daughters.

I then pulled out the performance agreement and went over what Red had to accomplish legally to get Cory back. Bernadette seemed to understand what had to be done and encouraged him to do it. Red, however, acted confused and resistant. Bernadette patted his hand and explained why it was time to put all that aside for "Cory's sake."

Bernadette mentioned that she was looking forward to spending time with Cory during the weekly supervised visits. "I know the importance of doing well in school and I am working on an advanced course at night, so we can study together."

After we left, Lillian and I agreed that having Bernadette in the home might be a positive influence. But I was nagged with one further doubt. Red Stevenson had undergone extensive psychological testing. I needed to know if this had revealed any threat to Cory.

I called Walt Hilliard and introduced myself as one of those "well-meaning women" on the benches, congratulated him on his splendid defense, and said that I was not concerned with his client's guilt or innocence, but in the welfare of his children. "I want you to know that the position of the Guardian ad Litem office is that Cory should be returned to his home. However, I have one serious concern."

"And what is that?" he asked cordially.

"Before I can go before the judge and unequivocally recommend Cory's return to his father, I must see the psychological that Dr. Osterman has on file."

"I can assure you that there is nothing in that record that would indicate a problem for Cory."

"I need to see it for myself."

"I'll have to ask my client for a release."

"As per my court order, he doesn't have to give one, but if that will expedite matters before the judicial review, fine. Mitzi Keller has announced that HRS's position will be to oppose Cory's return home. However, if I am satisfied that Red offers no danger to Cory, I will join your side to return Cory home under the condition that you will encourage your client to continue therapy for himself as well as his son.''

Not long after I hung up the phone, Mitzi Keller reported that Cory had been asked to leave the Castillos' that afternoon. He had cut school again and they didn't want to be responsible for him if he was going to be a truant.

''Where will you take him?''

''Anyplace that will hold him long enough for us to procure a one-way ticket to Spokane.''

''Wasn't Cory supposed to have a visit with his father last night?''

''That was canceled because he was on in-school suspension for cutting classes.''

''But that was going to be the first scheduled visit in more than three months. He was really looking forward to it.''

''We're not going to reward the kid for being a jerk.''

''Don't you think his actions might be related to his anger at not seeing his father as promised?''

I called Mrs. Castillo to see if Cory might be able to remain with her until we were able to see the judge, and was surprised to learn she had gone to Texas to pick up her niece and nephew. Apparently their single mother was in the military reserves and had just been drafted for duty in the Gulf War. Marta had volunteered to care for her children. Knowing how many beds were available at the Castillo home, I understood why the rush to get rid of Cory. Despite all of Marta's promises to him, a foster child was still expendable.

Lillian helped me arrange a special emergency hearing the next day to decide Cory's placement.

''Where do you think he should go?'' Lillian asked me.

''Cory's been a dismal failure in foster care, or perhaps the fault is the other way around. In any case, this child has two parents, both of whom want him.''

''Do you think his mother will take him?''

''I'll check, but he won't go there unless he definitely isn't permitted to live with his father, and even then, I think he'll rebel until he gets his way eventually.''

Lillian said she'd back me any way I wanted to go. In the meantime Cory was moved to a shelter home for the night. I phoned Tammy Spate to ask whether she would take Cory immediately. "Of course," she replied, "you didn't even have to ask."

As I readied for the emergency court hearing I realized how ironic it was to be fighting to send a child back to live with his abusing father, and yet I saw no other solution. To me Cory was a young wildfire almost out of control. Dousing with water had not sufficed. The way to cut this conflagration off was to set a backfire to contain it. In doing so, though, there was always the risk that matters could become worse.

Fortunately, Lillian was there for support, but everyone else was openly hostile. The HRS attorney insisted he was not prepared and that his witnesses, including Mitzi Keller, were away at a conference, and so he asked for a continuance. I told the judge that I could see no harm in a preliminary two-week visit because the father had been judged not guilty and that HRS had no better plan for Cory. The judge concurred, and that afternoon Cory went home with his father for the first time in almost one and a half years.

In the corridor Walt Hilliard shook my hand and told his client, "the guardian program is the shining star of the judicial system."

Mitzi was furious. "You are the only Guardian ad Litem who has ever recommended a child be sent back to an abusing home." I stated that it had been what Cory wanted. "Since when do we do what kids want? I've had abused kids claim they want to go back to parents who have cut their fingers off. Are you going to recommend that Alicia go home as well?" I shook my head. "Why Cory and not her?"

Lillian suggested that for more ammunition to use in the judicial review, I talk to a forensic psychologist whose specialty was reuniting children with abusive parents. The expert listened to my description of the case, then she asked, "Is the father scared? If he is, so much the better. Warn him he will be constantly under your scrutiny. Tell the kid that if his father hurts him, he should tell someone so his father can get help, and insist that the father and son must remain in therapy. Inform the therapist and significant teachers to report any unusual behavior or nonverbal acting out promptly." She suggested that I enlist Bernadette's help in reporting problems with Cory or evidence of abuse, "if only to protect the father from more legal entanglements."

The next day I steeled myself and drove alone to the groves in our pickup truck. There was a noticeable difference in the house. The musty odor had been relieved and the whole place was picked up and tidy with a neat stack of magazines on the coffee table. Red, Jeremiah, Bernadette, and Cory sat around drinking iced tea from clean glasses while I discussed the antagonism that we all faced with HRS. Red became infuriated and blamed everything on "that bitch, Mitzi. If she comes around here, I can't be responsible for what happens." Bernadette calmed Red down, saying, "Listen to Gay. She is trying to help."

I took Cory outside and talked to him. He said he was happy and wanted to remain, but I could see tension in his face. I told him to come inside the cab of the truck. "I'm not going to beat around the bush. I believe that your father may very well have harmed other children, including your brother and your sister. I also think that if he tries anything, you are old enough to protect yourself. Now, I am willing to go back to court and fight to allow you to stay home, but only if I know you will be safe, or if you feel threatened, you will get the hell out of there as fast as you can."

"I already have a plan," Cory told me, then explained where he would go and what he would do if anyone tried to hurt him. I took out something I had written and showed it to Cory.

A CONTRACT OF TRUST

I, Gay Courter, as Guardian ad Litem for Cory Stevenson promise to continue to work for Cory's best interests no matter where he is living or how he is doing. I will pass on information between all family members including parents, sister, and brother, and will assist family members in visiting one another. I will do my best to come to see Cory whenever he says it is important to do so. I will be available by telephone and will accept collect phone calls. [I then listed three telephone numbers.]

I, Cory Stevenson, promise to stay in touch with Gay Courter and let her know how I am doing, both during good times and bad. I promise to call her whenever my situation changes, if I move my residence, if I run away from any home or facility where I am living, if I am in any trouble at home with either of my parents, or grandparents, in a foster home, or living elsewhere. I will contact her if I am in difficulty in school or have been picked up or arrested by authorities, or will have my attorney contact her within 24 hours of an arrest. I will let her know if anyone harms me physically or if I feel unusually upset or unhappy, within 24 hours of the problem. I will also let her know of special things that happen too.

The first copy was on regular paper. We signed it together, then I handed him a copy I had reduced several times on my copy machine so it would fit in his wallet. We both signed this as well and shook hands.

* * *

Three days later Cory called. His voice sounded scared and wavering. Something had happened already! My heart pounded wildly until he explained that he was home from school with a fever. I thanked him for letting me know why he was home and was pleased he had "tested our contract."

The regularly scheduled six-month judicial review to discuss Cory's placement in foster care was set for the anniversary of the week Cory had become a foster child a year earlier. But this was anything but a routine hearing. Lined up on one side of the table were Lillian Elliott, Nancy Hastedt, me, the guardian program attorney, Kit Thorndike, Walt Hilliard, Red Stevenson, and Cory. Jeremiah Stevenson, not officially a party to the case, was kept in the antechamber, where Alicia and Ruth Levy also were waiting to testify. Mitzi was flanked by the HRS attorney, Calvin Reynolds, as well as her supervisor.

As perfunctorily as possible, I reviewed recent events for the judge. "Cory flared up with emotional problems, got in trouble with teachers, went through in-school suspension, and cut school with an older boy, a friend of his last foster family. He also was accused of mischief around the school, but no charges were pressed. This was due in part to a rejection by this foster family because they had to take in two small children of a relative on an emergency basis. He also was denied the first supervised visit with his father in more than three months, which made him extremely angry. The sum of these events caused him to lose his placement and resulted in the emergency hearing, after which he was allowed to visit his father. While I realize that Mr. Stevenson has hardly been a model father, HRS, due to various administrative problems, has failed to provide any but the most rudimentary services for Cory. No counseling was offered until I enrolled Cory myself."

Calvin Reynolds insisted that these facts had nothing to do with the problem at hand. "We maintain that Mr. Stevenson has a history of abuse dating back more than ten years. He has been confirmed as a perpetrator of crimes against several children and these cases have been disposed of in juvenile court, where the standard of proof is a preponderance of evidence. Simply because Cory has not made allegations of sexual abuse does not mean that he would not be at risk for such abuse."

I pointed to the third page in my report. "I know there are concerns about whether Cory might be at risk for sexual abuse in his father's home. Cory's therapist, Dr. Farrington, has felt that Cory may be at risk if he returns there, since he thinks Mr. Stevenson may have pedophiliac tendencies and these have never been treated. The psychological report prepared by Dr. Osterman reveals a long history of Richard Stevenson, Sr.'s, problems. Mr. Stevenson has been married at least five times, has had a traumatic childhood, and was sexually abused himself. All three of his offspring are experiencing psychological problems, some in the extreme. If Cory were to have permanent placement with his father, I would like to see an updated and more complete evaluation along with evidence of ongoing therapy for his current presenting problems and an analysis of Cory's jeopardy in his care.''

"What about the mother in Washington state?'' Mitzi's supervisor asked.

"Tammy is a long shot, '' I agreed. "I'd prefer that Cory return home first, but I'd rather send him to Spokane than back into foster care.''

"Then could we agree on an immediate transfer of custody to his mother in Washington?'' Calvin Reynolds asked.

"No, not if Cory won't accept it,'' I answered. "Look, since everyone is worried about the risk of sexual abuse to Cory, we also have to ask whether Cory is at risk for sexual abuse in the custody of HRS.'' I listed the two sexual abuse incidents he may have had in foster care. "Obviously HRS cannot guarantee his safety either. So, is Cory at risk for sexual abuse in his father's care? While it is likely that Mr. Stevenson has sexually abused children at some time, he has never been convicted of a sexual offense against a child. Further, Cory maintains his father has never abused him in any way. Also, Cory is almost fifteen, of normal intelligence, has good coping skills, and friends in the community he trusts including his grandfather, teachers, a guidance counselor, a therapist, a former foster mother, as well as his Guardian ad Litem. It is unlikely that Cory would subject himself to serious abuse without contacting someone who could help him.'' I told about my recent conference with the forensic psychologist, who discussed the importance of not destroying bonding even in dysfunctional homes. "In reuniting families in which abuse (including incest) has occurred, she felt that it can work providing the child is over twelve, that the abuse is out in the open, that the child is old enough and capable of defending himself, the perpetrator has been scared by the legal proceedings, and if the parent and child receive therapy after they are reunited. Cory Stevenson fits exactly into her definition and I believe he has a better chance of success in his home than in any other environment currently available to him.''

After very little further discussion, Judge Donovan ruled that Cory could return home for six months, to be supervised by HRS. He was to continue with his weekly therapy sessions and was permitted to go on a trip to Spokane for two weeks with Alicia to see Tammy.

Cory left the judge's chambers and fell into the outstretched arms of his grandfather. Red Stevenson came out and shook my hand. Alicia was standing by, in tears. Not only had she lost her criminal case, she had lost the ability to protect her brother.

I walked Cory to the elevator. "Remember the deal!" I said and he gave me a salute as the elevator doors closed.

Then I went back to his sister in the antechamber and said, "Alicia, I know this seems crazy, but this is a step on the journey. Cory won't last with your father, but he has to learn that for himself."

"So, now what?" she said, giving me one of her most petulant pouts.

"We'll go on from here," I said with more conviction than I felt. "You'll both visit your mom in Spokane. Then you each can decide where you want to live. Maybe you'll end up there together."

"I don't ever want to leave Ruth," Alicia said loyally as Mrs. Levy came to her side.

"Then, just like I fought for Cory, I'll fight for you to remain where you want to stay."

"You won't make me go live with my mother?"

"No. You'll have a visit—a vacation—that's all. And you won't even have to do that if you don't want to, but hey, why pass up a free trip?"

"Do I have to decide that now?"

"No, Alicia, there is plenty of time for that."

We hugged and she left with Ruth.

Mitzi was standing beside Lillian complaining about having to supervise Mr. Stevenson. "This will never last," Mitzi warned me.

"I'm not expecting it to," I said.

"Then why . . . ?"

"Because Cory has to learn things for himself. Nothing else will work."

5

Saying "No" to Never

The Colby Family

Listen to the mustn'ts *child*
Listen to the don'ts
Listen to the shouldn'ts
The impossibles, *the* won'ts
Listen to the never haves
Then listen close to me—
Anything can happen, child
Anything *can be.*

—SHEL SILVERSTEIN

THE DAY I WAS IN COURT waiting to clear Lydia Ryan of her unfair criminal charges, I sat through several other dependency cases. Without knowing their background, it was difficult to follow the proceedings, which were conducted in a legal shorthand referring to petitions and motions before the court. My interest was piqued, however, when the bailiff led in a prisoner dressed in pumpkin orange. As he took his seat next to his attorney, the man's leg shackles clanked against the metal chair frame. A woman sitting nearby with her attorney glared at him.

"The happy parents?" I asked Lillian, who was beside me.

Lillian nodded her head morosely. "They're the Colby family. HRS calls them the case that won't go away."

The agitation at the moment revolved around the parents giving another caretaker a power of attorney in case of a child's medical emergency. Since a child in regular foster care would be covered by Medicaid, I was confused.

"These Colby children are under the protective services department, not foster care," Lillian explained. Protective supervision is a court-imposed condition used as a tool to monitor families in crisis, hoping to keep the children out of foster care.

Lillian then explained that the original Guardian ad Litem for the Colby children had moved and she was acting as the guardian until another could be appointed. "Would you mind reading the file and giving me an opinion on what might be done here?" she asked.

Distracted by Lydia's impending case, I must have nodded in agreement, for the file came in the mail two days later.

There were three Colby sisters: Simone, sixteen; Nicole, fourteen; and Julie, twelve. Currently Simone was living with a family named Baldwin, Nicole with a Mrs. Lamb, and Julie was back with her mother, Lottie Colby Delancy Hunt. During the past six months Julie had also been to the Holy Family Children's Home in Miami twice, and had also lived with Whitney Sutton, identified as a stepsister; her father, Mervyn "Buddy" Colby; and someone called Mrs. Hopper. Nicole had also been to the same homes and to Miami once. Fortunately Simone had been able to remain in the Baldwin home for more than a year.

"This is ridiculous!" I said furiously when I called Lillian. "Do these girls live out of suitcases? What the hell is going on?"

"It is complicated . . . ," Lillian responded demurely.

"Well, give me the short course, okay?"

"Did you read the police files yet?"

"No, I am still on the itineraries. How can these girls have anything like a normal life? Why, Julie alone has had four—or is it five?—school transfers this year, and it's only February."

"The father and mother have been divorced for about eight years. Custody went to the mother, and she has remarried twice in that time, maybe more than that, I've lost track. At least one of the stepfathers, Jeb Delancy, was violent and abusive. He broke one kid's nose, beat the other with a two-by-four to the point where she was hospitalized, and terrorized the youngest so badly she developed a stutter and an ulcer. Custody then reverted to the father, who has a serious problem with alcohol. He's incarcerated now on a drunk driving violation, not his first and probably not his last. He's fine with them, unless he's drinking, but then he gets mean. He's beat them so hard with his favorite instrument, electrical cords, that he's left loop markings on their torsos. Somewhere there should be some Polaroids of the bruises, including one of Simone's eye swollen shut."

While Lillian spoke, I thumbed through the file and found an envelope containing the photographs. "Oh, God!" I said. "How could anyone . . . ?"

Lillian did not reply. Finally, I broke the silence. "Both parents are unfit, right? So, why don't we terminate their parental rights and find these girls a permanent home together somewhere?"

"HRS doesn't have a foster home that would accept three teenage sisters."

"What about an adoptive home?"

"Hardly anyone wants to adopt teenagers. It's rare to place one child, let alone three of them, Gay."

"Rare! Where have I heard that before?" I snapped. "Supposedly it was 'rare' to get a dismissal on a case, but we got one for Lydia. I'll bet there is a home in this community for three sisters. What are the kids like?"

"Darling, absolutely adorable. I've had to resist taking little Julie home myself. They are affectionate, bright, pretty children."

"Drugs, pregnancy, diseases . . . ?"

"None."

"How are they doing in school?"

"Considering the interruptions in their lives, remarkably well."

"Then, let's go for broke."

"But, Gay, you know the system is set up to be adversarial. As soon as you bring up the idea, the lawyers for the parents are going to fight you tooth and nail. Their job will be to protect the 'rights' of their clients, and they won't give a damn about the children's feelings."

"Why can't we change that? These aren't little contracts, these are children who need love and care and permanency. Let the biological parents continue to provide what little affection they can while allowing someone else to offer the nurturing and home they, for whatever reason, cannot. If a parent does love her children, she will want the best for them. If she doesn't, then she shouldn't give a hoot about signing them away."

"I love your spirit," Lillian said. There was a long pause, then, "I gather you are accepting the Colby case."

I laughed. "Did I ever have a choice?"

The moment I read the prodigious file, I decided that these children had been jerked around long enough. It was the Stevensons all over again. The siblings were separated. Each was having more and more severe problems. Nobody was attempting to reunite either the family or the sisters. Soon it would be too late for any of the girls to recover. If this had been one of my first cases, I might have felt the necessity to check everything with each department in HRS, working my way up the ladder from caseworker to supervisor to manager and allowing each the polite amount of time to get back to me. But I was fortified with an overwhelming sense of urgency. These three sisters were waiting to be settled so they could mature and flourish. When children were without a family, they were like potbound plants cramped in portable containers on a shelf.

They needed to be taken home, replanted in a fertile, sunny garden, and nourished before they could grow strong roots, sprout fresh stalks, and begin to flower. Unwilling to take the chance that these tender seedlings might wither away, I plunged right in, taking steps out of order and pursuing some shortcuts and making unorthodox detours.

After another briefing with Lillian, as well as a thorough study of the files, I called the Colbys' protective services caseworker, Iris Quinones.

"Simone has found herself a lovely home with the Baldwin family," Iris said in a singsong voice. "Their daughter, Eliza, is Simone's best friend. Ken Baldwin is a contractor, who built his family a large home on the Brookside Golf Course. Carol Baldwin is a speech therapist specializing in stroke victims. She's worked with Julie on her stutter with remarkable results. While the Baldwin family has promised to keep Simone until she graduates high school, they also have two younger sons and cannot accept any more children into their home."

"Do the Baldwins receive any money from the parents or HRS?"

"No, they cover Simone's expenses personally. Although they have asked the Colbys to contribute a modest amount every month, so far they haven't received a penny. They even paid for Simone to have some plastic surgery on her eye to repair the damage from one of her father's attacks."

"Does Simone have medical insurance?"

"No, none."

"That means she's utterly dependent on the kindness of strangers."

"Yes, and so is Nicole. A neighbor of her mother's took pity on Nicole when she was beaten a few years ago by her stepfather, and to get her out of the house started taking her to their church, where she met the Lambs. They have an older married daughter living with them while her husband is in the Middle East on a government contract, and they use Nicole to help care for the daughter's two-year-old child."

"How does Nicole feel about this arrangement?"

"The last time Nicole lived with her mother, they clashed so much the mother threw her out in the middle of the night. She claims she is willing to put up with the Lambs' strict rules and her duties as a babysitter to stay there because they are kind to her."

"Isn't there something exploitive about it?"

Iris sighed. "She's known much worse."

"What about Julie?"

"She started out the school year living with her mother in a trailer on the south side, but then her mother had the big fight with Nicole. Because

Lottie didn't think she could cope with Julie either, she sent her to the Catholic home, but they mostly take in unwed young mothers and girls with addictions, so it was unsuitable for a twelve-year-old, to say the least. Then, when Lottie married Mr. Hunt and moved to his much nicer house in the Sawgrass district a few months later, Holy Name sent her home for a trial visit.''

''How is it going?''

''Hard to say. Julie calls me almost every day after school because she is home alone and doesn't know anyone in the area.''

''Where's Mrs. Hunt?''

''She likes to fish. She and her new husband have a bass boat and they spend every spare moment on the various lakes around here.''

''What does Mr. Hunt do?''

''He's a night watchman at the mall.''

Next, I put in calls to the three children. Two weren't home, but Nicole, the fourteen-year-old, was. I told her I was her new Guardian ad Litem and asked when it might be convenient to visit her.

''Right now?'' she asked in a sugary, yet slightly leery voice.

''Fine with me,'' I said, then was delighted to discover the Lambs lived only a few miles from my home.

Fay Lamb opened the door wearing an apron. The house was filled with the aroma of baking apples and cinnamon. Nicole came into the room, greeted me with a tense smile, then curled up on the couch and pulled a knitted afghan over her bare legs. She had gray eyes fringed with thick lashes and long, dark straight hair, pulled back with a series of combs. Her face was ivory, her cheeks blushed pink, but her posture was as tense as an animal trying to choose between fleeing and standing off the intruder.

Nicole listened alertly while Fay Lamb spoke—or rather preached— about the Colbys' predicament. ''It's a shame the girls cannot live together. They are sisters and it isn't right. But that mother!'' Fay shook her blonde ringlets disapprovingly. ''She marries the first man she meets by the docks and thinks more about hooking a fish than feeding her children. And the way she puts down Nicole! I mean she does have what we call her 'moods.' We can deal with those, but her mother claims that Nicole is a threat to her safety, which is utterly ridiculous.''

Just then there was a knock on the door. Fay went to get it. When Nicole heard the voices in the foyer, she pulled the blanket over her chin. ''That's my mother!''

Lottie Hunt walked into the room, noticed her daughter huddled under

the coverlet but didn't say a word to her. I stood and introduced myself
as the new guardian for "all your children."

"Didn't I see you in court?"

"Yes, but I was there for another case. I was assigned to your daughters a few days later."

Mrs. Hunt opened her purse and removed a paper and showed it to
me. "Will you tell Iris that I brought it over like I said I would?" she
asked me. I took one look at it and handed it to Fay. It was the power
of attorney Mrs. Hunt had been ordered to produce in court. A few weeks
earlier, Nicole had fallen getting off the school bus and the Baldwins
had wanted her wrist and shoulder x-rayed. Without parental permission,
she could not be treated at the emergency room, and no private doctor
would see her because there was no insurance. Fortunately, they had
been able to locate Mrs. Hunt, and she went to the hospital and signed
the papers. "What if it is a more critical problem next time?" Mrs.
Baldwin complained to Iris Quinones, who had taken the matter to court
to force Mrs. Hunt to comply.

"I hope there won't be another emergency so these won't be needed,"
I said to fill in the silence. When nobody else spoke, I told Mrs. Hunt
that I had been trying to reach her that afternoon to set up an appointment
to meet Julie. She said to come the next day after school, then left
without another word to Nicole.

Obviously distressed, Nicole went to the bathroom with the blanket
still clasped around her shoulders.

"See what I mean?" Mrs. Lamb said as soon as the car backed down
the driveway. "How can a mother be so cold to her own daughter?"

"It's very kind of you to keep Nicole," I said softly. "But how long
can you accept full financial responsibility?"

"My husband and I are talking about it. What with having Stacy—
that's my daughter—and little Stevie here, we don't have much room.
Nicole shares the room with the baby, so she's a help with him, especially when Stacy works at night, but she should be with her sisters. I
can't take any more in, what with my mom having Alzheimer's and my
church work."

Nicole returned to the room and leaned against a doorway. After Fay
had prattled on for some time about her missionary committees, I asked
Nicole to come out to my car so I could give her some phone numbers.
She put down the blanket, but as soon as we were outside, she began to
shiver. I told Nicole to sit in the car and I turned on the heat. "So, how's
it going?"

''Not too bad,'' she said nervously, ''except their church is really strict.'' She told me about the ultraconservative denomination and how all the Lambs ''spoke in tongues'' and believed there was a biblical response to every issue. ''They don't approve of me seeing Simone because the Baldwins allow her to go to parties and to the movies. She even got to go away with her boyfriend's family for a weekend to Disney World, which Fay said was sinful.''

''Disney World?''

''No, going to a hotel with her boyfriend, even though she had her own room and the boy slept with his parents.''

''Do you ever see Julie?''

''No, Mom thinks I might corrupt her.''

''Sounds like you've had a hard time during the last few years.'' Nicole's eyes darted from side to side but she said nothing. ''What's the worst thing that ever happened to you?''

''Standing in a corner for a month, I guess.''

''When was that?''

''When Mom was living with Jeb Delancy, the one who beat me later on.''

''Why did he punish you?''

''For throwing my vegetables in the garbage without eating them.''

''How can you stand in a corner for a month?''

''He'd let me have two bathroom trips a day, sleep five hours a night, and go to school, but if I even leaned against the wall or complained, he'd whip me.''

''What did your mother do?''

''She said that somebody had to control me, and anyway, she knew better than to interfere, or he'd smack her around too.''

''Did he ever hurt your sisters?''

''Sometimes, but mostly he had it in for me.'' She lowered her eyes and whispered, ''because I was the only one who'd stand up to him.''

Since Nicole had known her previous guardian and Lillian, she understood the program. I gave Nicole information on how to reach me and told her that I lived nearby and would come over often. I asked how I could help in the future and she said she wanted to see both her sisters. I promised to arrange a lunch together soon.

When I arrived at Lottie Hunt's home the following afternoon, Julie was ''off somewhere on her bike.'' The blue stucco house had a window box planted with plastic flowers and a manicured lawn. Mrs. Hunt explained that she had moved there a few months earlier when she had married Mr. Hunt. Then she launched into complaints about Julie's unruly behavior, her tendency to talk back, and the fact that she was "turning out like her sisters" and it wouldn't be long before she became belligerent "just like Nicole" and would have to leave too.

"Would you like to be reunited with all three of your daughters?" I asked.

"No, it wouldn't work. Simone is better off where she is and I'm afraid of Nicole."

"In what way?"

"Do you know about the gun?"

"No . . . ," I admitted. "Tell me about it."

"I was having this discussion with Nicole about modeling school. She wanted to go and I told her I couldn't afford it. We worked out a plan. She went from door to door getting friends and neighbors to help pay her tuition, and when she had enough, she enrolled. But the day before she was to have her first class, she backtalked me, and I wouldn't allow her to go. Well, she became furious and her face got purple and she was screaming at me. She backed up to the cabinet where she knows we have guns and she pulled one out and pointed it at me."

"Was it loaded?"

"I don't know, but I managed to grab her arm and she dropped it. That's when I told her to leave."

"And then she went to live with the Lambs?"

"Right."

The front door opened and Julie came in. She was a slender, waiflike child with straight straw-colored bangs and a Prince Valiant haircut. With her huge green eyes and pink pointed bow lips, she looked ready to be cast as Cinderella.

"Hi," she whispered.

I told her that I was her new guardian.

"Tell the lady why you didn't bring home that form for me to sign," Lottie Hunt said with a snarl.

"I forgot, Mom," Julie replied with a slight whine.

"She's always forgetting everything. If her nose wasn't attached, she'd leave it in the bathroom. Is it so much to ask a child to take care of the few responsibilities she has?" Lottie asked me, then turned to her daughter. "What are you going to do about it?" she added in a much meaner voice.

"How can I go back to school now?"

"Why didn't you think of that while you were there? But no, the problem is you never *think*, do you?"

Julie noticed a black cat with white paws walking by and scooped it up. Burying her face in its fur, she said, "I'm sorry, Mom." Tears from Julie's face slipped onto the cat's shiny back.

"See, she loves that cat more than she does me. Don't you?" Julie shook her head in agreement. "What's the matter with her?" she shouted at me.

"Sounds like a typical twelve-year-old," I said to let Julie off the hook.

"Everyone always takes the side of the kids; nobody ever listens to me. Do they think I don't have feelings? I try my best. It's been hard. Their father was a no-good drunken slob who'd get repentant and religious in the morning, but by dinnertime would be ready to haul off and hit anyone who looked at him crosswise. Now I have to put myself first and settle my own issues. That's what I've learned from being a counselor at the spouse abuse center."

I did a double take. "You mean you counsel other people?"

"Yes, I'm a peer counselor. I work with other abused spouses. By doing so, I also help myself."

"What about the children? Do they see therapists?"

"They sometimes see my therapist, Wanda, too."

"I hate that lady!" Julie seethed. "She never listens to us."

"Wanda thinks you need some discipline. Like yesterday. I came home from fishing and you weren't here, were you?"

"I was at Donna's."

"Who's that?" I asked.

"A neighbor's brat," Lottie replied.

"Why were you there?" I questioned Julie gently.

"I heard some noises in the bushes and got scared, so I called Donna's mother—their house is over the back fence—and asked her if she knew what was out there. She came over to see if I was okay and invited me for dinner. I left a note for Mom, but she was angry about it."

"What time did you get home?" I asked Lottie.

"Around nine."

"What would Julie have done about dinner?"

"There were leftovers and frozen pizza here."

"Maybe she was lonely."

"The point is she defied me. She is not supposed to be wandering around the neighborhood."

"I was scared," Julie moaned, her tears flowing more freely. The cat jumped off her lap and she pulled her knees up and hugged them to her chest.

I realized that it was almost six. My husband expected me home, but I made a sudden decision. "Could Julie have dinner with me tonight?"

"I guess," Lottie said, shrugging.

"Do you want to?" I asked Julie. She wiped her eyes and nodded.

In the car Julie brightened. "How come I get to go out with you?"

"Because you looked so sad, I wanted to do something to cheer you up."

I used my car phone to call Phil and explain I wouldn't be home for dinner and directed him to some leftovers. Then I asked Julie where she would like to eat.

"McDonald's is the cheapest."

"Actually, I'd prefer Italian, Chinese, or seafood."

"I love fish!"

I headed for the Waterside Inn. Julie knew people who worked there as waiters, but had never eaten there. She ordered a fried grouper dinner, a salad with blue cheese dressing, and was surprised I allowed her to have a large Coke.

"Thank you for taking me here," she said with a solemn politeness unusual for guardian children.

While waiting for the meal to arrive, her whole demeanor changed and she became chatty, telling me about movies she liked to watch. "I love R-rated movies like *Friday, the 13th.* Jason is so cool, don't you think?"

I admitted I didn't care for that sort of violence.

"I liked to be scared."

"You were scared the other night when you went to the neighbor's house. That didn't sound like fun."

"I hate being alone all the time. We only have a hot meal on Saturdays when my stepfather has his kids over for visitation. My mother eats sandwiches and drinks beer all day when she is fishing, so she doesn't feel like cooking at night."

As Julie spoke, she was attacking her salad. I watched as she lathered the dressing over the top like a blanket, then gobbled the onions, tomatoes, and every leaf of lettuce with gusto. She used the crackers in the bowl on the table to finish the last vestige of salad dressing.

When the fish platter came, she was equally aggressive, which seemed surprising in a skinny and pale child who seemed more the type to have a picky appetite.

"Do you remember Jeb Delancy?" I asked.

"I would prefer to forget him," she said between bites.

"Did he ever hurt you?"

"Not really . . . well, I guess he spanked me."

"Did you stand in the corner?"

"No, he only did that to Nicole."

"Not Simone either?"

"No. Our father is the one who smacked Simone around, but she did whatever Jeb said. Nicole is the one who would talk back, and then she'd really get it."

"What did you think of Jeb?"

"I hated him, but what could I do? I mean, even Mom let him do whatever he wanted, and she even made Nicole lie in court so he wouldn't go to jail."

My appetite was gone. I put my fork down.

"In what way?"

"One time Nicole was so bruised a teacher asked her what happened, and she said Jeb hit her with a board, which was the truth. By the time she had to go to court, Mom convinced her to say it was only this yardstick and that she bruised easily. Which isn't true. I'm the one with the sensitive skin."

While Julie was working on her french fries, I took out a pencil and paper and said, "I am making a wish list for Julie. If you could have anything you want, what would it be?"

Julie put down her fork and tilted her head to check whether I was serious. I showed her that my pen was poised. "Okay!" she beamed. "Number one . . . I want to go live with Mary Lee. She's my best friend."

"If that wasn't possible, where would you like to live?"

"Anywhere but with my mother."

"Would you want to live with your sisters?"

"Of course, but that will never happen. I mean there are lots of things I want, but will never have."

"Like what?"

"My own TV and my own phone and lots of clothes in purples and greens, and a little dog with a wrinkled face."

"You mean a shar-pei."

"Yeah! How did you know?"

I diligently wrote this all down. "Now, let's go back and you tell me which to work on for you first."

"You mean some of this could come true?"

"I don't know, but if I don't try, nothing will happen. What are the most important things to change?"

"I want to see my dad," she said suddenly. "I know he's in jail, but they said I could visit if I proved I was his child. That means I need my birth certificate, but Mom won't give it to me."

"I can help with that. Next?"

Julie looked at me soberly. "Really, I need another place to live. Any home where they are nice and fair and where there is dinner every night."

Julie was a hungry child. Not only was she hungry for affection and company, she was not getting enough to eat. Every time I visited she showed an unusual interest in food. Something as simple as pizza topping choices could become a topic for a dissertation on extra cheese and thicker crusts. She qualified for free lunches but had moved so many times that year, she had not been placed in the program.

There seemed to be enough money for Lottie Hunt to live in a pleasant neighborhood and to spend her days in leisure activities, so the lack of plentiful food fell into the category of neglect. I was even more disturbed by the mother's behavior toward her daughter in front of me. I had not only been a stranger in that home for the first time, but also a court-appointed visitor who would be reporting the conversation, and yet Lottie had launched into an unrelenting diatribe on Julie's supposed sins in so ugly and angry a fashion, I could only wonder what went on when mother and daughter were by themselves. To me, this had been a clear demonstration of emotional abuse. I documented every word of the conversation I could recall. Then I phoned Lillian to ask if she had seen anything similar.

"This is a very disturbed woman," Lillian admitted, "but I didn't want to prejudice you beforehand."

"Do you know anything more about the incident with Nicole and the gun?"

"Yes, I have heard several versions of the story. Every time Lottie tells it, though, it becomes more exaggerated. The only part that appears to be true is that Nicole became enraged when her mother pulled the plug on her going to modeling school. She had been working for months to beg or borrow the tuition. Can you imagine sending that pretty young

thing to knock on neighbors' doors to ask for money? I was afraid someone might take advantage of her. Anyway, when she was yelling at her
mother, she did back up until she was against the cabinet where the guns
were kept. She admits to thinking about the guns in there, but she never
opened the door, never took out a gun, never pointed it at anyone. That
part is the mother's paranoid fantasy.''

''Are you sure?''

''I suggest you call Brigitte Rouelle, the therapist who counseled the
family in their home.''

''Is that the woman from the spouse abuse center?''

''No, that's Wanda, who has a degree in basket weaving or something,
but she's no psychologist. Mrs. Rouelle is from a special HRS intervention program designed for crisis counseling.''

In the file I found Mrs. Rouelle's report, which stated that she had
spent six weeks working in the home to try to resolve family conflicts.
At that time both Nicole and Julie had still been at home. The cover
sheet for her notes was a checklist that indicated the family was in need
of further treatment but no appropriate referral was available. As to the
rate of improvement, Mrs. Rouelle had indicated that the Colby family
was worse off after her visits than before, and stated that the family was
at high risk for emotional and psychological neglect.

After a few tries I reached Mrs. Rouelle on the phone. She gave me
many other examples of Lottie Hunt's barrages against her daughters.

''At one point it was so destructive,'' Mrs. Rouelle said in her French
accent, ''that I refused to leave the house until an HRS worker was
summoned for the children's protection.''

''You mean you called HRS and said the situation was abusive?''

''Absolutely. I knew that if I left the house, Mrs. Hunt would hurt
one of the children, or one of the children would have hurt her, or
worse.''

''What is the mother's problem?''

''She's a very immature, complicated woman. While I did not do
private work with her, she is symptomatic of a person with borderline
personality disorder. She has a very shaky sense of identity, has frequent
violent outbursts—as you and I have both witnessed—is oversensitive
to imagined rejections. She keeps blaming the children for not loving
her enough.''

''She told me that Julie loved the cat more than her.''

''People with her syndrome often have many intense love affairs,
which may explain why Mrs. Hunt has been married so many times in

recent years and why she has stayed with men who have been abusive toward her and the children. Has Nicole told you about what she had to endure from Mr. Delancy?''

"She started to."

"It's horrifying, isn't it?"

"Could they live with their father when he gets out?"

"No, he's too violent. Julie, who stayed with him the shortest time, still believes he might be there for her, but he's only allowed supervised visitations and that won't change for a long time."

As I typed up my extensive notes from the conversation with Mrs. Rouelle, I was pleased to have clinical confirmation for the upcoming hearing.

By the end of my first week on the Colby case, I was able to get an appointment with the eldest sister, Simone, and her "adopted" family, the Baldwins. The Baldwins' recently built house was by far the nicest of the Colby children's residences. Carol Baldwin met with me in her husband's home office. The sliding glass doors opened onto the fairway of a golf course and ducks from a nearby pond waddled across the lawn.

"Although Nicole is fairly stable with the Lambs, I don't think that is going to last," I began. "But right now I'm more worried about Julie, who seems miserable, hungry, and her mother is out of control."

Carol gave me a strained smile. "We've made a commitment to Simone, but we can't include the other girls. Ken adores Julie, too, but we can't accept another child into our home."

"I was not asking you to."

"Well, maybe I was asking myself. Ken has allowed me to buy the three of them school clothes and Christmas presents, but that is the most I can ask, considering we have three of our own. I feel for those children, every one of them. It took a year before Simone trusted us to tell us some of what has gone on in her life, and it is more harrowing than you can believe. If I won the lottery, I'd adopt them in a minute."

"Do you think someone might step forward who would adopt all three?" I asked as the idea began to form in my mind.

"It could happen, but when I asked Iris about legally adopting Simone, she said that neither parent would relinquish their rights."

"Even if adoption is out of the question, if some family were to offer the three of them a permanent home, how would you feel about losing Simone?"

"We would always want what is best for her."

The door to the office opened and Simone arrived with her friend Eliza. After I was introduced, Eliza ducked out.

Simone had large, soft brown eyes that had the look of a young, startled doe and was the only Colby to have curly hair, which cascaded prettily down her back. It was the same cornsilk shade as Julie's, but the effect was less storybook and more sensual. "When can I see my sisters?" Simone asked, then went on to complain that the Lambs were making it impossible for her to get together with Nicole. "They even listen in on her phone conversations," she said with exasperation, adding, "if I try to see Julie, I'd have to deal with Mom, so it isn't worth it."

"The arts and crafts festival is on this weekend and I could take the three of you."

Simone gave me a doubtful look. "You think the Lambs or my mother will agree?"

"They won't have a choice," I said, and meant it.

My car was filled with exuberant girls. In contrast to the Stevensons, Nicole, Simone, and Julie were delightful companions. As we walked around the fairgrounds, they kept running into friends from school and extended family members. Everyone greeted one another warmly, and I could see how rooted they were in this town. Even more intriguing to me was their curiosity about every artisan's booth. They studied the sculpture, stained glass, and other pieces, asking what techniques were used and commenting on what they liked and disliked. Simone, in particular, kept saying she would like to try her hand at various crafts. Julie was fascinated by everything having to do with the sea, and Nicole talked about decorating her dream house someday. Nicole was in the school and church chorus and wanted to join the band. Simone already played in the school orchestra. The older sisters kidded each other about boys and mutual friends, while making certain Julie was included. Whenever I bought them a slice of pizza or dish of fresh-churned ice cream, they looked on the treat as something special. I began to fantasize about how they might react if I could have walked into the next stall and arranged an adoptive home where they could all live together again.

Well, why couldn't I? Wasn't this in their best interests? Mrs. Lamb and Mrs. Baldwin had agreed the sisters needed one another. The therapist had stated that neither biological parent was suitable. There had to be a family who would welcome these attractive, intelligent, talented, kind, and considerate sisters. I looked around at the passing crowd. This was a small, family-centered community. Surely there was a home for these terrific girls. Somehow, somewhere I would find them a family, I promised myself.

Here is precisely what happened next.

After delivering the Colby sisters to their respective families, I stopped by the home of friends, Darla and Stanley Brandon, who had adopted an infant two years earlier.

"Ready for another kid?" I asked.

"Maybe . . . ," Darla said slowly as she pondered whether or not I was serious.

"How about three of them?" I went on to explain about the Colby sisters.

"Well," Darla said, laughing easily, "we were thinking of something a little younger, but I could ask the pastor at church if he knows of anyone else."

That was Saturday. Keeping her word, Darla stood in line after the service and mentioned to the minister that three sisters were looking for a permanent home. He asked if he could give it some thought and call her back. That Monday I left town on business. Thursday morning, my secretary gave me a message from a Mrs. Slater who "wants to adopt your three children. She requested that you phone her from New York."

"This is absurd," I said aloud, but dialed the number in Florida anyway.

After introductions, Jeanne Slater explained that she and her husband had been to Bible study that Wednesday evening and "the pastor had asked for prayers for three separated sisters who need a home together. I glanced up at my husband, Vic, and he looked at me. I can't explain it, but at that moment we just knew that we were the ones. We'll take them."

"Wait a minute, you don't know their names or ages or background."

"That's true, but we're ready to accept them into our hearts and home."

"That is very kind of you, Mrs. Slater," I said, thinking I was dealing with some sort of nut. "I'll be back over the weekend and I'll call you then."

"We'd like to meet you. Could you come over on Sunday?"

Deciding I had better clear this with Lillian first, I pushed the appointment until Monday evening. When I hung up the phone, I was shaking my head. "This is incredible. This is so crazy." I waited, trying to dispel

the feeling that something momentous had happened. Instead I was overcome with a calm certainty that somehow in some way this was going
to work.

Lillian couldn't see any harm in a meeting, although she doubted anything would come of it. On the way to the Slaters', I picked up some
snapshots of the sisters I had taken at the craft fair. Vic and Jeanne lived
in the Country Farms section of town that bordered rolling pastures.
Their three-bedroom ranch house hugged the curve of a cul-de-sac. I was
surprised to see two children's bicycles out front.

Jeanne and Vic Slater were in their late thirties or early forties and
both were slim and tan. Vic was wearing emerald golf slacks and a polo
shirt with the collar turned up. His wife's shirt matched his, but she wore
a wraparound twill pink and green skirt, pink ankle socks and expensive
leather sneakers. Their clothes were color coordinated to the poker-felt
green rug, rose and green sofa, and matching shell paintings and decorations. An adorable pug puppy snapped at my feet.

"Hey, Squire, cool it," Vic said to the dog.

As I pushed the dog off, I realized that although this was not a shar-
pei, he did have a wrinkled face.

Impossible, I told myself. Don't get your hopes up because none of
this makes any sense.

Mrs. Slater served coffee and homemade lemon squares. I filled the
Slaters in on the girls' first names and general background. "They've
been subjected to various forms of abuse, but as far as I know, there has
been no sexual abuse." I passed out the pictures.

Vic pointed to Nicole's and handed it back to me. I looked from the
photo to Jeanne and back again. There was no question that the resemblance to his wife was startling, especially since they had the same dark
hair and soulful eyes.

"Simone was my grandmother's name," Jeanne said softly. "She was
French-Canadian, but I grew up in Maine."

"Where are you from, Mr. Slater?"

"I was born in Ohio, but met Jeanne in Washington, DC. We both had government jobs and took early retirement." He explained that they had sunk
their savings into a sporting goods franchise, sharing the management duties.
Vic handled the accounting while Jeanne organized the stock and personnel.

In about an hour I had learned that Jeanne had been married at fifteen
and had one grown daughter. Vic had a teenage son, who lived with his
mother in Virginia. Both hinted at unfortunate first marriages at a young

age but stated that their twelve-year relationship was stable and happy. Jeanne explained that they had temporary guardianship of her two grandsons from Maine, so they knew a bit about taking in other people's children. It looked as though they might keep them for many years to come due to "a drug problem with their parents."

"Why would you want these girls too?" I asked.

Vic stroked his Van Gogh beard. "We feel a spiritual calling to take them."

I passed back a picture of Simone with her arms around the waist of one of the boys she had seen at the fair, the one with whom she had gone to Disney. "They come with boyfriends at this age."

"I know about that," Jeanne remarked flatly.

After reviewing the children's legal situation, I explained that Julie might need a home on an emergency basis. "We're ready," Vic replied, "just tell us what we have to do."

I conferred again with Lillian. She reminded me that the Colby children had a routine court appearance for their six-month case review the following week. "Make sure everything is in your report," she counseled. "Don't mince words. Don't worry about hurting feelings. This document will start the process rolling."

Because Guardians ad Litem have access to so many files, we can synthesize them in ways that the social services and legal people cannot. While our reports are always centered around the best interests of the children, I made certain that the Colbys' material also hinted at the direction the case might take even though it was far too early to mention termination of parental rights or adoption. As part of the "information received" introduction I included an outline of the history of the case. Regarding their father I wrote:

> Mervyn Colby is currently incarcerated, and even when he is free, is not able to provide an appropriate home for these children. He has had many opportunities to remedy his substance abuse problems, but there does not seem to be any change in this area. Despite his problems and the abuse they suffered, the children speak of him with some affection and wish to remain in touch with him.

About the mother I stated:

Mrs. Lottie Colby Hunt has had custody of her children intermittently. Simone has been out of the home for more than 18 months, living with the Baldwins, who are the parents of a friend. Simone is adamant that she would never wish to live with her mother again and she does not feel that her mother is an appropriate parent for either sibling.

Nicole would not return to her mother or her father and does not feel Julie should remain with her mother because of a risk of psychological abuse in that home.

Julie is currently living with her mother. She was sent to the Holy Family Home in Miami last August; however, the administrator feels this is not a suitable placement because the other students have addictions and other severe problems. When Julie's mother married Mr. Hunt, it was felt she might do better at home than in an institution. Since then, Julie reports being extremely unhappy and would rather live "anywhere else." Her choices include being returned to the Holy Family Home where the rules were "strict, but fair" and where they treated her "like a real person, with respect." She felt loved there.

Mrs. Hunt states that she might consider having Simone back and wishes to keep Julie, but that she does not want Nicole again because she is afraid Nicole might become violent and hurt her. She thinks the Baldwin and Lamb families are taking care of her daughters because of "what they are going to get out of it financially."

Under my "summary and recommendations" I stated:

Ultimately, the best solution for the Colby sisters would be a permanent, stable home where all three could live together and be financially secure.

I then presented separate recommendations for each child. For Simone and Nicole I suggested that they remain in their current homes and have more frequent contact with each other. When it came to Julie, I stated that I had been a witness to the extreme nature of the clash between mother and child. Mrs. Hunt had not been the primary parent for most of this child's life, and the bond between mother and daughter was tenuous. Julie was sad, distressed, possibly malnourished, and depressed. She was unable to concentrate in school and was underachieving. I wrote, "Julie desires to live anywhere but with her mother, including to be returned to the Holy Family Home in Miami, to live with the family of one of her friends, or any other yet unknown, but caring family. Ideally she would like to be reunited with her sisters in a home where she would be cared for and trusted, not be left home alone, and would receive dinners every night.''

My recommendations included that Julie be moved to a temporary, nurturing home for a cooling-off period between mother and daughter, and that it should be in the county to facilitate stability at her current school as well as to enable the sisters to see one another often. I wanted her to receive counseling from a qualified therapist with at least a master's degree and receive testing and evaluation. Most important was that a more permanent long-term placement, with a genuine commitment from another family, be sought for Julie. I suggested that a placement that might include Nicole and possibly Simone be given primary consideration, rather than just looking for a home to place Julie. In any case, I wanted HRS and the families concerned to facilitate frequent contact among the sisters. There was a notation to ask Mr. Colby and Mrs. Hunt to contribute at least fifty dollars per month each for Julie's upkeep.

This report, like all other official ones, was submitted with a certificate of service to all parties in the case including the HRS attorney, the caseworker, the parents, their attorneys, and the Guardian ad Litem.

Two days later, I received a phone call from Mrs. Baldwin. ''Julie is gone.''

''What do you mean?''

''Her mother was so upset when she read your report saying that Julie didn't want to live with her, that she shipped her off to that place in Miami last night. Can she do that?''

''She still has legal custody of her children.''

''Now Simone is worried that her mother might do the same with her.''

''She could.''

''You mean that after eighteen months with us, Lottie Hunt could march in and send Simone to Miami?''

''Until the court changes the children's status to foster care, HRS only will intervene in a crisis.''

''A lot of good they've ever done,'' Carol Baldwin said with a sniff.

''My goal is to get the kids into a much stronger legal position and my report was the first step.''

''What about poor Julie? She wasn't even given a chance to say goodbye to anyone.''

''I want her back in the county, but not with her mother.''

''We're in her school district.''

''Would you take her?''

"For a few weeks."

"Thanks, Carol. It would help if she could be with Simone, and you've worked with her speech problem so she knows and trusts you. Court is on Tuesday. We'll tell the judge exactly what happened and let him decide."

Judge Donovan was not pleased. No matter how Mrs. Hunt or her attorney tried to explain it, it was obvious that Julie had been sent away to spite both the guardian and the child. The judge ordered that Julie be returned to our district immediately.

I conveyed that the Baldwin family was willing to keep her until something else could be found. The HRS attorney added that since the agency already had approved the Baldwin family for Simone's care, he had no objections.

The judge ruled that Julie be returned from the Holy Family Home and placed with the Baldwin family, where Simone resided, that protective supervision by HRS should continue, and that Mrs. Hunt should select a mental health counselor for her children to see.

As we were leaving the judge's chambers, Mr. Colby, still in his prisoner's suit, clanged by in his leg irons. "May I talk to my girls?" he asked the bailiff.

The bailiff looked at me. I introduced myself to Mr. Colby. "Only Simone and Nicole are here. I'll get them."

Buddy Colby kissed each daughter on the cheek and put his arms around them. "I love both of you, you know that?" They nodded but were clearly uncomfortable being hugged in a public hallway by a man in an orange uniform.

"You miss them," I said matter-of-factly as I moved to extricate the sisters from his grip. "When you are free, I'll help you to see them as often as possible."

Just then Mrs. Hunt walked by. Mr. Colby turned to face the wall rather than confront her. I led the girls back to where Mrs. Baldwin was waiting to take them to school and told them I'd call that night.

On the way out of court, the HRS attorney, Calvin Reynolds, stopped me. "Mrs. Courter, when I saw that you had been assigned the Colby case, I knew that it was a lucky day for those girls."

"Thank you." I was taken aback because Calvin wasn't usually complimentary to guardians.

"These children take up an entire file drawer in my office," he said shaking his head sadly.

To me this drawer represented a family's painful past. "Want to clean it out for good?"

"You bet!"

"Then don't fight me when I ask for a termination of parental rights."

"Why go to that trouble?"

"So they can be adopted."

"Individually?"

"No, as a family group."

"Nobody will ever adopt three adolescent girls."

"Don't you believe in miracles?"

Calvin's face changed from dubious to challenging. "If anyone can do it, you can."

"If this works, I won't be able to take the credit."

"Who then?"

"I leave that to you to figure out."

My first phone call was to the Slaters. "Julie's coming back!"

"Great!" Jeanne said. I had to remind myself that they had never met.

The Slaters and I made plans to have dinner with the sisters a few days later. Before then, however, I took the girls out for burgers and played a game of "what if."

"What if you could live together with one family, is that what you want?"

"Yes," they chorused.

"Even you, Simone? You have a good deal with the Baldwins."

"I'd rather be with my sisters."

Nicole had a faraway look.

"The Lambs aren't working out, are they?" I asked her.

"No." Nicole's lips narrowed into a tight, angry line. "Now they won't let me call Julie because she's with the Baldwins." She started breathing rapidly and I could sense the rage beneath the surface. I gently rubbed her neck and shoulders until she relaxed slightly.

"Listen, girls, there is a family I want you to meet. They heard about three sisters who weren't living together and wanted to help out. I don't want to get your hopes up because there are many legal steps to go through and lots of ways this could fall apart. Plus, your mother is still in charge of you and can make any final decision about where you live."

"Do they have a dog with a wrinkled face?" Julie asked.

"Come on, Julie, don't be stupid," Nicole said.

"Well, Julie," I said with a tense laugh, "actually they do. His name is Squire."

We met at the Pasta Place. I brought Julie, Nicole, and Simone. The Slaters arrived with their grandsons, Jared and Zane, who were six and seven. Both were freckled redheads, but Jared was skinny, serious, and wore glasses, while Zane was considerably taller, more robust, and talkative. Julie plopped herself down between them, saying, "I always wanted two brothers."

My heart fluttered. Had I set them up to expect too much? Soon they were chattering away. Nicole was next to Jeanne and their resemblance in person was even more striking than it had appeared in the photos. Even their bodies had matching curves, and I could see Nicole raiding Jeanne's closet at the first opportunity. Vic and Simone were talking about sports. Both liked the Miami Dolphins and the Atlanta Braves. Vic coached the boys' ball team but said he preferred golf, and Simone admitted she was on the school's golf team.

Considering what was at stake here, everyone was remarkably relaxed. There were jokes and giggles and tastes of different pasta sauces and lots of thank yous for the garlic bread and extra sodas.

During a lull in the chatter, I overheard Zane talking to Julie. "We haven't seen our father since we were babies and we can't live with our mother anymore, so we're going to stay with Granny and Grampy forever."

"You don't know that for sure," Jared said.

"Yes, I do, right, Gramps?"

Vic nodded while he chewed. After he swallowed, he said, loud enough for everyone to hear, "We have custody of these boys. They've been here three years already, and as far as we are concerned, they'll grow up in our house."

"That's because of what happened to our mother," Zane continued.

"Zane!" Jared admonished under his breath.

"I can tell them anything I want," Zane protested. By now he had everyone's attention. "You see, our mom's in jail for a long time, at least until we grow up."

Nobody moved. This was news to me. I saw Julie staring at Nicole. Simone turned away. Nicole glanced down at her plate. Julie looked at me for permission. I gave her a little nod.

"That's okay," Julie said. "Our dad's in jail too."

* * *

The phone rang within fifteen minutes after I had returned home. "We want them, any time, any way," Vic said.

"Well . . . we do have a problem right now with Nicole." I explained that the Lambs were putting too much pressure on Nicole to conform to their way of life.

"I thought so," Vic said. After the spaghetti dinner, the Slaters and Colby girls had exchanged phone numbers. Already Nicole had called to talk to Jeanne.

"Jeanne said Nicole sounded lonely."

"She is."

"We have a bed ready and waiting."

I explained the problems with informally moving the children around, the fact that Nicole would come with no financial subsidies or medical insurance, and her mother could jerk her away at any time.

"How can I say this without sounding like a lunatic?" Vic asked. "We just feel that somehow it was meant to be."

"Me too, but that isn't going to hold up in court."

We laughed. Then I became more serious. I explained about my court report and the fact that Mrs. Hunt deeply resented me at the moment.

"May I have your permission to call Mrs. Hunt myself?" Vic asked.

"It can't hurt," I said, then wondered what in the world he would say to Mrs. Hunt.

"It's done," Vic said on the phone two days later. "Nicole is moving here this weekend."

I was astonished by his explanation. Nicole had spoken to Jeanne again and had had a heart-to-heart talk. Jeanne had called Fay Lamb at work that afternoon, who admitted that they were tired of being harassed by Nicole's requests to see her sisters. Then, without consulting me or anyone else, Jeanne had phoned Lottie Hunt, introduced herself, and asked permission to take her daughter. Mrs. Hunt said she never did like Fay Lamb, but didn't know the Slaters. Jeanne agreed that Lottie should not make a decision until she met her, but Mrs. Hunt said she was in a fishing tournament that afternoon. Jeanne left work early and went to meet her at the marina. Using a copy of Mrs. Lamb's power of attorney, Jeanne whited out the Lambs' name, made another copy, wrote in hers, and took it to Mrs. Hunt, who after fifteen minutes with Jeanne, signed on the dotted line.

"Amazing," I said. "Jeanne's incredible."

"I was worried you might think that she stepped on your toes," Vic said.

"Not at all. I'm impressed by her determination."

"When Jeanne wants something, there's no stopping her."

"Then we're going to get along fine."

As I wrote up my notes, I realized that I had been the Colby children's Guardian ad Litem for one month and three days. Because of my experience with other cases, I had resolved to make some changes fast, but I could never have predicted that so much could have happened in so short a time. Totaling my time sheets, I already had spent sixty-seven hours on the phone, at meetings, and with the children, and had driven 354 miles. That was a lot for a given month, yet thirty-three days later the sisters were in better homes, two of the girls were reunited, the HRS attorney was on my side, and the family that had come forward to offer the three children a permanent placement was now caring for one of the girls. Buoyed with so many successes, I felt the best course was to forge ahead so that all three could live with the Slaters under some legally binding ruling. As yet, I knew nothing about adoption law, nor the process of getting the rights of the natural parents terminated.

In recent months, though, the nation had been privy to the most famous termination of parental rights case ever: Gregory K., which had influenced my direction on the Colby case. Gregory K. had been living at the ranch where Cory Stevenson had been placed for a while. While at the ranch, a local attorney, George Russ, came for a tour and spent some time with Gregory. Shortly thereafter he became Gregory's foster parent and wanted to adopt him. Early on, before the media became involved, I had heard about the situation. Mr. Russ's law partner's daughter and my son had both attended the same boarding school and now were at the same university, and our families had become fast friends. In fact, I had asked George Russ's partner to take Lydia, the girl who had been falsely accused of a crime, when I had been searching for a home for her. They might have been interested if Lydia hadn't required a Pentecostal home. Knowing my interest in child abuse cases, this family had told me about Gregory being taken in by the Russ family even though they already had eight children of their own.

A few weeks after hearing the Russes' side of the story, Nancy had called me about a "special case" she wanted me to handle.

"This situation originated as a typical termination of parental rights case," Nancy began, "but has developed another unusual dimension."

She explained that before the case had been transferred to the county where the Russes resided, it had originated in the Orlando area, the one county in Florida where the bar association had determined that only pro bono attorneys could serve as guardians. In theory this provided legal representation for every child, but in reality the lawyers did not have time to investigate or monitor cases the way the volunteers could. Gregory K.'s first Guardian ad Litem had never visited him and had made his recommendations by reading the file. I laughed at this, as did Nancy. If I had gone strictly by Lydia's file, for instance, I might have believed that she had put a baby in a microwave oven. Also, if a guardian did not know the child, she could not feel the urgency of her loneliness or see for herself what had to be done. If the guardian did not meet the natural parents, she could never fathom how irresponsible or self-centered or, on occasion, well meaning they were. If the guardian never visited the foster parents and siblings, she could not evaluate what might be in a child's best interests.

While this seems obvious to experienced guardians, it apparently is not to a vast portion of those who have the legal responsibility for children in the justice system. Many "advocate programs" work from the papers only. Gregory K. was to prove—in headlines—the foolishness of this approach.

Nancy told me that Gregory K. needed a guardian to replace the one who had neglected him. However, because the system (and his first guardian) had already failed to perform on his behalf, Gregory K. had hired his own lawyer, Jerri Blair, to terminate his parents' parental rights in civil court. While dependency cases are sealed from the press, civil cases are not. When the local reporter on the courthouse beat saw the docket, he asked the clerk what sort of proceeding this was to be.

"The kid wants to divorce his parents," the clerk said by way of a flippant explanation. What Gregory really desired was to have his mother's and father's parental rights terminated so that he could be adopted permanently by the Russ family, and since nobody with the authority to do so (either HRS or his attorney guardian) had taken these steps, his attorney had devised a clever way around the problem by filing the papers in the child's own name.

The reporter filed a small story with a provocative headline: BOY WANTS TO DIVORCE PARENTS. "A few national papers have already picked up the story," Nancy said, "and I'm afraid the guardian on this case might not only have to handle a tricky legal situation but will also have to deal with the media. Besides myself, you're the only one around here with that experience," Nancy concluded.

"What's the story with his parents?" I asked.

"They've been totally irresponsible, and finally this kid has decided that he has been kicked around long enough by both them and the system. The file shows that during one eighteen-month period in foster care, he was placed in five different foster homes, shelters, and institutions."

"Sounds like Cory Stevenson all over again."

"Is there any hope that his mother will mature?"

"I doubt it. There's no evidence that she has written, phoned, or visited him in more than a year."

"Poor kid."

"You'll take the case?" Nancy asked hopefully.

Inwardly I groaned. Gregory K.'s home was a round-trip of over a hundred miles on two-lane country roads. Still, I wanted to champion a kid who'd made it out of the same institution where Cory Stevenson had been so miserable. Also, if it did make sense to support the termination decision, the Guardian ad Litem could file papers on Gregory's behalf. So even if the court did not accept the child's petition in his own name, they could consider one filed by a guardian.

"The kid is really happy at the Russes. They are a warm, loving family and they've gone through the licensing procedure to become official foster parents just to make a stable home for him. He told George, and his foster mother, Lizabeth, that he did not ever want to live with his mother again. Who can blame him? He's only stayed with her a total of eight months during the past eight years and his father is an alcoholic."

Nancy went on to explain that Gregory, like all children, are literally the tangible property of parents. His mother, Rachael, had signed a performance agreement with HRS that required her to attend parenting classes, seek psychological counseling, and to prove that she was emotionally and financially stable before she could regain custody of her three sons. After she moved to another state, leaving Gregory in Florida, she did not meet her commitments. HRS assumed that she would be willing to terminate her parental rights, but as soon as Rachael heard that his foster family was considering adopting Gregory, she hired an attorney to win him back. (Gregory's father, Ralph Kingsley, agreed to a voluntary termination because he thought it was in his son's best interests, and subsequently Ralph died in an accident before the appeals process was finished.)

"Gregory has made up his mind that he will never agree to live with his mother again and asked to be the one to determine where he would live. George Russ gave Gregory the phone number of Jerri Blair, a local attorney, and she agreed to take his case."

"I think I have a conflict of interest," I said slowly. "I'm already prejudiced in favor of George Russ because of my friendship with his colleague," I admitted. "I'd still do it," I said, "but if the press is going to crawl over this, they might uncover the fact that he has a compromised guardian."

Nancy agreed and accepted the case herself but asked if I'd work with her as a consultant, especially about media matters, which I agreed to do. Later, I would be grateful I did not take on this all-consuming case, which became a *Newsweek* cover story, a "20/20" special piece, the subject of two movies-of-the-week, as well as a high-profile broadcast trial. Through the legal process, both of Gregory's biological parents made the rounds of daily talk shows and George Russ had to do the same to get Gregory's story told. I had many reservations about how healthy this was for the family, or the legal situation, which became more adversarial with every round. (Eventually, Gregory's case was transferred to Orlando, and a third Guardian ad Litem, also an attorney, was appointed for him. But unlike her predecessor, the last guardian did a thorough job of representing his interests. Her report clearly stated that Gregory K. should remain with the Russ family and that his parents should terminate their rights.)

What was clear in the story of Gregory Kingsley was that this eleven-year-old boy had been neglected and abandoned by his parents. Much like Buddy Colby, Ralph Kingsley had a serious alcohol problem. And as with Lottie Hunt, Rachael Kingsley had a life complicated by poverty and difficult relationships with lovers and spouses. Now the Colby children had an offer of a permanent home, only they were luckier, because Gregory's two brothers had not been included in his deal with the Russes.

Gregory K. is a lesson in what typically happens when parents are asked to terminate parental rights. Suddenly these parents, who for years have ignored their children, decide that these same children are their most precious darlings and they will do anything to get them back again. Aided by court-appointed attorneys, the parents often take positions contrary to the best wishes or best interests of their child. Suddenly it becomes more important to reestablish their claims to the child than to place the child in the best possible situation. Because the attorney works in the best interest of the parent's rights, the parent is placed in an antagonistic position to the child. This fighting does nothing but delay safety and permanence for the child.

Parental rights. The precious right to be the parent to your own child. When the Gregory K. situation exploded, I had felt that if everyone— including the biological parents—worked together as a team, Gregory's adoption might have been worked out amicably. Might there be a way to present adoption to the Colby parents so they would understand that it was in their own best interests to promote a stable environment for their daughters? After all, it was only a few years until Simone was eighteen. At that time she could live wherever she wanted—with either parent or anyone else. Thus termination of parental rights is merely a temporary maneuver until a child came of age.

What if Gregory K.'s mother had been willing to vacate her ''temporary'' rights to control her child so he could remain at the Russes? What if Gregory had wanted to continue visitation with his mother, his two brothers, his father, while still returning to the Russes as his home base? I realized that Gregory came from a very conflicted family, but perhaps mediators could have found a way for everyone to have many of their needs met. Gregory had required stability. He needed to know that someone would be there for him, but would it have hurt him to retain the love of his parents while adding the Russes to his list of people who cared for him?

The media attention fueled the feud. The Gregory K. case disintegrated into a shouting match on talk shows and became fodder for debate by columnists. Yet only one person knew what was best for Gregory—and that was the child himself. Gregory made certain that he was listened to.

On September 26, 1992, Circuit Judge Thomas S. Kirk stated that Rachael Kingsley, Gregory's mother, had ''lied consistently'' and announced that he believed ''by clear and convincing evidence, almost beyond a reasonable doubt in this case, that this child has been abandoned . . . and neglected . . . and it is certainly in his best interests that her [the mother's] parental rights be terminated immediately.'' (His father had done so voluntarily.)

Gregory won—not only his new family, but the right for a child to fight a case in his own name. Judge Thomas Kirk ruled that since ''Gregory has the greatest interest in the outcome of this litigation'' he could be given standing to pursue his petition for termination of parental rights in the lower court. When the case was appealed, the State of Florida argued that Gregory had no direct capacity to question the state's conduct toward him, even though he was permitted to remain in foster care considerably longer than the mandated maximum times allowed by statute. Thus the Florida appellate court reversed Judge Kirk's decision. The ruling stated that Gregory K. never had the legal right to ask for termination of parental rights in his own name, since children have no cause to file lawsuits because HRS and adult representatives (i.e., guardians) are responsible for filing cases that represent a child's best interests. However, the termination of parental rights from his mother was upheld on the grounds of abandonment. The adoption by the Russ family went back to the trial court for further proceedings without disrupting Gregory's placement in that home, and eventually he was adopted by the Russ family.

The Colbys didn't need to make either headlines or case law, but they required a permanent adopted home just as much as Gregory had. In order to make this happen, I would have to devise a structured approach and unite the participants in a common goal. Also, the standard rules of HRS procedure would have to be bent. To prevent the animosity that flared in the Gregory K. case, these maneuvers would have to be accomplished before the respective attorneys became creative with their petitions, or before the children wilted and became discouraged.

Once I decided what had to be done, I phoned Nancy and worked on a strategy.

Iris Quinones, the protective services caseworker, had been polite, but unhelpful. She felt the Slaters were as good as the Baldwins or the Lambs for temporary care, but doubted whether it would ever be enduring. "They'll never take all three, nobody would."

When I talked to Iris about placing the girls in foster care so that HRS would partially cover their financial support and health insurance, she said the Colbys didn't meet the qualifications to become foster children. When I asked about doing the paperwork so they could be adopted, Iris claimed a child couldn't be moved from protective services directly into adoptions because the procedures for that transition didn't exist, and besides, it couldn't be done until parental rights were terminated, and that would never happen because the parents had not done anything so egregious as to have their rights removed by force. When I suggested that the parents might be convinced it would be beneficial for their children, Iris laughed and said that once their attorneys became involved, the Colby parents would hold on to their claim for dear life.

"They always love their 'rights' more than their children," Iris quipped, then became more serious. "Look, the point is that nobody will adopt three teenage girls."

"Why? They are great kids, no arrests, no drugs, no illness, and the Slaters are willing."

"That's this week. They only have Nicole, and she hasn't shown her true colors yet. Wait till she pitches one of her fits or lunges at them with a pistol."

"The gun story was a fabrication."

"That depends on whom you believe. Anyway, she's unstable and bound to be a troublemaker."

"She's been brutally abused. I heard what Jeb Delancy did to her."

"And you fell for that?"

"Julie confirmed it."

"Those kids have learned the system."

"Iris, are you saying that you don't believe they were abused? What about the police reports and photographs?"

"Those maybe, but not the rest of it. There was also contradictory testimony at Mr. Delancy's trial. "

"I checked on that. He actually beat Nicole with a two-by-four, but her mother forced her to recant and say it was only a yardstick. So he got off."

"Maybe it was a yardstick."

"Not according to medical testimony." I groaned. "Why are we arguing? These kids need a home. Carol Baldwin is not going to keep Julie for more than a few weeks. What then?"

"She liked it in Miami," Iris suggested.

I gave up trying to convince the caseworker and called Lillian, who explained that someone at Iris's level was locked into following the rule book. "If we need exceptions to the rules, Nancy will have to negotiate with the district managers of foster care and adoptions," she said.

Because Nancy had once worked for HRS, she knew their procedures almost as well as they did. "I'd like to meet the Slaters," she said, "then I can figure out the best situation for them."

We met back at the Pasta Place. I had expected that Nancy would discuss how to arrange the most uncomplicated adoption or foster care placement. Instead, she hardly waited until the beverages were served to put the situation "in perspective."

"Before coming this evening, I had a conference with Mr. Thorndike, our program attorney. He wants you to know the pitfalls of your actions.'' Nancy began grilling Vic as though she were accusing him of something. ''For instance, do you realize the liability you have already incurred by having Nicole in your home?'' Nancy then launched into how, if something happened to Nicole in the Slaters' custody, either natural parent could sue them. Even worse, if Nicole created a disturbance or hurt anyone, they could also be held responsible.

I shot daggers at Nancy, but she averted my eyes and continued to delineate the cost of raising three additional children. Then she reviewed the steps to adoption, including becoming foster parents. The Slaters would have extensive background checks, their home would be under scrutiny by counselors, and the sisters could be removed at any time prior to the adoption. Parental rights would be difficult to terminate, and even if they were terminated, nobody could promise the parents that they would ever see their children again.

Vic stopped Nancy. ''That's ridiculous. These kids can use the phone and call whomever they want.''

Nancy's lips almost broke into a tiny smile, but I saw her steel herself back into her most authoritarian role.

''Are you saying that it would be impossible for us ever to adopt these girls?'' Jeanne asked, her dark eyes shining with tears.

''No, not impossible, but difficult. Gay's kicking me under the table, but I am here to give you a harsh dose of reality. This isn't going to be a picnic, either legally or in terms of raising three abused children. I don't know why you, or anyone else, would want to do it. Take all the time you need to think this through before we get the children's hopes up.''

Vic studied Jeanne, then turned back at Nancy. ''We needed to hear this,'' he said in a voice choked by emotion.

Jeanne reached across the table and took her husband's hand.

''I'll get you for this,'' I said to Nancy to break the tension.

Nancy didn't budge. ''This is not a romantic dream, Mr. and Mrs. Slater. What we decide tonight affects three children, your grandchildren, your marriage, the Colby parents, and their families. If we're going to drop a bomb, we need to have a darn good idea what the fallout is going to be. If we're going to fight this out with HRS, as well as in court, I want to be convinced that you're going to be there for these girls during the stormy times as well as the sunny ones.''

Jeanne looked at Vic. He squeezed her hand and spoke for them both. ''I've been through a lot, and so has Jeanne, and I think we can help these girls in a special way. We know it isn't going to be easy, but already we can't imagine Nicole leaving.''

Nancy's shoulders relaxed. She took a sip of iced tea. "Okay," she said as if she had accepted defeat gracefully, "here are your choices."

By the end of the meal, the Slaters had determined that the most logical course was to take the classes required of both adoptive and foster parents, and at the same time apply to become the preadoptive foster parents for the Colby sisters. As soon as possible, they would get Mrs. Hunt's permission and powers of attorney for Julie and Simone to move from the Baldwins. Jeanne was certain she could talk Mrs. Hunt into this, and then Jeanne would also initiate the idea of Lottie terminating her parental rights voluntarily. As soon as Buddy Colby was released from jail, I would facilitate visits with him and approach him about his termination. In the meantime, I would prepare a case to have the children become foster children. Timing was crucial, for if they were ordered into foster care before the Slaters were licensed as a foster home, HRS would move the sisters to temporary foster homes, probably separating them again. Once the Slaters were foster parents, they would be able to have the girls indefinitely, even if they were never legally freed for adoption. In the best scenario, their parents would terminate parental rights and make it possible for the Slaters to adopt them. Also, because as a group of older siblings they were considered a "special needs case," they would qualify for a state-subsidized adoption and would receive monthly support payments, Medicaid, and psychological counseling.

When the Slaters left, Nancy walked me to my car. "You understand why I had to do that?"

"Yes, but you had me scared."

"I know you see this whole process as a straight line, Gay, but it has many twists and turns—and even worse—people just waiting to trip you up."

"Like the parents?"

Nancy gave a sardonic laugh. "They are the least of your problems. HRS is going to resent this."

"Why?"

"They are not going to welcome three more kids on their support rolls and they are not going to want to see kids adopted by a family that a guardian dredged up with one phone call."

"What about Calvin Reynold's file drawer?"

"He's your ally for a change, which is terrific. Keep him on your side. But watch your blind side."

"Nancy, you know something, you're paranoid."

"Nope. I'm realistic."

* * *

Everybody bought the Colby children Easter presents, everybody but their parents that is. Carol Baldwin routinely bought clothing for the three girls, so she made sure they each had new dresses. Jeanne also took them shopping, then sewed matching hairpieces for each sister and had their hair cut and styled. Mrs. Lamb gave them each Bibles with their names stamped on them.

The Slaters and Baldwins had worked out a gradual transition. On Wednesdays, Julie and Simone, who were doing well together at the Baldwins', spent the evening with the Slaters and then they visited every weekend, unless it interfered with the Baldwins' plans. Soon Julie, in particular, was joining Zane and Jared at their ball games and the boys were attending Nicole's concerts. Vic made certain he was at Simone's first golf tournament. The best part of this, as far as I was concerned, was that almost everything was arranged between the children and the families without consulting me. Jeanne and Vic were determined to make this their family, and so far their choices and decisions had been right on the mark.

Nevertheless, nothing was simple. Nicole was not in the same school district as the Slaters, but she found rides to school with the Lambs and others who were willing to help out. Julie and Simone were in the Baldwins' zone, but not the Slaters. Finally it was determined that Julie could not survive a fifth change in her sixth grade year. Mrs. Baldwin said she should remain with them until June. Then both Julie and Simone would move in permanently with the Slaters, who would presumably have their foster care license by then.

There was another hitch when Jeanne and Vic signed up for foster parent classes and learned that one series had just ended and another wasn't beginning for six months. The only possibility was to travel forty-five miles each way for the nearest class, but since they would have to go together, this would mean leaving the children alone, something they felt was unwise.

"Isn't there somebody who is qualified to teach the course who might do it on an individual basis?" I asked Nancy.

"Actually, I can," she said with a ringing laugh. "Also, Alicia Stevenson's foster mother, Ruth Levy, has certification."

Before the day was out the two of them had "volunteered" to work with the Slaters privately. With everyone pitching in, Vic and Jeanne completed the eight sessions in three weeks.

There were endless stumbling blocks to getting a foster home license.

A fire inspection was going to take three weeks. When I investigated, I discovered that the regional fire marshal had to be contacted, then he had to send someone from seventy-five miles away to tell the family where they needed to place smoke detectors and fire extinguishers.

"We have a county fire marshal whose station is less than a mile from the Slater home. Isn't he qualified?" I asked Iris.

"Not unless he has the correct form for HRS," Iris explained.

It was a simple matter to have the paperwork faxed to me, then delivered to the fire marshal, and sent back to HRS within two days, thus shaving a month off the licensing process.

Calvin Reynolds's paralegal chuckled at my frustration. "If you think that is bad, you should see the paperwork I have to fill out to order a pencil. And did you know that each foster care check passes through fourteen payment steps in five cities?"

This concerned me. I had to cut through the bureaucratic barriers somehow and looked around for a likely ally. Skipping the caseworkers and supervisors I normally dealt with, I went directly to the head of HRS in our county, Lauren Lorenzo, who was one of the few people who had not been "Peter principled" into her position. I had met her briefly at a meeting and a social occasion, but usually she had no direct contact with volunteer guardians. When I called her secretary for an appointment, I said, "Tell her I'm not making a complaint, I'm offering her an opportunity."

At first Lauren Lorenzo was a bit tense. Guardians rarely saw her, and when she was in touch with our office, it was usually to speak to Nancy about a disastrous situation.

"I've come to you for help," I said candidly when I took a seat in her office. "We have a group of children who need special handling to make an adoption work." After giving her a précis of the situation, I said, "Iris Quinones is confused, as is everyone from the fire marshal to the adoptions worker. I need a team leader for this project to move the kids into a permanent home, someone who knows the system from the inside who can deal with something that does not follow standard procedures. Also, the timing has to be coordinated. We can't allow these children to be placed into foster care before the Slaters are licensed or they will be moved, which would be cruel and destructive, especially since there are no current foster homes that will accept three teenage siblings."

"I think I can be of use," Lauren said enthusiastically. "Who else is on the team, coach?"

"The Slaters, of course, plus the Baldwins, and if I can enlist them, the Colby parents."

"Isn't that asking for the impossible?"

"Not if they are approached the right way."

"I've heard the father is a real bear and the mother isn't mentally stable."

"That's true, but I think we have a hidden weapon: the children themselves. They know how to handle their parents."

"Isn't that asking a lot of them?"

"Yes, but they are the stars of this team. They are in charge. Everything will be checked with them. They will not go into foster care or be adopted by anyone without the permission of each one. As their Guardian ad Litem, I will not recommend anything with which they do not agree."

I watched Lauren for her reaction. For a moment she was thoughtful, then she smiled. "I'll do whatever needs to be done. Count on that."

There were rumblings of typical adjustment problems with each of the sisters. As terrific as they were, the Slaters represented one more in a long line of caregivers, most of whom had made promises to them that turned out to be hollow. The Slaters had to prove themselves. The honeymoon period had to end. Testing about bedtimes and petty rules had been recent issues, so I knew it was a matter of time before there would be something that would cause Vic and Jeanne to question what they were doing.

The call came sooner than I had expected.

"You won't believe what happened," Vic said, so distraught his voice cracked like an eighth grader's. "This weekend, when Simone and Julie were here, Simone and Nicole went for a walk after dinner and didn't return."

He explained that they had passed the home of a boy Nicole knew from school and he invited them in to watch a video. They stayed for two hours, never once thinking to call Vic or Jeanne, who had been occupied with visiting relatives. At first they assumed the girls had returned and were watching television in the den. When Julie came out looking for her sisters, it dawned on Vic that the girls had been missing for over an hour.

He jumped in the car and began cruising the neighborhood. Then he started to panic. His worst fears had come true: the girls had been kidnapped by a pervert. He was liable for them and he saw everything he and Jeanne had worked for go down the tubes. On the way back to the house he met a boy, whom he recognized as one of the girls' friends, and stopped him. The boy had come from the house where the girls were watching the video and directed Vic there. Vic burst in screaming. The boy's father, who had thought Nicole and Simone had permission to be there, was furious at the boy as well as at Vic for carrying on. A row ensued, with Simone and Nicole being packed in Vic's car and brought home in disgrace.

"The worst part," Vic explained, "is that they didn't see what they had done wrong. They thought they were in a safe place and it didn't matter. When I tried to talk some sense into them, Nicole shouted at me saying I had no right to tell her what to do." He was silent for a while, then he decided to tell me more. "Nicole changed right in front of me. One minute she was this adorable child, the next her face contorted like a monster and nothing we could do or say would calm her down."

"I realize how upset you must have been, and of course I can't condone what the girls did, but maybe it would help to understand that they are going through a typical stage of adjustment called active resistance, in which they become defiant and try to set up power struggles as a way of discovering your level of commitment to them."

"But we've told them we love them and want them with us."

"Those are words. What they want is a demonstration that you not only care, but that you'll also be there for them no matter what they do . . . good or bad."

"What if something had happened to them?"

"Vic, these girls need counseling, and maybe a family therapist would help you and Jeanne understand more about the dynamics of these actions."

"How could we pay for one when we haven't had the first dollar from HRS, their parents, or anyone?"

"Their mother was court-ordered to put them in therapy, but she didn't follow through, as usual. Frankly, I wanted her to fail at that task as proof that she can't care for them. But enough time has passed. I'll see if I can find some private money for therapy."

Since the girls did not qualify yet for Medicaid, there were no funds for counseling. The best children's therapist in our area was Jayne Abernathy, a private clinical psychologist. I phoned her, and after explaining the situation, asked her for a reduced rate. Then I talked to Nancy about getting some emergency funds from the Guardian ad Litem Foundation, a new nonprofit group that raised money for the special needs of guardian children. For instance, the foundation had bought shoes for a child in shelter care who could not wait weeks until an HRS check provided sneakers for his bare feet, and paid the funeral expenses for a child who committed suicide while in foster care, because there were no HRS funds to bury a foster child. If the foundation had been in place when Alicia's mother needed a plane ticket, I could have applied for those funds. A few days later the foundation director agreed to send Dr. Abernathy funds to cover the initial therapy sessions.

Before the first visit, I had sent the doctor a letter outlining the past and present situations of these girls and the possibilities for the future and enclosed my court order that allowed me to share files and consult with her.

After her first meetings, the psychologist reviewed the case with me and said, "The Colby sisters have the most potential for change I've ever seen in kids with their disastrous background."

At the same time I was trying to prepare the Colby parents for the termination of parental rights on an entirely voluntary basis. As soon as Mr. Colby was released from jail, Julie wondered whether she could contact him. I told her that would be a fine idea, and offered to supervise the visit.

Buddy Colby asked to have the children at his home for a barbecue. Julie wanted to go, but the others balked. I told Nicole and Simone I would not force them, but asked, "Do you want your father to terminate his rights?"

"Yes," Simone said loudly, and Nicole agreed. Julie wasn't so sure.

"But wouldn't you like to remain friends with him whatever happens?"

Julie nodded. "If I could still see him, I'd rather have someone else as my parent."

I looked at Simone and Nicole. "Someday you might also want him to be involved in your life, to come to your concerts and school events, to have meals with you, to talk on the phone, and stay friends even when you are older with families of your own. If he can see that might happen easiest if he gives up some legal rights, he might go along with the plan."

"You don't know my father," Simone added ominously.

I realized she was right. I had talked to Buddy Colby a few times on the phone trying to make arrangements, but had only seen him briefly in court. "We can fight him, but then he's likely to want to fight us back. That will take time, energy, and make everyone sad in the end. Let's try to be friends and see if that works. If it doesn't, we can always go into combat later. But if we argue first, it will be almost impossible to put the pieces back together."

Nicole was trembling. "What if he's drinking or gets out his gun?"

"Does he have a gun?"

"Lots of them," Julie said, piping up. "He chased an HRS lady away with one once."

"Then I had better remind him I'm not with HRS," I said with a forced laugh. "But seriously, if anyone feels uncomfortable, let's have a signal and we'll leave at once."

We decided that if anyone was upset, they'd refer to having a stomachache and we'd go home without another word.

Julie sat in the front seat and directed me to her father's home. After a few turns down sandy roads in the pine forest, she pointed out the traditional "cracker" house with a tin roof and wraparound porch. Although quite old, it was in good repair, and except for needing a coat of paint, was immaculate inside and out. The porch had a swing and some willow rocking chairs. In the back garden there was a dilapidated lean-to on stilts that Julie called her playhouse. I knew that Buddy Colby was the grandson of the founder of the Colby Roofing Company, a well-known firm, but the girls said that an uncle ran the business and wouldn't give Buddy a position unless he cleaned up his drinking problem. Apparently he lived on handouts from his mother and part-time work when the crews were short.

I took a tour of the house with Julie so the others could have some privacy, then asked Nicole to show me the playhouse, so Julie could spend time with her father. When we were alone, I asked Nicole if she wanted to leave, but she said it was going better than expected.

Mr. Colby served up spicy broiled chicken, coleslaw, potato salad, rolls and butter, and offered sweet ice tea and coffee. The kitchen was clean and perfectly organized, and Mr. Colby reminded the girls that the utensils were in the places they remembered and they were to put them back that way.

When everyone had just about finished the meal, I brought Mr. Colby up-to-date on the legal situation. I stated why I wanted the girls to go into foster care and move in with the Slaters. "This way your daughters will have every financial advantage. Because they will qualify for a subsidized adoption, there will be health insurance and several hundred dollars a month per child for other expenses.''

"Nobody ever offered me no money to care for the girls." I explained that able-bodied parents did not receive subsidies for their own children. Then he launched into his ex-wife's failure to support the children and recounted her deceptions and lies. The sisters were uneasy with this turn in the conversation, so I attempted to steer it back to the issue at hand.

"Mr. Colby, you have wonderful daughters, who care about you, but under the circumstances, they cannot live with you. There is no reason why you can't contact them by phone or see them at any convenient time as long as the visits are supervised."

"I ain't never going to HRS again. Those people have done me dirty."

"If you prefer, I'll be available. I want you to be informed about everything that happens. Nobody wants to exclude you from their lives."

He looked at me warily. "And nobody is going to stop me from seeing my flesh and blood."

"I'm trying to make that as easy as possible."

"Nicole and Simone didn't want to come here at first, but Gay talked them into it," Julie said in a burst.

Buddy Colby began to cry. I gathered my purse and car keys and told the girls I'd back the car around while they said good-bye. From a distance I watched the hugs and farewells. Simone's and Nicole's were perfunctory, while Julie's lingered the longest.

In the car Simone took the front seat. "Did you know my father was drinking booze the whole time you were there?"

"No," I admitted.

"He tricked you," Nicole added. "Remember when he brought you that photo album? That's when he went over to the liquor cabinet, pulled out some whiskey, and dumped it in his coffee cup."

"You saw him pour it?"

"Yes," Nicole said.

"Does he drink a lot?"

Simone groaned as if this was the most obvious question in the world. "At least we got out of there in time. In another hour he'd be either cussing or praying. Trouble is, we never knew which it would be."

Jeanne Slater and I discussed how to best approach Lottie Hunt. I knew the woman still resented me because of what I said about her in the report. Jeanne said that so far she had developed a good relationship with Lottie regarding Nicole. So it was decided that Jeanne would be the liaison to Lottie

Hunt and would make her feel included in all the developments regarding her children. She told her about the foster parent classes, the fire inspection, and when she finally asked whether Mrs. Hunt might allow someone to adopt her three daughters, Lottie had said that she would consider it if the Slaters were the family, and nobody else.

After Jeanne reported this conversation, I asked her to see whether Mrs. Hunt would be receptive to officially terminate parental rights. Jeanne called back to let me know that Mrs. Hunt consented to sign the papers ''any time it was convenient.''

I knew we were jumping the gun because the Slaters were not even officially foster parents, but it was important to have at least one parent agreeable, especially Mrs. Hunt. Although the children had been abused in her care, she had not been the perpetrator and the culprits were no longer in her life. Even if she had psychologically injured them or had failed to provide for them adequately, it would be almost impossible to get a court to terminate her rights involuntarily. Mr. Colby, on the other hand, had been the abuser, and we had documented proof, police reports, and children who feared living with him. There might be a case to get his rights revoked, but it would be a long, messy, Gregory K.-style fight. Still, I felt we might win his cooperation if he was approached correctly.

The next hurdle was the adoption department at HRS. Nancy had set up the meeting with the district head of adoptions, the adoptions case-worker assigned to our county, and the attorney who handled these cases. Iris Quinones was also invited. We had done much preliminary work and had the promise of one termination, so I expected the adoptions unit would be receptive to a favorable ending to a complicated case.

Adoption seemed the best solution, for only with adoption did children receive a guarantee of permanency. Otherwise they lived in the limbo of foster care, never trusting that they wouldn't be moved, thrown out, or returned to a natural parent in the next court proceeding. The cost to the federal government for foster care is 2.3 billion dollars annually. Of that, only 1.4 billion goes to the children's maintenance, while the other billion is used to administer the funding. That does not include the dollars added in to support foster children at the state and local level. These numbers add up to a sizeable industry with the foster care children being commodities. Obviously some people have a vested interest in making sure that children remain in foster care or they will lose their jobs. This situation is compounded in areas where foster care is contracted to private child welfare agencies—agencies that would go out of business if these children magically disappeared into adoptive homes or were returned to their families. Even worse, foster care is a growth industry. The foster care population increased from 269,000 in the mid 1980s to 460,000 in 1992. At the same time, the number of children freed for adoption has stayed constant in the 30,000 to 40,000 range. About 100,000 additional children have adoption as their long-term plan, but most of these children never find permanent homes.

Why? Is it true that nobody will take these hard-to-place children? In the 1950s and 1960s the point of adoption was to provide babies to infertile families based on matching characteristics including appearance, religion, background. These days, when there are far more people who want to adopt than children, the affinity is based on tolerance. What behaviors might parents abide? Might they accept a hyperactive child? A child with a learning disability? A child of a different race? A child with a physical handicap? Would they take a sexually abused child? A child who has committed a crime?

If you get a group of adoption advocates together, they soon get into a game of one-upmanship describing their least adoptable case. The most recent prize story was about a child who had been in an automobile accident that severed her spine from the neck down. She was a quadriplegic who could neither control her bodily functions nor speak. The biological family had long ago signed their daughter over to the state because they could not afford her medical costs. They had stopped their visits because they thought the child did not know them anyway and they couldn't deal with their pain. The practical nurse discovered that the child could signal with blinks and eye movements. This breakthrough in communication bonded the child to the nurse, and soon the nurse was inquiring about adopting the child. She was told she was crazy to accept this massive responsibility for a child who would never recover any further functions, but the nurse persisted. Eventually the nurse became this very disabled child's foster parent, and later her adoptive parent, with a state subsidy for her home medical care, which was tens of thousands of dollars a year cheaper than nursing home living. If this impossible-to-place child had found a permanent home, surely there were many more families willing to take other children with complications.

One distressing statistic is that the younger the age of a child entering the foster care system, the longer he stays a foster child. Fifty-three percent of the children who come into foster care remain without a permanent home for over four years. Doesn't it seem more likely that the cute infants would be the most adoptable? It would, except most are not available for adoption. Family preservation is the hallmark of the "mod-

ern'' social services approach. Foster care and protective services caseworkers are supposed to use their best efforts to reunite families. (The
former work with the children who are already court-placed in foster
homes; the latter work with children who are merely being supervised
either in their own homes or in some temporary informal placement.)
Caseworkers might allow a drug-addicted mother a year or more to get
her life together or give a young teen mother a chance to mature, not
considering that a two-year-old, who has spent a year in foster care, has
lived half his life being parented by someone else. When a caseworker
finally accepts that parental rights must be terminated, the attorney for
the agency often looks at the case and says he cannot win it because
some steps haven't been covered to document parental neglect, thus the
process is delayed yet again. If, for instance, the child's mother is chem-
ically dependent and the goal was to get her into treatment and reunite
the family, but the agency did not have the resources to help the mother,
the mother's lawyer can probably get a continuance in the case, leaving
the child in limbo even longer—years longer.

My mother, who was a social worker and now lives nearby in Florida,
also became a Guardian ad Litem, and we enjoy having this in common.
One of her cases was a baby abandoned by both parents at the age of
six months. The relative who had been stuck with the infant turned her
over to foster care. Her first foster mother adored the child and immediately applied to adopt her. But as soon as the process began, the missing natural mother showed up—or at least her attorney made a court
appearance—and claimed the mother wanted her baby back. Visitations
were begun, with the mother only showing up for one out of five appointments, and then demonstrating very little interest in the child, who
clung to her foster mother because she did not know her real mother.
Finally, when the mother did not appear for two court hearings, termination of parental rights procedures were begun in preparation for the
adoption. At the last minute a grandmother demanded custody of her
granddaughter, and HRS changed the child's plan from adoption to
placement with a relative. My mother's diligent investigation of this
grandmother revealed she had given up three of her children to foster
care and had lied about several other essential matters. After more than
a year of constant prodding by the Guardian ad Litem, finally this little
girl was adopted by her foster family, the only family she had ever
known.

Sometimes the appeals process can last years and is definitely not in
the best interests of children. Nancy had warned me that this delay would

be the result if either Colby parent contested termination. By the time the appeals would be heard, Nicole and Simone could have turned eighteen, making the issue a moot point. This had given me the idea that termination of parental rights was not a permanent state, but a temporary one until the child was eighteen. Thus, after that age, a mother could continue a relationship with her child without anyone's permission. Being a parent did not end at some magical birthday. When the Colby girls grew up and had families of their own, they might choose to socialize with their biological parents if a friendly relationship could be maintained. If I could help the Colby parents to see it in this light, perhaps they wouldn't fight the adoption.

The problem was that what I had in mind was called an "open adoption," in which the biological parents would be welcome to stay in touch with their offspring. But when parents signed the termination papers under Florida statutes, they had to agree to relinquish the child to HRS and consent to "give up all right to further information concerning the whereabouts of this child, or the identity or location of any adoptive parent of this child," thus legally creating a "closed adoption" situation. For many years it was believed that it was in the best interests of the families involved to keep a child's whereabouts secret, but in the United States there are more and more cases of "open adoptions" in which the mothers relinquishing newborns continue to have some knowledge of or contact with the adopting parents. This is due in part to the scarcity of babies for adoption, which leads to families meeting the birth mothers as a way to convince them they would be good adoptive parents for their children. Also, with less stigma attached to unwed mothers, the young mothers are not cloistered and do not feel the terrible shame that makes them refuse to reveal their identity. However, under the HRS adoption rules, nobody is allowed to promise parents that they can have continuing contact with their children. Even so, there was no way anyone could prevent the Colby children, who could use a telephone and soon would be driving, from contacting their parents. Also, the Slaters were not opposed to the children continuing whatever relationship with their parents that they desired.

I knew there was something wrong the minute I entered the HRS boardroom. Iris Quinones sat between Scott Keefer, the head of adoptions, and Dolly Lemoine, our county's adoption caseworker. Nancy and I took the empty seats opposite, while the HRS adoption attorney, Myra Garland, stood at the head of the table. Nancy made the presentation of the Colby case, then asked me to fill in anything she had missed.

"We can't do anything without signed terminations," Myra Garland said.

"How are those coming, Gay?" Nancy asked me.

"Mrs. Hunt said she will sign any time it is appropriate and Mr. Colby hasn't been approached directly yet."

"They'll never sign voluntarily," Scott Keefer said emphatically. "How does it look for a court-ordered termination?"

"A very weak case," Myra replied rapidly.

"The man just got out of jail," I said.

"Not for hurting his kids," Myra snapped.

"There are documented abuse reports."

"They were a long time ago," the lawyer said to prove she had read the file.

"The kids refuse to ever live there again."

"Not true," Scott said, flipping through one of Iris's reports. "Julie says she would like to live with her dad."

I shot a glance at Iris, who looked away. "When did she say that?"

"Last week."

"After she was grounded by Mrs. Baldwin for refusing to help with chores?"

"These kids know the system and how to jerk everyone around," Iris said.

"They're in therapy to work on that, but they aren't going to improve by staying in the system for the rest of their lives," I added.

"Look, Nancy," the attorney said, spitting the words like machine gun bullets, "I know you have the best intentions, but I don't think your guardian has the experience to see the pitfalls. This is a classic setup for a failed adoption."

"What do you mean?" I asked.

"Adoption sounds like a panacea. The papers are signed and everyone lives happily ever after, but adoptive parents get fed up, particularly with adolescent behaviors, and they turn the kids back to us and we have to accept them. Then we're stuck with three kids who will take this next failure so hard emotionally they will be worse off than before, and will probably spend the rest of their minority in foster care."

"I don't see the difference," Nancy responded. "They'll be in foster care in a few weeks anyway. Adoption is a chance, maybe only a slim one. Why should we second-guess it and deny them this little window of opportunity?''

"There is a tremendous amount of work putting one of these adoptions together," Scott continued. "I like to direct my limited resources at children who have more of a chance at success."

I looked around the room wondering why everyone was so antagonistic. Dolly Lemoine had her back turned so she would never have to look at either me or Nancy. I could not understand why none of them would give this situation a chance. "You don't know these girls," I said, pleadingly. "Their therapist has stated that they have more potential for change than any kids she's ever seen. If I put them in a group of high-functioning children from stable homes and asked you to pick them out, you wouldn't be able to." I fumbled in my file for the snapshots from the craft fair and passed them around. Nobody seemed to care, but I left the photos faceup in the middle of the table.

Dolly Lemoine spoke up for the first time, but she still didn't face the gathering. "We have other sibling groups who have been on the waiting list for years that the Slater family might be interested in."

Nancy saw my back stiffen and leaned over as if to soothe me. "The Slaters are only considering these children," I snapped. "You heard the story of how they felt compelled to take them in."

"That's what worries me the most," Scott said. "They sound unstable to me. One of these kids is going to pull some typical teen stunt, and they are going to toss her out."

"This theorizing isn't getting anywhere," Nancy said. "Let's formulate a plan for proceeding. If it begins to unravel, we can reevaluate then."

Scott Keefer deferred to the attorney. "I want to see those terminations," Myra said. "And I don't want them tainted." She stared meaningfully at Nancy.

"You want them vetted by the parents' attorneys and without guardian involvement, right?"

Myra nodded, then said she had another appointment.

"There are many other obstacles," Scott added after she left. "Our budget has been cut and we won't be able to do a home study for at least three months. In the meantime, the children need birth certificates, psychological reports, and medical and dental examinations. I'm afraid we do not have funds for any of those right now."

I was smiling. I had copies of the birth certificates all ready. Dr. Abernathy could write the psychologicals. I had friends who were doctors and dentists who would gladly perform exams for the children to be adopted.

"Your guardian thinks this is some sort of joke," Scott Keefer said with obvious annoyance.

I flushed. He had mistaken my relaxation for impudence. "I'm sorry, I wasn't laughing at you, I was just happy that none of those items are difficult." I told him who would provide those services. "Just give me the forms and it will be done."

"The birth certificates have to be certified originals."

"I can take care of those," Iris Quinones said to be helpful. "Gay can handle the rest if she is willing."

"Then it is settled," Nancy said and recapped everyone's responsibilities.

Without another word, Dolly and Scott left the room.

In the parking lot, Nancy was furious. "See what I mean? They want to sabotage this adoption. And I don't like the way they were condescending to you."

"I didn't mind."

"Well, I did! You are a volunteer and deserve to be treated with respect and gratitude for everything you have already done. I'm going to call Scott tomorrow and demand an apology to you."

"I guess they were fairly hostile, but it seems absurd to me. We're taking three kids out of the system. We've found the placement for both foster care and adoption. We have private funds for the medical and psychological. I'm doing most of the work for free. What's the big problem?"

"It wasn't their idea. It's not their adoptive home. It's not being done in the right order or by their rules."

"Surely they wouldn't deny these girls a home because of that, would they?"

Nancy didn't reply at first. Then she looked at me with fire in her eyes. "Not if I can help it."

The case of the three birth certificates classically illustrates the bureaucratic web that ensnares children. Getting certified original copies was the one job Iris Quinones had agreed to undertake.

Two weeks later, she called me. "Can't get them. They will only give them to a natural parent or guardian."

"Aren't the Colbys dependent children under HRS and isn't the health department, which issues the certificates, an HRS agency?"

"Yes, but the clerk said I'd have to fill out the forms and apply through Tallahassee. That will take six months."

"That's ridiculous. Why don't you ask their mother to do it?"

"She hasn't returned my phone calls, but as her guardian you could get them."

"I'm not the legal guardian of the child, the state is."

"The clerk said they'd give it to the Guardian ad Litem."

Exasperated, I got into my car and drove twenty-two miles to the health department, where I presented my court orders, showed my identification card, my driver's license, and copies of the children's birth certificates.

"One of the children was not born in this county. That requires an eleven-dollar fee," the clerk said. I took out my checkbook. "Cash." I handed her a ten and a single bill. "It's ten dollars for each of the other ones."

I gave her twenty more dollars, leaving myself only change in my wallet, and demanded a receipt. Then I drove two miles to the HRS headquarters and asked for Iris Quinones. After thirty minutes, she still had not appeared. Finally I had to leave. I asked the receptionist to make copies of the birth certificates and my receipt. I impressed upon her the value of these documents and she promised to deliver them to Ms. Quinones at once.

Two weeks later Myra Garland still did not have the birth certificates. Later I had learned they had traveled from Iris's desk to the county attorney, then on to Lauren Lorenzo, Dolly Lemoine, then Scott Keefer, before landing on Myra's desk. She had decided to have Calvin Reynolds manage the legal proceedings locally, but we had to wait for the certificates to make their way back to his office, which took six weeks.

If I had not "interfered" with this process, it could easily have taken six months, or longer, for this tiny step to have been made. Instead of being annoyed by this, however, it energized me. Everything was falling into place. School was ending and the Slaters were about to become licensed foster parents. Soon the children would be reunited under one roof with people who wanted them to stay forever.

The rest was nonsense.

I could handle nonsense.

A few days before Mother's Day, Nicole called me and asked, "Which one should I send cards to?"

"You have two mothers, why not send them both cards. It would make each one of them happy."

"What about Fay Lamb? She was also my mother this year."

"Sure, her too."

All three women made a point to tell me they had received "special" cards from Nicole. The other girls also gave cards to both Jeanne and their mother. At church Jeanne was called to the front of the congregation to receive the Mother-of-the-Year award. Her picture was taken surrounded by Julie, Nicole, Simone, Zane, and Jared.

When Father's Day rolled around, Julie asked her father to lunch and I took the sisters to McDonald's. Buddy Colby bought us Big Macs. I gave him a stack of photographs of the girls and we talked about how well things were going in the Slater home and the fact that they would officially become foster parents in a few weeks. We kept the conversation centered around the financial benefits of foster care and adoption, but I said that nothing would stop him from opening bank accounts in the children's names for their future. At this, Mr. Colby changed the subject.

At the end of the meal, Buddy said, "I know you want me to give up my rights to these girls, but I think it's one of Lottie's tricks to get me out of the picture."

"That's not the case," I said, "but I understand your concerns. What would make you more secure?"

"If I saw that she signed the papers first and that she couldn't grab them back."

"Okay, I'll see what I can do."

"That still doesn't mean I'll give away my daughters."

"I'm not going to try to talk you into it. You discuss it with the girls and then you pray about what you think will be best for them. I know you love them and because of that love you will do what is right for them."

A week later I had a call at the Guardian ad Litem office to contact Mr. Colby. I reached him after dinner. His speech was slurred.

"Been thinking about what you said about my girls."

"About what is best for them?"

"Yes." There was a long pause. "I like you. You are the only one who ever seemed to really care about my children. Do you actually think it would be better for them to be adopted by strangers?"

"I think it would be best if they could live together with one of their parents, however they don't want to go back to their mother."

"I don't want them to do that either."

"And the court won't send them back to you in the near future."

"I know that."

"If they stay in foster care, they could be moved around and separated. Adoption is the only possibility of permanence. Also, once they are adopted, HRS is out of the picture—and by the way, I am too. That means HRS won't be able to control your access to them and you won't have to answer to HRS."

"I think I am going to do it."

"What's that?"

"You know, what you want me to do."

"I want what is best for the girls."

"I'll do it, if they tell me that's what they want."

"Okay, we'll talk again. Call me anytime."

He hung up the phone and I held the dead receiver for several seconds, then threw the portable phone in the air. "Yes!" I said aloud. Then I dialed Vic Slater and told him the news.

A court date for the change of placement hearing was set. As soon as Calvin Reynolds heard the Slaters' foster care license was in the mail, he filed the papers to order the Colby sisters into foster care. For once, HRS and the Guardian ad Litem office were in agreement. In preparing my report for the court, I took special pains to write complimentary words about the natural parents as well as the HRS workers.

> Many departments of HRS, including foster care licensing, protective services, and adoptions have worked hard to facilitate this atypical case. Everyone, including the children themselves and their birth parents, cooperated to make this special placement work. Complex procedures were done rapidly and communication between everyone has been excellent, allowing this favorable outcome in a challenging situation.

The girls prepared to come to court because they wanted to tell the judge that this is what they desired. When I took them into the judge's chambers, I said, "Usually ordering children into foster care is an admission that all other avenues have been blocked, and Your Honor's decision is the least detrimental alternative. However, this is a happy day because foster care is merely a technical step on the way to an adoption and everyone present is in accord that this is the best course of action."

Calvin Reynolds nodded. The lawyer for Mr. Colby, who was not present, and the lawyer for Mrs. Hunt, who was, stated they had no objections.

We were out of court in less than five minutes.

In the hallway, Calvin said, "What about the terminations? Who is handling those?"

"Send them to the parents' lawyers. We're ready to go."

"Are you certain they will sign?"

I saw Mrs. Hunt coming out of the rest room and motioned for her to come over. "Mr. Reynolds wants to know if you are ready to sign the terminations."

"I could do it now," she said.

"Sorry, I don't have the forms," Calvin replied, a bit taken aback by her enthusiasm. "I'll send them to your attorney tomorrow."

"Thanks, Lottie," I said. "Call me if you have any questions."

"What about the father?" Calvin said after Lottie left.

"He'll sign, but he wants to be certain their mother does it first, so this isn't some sort of ploy for her to get them when he can't."

He pressed the elevator button. "Why don't we bring them back to court and have them execute the consents simultaneously?"

"Mr. Colby doesn't like coming here because the last time he was in shackles. Also, he hates to be in the same room as his ex-wife."

"What if he doesn't sign?"

"He'll sign. He told me he would."

Calvin shook his head in disbelief. "It never happens this easily."

I headed for the parking lot where my car sizzled in the midday Florida summer sun.

The girls were waiting for me with their mother. "Want to join us for a burger?" I asked Mrs. Hunt. She beamed. "Who wants to ride with her mom?"

"I do," Julie said.

"Okay, Nicole, you come with me and Julie and Simone go with your mother."

In the restaurant everyone was cheerful. Simone talked about her summer job, Julie about taking horseback lessons, and Nicole about babysitting for Zane and Jared, who were "a pain" but it was worth it because of the money.

Lottie Hunt glanced at a newspaper that had been left on the next table with two headlines about custody cases. During the summer of 1993, there were several high-profile children's rights cases: Baby Jessica, the two-year-old child, who the court in Iowa had demanded be returned to her biological father from her adopted parents in Michigan; and Kimberly Mays, the fourteen-year-old Florida girl who had been switched at birth. Kimberly was asking that her natural parents, the Twiggs, be restrained by the court from seeking custody of her.

"What do you think about those cases?" Lottie Hunt asked me.

I deflected the question. "What do you girls think?"

Nicole spoke up first. "I think Baby Jessica should go back to her birth mother."

Lottie seemed surprised. "Why?"

"Her mother has been trying to get her back since she was a few weeks old and the courts have been holding it up. That wasn't fair to either the real parents or the baby."

"But the mother lied about who the father was," Simone interjected.

"So, should the baby suffer for that?" Nicole countered.

I was surprised that the Colby sisters knew so many details about the case.

"What about Baby Jessica?" Lottie asked me. "Did she have a guardian?"

"Actually, I think she eventually was given one, but it wasn't very meaningful. Her rights haven't been considered. In law children are the property of their parents."

"That's not fair," Julie said.

"If you were Baby Jessica's guardian, what would you do?" I asked Julie.

"I would allow her to live with the people she knows but to visit her mother sometimes too."

"I agree with Julie," Lottie said. "You've got to think about the baby first."

I popped some of Julie's french fries in my mouth, thinking: I cannot believe this conversation. We've just taken this woman's children and put them one more legal step beyond her reach, and she's thinking about their needs rather than her own for a change. "What about Kimberly Mays?"

"That's different," Simone said. "She should visit her birth parents because none of this was their fault."

"How can you force a fourteen-year-old to stay with people she doesn't like?" I wondered.

"They could see her at someone like Dr. Abernathy's office," Julie said.

"What about Gregory K.?" Lottie Hunt asked me. "Do you think he had the right to divorce his parents?"

"All he wanted was termination of parental rights, the same paper you have agreed to sign."

"I know. I didn't want to put my kids through that. If Gregory's mother had really cared about him, she would have done the same."

"You really love your daughters, don't you?"

"Yes," Lottie answered steadily. "And I'm showing everyone you can do something like what Gregory K. wanted, and do it right."

"We have a little problem," Vic said three days later. "Julie wanted to stay overnight with a friend of hers, but we did not know the family and suggested that her friend could come to our house instead. She had a fit and cried and said we were being mean to her. Then, when we thought she was calling her friend, she phoned her father and told him she didn't want to live here anymore and didn't want to be adopted."

"I guess she'd better talk to Dr. Abernathy about this. In the meantime, I'll take Julie out for a while. Would tomorrow afternoon be all right?"

The next day Julie and I went for ice cream sundaes at Dairy Queen. "Complaint time," I said.

"What do you mean?" Julie asked tensely.

"I bet you have a whole list of complaints. Lay it on me. That's what I am here for."

"Well, I hate it when Jared and Zane use the bathroom first. They leave a big mess and then I get blamed for their towels on the floor."

"Yeah, and if you pick them up, they'll expect you'll do it every time and if you don't, you get in trouble, right?" She nodded somberly. "What else?"

We went down the list. I made certain to reflect back Julie's problems to demonstrate that I took them seriously. I didn't consider them trivial and I didn't blame her. After all, I was not her parent or her therapist, I was her voice, and what I was trying to do was to help her see ways she could deal with the complexities of her new family. I sympathized with the fact that she suddenly was the middle child, when up until then she had been the baby. She was also distressed because she was going to have to repeat sixth grade. I reminded her that the situation was hardly her fault and that she was young for sixth grade anyway and would be at the top of her class the next semester.

When we were back in the car, Julie said, "I thought you were going to be mad at me for calling my father."

"You can phone him anytime you want."

"What if I don't want to be adopted?"

"Then you won't be. Since you are over twelve, you have to go to court and sign your own adoption papers anyway. Nobody can force you to do it."

"What if my sisters want it?"

"Then they will be. But you are an individual and you will do what is best for Julie and nobody else."

"What if I don't want to live with the Slaters anymore?"

"That's a problem, but not an insurmountable one." I then told Julie about some of the other foster homes and that she wouldn't necessarily remain in the same school district or be near her sisters.

"I don't want to leave the Slaters," she said.

"Okay, so you won't leave this week. Tell me how you feel next week."

The next one to blow was Nicole.

Vic called and said, "I don't know if we are going to be able to keep Nicole."

"What happened?"

"I'm not sure, that's the crazy part. Nicole had been folding laundry and putting it out on everyone's beds like we do around here, when Jeanne told her she should also pick up the clothes that were draped across the furniture. She flew off the handle and tossed the boys' clothes at Jeanne and began screaming at the top of her lungs, 'You can't make me do anything I don't want to do.' She turned purple and her whole face was twisted. She backed into a corner and crossed her hands over her face and kept screaming and screaming, then she ran into her room and didn't come out for the rest of the night."

"She needs to talk to Dr. Abernathy about this right away, but I'll be seeing her tonight when we go to her father's for a barbecue. Maybe she'll have something to say about it then."

"All right," Vic said, "but we don't know if we can take this. Jeanne was frightened and nobody could calm Nicole down."

"You have to remember that Nicole has been the most brutally abused of the children. Maybe something that happened triggered a memory or maybe a lot of other tensions just built up and exploded. In a way this might be a compliment to you and Jeanne."

"How could that be?"

"If she wasn't beginning to feel secure in the relationship with you, she might not have felt she could let out her feelings of helplessness and rage."

"She's normally so sweet and helpful . . ."

"I know, Vic. She thinks she has to be that way or nobody will take care of her. This could be a breakthrough in your relationship."

"Felt more like a breakup to me."

"Why don't you make an appointment with Dr. Abernathy too? She might have hints for how to deal with your confusion as well as how to manage these outbursts better."

The next evening Nicole was in the front seat as the three sisters and I headed toward Buddy Colby's house. I didn't bring up Vic's conversation, but Simone did.

"Now don't you go telling Daddy about what happened with Jeanne," Simone warned Nicole in her big sister tone. "Julie's already caused enough trouble."

"Simone, I know you want everything to work out with the Slaters," I said, "but Julie and Nicole are separate individuals and each will make up her own mind."

"It's time they thought of someone else besides themselves. I left the Baldwins' to be with them and what thanks do I get?"

"Would you rather be there still?"

"No, I like the Slaters. They are trying to do their best and they want us all to get along."

"Why do you think the Slaters are doing this?"

"To show off," Nicole responded snidely, "to get the precious Mother-of-the-Year award and prove they are so wonderful to everyone in church."

"Why else?"

"For money?" Julie asked.

"No, definitely not for money. They haven't even gotten the first foster care check and they've fed and clothed Nicole for months, and the rest of you for many weeks, not to mention the trips, church camp, riding lessons, and everything else. They've sold their house and are moving into an inconvenient rental so they can build a bigger house. They need to trade their compact car for a van."

"They are doing it for God," Simone explained matter-of-factly. "The Lord came to them and told them to take us even before they met us, so it is spiritual."

"If that is true, why did Jeanne attack me last night?" Nicole snapped.

"She didn't attack you," Simone retorted. "You freaked out."

Nicole began to tremble. We were almost at the turn for her father's lane, so I pulled over on a grassy lot, and parked the car. "What happened, Nicole?"

"Jeanne came at me."

"No she didn't!" Simone shot from the back.

I turned around. "Simone, let's hear how Nicole feels about it." I placed my hand on Nicole's shoulder. "Show me what Jeanne did."

"That's how it begins. That's how it always begins . . ." Nicole's voice had become lower, more ominous. Her eyes flashed and her knees were shaking. She shook her finger at me and her mouth twisted. "She had this smirk on her face. I hate it when they get like that. That's when they hit you."

"Who hits you?"

"People who don't like what you do."

"Did Jeanne hit you?"

"She was going to."

"Did she hit you?" I repeated.

"She wanted to. It was like a hit . . . I don't know. It hurt like a hit."

"Then what happened?"

"I screamed at her to get away. Nobody can come at me like that, nobody!" Nicole's voice became more normal. "I lost it. Do you think I am crazy?"

"No. I think you have scary memories. What did Jeanne do?"

"She yelled at me."

"That didn't help, did it?"

"No, it was like adding sticks to my fire."

"How's the fire now?"

"Better."

"Are you ready to see your father?"

"I guess."

I gave Nicole a hug. "There's nothing wrong with you."

"Are you sure?"

"All you need is some extra attention."

"How can you tell?"

"Because there are times when everyone does. And you know something? Your father loves you in his way, your mother loves you in her way, the Slaters love you, even the Lambs do too. And don't forget you are very special to me. I'm sure there are others on that list. Here's a little secret: you can never have too many people who love you."

* * *

Buddy Colby barbecued pork chops and served sweet ice tea, baked beans, and sliced tomatoes. The television was on during the meal and from time to time he glanced up at the country music channel. He talked about the problems he was having with his car, his abscessed tooth, and a relative who arrived for a few days but showed no signs of leaving. I mentioned that Julie was learning to ride a horse, Nicole was earning money baby-sitting, and Simone had an application in to work for a fast-food restaurant. He listened, but never asked his daughters any questions.

While the girls were cleaning up the paper plates and putting away the television tables, Buddy Colby turned. ''You sure this is the right thing to do?''

''You mean signing the papers?''

''Yeah. My lawyer sent me a big packet of crap and I burned it, but now I'm thinking on it again.''

''You burned the termination papers?''

''No, I just said that.'' He glanced up at Garth Brooks singing, ''The Dance.'' As he sipped from his cup, I wondered if he had spiked it this time as well. ''What do my girls want?''

''Ask them.''

I called the sisters into the room and waited, but Buddy Colby was silent. ''Your father wants to know if he should sign the termination papers.''

''It would make everything easier, Dad,'' Simone said.

''HRS tells us where we can sleep overnight and I can't visit my friend in Alabama unless I get out of foster care,'' Nicole added.

''What about you, Julie?'' he asked. ''You told me they weren't being nice to you.''

''They are, Dad. I just was mad at them.''

''The Slaters are planning to live in this county so you can watch your girls grow up. Simone is driving now. She can come over to visit you whenever she wants. Nobody will keep you away from them.''

''They'd better not,'' Buddy replied in a guttural voice. Then he wiped his eyes. ''Okay, girls, you win. I'll do it whenever the lady says I should.''

''What lady?'' Julie asked.

Her father pointed to me.

''The time is now, Mr. Colby.''

''Has their mother done it?''

''She has an appointment this week. Why don't you go to your attor-

ney's office and sign and then ask him to hold the papers until he sees
Mrs. Hunt's papers? That way you are protected."

"Got to go nearby there on Tuesday. Is that soon enough?"

"Tuesday would be fine. And thank you."

Two days later Julie called me. "Is it normal to wake up from a dream
and you've been crying in the dream and then you find out you are crying
for real?"

"If the dream was very sad. Want to tell me about it?"

"We were having dinner at Daddy's house, just like the other night.
You were there and Daddy and my sisters." Her voice splintered and
she continued in a whisper. "Then there was a big storm, like a tornado.
Branches were flying off the trees and then a huge one fell on the house.
We ducked under the table, but when we looked up we saw that the
trunk had come through the roof and killed Daddy. It was raining really
hard, but you said we had better bury him, so we dragged him outside
near the dog pen. Simone and Nicole dug a deep hole and I was sliding
around in the mud. Finally, we pushed him in the hole, although it was
harder than we thought it was going to be. We were standing there saying
some prayers and I started crying and then I woke up."

"That's a really sad dream, isn't it?"

"What does it mean?" Julie sobbed.

"You want to think about it and tell me?"

"No, I want you to say it."

"You want me to say that the other night was like killing off your
dad, that by signing away his rights he is no longer going to be your
daddy anymore."

"I want a regular life like everyone else, but I don't want to hurt
anyone."

"You deserve that, but your father is not gone forever. He wants to
see you and you want to see him."

"What if Vic and Jeanne have been lying and as soon as they adopt
us they turn mean and break their promises?"

"I suppose it could happen, but what would they get out of it?"

"Why does anyone want to hurt a kid?"

"Good question, but I think Vic and Jeanne have the best intentions.
They aren't perfect, but then nobody is. And if you can't stand living
with them, you can always go back into foster care."

"I can?"

"Sure. Nothing is forever."

"Okay!" Julie said so much more brightly that I marveled at her resilience. "Talk to you later," she said, then hung up.

I remained with my hand on the phone for a long time. The image of the tree hitting Buddy Colby, of the grave in the garden, the rain, and Julie's tears soon had me crying. In a way she had been telling me that I had helped to kill her family.

The next court appearance after the Colby children were ordered into foster care was for the review of the permanent placement plan. Since parental rights had not been terminated, adoption was not yet legally possible. Every child put in the state's care is supposed to have a plan to get out of foster care. Usually the first goal is family reunification, but those days had long passed for the Colbys. Everyone agreed that foster care would be continued with the goal being the termination of parental rights.

Only the attorneys for the parents were present. Mrs. Hunt's lawyer stated that she was ready and willing to sign the terminations when Mr. Colby executed his. Mr. Colby's attorney said that his client had not yet agreed to do so. I explained that on two occasions Mr. Colby had told me that he was ready to sign, and in fact, had said he would see his attorney before this hearing. The attorney claimed this was news to him. The judge continued the case for two weeks to give Mr. Colby an opportunity to sign the papers. I also used the hearing to get the Colby children an exception to the strict foster care rules that did not permit them overnights in unlicensed foster homes. I wanted them to have visits with their mother, if desired, for Julie and Simone to stay with the Baldwins, as well as for them all to be able to attend slumber parties like other normal teenagers.

"What if they are sexually abused in a friend's home?" asked Jenny Clinch, the new foster care counselor, who had replaced Iris Quinones because the children were now in another department.

I rolled my eyes. "The goal is for these children to have a regular life for a change. They have friends at their church and their crowd is one of the best in town."

The judge asked Calvin Reynolds what he thought. "As long as we are informed about where the children are staying, it is fine with me."

"So ruled," said the judge, annoying Jenny Clinch.

After court Jenny said to me, "The father didn't sign, and I bet he never will. This case is going to blow up in your face, and then I'll be the first one to say I told you so."

In the past I had locked horns with Jenny over several other children. For some reason we never agreed about the disposition of a case. I tried to smile as I replied, "I shall take full responsibility, but I cannot understand why someone in your position wouldn't want to root for the team that has put this together. We'd like you to join and make this transition as easy as possible, but if you won't, why would you bet against us?"

"Adoption is hardly a football contest. It's damn serious business."

"Have you met the Colby children yet?" I asked to defuse the moment.

"No, I'm going out to the Slaters' tomorrow."

"Then I suggest you talk to them and then get back to me. In the meantime, I have the terminations to worry about."

Mrs. Hunt accompanied her attorney to the next hearing to review the permanent placement plan. She also brought along Wanda, her therapist, as a support person, and the judge allowed Wanda into his chambers even though she wasn't a party to the case. Mr. Colby didn't appear, although he had promised his attorney he would. Embarrassed, the attorney phoned his office. Mr. Colby had left a message that he was having "car trouble."

Mrs. Hunt's attorney demonstrated that she had signed the termination of parental rights forms, but these would only be given to the court when Mr. Colby had done the same.

"Your Honor," I said, "Mr. Colby has stated to me that he does not wish to come to court or to be in the same room with his ex-wife, so this no-show is part of a pattern. I don't think it is fair to leave these children in limbo." Then I reiterated the history of the case. "I'd like to suggest that if Mr. Colby does not do what he promised, then we take steps to begin an involuntary termination proceeding against him. I do not think this would be in the children's best interests, though, because I hoped they could continue to have friendly relations with their natural father. However, they have told me they are willing to testify against him if necessary."

"I'll continue the case for one week," Judge Donovan said. "By then I expect both parents to have the terminations signed or I will expect the department to have the documents ready to proceed against Mr. Colby."

"May I have the court's permission to go to Mr. Colby's house to get the consents?" his attorney asked, since he was court-appointed and this would probably incur an additional fee charged to the court. The judge approved the motion.

Four days later Lillian phoned me at eight in the morning to say that Mr. Colby was trying to get hold of me. I called him back at once.

"I fired that damn lawyer," he said, then explained how his attorney had come to his house to get the papers signed, but he hadn't been there and had told his visiting relative to tell the attorney to leave the papers, but the attorney had refused. Then the lawyer had called him and dressed him down for not being there at the appointed time. ''And he lied about the papers. I thought I was giving my girls to the Slaters, but it says here that the children are released to HRS. What kind of a dirty switch is that?''

''The adoption cannot go directly between you and the Slaters and still receive state subsidy. We're doing it this way so the children have financial support and medical insurance until they are eighteen.''

''I won't give HRS my children.''

I explained what the judge had ruled and that if the papers were not signed by the next day, HRS would proceed against him. ''That is not what your daughters want. They will resent having to tell their story again in court. Why not make it easier for them?''

''That's what Vic Slater said when I talked to him last night.''

''You called him?''

''Yes. I wanted to make sure he wasn't going to shut me out.''

''What did he say?''

''He promised he would protect and take care of them, and that I would always be welcome in their lives.'' There was a long pause. ''I don't want to hurt them, you know that.''

''I know, but this is hard for you.''

''It is tearing out my heart.''

''You feel like you are giving up your children forever,'' I said in my most sympathetic voice, although my patience was waning fast.

''You're the only one who understands. I'll sign the papers with you.''

''We can't do that, Mr. Colby. I represent the best interests of the girls and your attorney needs to advise you of your rights in the matter.''

''He's a fool. He's filing the papers to withdraw from the case. Can't you come to the house?''

''I'm not a notary and you also need two witnesses.''

''We could meet at the bank.''

''When?''

''In twenty minutes?''

''Okay,'' I said, although my hair was dripping wet and I hadn't had breakfast.

I hung up, called Nancy, and explained the problem. ''I warned you that you can't be connected with the signing of the terminations,'' she said, not cloaking her annoyance.

''I know, but Mr. Colby said he will only give them to me.''

"He could later claim he signed them under duress."

"We'd be in a public place, with witnesses to what was said."

"If there was an appeal, he could contend that you met him earlier and talked him into it or made promises that he could see the children or have some control over them."

"Well, he could assert that I did the same thing last night or last week."

"I don't want these consents to terminate parental rights compromised, Gay. You heard what Myra Garland said about them being 'tainted.' "

"The alternative is to force the kids through a termination hearing." Just then my housekeeper arrived. "How about if I bring a personal witness who could attest to what I do and say at the bank?"

"All right," Nancy said with a sigh. "Just be very careful."

I asked Mary, my wonderful housekeeper, to come for a ride and explained that she should remember what I said to the man we were going to see at the bank.

I left the car window open for the six-mile drive, hoping the breeze might blow dry my hair to some extent. Then, in the bank parking lot, I made a hopeless attempt to comb it back, but I could see Mr. Colby waiting impatiently and gave up.

I shook Mr. Colby's hand. "This is a friend of mine," I said introducing Mary. "She is here to witness that I am not talking you into anything."

"You want me to do this, don't you?" he asked plaintively.

"I want you to do what you think is best," I said and followed him into the bank.

I stood in the foyer with Mary. Mr. Colby went to the other side of the velvet ropes and took a seat in a bank officer's area. She read the forms and then asked Mr. Colby for identification. Next he signed one paper for each of his children agreeing that "it is in the best interests of this child to release the child to the Department of Health and Rehabilitative Services to be adopted" and also that "I hereby acknowledge that I have read this form concerning this child, and I clearly understand its meaning and it is correct and true to the best of my knowledge and belief, and I have freely and voluntarily signed this Affidavit and Acknowledgement of Surrender, Consent and Waiver of Notice in order to release this child for adoption."

When the papers were signed, witnessed, and notarized, Buddy Colby came around the ropes and handed them to me.

"You are handing these consents to terminate your parental rights to me. I will bring them to your attorney's office and he will give them to the judge at the next hearing, is that correct, Mr. Colby?"

"Yes."

"Thank you, Mr. Colby," I said softly, then opened the door to the parking lot. On the curb, I asked, "Do you want to call the girls, or shall I?"

"Will you?" he asked, tears shining in his eyes. "And tell them I love them."

Lottie Hunt had come to court with Wanda. Lillian was there with me, but Nancy was not available. Mr. Colby's attorney had agreed to fulfill this final duty, after Mr. Colby apologized to him on the phone.

When our case was called, I walked up to sit in the guardian's seat next to Lillian. But Calvin Reynolds waved me forward to his table on the right side of the courtroom. "This is your day, Gay. Come sit beside me."

Calvin had worked out a way to accomplish several legal procedures simultaneously. First he filed the permanent placement plan that had been in suspension putting the children in a preadoptive placement, and requesting terminations from the parents. Then he filed the voluntary terminations of parental rights for each of the three children along with waivers of notice of future hearings and proceedings. It was determined further that it was manifestly in the best interests of the children to continue in HRS custody. The proof of this was the list of the children's placements over the past five years. The termination form mentioned eleven moves for Simone, thirteen for Nicole, and eleven for Julie. The court then retained jurisdiction over the children until the time when they would be adopted.

"Does anyone else have anything to add?" the judge asked.

"May I approach the bench, Your Honor?" I asked.

He was taken aback but nodded. I handed the judge a photograph of the children at the craft fair. "I wanted you to see the children whose lives are being changed at this moment," I said.

He smiled broadly. "They are handsome, aren't they?" He handed the photo to his clerk, who passed it to the court reporter. At the end of the chain was Lottie Hunt. I nodded that she might keep it.

The judge directed his words at her. "Mrs. Hunt, the court recognizes that this has been a difficult and painful decision for you to make. It has taken courage to relinquish control of your daughters and I want it on the record that your contribution has been one of caring. Thank you for putting the interests of your children first.''

The courtroom was silent in recognition of what had just happened. Calvin Reynolds stood and shook my hand.

''Now you can clean out that file drawer, Calvin,'' I said, then turned and saw Lottie being helped to her feet by Wanda. I went up to Lottie and hugged her.

''Thank you for doing this, Mrs. Hunt.''

''I feel better after what the judge said. It's like he took a weight off me. Now I can still be their mother, just differently.''

''Yes, you can.'' I said, then hugged her again. ''We did it. We did the best for the girls.''

On that day two boxes of Colby files moved from the county office to the adoption unit. Dolly Lemoine began her adoption home study and the Slaters faced another round of paperwork.

During the next few weeks, Lottie Hunt had Julie for an overnight on her birthday weekend and took Simone to the dentist twice because Mrs. Slater was working. Lottie attended Nicole's sports day and Simone's concert. When Julie's class had parent's day, it conflicted with both Jared and Zane's, so Vic went with Zane, Jeanne with Jared, and Lottie Hunt attended the activities with her daughter.

Mostly Julie calls her father on the phone, but on a recent school holiday morning, I took two of the sisters to a restaurant breakfast with their father. Simone had to work a shift at her new job. While the girls may have unsupervised visits with him now, they still prefer to have me along.

Sometime after Christmas the Slaters and their five children expect to move into their new home. Jared and Zane will share the pool side bedroom, Julie and Nicole have the garden side, while Simone gets her own room. When she goes to college, that room will go to Nicole. Now they were trying to coordinate Christmas visits with the Slaters, the Hunts, the Baldwins, and their father.

''We'll work it out,'' I assured them. ''This is the sort of problem I enjoy.''

6

All Victories
Great and Small

The Rights of Children

❖

I beseech you to treasure up in your heart these my parting words:
Be ashamed to die until you have won
some victory for humanity
—HORACE MANN

WHEN I BECAME A GUARDIAN AD LITEM, I was looking to help individual children. As soon as I became actively involved in their lives, I began to receive a practical course in the social and economic issues that helped create the acute problems many children face and how little is being done to remedy the root causes of abuse and neglect as well as the dearth of programs to assist families in crisis. The fact that the Stevensons were not kept in the same foster home or that the social workers gave no consideration to continuity of schools in placing them astonished me at first. When I learned that this was routine management, I no longer could content myself with merely putting out the fires as they threatened to engulf the children in my charge. I had to begin to address how citizens could take the lead in local action in the areas of prevention and recovery. Like many advocates, I felt I had to pass on what I discovered to the much wider community. The outrage all the guardians feel during our personal encounters with the cruelty and injustice our children have suffered spills over to a much wider base of friends and families, all of whom vote for legislators and judges. Because we feel viscerally connected to the families in the system, we are less likely to accept platitudes from bureaucrats. We bristle when children are referred to as "files," homes as "beds," families as "placements." We refuse to accept shoddy work, lazy excuses, convoluted paperwork, unconscionable delays, and idiotic rules or fragmented authority when they impact negatively on any child's life—especially one assigned to our supervision.

The children entrusted to me were not particularly difficult or unusual cases. I received whatever the office had to have covered at a time I was willing to accept a new case, although once I had some success with teenagers, I was given more of them. There are family problems even more convoluted and acute than the ones I handled, there are court cases with uglier perpetrators, there are children with more tragic lives. In a sense, I have had a random sample of what happens in social service agencies and courtrooms throughout the country on a daily basis.

Nationally, one-third of all children in foster care are between thirteen and eighteen and about one-half are over the age of ten. Many guardians, especially the older ones, feel more comfortable with younger children, who are not as expressive about how they feel or have as many ideas about where they want to live. Yet the severe problems of older children do not suddenly erupt with their hormones. Years of unreported abuse and neglect take their toll and foster care does not begin to solve their problems. At least half of all runaways (an estimated 500,000 teenagers) in the United States have fled from state-supported foster homes or correctional institutions. Lydia Ryan and Alicia Stevenson preferred to live on the street rather than return to the "system." No matter how hard I tried, I could not secure the individualized mental or medical health or educational programs they required. Their injuries did not stop when they were removed from their parents' homes but were compounded by the ineffectual way the state managed their care, and they were irrevocably harmed when they were dumped without any resources the day they came of age. Nobody would listen to what they wanted when they were under eighteen. Nobody would help them when they were over eighteen. In the end I also failed to provide either of them with a permanent, loving family. What would have to change to improve the outcome for troubled children in the future?

A CHILD'S RIGHT TO A PERMANENT, SAFE, CARING HOME MUST BE ESTABLISHED LEGALLY

As societies evolve, the first rights are given to men, then animals, followed by minorities, women, and finally children. In twentieth century America, the first wave of rights reform went to minorities while the second wave established parity between men and women. There seems to be about a ten-year span between the early work to establish these rights, national legislation to guarantee them, and court cases to interpret and insure them. Now comes the third wave: the rights of the most tender citizens. We are in the early stages of establishing that children should have guaranteed constitutional rights.

Until recent times, parents could do anything they wanted to their progeny. In ancient Rome, fathers could legally kill their children because the person who gave life could also take it away. The first child abuse case in the United States was prosecuted in 1894 only after the head of the Society for the Prevention of Cruelty to Animals persuaded a judge that the child, Mary Ellen, was a member of the animal species and thus deserved protection under the cruelty to animal laws. In the landmark Gault decision in 1967, a judge reversed the conviction of a boy accused of making lewd telephone calls who had been sentenced to seven years in a juvenile detention center without being allowed to argue or appeal his case. His victory won minors the same rights as adults to due process. Since then, children's legal rights have taken a few baby steps forward, then have regressed in an ancient struggle with those who refuse to relinquish total parental authority.

While parents have an abiding personal interest in enjoying the companionship of their children and the state has a compelling interest in the health, welfare, and safety of all its citizens—including children— the child should be entitled to mental, physical, and emotional health, safety, and well-being, and in these days of broken homes and battered babies, that entitlement must supersede the interest of its parents as well as the state.

CHILDREN'S BEST INTERESTS AND WISHES MUST BE GIVEN A VOICE

Article 12 of the Convention of the Rights of the Child (ratified by over 130 nations, but not by the United States) states that children should have the right to express their views freely and be given a meaningful opportunity to be heard, especially in court. With a volunteer or attorney advocate by her side, a child should be able to request a stable, sober parent who will not abuse her and who will at least make an effort to meet her needs or find her additional services. The child must also be legally protected from social service agencies that hide behind paperwork and confidentiality laws to do the minimum for the child, or worse, harm the child further as she is shuffled through the system.

In a 1973 *Harvard Educational Review* article "Children Under the Law," Hillary Rodham Clinton wrote that children, like wives, slaves, and Indians, have historically been treated as dependents who are incapable or undeserving of the right to take care of themselves, thus they require social institutions specifically designed to safeguard their position. The legal system of the United States only began to focus on a child's need to have legal representation during court proceedings after the passage of the Child Abuse Prevention and Treatment Act (CAPTA) in 1974. This legislation mandated that "in every case involving an abused or neglected child which results in a judicial proceeding a Guardian ad Litem shall be appointed to represent the child . . ." Any state receiving federal money for abuse and neglect services is required to follow this rule, but no guidelines as to who will perform this function are included, nor is federal funding sufficient to support the appointment of an advocate for every child. Although there are now court-appointed special advocates (CASAs) or Guardians ad Litem (GALs) in every state, there are many different interpretations of how this need is best served.

The supreme court of Florida has determined that minors under the law are persons and that constitutional rights do not mature at eighteen, the state-defined age of majority, but they have not yet given children party status in court. Gregory K. did win the right to argue his own case, but this was overturned by the appeals court. Even those people who do not want to see children bringing legal actions in their own name wonder why children's desires and feelings are not given more consideration by the powers that be. Why, for instance, wasn't Cory Stevenson asked where he wanted to live when he had to leave the Rose/Perez foster home? All children in foster care should be allowed to participate in decision making about their future and they should be given honest answers to any matters that will affect them. Of course, communicating with a three-year-old will be different than a fifteen-year-old, but at any age a child can be listened to in a way that validates his feelings and, one hopes, elicits his cooperation.

In "Children's Rights: A Legal Perspective," (Teacher's College Press, 1979) Hillary Rodham Clinton addressed the question of when a minor child might be mature enough to be heard. While it is obvious that newborns are incompetent to present their own views, "it is more difficult to prove a twelve-year-old child totally incompetent, and I think impossible to presume the typical sixteen-year-old incompetent." Yet the law "treats all these children, at their dissimilar stages of life, as incompetent and ignores psychological and social realities." Whether or not a child can speak for himself yet, the court should always listen to what a child has to say, both on his own as well as through his advocate or legal counsel. Then it is up to the judge to weigh a child's interests and wishes in view of his unique circumstances—including his age and maturity—and then determine how to rule on the child's behalf.

Some argue that nobody under eighteen has any idea what is best, as though some maturity surge on a given birthday makes a person more competent than he was the day before. Others arbitrarily select age twelve or fourteen, when actually very young children may be able to state or express what they want. A few very progressive advocates suggest listening to a child of any age, even a toddler, and then making a wise and educated decision taking the child's statements and feelings into account.

While most people bristle at this concept, I recall our three-year-old son carrying on when he was left with a certain baby-sitter. I had checked this woman out thoroughly and was utterly convinced she was a responsible caretaker. It took many weeks before I saw through her two-faced behavior and realized she was mean and neglectful, and I am thankful this discovery was made before she actually harmed our son. If instead of discounting his complaints I had listened to him, he would have been far better served. On the other hand, adults have extraordinary power to influence what children express, feel, and recall. One side can easily persuade a young child to say something against another caretaker, and recent studies have proven that children can be manipulated to believe certain abuses have taken place that actually did not. Anyone representing a child's best interests needs to take the time to investigate all claims and arrive at a measured, thoughtful, nonemotional, unbiased decision on how to best accommodate that child.

When the guardian program began, judges began appointing attorneys—either paid or pro bono—to the task of representing children. After Judge David Soukup of King County (Seattle), Washington, developed a program in which volunteer advocates were supervised and trained by both attorneys and social workers, as well as represented by an attorney in court, it was endorsed by the National Council of Juvenile and Family Court Judges. Florida was first to pass legislation requiring a statewide program that allows either an attorney or volunteer to represent a child. In some regions an attorney is required by law, but a volunteer may assist that lawyer, while in other states both an attorney and volunteer work on every case. Experts disagree about which model is best and debate continues over who should fund these programs. There have been two studies comparing various advocacy programs (*National Evaluation of the Impact of Guardians ad Litem in Child Abuse or Neglect Judicial Proceedings*, 1988, and *Who Best Represents the Interest of the Child in Court?* by John Poertner and Allan Press, 1990). Both determined that volunteers performed as well as attorneys with the exception that there were more adoptions in the cases handled by volunteers. Over and over again it has been shown that volunteers who are able to focus their concern and dedicate their time to a few cases are usually able to interview more people involved with a case, spend more time with the child, and thus make more reliable recommendations to the court.

Attorneys are still an essential part of the legal process, but their professional rules of conduct regarding their relationship with the client become confused when the attorney accepts the Guardian ad Litem role. Often a lawyer feels compelled to represent the child's wishes rather than what he feels to be in the child's best interests. And attorneys can be caught in conflicts about privileged communications because they are ethically bound not to reveal confidences of any client, whether adult or child. There is no problem if the attorney is hired to represent a child's wishes, but when the attorney acts as Guardian ad Litem the situation becomes muddled. Also, occasionally the Guardian ad Litem is required to be called as a witness, something an attorney cannot be asked to do. Finally, if Guardians ad Litem learn of any abuse or neglect to the child, they are required to breach confidentiality, while an attorney does not have to do so.

The solution in our district's program is to have volunteer child advocates who are supervised by professionals and sometimes are represented or advised by attorneys. The volunteer also offers continuity for children through the court process and often many years thereafter, while the attorney generally only provides legal services, but not monitoring or long-term involvement. In every case where I was the Guardian ad Litem, I became the most stable adult in the child's life. As appalling as it is to consider, the fact is that parents, foster parents, attorneys, case-workers, and therapists faded in and out of their lives. Only their advocate remained the same and was always there.

One of the most valuable contributions of lay guardians is their independent and objective viewpoint. When I write a report for a child, I do not consider my remuneration, job security, status in an organization, or professional reputation. I cannot lose money. I cannot be sued. The worst that can happen is I won't be asked to be a volunteer any longer. If the advocate can mask the noise of the disparate parties and reflect solely on what is best for a child, a very untainted—often creative— solution emerges. For years the Colby sisters languished in one impossible situation after another under the ''watchful'' eye of HRS's protective services department. Another guardian assigned to the case might also have seen that the three girls needed to be together in a loving home. But there was no clear administrative path to this outcome. An advocate with perspective was the best way to mobilize unrelated community resources rapidly and turn that situation around.

Court administrators are quick to point out the economic value of volunteer programs. When the Florida legislature was thinking of cutting funding for the Guardian ad Litem program, researchers demonstrated the program saved millions of dollars over what it would cost to pay attorneys to represent children in court. But the fact that an area does not currently have a volunteer children's court advocate program should not be discouraging. New programs continue to be developed and older models are beginning to integrate volunteers. In 1992 the National Court Appointed Special Advocate Association (NCASAA) reported that sixty percent of the programs that use volunteers place them in the capacity of Guardians ad Litem. Other groups use the volunteer as a friend of the court, who makes recommendations but does not have the legal clout of a Guardian ad Litem. A friend of the court is someone who follows a case but cannot insist that the court's orders are followed.

Once in a while a child might require one advocate to represent his wishes and another to speak for his best interests. For instance, the care of a parent or facility may be suitable in every way, but the child has a strong aversion to it. That child has a right to have his position argued in court by an attorney so that a judge can make the final decision. On the other hand, both attorneys and advocates must guard against behaving like ventriloquists who pretend to be acting either in the child's best interests or speaking for the child's wishes, while really using the child to promote their own agendas.

The U.S. Advisory Board on Child Abuse and Neglect believes that children can become ''partners in the pursuit of justice.'' Who will speak for these children? More and more people must volunteer and take an active interest. Making certain every child in need has an advocate is the first step. With the recent high-profile children's rights cases in the media, American law is on the cutting edge of children's rights and most of the western world is watching to see what happens.

CHILDREN HAVE A RIGHT TO LIVE WITH THEIR "PSYCHOLOGICAL PARENT"

The time has come to establish who a child's psychological parent is and what constitutes a person's true family. A family begins with a biological basis but flourishes with emotional bonds. The members of a true family make serious attempts to love one another and meet one another's needs. Yes, the custody, care, and nurturing of the children reside first with the biological parents, but children also are entitled to be protected from abuse, neglect, or exploitation by any adult, as well as to have the right to act independently of parental control under certain selected circumstances. The latter becomes controversial when a fourteen-year-old girl wants an abortion against her parents' wishes. Yet even those who disagree with a child's right in this case might be sympathetic if that same girl wanted to defy the beliefs of her parents' religion if they mandated the end of formal schooling at age fourteen, or side with a child whose parents tried to deny her lifesaving treatments because of their faith. Almost everyone would find some reason to agree that there are times when the manifest best interest of the child might differ from the parents' wishes. One look at the tragic consequences to the children of the followers of David Koresh or Jim Jones demonstrates this point vividly.

The Florida Constitution declares: "All natural persons are equal before the law and have inalienable rights among which are the right to enjoy and defend life and liberty, to pursue happiness." In order to protect those rights, then, children must be able to live in surroundings that do not violate their pursuit of happiness. Likewise, we cannot be biased against families simply because of limited economic circumstances or because their family does not function at optimum levels. There is a vast difference between the problems that poverty or misfortune inflict on a family and the sadistic discipline of overly strict parents or the neglect of totally inept caretakers. A genetic connection alone must not be an irrevocable license to allow brutal or incompetent parents to control a child.

Yes, the vast majority of families are much better than the state at raising children, but as Hillary Rodham Clinton wrote in "Children Under the Law," "the state, representing the community of adults, has the responsibility to intervene in cases of severe emotional deprivation or psychological damage if it is likely that a child's development will be substantially harmed by his continued presence in the family." Just as a child must sometimes undergo the pain of surgery to be cured of a dreadful disease, sometimes it is essential to inflict the pain of separation and loss to have a healthy outcome.

In speaking with people about the plight of our youngest citizens and the need for more children's rights, there is an immediate backlash that imagines that children who are represented independently from their parents will bring frivolous actions against them as a way to acquire more material possessions or to subvert the parents' ability to discipline them. Protection of individual family values is touted as a reason to halt the interference of the state in family matters. We should, in fact, respect every family's uniqueness as long as they make a strong attempt to give their children love, care, security, and try to meet their offspring's essential needs for food and shelter and affection.

There is also the fear that the state will impose standards that do not permit a wide variety of parenting styles and family beliefs or that children will be removed from poor parents and handed over to wealthier ones. Part of the argument used by Gregory K.'s natural mother was that the foster family offered her son financial benefits she could not give him and that they were seducing him with their more affluent lifestyle. This ignores the fact that Gregory K.'s mother behaved irresponsibly for many years and that he had been languishing in foster care for thirty months with no hope of a permanent family on the horizon. For a few dollars she could have maintained some, if tenuous, contact with Gregory K. and could have made a more earnest attempt to keep him in her home.

Almost everyone concerned about families understands that under most circumstances a child will grow best in his own family, even in a very imperfect family. Rachael Kingsley, Gregory K.'s mother, complained that if some of the money used to keep Gregory in state custody had been given directly to her, she might have been able to care for him properly and would not have had to give him up in the first place. While experts could argue that case forever, it is clear that families in crisis would benefit from a different approach to protecting children at risk. Until recently, $2.3 billion a year was spent nationwide to maintain children in foster care, but only $274 million was allocated to try to keep families together. New legislation provides a $2.5 billion allocation for "family preservation" but does not clarify what constitutes a family. Blind adherence to any one policy must be avoided. Every family's situation is different. Every case should use only one pure standard: what is in the best interest of that child.

When I was in court waiting for the Colby case to be called, I happened to hear the case of four-year-old Darryl. He limped into court. "Hiya!" he said to anyone who would listen, including the judge.

"Hi, Darryl," came the response from the bench.

Testimony revealed that Darryl had a life-threatening medical condition. He was placed in foster care because his young, untrained, and poor mother had not yet been educated in how to give him the special care he needed, and she did not have a telephone to call for emergency help.

The fees for home visits by a nurse and the cost for a telephone installation were far less than the foster care expenses of this child, but HRS did not coordinate these services until the judge ordered them to do so. If the social workers had simply pulled together the services that his mother needed, Darryl might have been able to remain in his own home without a long, deleterious detour into foster care.

Foster care was meant to be a temporary solution between solving a family's problem or changing the child's home for good. In many cases foster care has become the only way of life a child ever knows. While children often need to be removed from their homes for good reasons, foster care rarely is the final solution. In retrospect, sometimes even a rotten family turns out to have been better than no family at all. When Cory, who insisted that he was never abused by his father, went into foster care against his will for his own "protection," he suffered an emotional deprivation that was never dealt with. The moment Cory was taken from his home, the state became the perpetrator of further damage. Cory not only lost his abusive father but also lost his sister and brother, his grandfather, his teachers at school, his neighborhood friends, his bedroom, his toys, the smell of orange blossoms in the groves, the bumps on the dirt road that led to his house. Cory didn't understand the state of suspended animation he was supposed to live in until the courts tried his father. Nor could he comprehend why he was treated punitively at the MacDougal home. (It is extremely common for these children—who are actually the victims—to be punished more than the perpetrators. This certainly was the case with all the Stevenson children, as it is with battered women and other casualties of violence in our twisted society.) But as bad as the MacDougal home was, Cory was so afraid of another separation, he did not instigate that change on his own.

Instead of thinking that the only thing we can do is to remove the child from a hazardous condition, we need to remove the hazard from the child. If, despite the incest allegations leveled at his father, the family had been given some psychological assistance, Cory might have been able at least to have continued living with his grandfather. Initially the family would have had to have had intensive counseling and ongoing supervision. Cory would have had to know he had a way out if he was in an abusive circumstance. He would also have had to decide whether or not he was going to visit his brother and sister. That situation was complex and there were no programs in place or counseling funds available. The only officially responsible choice was to remove him precipitously from his family. Even so, every effort should have been made to maintain consistency in Cory's life. He could have been placed in a foster home with Alicia, and if the foster parents had been trained and a support system had been in place, they might even have been able to have cared for Rich as well. The curative value of reuniting these siblings might have been immeasurable. Maybe Rich would not have had to try to create his own little family by marrying Janet so early. Alicia's brothers may have offered her the love and security she only found during sexual encounters with boys.

A CHILD'S SENSE OF TIME MUST BE HEEDED

Another problem with family preservation initiatives is that a high percentage of children reenter foster care after failed attempts at reunification with the family. Fewer than ten percent are ever adopted. And sometimes even adoptions put together with the best intentions fail. How can this be remedied? If we allow the system to move at its usual sluggish pace, the family and child become weaker and weaker. Families in trouble cannot begin to deal with the power differential between them and the authorities and eventually give up unless they get tremendous support. Advocates can make certain that both sides are communicating and can also point to the hands of the clock and issue warnings when either the parent or the social service agency is not meeting the child's needs in a timely fashion. Once a child is in a foster home, there is a tendency to compare the comfort and control of that environment with the risk of allowing the child back home. As long as Cory was in foster care—no matter how badly he was doing—the caseworkers could believe they were protecting him from his "monstrous" father, and they could deny the harm that he was suffering by feeling so unattached. The system never dealt with his grief and loss because the professionals were utterly—and blindly—convinced they were doing him a favor.

Few discuss the fact that children grieve when they lose their primary attachment figure, even if that person was an abusive parent. Grieving children do not behave normally. While some seem to adjust well, eventually their behavior deteriorates. Some may actually act sad or talk about the loss, but most hide it with behaviors. To cover the pain some keep as active as possible and are labeled hyperactive. Others become defiant or negative. Many perform poorly in school. Julie Colby was so consumed with her problems that she found it impossible to focus on her academic work and failed a grade. When she had a solid year at the

Slaters, she did very well, but even then the uncertainty of her position gave her depressive periods when she ignored homework and misbehaved.

Rich Stevenson was a boy who had learned that sadness was unacceptable, so when he acutely felt the loss of his family, he became angry and behaved in ways that got him into serious trouble. He never was able to have friends or develop any long-term relationships because as soon as someone came close, he feared he would lose them. To remain in control Rich acted out first to instigate the break.

His brother, Cory, had no help getting over the initial grief of being removed from his home. Until he was reunited with his father, Cory idealized Red, which is common when children are displaced from their families. They need guidance to mourn the disappearance not only of the home they actually lost, but also of the dream family that they fervently had hoped it might someday become. Then Cory was thrown out of the MacDougals' home. Even though I knew he was better off in the Rose/Perez household, I realized that he suffered an injury from that rejection. "What is wrong with *me*?" is how he internalized losing two homes in a few short months. Unfortunately, when the Rose/Perez foster home moved out of our district, Cory was burdened with yet another layer of unresolved grief. By the time Cory suffered this third loss, he was well on his way to becoming an unsalvageable, nonattached child. And classically, unattached children turn against society through criminal activities.

No matter where a child is living, primary consideration must center on who is the child's psychological parent before he is moved. This has to be discussed the moment a court begins the process of extracting a child from his home and kept in mind through every change. Even if the psychological parent is someone other than the biological parent, the effects of removing the child from that parent can be just as devastating. Many children have spent most of their young lives with the same foster family only to eventually be "reunited" by court order with their rehabilitated parents, who are virtual strangers. This amounts to nothing less than a legalized amputation in terms of the pain endured by the child. Gregory K. had no emotional relationship with his biological parents and begged to be adopted by his psychological family, the Russes. The psychological parent is the person who the child feels understands him, whom the child turns to for assistance, the person with whom he feels secure. This parent knows a child's likes and dislikes and can interpret his moods. He knows a child's favorite food, toy, music. When

Woody Allen tried to obtain custody of his children, it was revealed that he didn't know the name of his children's doctors, friends, or even their pets. Julie Colby's mother did not even know what grade she was in— and that was when Julie was living with her! Julie's father professed deep love for her but hadn't the slightest idea of her likes, dislikes, or interests. Gregory K.'s mother claimed she desperately wanted him back but had not communicated with him by phone, letter, or even sent him a birthday card in more than a year. As Simone Colby told me regarding her father's reluctance to terminate his parental rights, "He talks a good game, but he never comes through and does what he says." Indeed, the Colbys know better than anyone that "parental rights" are spelled "responsibility."

Listening to people fight over their children, I've become acutely aware of two types of refrain. Some parents relate everything to their own needs and wishes: "I'm upset when I can't see my son" or "Nobody cares how I feel about this," while the other parents see beyond themselves: "She gets upset when her father doesn't show up for visitation" or "He hasn't done well in school since he's been in foster care." These child-oriented statements demonstrate that the adult is thinking about the concerns of the child. Sometimes it is surprising to hear who is doing this. It may be a grandmother, social worker, guardian, foster parent, neighbor, or even a sibling. It also might be a parent who has refocused her interest on her child, and this is a good indicator of potential success.

More and more guardians are having to fill the role of a mediator. As soon as conflicts in families begin, sides are taken and issues escalate with very little concern for how this affects the welfare of the child. Whenever we attempt to do something to help the child, we are also doing something to harm that child. The list of things we want our own children to have and the idealized way we expect our own family to be treated are not necessarily what is essential or best for another child. We must be careful not to inflict our values or assumptions on others. Young people require what is referred to as "minimally sufficient care." Even very inadequate parents can provide enough to meet a child's needs to grow and remain healthy and safe. Poverty makes many opportunities impossible, but there is nothing as debilitating to a child as the lack of someone who feels connected to the child. In weighing all the possibilities for a family in crisis, professionals must search for the least detrimental alternative. As heartless as it seems on the surface, the best interests of a child often end up being not the perfect solution but the least worst choice. A child removed from a violent home is still losing his home. If that transition is not going to lead to a much better future outcome, perhaps we should reconsider doing it in the first place. Every single intervention in a child's life has potential to bring harm, so we need to evaluate whether or not removing a child from a home or even trying to reunite a family might do more damage than maintaining the status quo and supplementing with services or other forms of aid. There are often less drastic solutions possible, and while caseworkers have manuals to follow and laws with which they must comply, creative solutions sometimes offer the best alternative.

An out-of-home placement should attempt to be the least disruptive possible. A child's family may be the most important place he receives security and socialization, but the wider community of neighborhood, friends, and school are part of his essential root system. If you try to transplant a tree, it will have the best chance for success if as much of the root structure as possible can be left intact. You can remove primary and secondary roots, but you cannot sever a plant stalk and expect it to survive in an entirely different climate and without having some of the taproot left to grow again.

The foster home should be culturally appropriate. Lydia insisted on a family that was of the same religious affiliation, and while this is not always practical, serious consideration should be given to race and religion. Proximity to the last address is vital so that a child can maintain school continuity, have the same friends, visit easily with parents, siblings, and other relatives. While this seems logical, in our jurisdiction attention to these factors is largely ignored. Next, services should be directed at remedying the problems that precipitated the child's removal from the home. In some cases a parent needs only to clean up the house, apply for the various services and benefits for which she qualifies, and learn some parenting skills. Having a mother educated, trained for a job, or employed might be best for the parent in the future but should not hinder reunification with her child. A family should be told what they must do to reach minimally sufficient goals. Service providers must act quickly to help them achieve those objectives, and evaluators must determine whether or not the parent has made a reasonable effort to do so. Sadly, many parents just cannot get it together. They are unable to wean themselves from drugs or attend parenting classes or restrain their angry outbursts. They may show little interest in visiting their children and their behavior with the children when they are together may continue to deteriorate. At that point, the child's need for permanence should take precedence and another long-term solution found.

PERMANENCY IS THE CRITICAL FACTOR

If, after careful consideration, it looks like it will be impossible for a child to be cared for by his family in a minimally sufficient way in the near future, getting the child into a permanent home should be the next mandate. In doing so, however, the child must be involved from the beginning. We should never mistrust empowering individual children. Nobody understands a situation better than the child who lives with it. He must be asked how he feels about visitation and to help evaluate where he is living and where he might like to live. Foster parents are often given the right of first refusal to decide if they want to adopt a child in their care, but these options are not offered to the child. The idea that Cory or Alicia might choose their foster home terrified the social workers, yet if a child participates in the decision-making process, he is much more likely to cooperate with the result.

Caseworkers are also apprehensive that the children will grow too attached to their foster parents. Sometimes children are moved when it is perceived this is happening, and foster parents, like the Fowlers with Lydia, are blamed for not maintaining distance from them. After Baby Jessica DeBoer had spent two years with her adoptive parents while a court fight raged in two states, who was most harmed by her return to her natural parents? While we can argue that the mother or father were denied their rights or that the DeBoers purposefully used every legal loophole to delay the case, thus making it harder on Jessica, the fact is that the process was set in motion and the decision was made by several courts entirely without Baby Jessica's needs being considered. Returning young people to their natural families because of the parents' "rights" means that we permit children to be repossessed like property.

Our federal funding structure actually hinders the resolution of foster care cases. As long as we spend more to reimburse agencies for maintaining children in foster homes and do not offer social services to either repair the family relationships quickly or facilitate adoptions, children will wither in transient homes.

Time is of the essence when it comes to moving children. Intervention in a family crisis should be a team effort. First the child should be worked with in the home, if at all possible, and services given to that family. If that fails—

or if the child is in jeopardy—a plan that considers intervention with constant monitoring should be attempted. Goals must be set, and a timeline established. A year-old baby living apart from her drug-addicted mother for six months has been out of her home for half her life. A three-year-old in a foster home for a year has spent one-third of his life attached to another family. Anyone who works with these children should hear the clock ticking loudly. Procedures must be speeded up accordingly. Children cannot be allowed to languish just because they are ''safe'' for the moment.

However, in order to terminate parental rights the state must prove by clear and convincing evidence that the parent is unfit and that it is in the best interests of the child to end that relationship. In Florida, we must demonstrate that the child was adjudicated dependent, a performance agreement was offered to the parent, and that the parent failed to substantially comply with the agreement for reasons other than lack of financial resources or failure of HRS to make reasonable efforts to reunify the family. In addition, the court must then determine that the termination is in the manifest best interests of the child. Judges are very reluctant to bear the responsibility for severing a family forever. A 1991 Florida ruling (*Padgett v. Dept. of HRS*) stated that while a parent's interest in maintaining parental ties is essential, the child's entitlement to be free of physical and emotional violence is more so, and the state has a compelling interest in protecting all citizens, especially a child, against the clear threat of abuse, neglect, and death. We must include emotional abuse and neglect in this rule. Once and for all the judiciary must discard the old maxim that whoever ''begets them gets them.''

PARENTAL RIGHTS COULD BE SPLIT TO PERMIT OPEN ADOPTIONS

When I worked on the Colbys' termination of parental rights, I saw how excruciating it was for the mother and father to sign those forms, which demanded that a parent agree to the ''permanent deprivation of my present parental right to this child'' and ''the right to further information concerning the whereabouts of this child, or the identity or location of any adoptive parent of this child.''

Perhaps there is a way to modify the termination of parental rights statutes to make them less onerous in some situations. To do this, though, there has to be a change in the perception of children as the property of parents. At birth children would be inalienably members of their birth family, and this status could change only if the parents did not want to raise their children or willfully and repeatedly seriously abused or neglected them physically or emotionally. But once a parent injured a child, the rights would shift from the parent to the child. From then on the child's right to a safe, constant, nurturing home would supersede the prerogative of the parents to have possession of the child.

With this in mind, it behooves the courts to move swiftly to provide for a child's needs. Much as a criminal has a right to a speedy trial, a child should have the right to be placed in a permanent home as quickly as possible. Some psychologists feel that ninety days is the limit a child should be in limbo. Unfortunately, that is far too short a time to make legal decisions. I would suggest a six-month window of time to analyze and locate the best placement for a child.

In order to make this more palatable and swift, as well as to include some of the complex issues of parenthood brought on by new medical technologies and family structures, I would propose a two-tiered termination of parental rights.

Every natural parent automatically possesses both rights: primary and secondary. *Primary rights* would be the right to have physical custody of a child and includes the responsibility to support and give loving, stable care to that child. *Secondary rights* would give the parent, or another party, the right to know the whereabouts of the child as well as for the child to know the whereabouts of that person, as well as the right to visit the child on a schedule that is agreeable to all parties. In actuality, secondary rights would virtually legalize open adoptions.

How might this work on a practical basis?

Let's say a cocaine-addicted mother gives birth to an addicted child with medical problems. The mother agrees to go through a detoxification program, but her history indicates that she has failed to keep these promises in the past. Besides, it will be at least eighteen months before she could be drug-free, have housing, and financial security. Under today's laws, the child would be placed into foster care until the mother got her life together. The mother would then be given many opportunities to parent the child, with the child returning to foster care again if she failed. After repeated problems, the social service department could reevaluate the situation, decide whether the mother had been given every chance to succeed, and then begin the long involuntary process of terminating parental rights. The mother would be assigned an attorney, who would argue for his client using every loophole to give her the benefit of every doubt. In the meantime, the child could reach three or four years old and may have only spent a few hours or days with his mother. The foster family who raised the child could be asking to adopt him, but there is no guarantee that they would be the final parents either. Or the child could have lived in a succession of foster homes. Shockingly, the children who come into the foster care system as infants remain there the longest, precisely because of these scenarios.

If, at birth, the mother agreed to relinquish only her primary parental rights, the baby would immediately be freed for adoption of his primary rights. He would go to an adoptive family within weeks of birth and they would know that he could *never* be removed from their household and offered back to his birth mother. This child would be guaranteed a safe, permanent home. In the meantime, the addicted mother would be given services to assist her. During her rehabilitation she could visit with her child and she would always be informed where her child was residing. She would know that her child was cared for and she would be applauded for her decision to offer her child security, but she would not be denied the possibility of ever again having a relationship with or knowledge of the child.

Young mothers who find themselves pregnant before they are ready to raise a family would have another option besides abortion, caring for the child themselves, or giving them up for adoption forever. If they knew they could have some limited contact with their baby, they might be much more willing to consider adoption.

When families are in crisis, as Gregory K.'s parents were, and children are placed into the purgatory of foster care, the parents might more readily consider giving their children to another family on a long-term basis if they were not being denied the last vestige of contact with their children. Certainly the Colby parents would have signed away their primary rights to their daughters years earlier. It was only because we created a de facto open adoption that they voluntarily agreed to terminate parental rights.

Division of parental rights also might have solved the Kimberly Mays and Baby Jessica cases. When the Twigg family learned that Kimberly was their daughter, they could have applied for and received secondary rights at once. They could then have been her secondary parents without threatening Kimberly's security. Of course secondary rights could not be abused. Guidelines for visitation would be set by mediators who work with families. Harassment or misbehavior on the part of the secondary parents would be grounds for the elimination or suspension of these claims. Older children would fully participate in the decision to see their secondary parents. However, in almost every case, the secondary right holders at least would always be notified of the child's location and vice versa.

This could become more and more crucial as medical technologies rely on genetic material and related biological products to cure diseases. Bone marrow and other transplants are best done between compatible family donors. Years after birth a child may need a parent's tissue or genetic contribution, or a parent may require a child's, in order to remain healthy. To deny access to this hereditary information could be life-threatening. Also, communication between birth and adopted parents would put an end to the frustrating decades of searching that some children (and birth parents) go through in order to understand their identity and offer closure to this mystery in their lives.

A situation like Baby Jessica's—the little girl who was given up for adoption until the mother changed her mind—might have been salvaged with this solution. Her birth mother gave up her parental rights, but lied about who the father was. When the real father surfaced, he sued and eventually won his right to have Jessica. However, had he been offered secondary rights immediately, he would have continued contact with his daughter, but she could have remained with her primary (and psychological) adoptive family.

Some parents would choose not to retain any rights to their children, and thus both primary and secondary rights would be relinquished for adoption. Some adopting families might not wish to continue a relationship with a birth parent and would only adopt a child who was totally free for the adoption of both primary and secondary rights. In egregious abuse cases, courts could involuntarily remove both primary and secondary rights. These hearings would be similar to those today for involuntary termination of parental rights with all parties being represented by counsel. However, in less drastic cases, judges could swiftly remove primary rights because of the fundamental belief that every child deserves a safe, secure home.

Gregory K.'s case made the plight of older children in the system more visible. Even so, when I brought up the idea of finding the Colby sisters a permanent home together, the social work professionals scoffed at me. Since then, though, many people who have heard of the Colby situation have indicated that they might consider doing what the Slaters did. Perhaps they might not take on three children but would consider one or two. Adoptive homes must be recruited aggressively. An African proverb reminds us that "it takes a whole village to raise a child." Respect for human rights begins with the way a society as a whole cares for its children. Throughout human history, tribal members pitched in to rear the children communally, especially when the parents died or were incapable of doing so. There are almost 100,000 children in this country waiting for adoptive families and another 300,000 in out-of-home placements, many of whom are unlikely to be reunited with their original families. Adoption is their best chance for permanence. While some experts doubt they will ever find homes for most of these children, I believe there may be a vast untapped group of families that might be convinced to open their hearts to a homeless child. For instance, as part of their mission to protect unborn children, the large committed corps of prolife advocates might adopt some of these unwanted children who need love and protection for quite some time after their birth.

Many people are not interested in becoming foster parents. They don't wish to be employees of the state and have their homes monitored by social workers. Nor are they willing to invest love and energy in a child for an indeterminate time. But if they knew that the child would receive both financial support and become a lifelong family member, their attitudes might change.

When she was eighteen, Alicia and I talked about what she wished had been different in her life and how I might have been a better guardian. "I wanted Ruth or somebody else to adopt me," she replied plaintively. I flushed with shame because I had never realized this. Red Stevenson had signed the consent to terminate his parental rights when his daughter first pressed charges against him, and Tammy had been out of the picture. The HRS workers told me from the beginning that nobody would adopt Alicia because of her age and background, and I took their comments at face value. Now, after my experience with the Colbys as well as learning more about other difficult-to-place adoptions, I don't believe any child is inherently unadoptable. Ruth might have considered adoption if she had known that this is what Alicia desired, and there might have been other homes we could have found. Without an adoptive family, nineteen-year-old Alicia has nobody to turn to because the Levy family did not remain her foster parents. Today I am the only person who accepts her collect phone calls.

More families need to know that they can receive subsidies if they adopt difficult-to-place and special needs children. Counseling and medical services can be provided. With open adoption made more viable, additional services may be required to help a child adjust to the various adults in his life. Therapeutic assistance to alleviate guilt and help with the new family's attachment process might be necessary in many cases, but this would be a bargain compared with the up-front and long-term costs of foster care. When people ask me how the Colby children cope with contact between their real parents and adoptive parents, I repeat what I once told Nicole, "You can never have too many people who love you." Also, it is important to remember that while termination of parental rights is legally forever, once a person turns eighteen, she is free to contact whomever she wishes. Less than two years after her adoption by the Slaters, Simone Colby will reach her majority. If she wants to visit—or even live with—either parent after that, she may. Both her birth parents realize this and also understand that by making their children's life easier now, they are more likely to have a relationship with them throughout their lives.

While lawyers are essential in preserving rights and representing clients, attorneys in cases that pit children against parental figures must try to find a way to be less adversarial and arbitrate more situations so they reflect the best interests of a child at the time of the current crisis while also keeping in mind the continuum of the child's life. However, if cases are settled too swiftly, attorneys will collect fewer fees. We know that the Colby sisters desire communication and contact with their biological family, but we do not know where this might lead. It is possible that they may become alienated from their natural father or mother, they may have a friendly, but distant relationship, or at some point in their lives one or more of the sisters might very well establish a stronger bond with their parents. As young adults search for their identities, reconciliation with their birth families is sometimes part of the process. Thus, it came as no surprise to learn that Kimberly Mays, who had claimed she "hated" the Twiggs and never wanted to visit them again, turned to them when problems with her custodial parents developed. I would not be surprised to learn that Gregory K. tried to contact Rachael to make peace with her at some time in his life. If these doors can be left open— if only a crack—the child is better served than if he feels he has to bolt one shut in order to move ahead.

The concept of dividing parental rights strikes fear in parents who think the state might move in to control their parenting or relinquish their children to others to raise. Nobody has any interest in telling functioning families how to bring up their children. Just as the Gregory K. case raised the specter of children suing their parents for "divorce" because they had too many chores or didn't get the right brand of sneakers, these suspicions are groundless. So great is the fear of abandonment, children will frequently plead to remain with abusing families. One visit to dependency court will convince anyone that the children who appear there have been so battered and bounced from home to home that any solution that gives them equilibrium and stability should be attempted. These terminations will not be casual decisions. They will be made by professionals and ordered by a judge. In fact, judges and attorneys who are bewildered by the complicated cases that broken and dysfunctional families create are already attempting to work out legal solutions by interpreting current parental rights statutes casually for the sake of the children.

The best interests of any child, then, should be reflected in the ultimate best chance for a permanent, safe, nurturing environment. There is no one right path to this end. Sometimes children absolutely cannot flourish in their families of origin. Sometimes a stressed family might respond to a galaxy of services and turn itself around to be able to provide for its children. Foster care must only be the most temporary of solutions, with every child in that status heading toward either a rapid reunification with the biological family or an intensive plan to find an adoptive home, possibly with an ongoing relationship with the biological parents, possibly with that relationship severed for the child's sake. Any local or national program that places the general goals of a prescribed scenario (i.e., family reunification) above the needs of an individual child will fail a good proportion of the children. That is why each child not only deserves—but should be required to have—an advocate firmly speaking out for him at the earliest possible moment.

WE MUST LIFT OUR VOICES LOUDLY FOR THE SAKE OF CHILDREN

Marian Wright Edelman, founder and president of the Children's Defense Fund, reminds us that "service is the rent we pay for living." In *The Measure of our Success* she warns that "individual service and private charity are not substitutes for public justice, or enough alone to right what's wrong in America. Collective mobilization and political action are also necessary to move our nation forward in the quest for fairness and opportunity for every American." Even if you do not have the skills, time, or ability to advocate for children one-on-one, you still can vote for candidates who really are for kids and not just kidding when they say they believe in family values.

While children without homes and families of their own rarely make the news when they are compliant, they blaze in the headlines when they retaliate at a society that denied them affection and caring. Abused and neglected children are the breeding ground for criminal activity. The worse the treatment a child receives, the more vehemently he strikes back in the crimes he commits. The social costs of ignoring these children include drug and alcohol abuse, gang violence, sexual promiscuity, teenage pregnancy, and every sort of crime. There is an outcry to build more jails and to have tougher punishments, but as Jesse Jackson remarked, "It costs twice more to send a child to jail than to send a child to Yale." It might be easy to ignore these children or label them as bad, but the background for each is much the same as that of Rich or Cory, Alicia or Julie. Many of the adults in our jails were children whom we have let down and ignored. Even when we intervened, they may have become products of a foster-care system that unwittingly became an abusive and neglectful parent. Because we never cared for them, they don't give a damn about us now.

If this sounds like the far-fetched rantings of a bleeding-heart liberal, let me tell you about the latest case I just received. Sharonda is a bright, lively girl of fifteen. Her mother was murdered when she was eight. Sharonda was in the room at the time. Sharonda's father is in prison, again. Sharonda and her younger sister were raised by her maternal great-grandmother, who is now almost ninety and blind. Most of the time the sisters either fended for themselves or helped their grandmother, but she can no longer care for them. Her paternal grandmother tried to raise the sisters, but they refused to follow her strict rules, so she threw them out. Since then, they stayed in various homes of friends, relatives, and men. Sharonda has never received financial support other than that received by her grandmother and great-grandmother from Aid to Families with Dependent Children. She has been in the juvenile justice system for several years. All her arrests have been either for stealing food or clothing or for running away from home. After her last arrest, the judge, thinking that part of her problem might be the lack of a parent or home, ordered her into foster care. Lillian noticed that she had never been assigned a Guardian ad Litem and asked me to take the case because "nobody else will."

HRS put Sharonda with the Fowler family (Lydia's foster parents), forty miles south of her school, family, and friends. She was the only African-American child in that home, neighborhood, or classroom and demanded to be moved somewhere in her own community. Reluctantly, her caseworker agreed. During a rest stop at a convenience store, the caseworker went inside and a taxi drove up. Sharonda got into the taxi and disappeared. Nobody found her for six months. She surfaced again when she was arrested for stealing food. Her juvenile justice worker has used the detention system to provide housing for Sharonda because there is no place else to put her. She has spent most of her time in state custody in a punitive environment. These programs do not even attempt to reform or educate. Each time Sharonda is committed, she emerges more criminally sophisticated than when she went in and further behind in school. When Sharonda became ill recently, she was seen in a hospital emergency room and given a prescription for an antibiotic. However, because she was given a legal status that put her in a limbo between foster care and a family placement, she did not qualify for Medicaid benefits and thus could not get the medication. When I complained that she needed services, her HRS worker told me (and her) that to qualify for help, she should get pregnant.

Sharonda is one of two million children who will be in state custody this year. More than 500,000 will enter the correctional system, and more than 400,000 will be in foster care. At least another 700,000 children will be reported as abused or neglected and will receive some services even though they will remain in their homes.

Sharonda has fallen into a crack where she receives nothing in the way of assistance or programs. She is currently living with a friend who has two small children. She receives no food stamps or any other financial aid. She is not in school because her caseworker has not done the paperwork to enroll her. She has not seen a dentist or doctor (except in an emergency) in years. The first time I met her she had not eaten in two days. A week later she was arrested again for stealing jeans. This child is technically in foster care, but who is the neglectful parent? And how can the state justify its actions? Ironically, unless Sharonda hangs herself in a cell or commits a gruesome crime, nobody will ever find out about her plight because the privacy laws that are intended to shield her protect the system instead. Since Sharonda's juvenile court records are sealed, the system avoids scrutiny and does not have to be accountable to anyone—except the guardian, now that she has one, and thus the courts. Yet even with my very late involvement in her life, what can we predict will happen to Sharonda in the months and years to come?

If you think that the world is fine because you have enough food, shelter, clothing, and love in your life, think again. If we don't raise strong healthy children who not only want to contribute but also have some skills to offer, we end up with parasites whom we will have to support with expensive back-end facilities like prisons. Studies conclude that most criminals were consistently mistreated, demeaned, and neglected as children. Also there is evidence that the degree of adult criminality may be in proportion to how seriously abused they were. The roots of crime are in the home. Alcohol abuse and family violence are found in the parents of most male rapists and robbers. Most female prostitutes had abusive, drunken parents. It costs more to keep one child in prison than in the finest prep school. With the exponential growth of serious crime, we will be paying a major portion of our tax money for prisons. And no matter how secure and healthy you are, you will not feel safe when those children who have been neglected and abused find illicit ways to settle the score.

In order to prevent a fear-ridden society, we have to prevent children from suffering through pitiful childhoods. These children deserve to be wanted. Unplanned pregnancies result in neglected children. Neglected children feel unloved. Unloved children don't care about anyone else. In fact, they hate everyone for making their lives miserable, and as soon as they are strong enough—or have access to weapons that make them feel strong—they vent that rage indiscriminately.

Lydia and Alicia, Rich and Cory, Simone and Julie, Nicole and Sharonda, and all the others in the system represent children in dire situations. These are children whose nightmares begin when they wake up each morning.

Who will chase their very real monsters for them?

Marian Wright Edelman entreated all of us to "offer your hands to them so that no child is left behind because we did not act." Don't think that one person alone can do nothing. There are many people who can point to such a one caring person who made all the difference in their lives. Advocate for a child, just one child, and start making a significant difference, for the ripple effect of little victories will help win the war and change the future for all our children.

7

How to Contribute

❖

The best effect of any book is that it excites
the reader to self-activity
—THOMAS CARLYLE

REPRESENTATION OF CHILDREN BY CHILD ADVOCATES varies widely throughout the United States. Currently Florida, North Carolina, South Carolina, and Vermont have statewide programs that use volunteers in almost every jurisdiction. Other states engage attorneys as the Guardian ad Litem, with volunteers assisting them. Programs are supervised through varied agencies including state judiciary systems, public defender's offices, or are independent. The Florida program is administered through the state courts and receives legislative funding. Other states' programs are funded through the courts or directly.

There are several national and international organizations, listed below, that promote child advocacy and children's rights. If you are interested in becoming a Guardian ad Litem or wish to advocate for children in a capacity that bests suits your interests, abilities, location, and time, your participation will be welcomed. Some commitments involve contact with children and the courts, others are more political in nature, but all need concerned citizens and active volunteers to promote the cause of children.

National Court Appointed Special Advocate Association (CASA)
Suite 220
2722 Eastlake Drive East
Seattle, WA 98102
(800) 628-3233

CASA is the national organization that supports the development and growth of court-appointed advocate and Guardian ad Litem programs. They are working to make certain every abused and neglected child who needs an advocate will have a CASA volunteer. They can put interested people in touch with their local programs or help start a new one in your community.

Children's Defense Fund
25 E Street NW
Washington, DC 20001
(202) 628-8787

The Children's Defense Fund provides a strong voice for American children, with particular attention to the needs of the poor, minority, and disabled. They encourage preventive investments before children drop out, get sick, suffer family breakdown, or get into trouble.

Child Welfare League of America
Suite 310
440 First Street NW
Washington, DC 20001-2085
(202) 638-2952

The Child Welfare League of America is an organization composed of over seven hundred public and private voluntary child-welfare agencies. Its goals include setting standards for child-welfare practice, proposing national policy initiatives, and providing assistance to member agencies.

The Legal Action Project (LAP)
(of the National Committee for the Rights of the Child)
106 Parrish Street, 3rd Floor
Durham, NC 27701
(919) 688-0268

The Legal Action Project is a broad-based coalition of organizations and individuals trying to improve the quality of life and development of children in the United States by carrying out precedent-setting litigation.

Defense for Children International
P.O. Box 88
1211 Geneva 20, Switzerland

The Defense for Children International promotes and protects the rights of the child and helped draft the United Nations Convention on the Rights of the Child, which entered into force in 1990.

The National Committee for the Rights of the Child (NCRC)
125 Cathedral Street
Annapolis, MD 21401
(410) 268-1544

The National Committee for the Rights of the Child is a coalition committed to improving the quality of life and development of children in America. They work to promote the rights of children on all levels, as exemplified by, but not limited to, the standards contained in the United Nations Convention on the Rights of the Child.

It All Depends on What You Mean by Home

Where Are My Children?

❖

Home is the place where, when you have to go there,
they have to take you in.
—Robert Frost

I SHOULD HAVE CALLED IT SOMETHING you somehow haven't to deserve,'' is the way Frost talked about a home, and yet most of my guardian children are homeless either in the mind, body, or heart. Deep inside,
in that place where we know who we are, they don't feel that they ever
deserved to be cherished and kept forever in a place called home. While
I know I would receive an unconditional welcome in many homes of
family and friends, Alicia and Lydia and Cory and Rich really have
nobody they can trust who will take them in. Sadly most children who
graduate from foster care end up with no place to go home to in times
of trials, triumphs, or even for school vacations or work holidays.

What happened to the children in this book? Though their stories end
with tidy chapter conclusions, almost daily their situations change. Most
of them are in flux, without permanency or homes. Looking into what
happens to foster children when they are eighteen, I am shocked to find
that in some areas almost fifty percent wind up homeless in their first
year. If the state, in its wisdom, accepts the burden of becoming a parent
for abused and neglected children, we must insist that they not abandon
their progeny on the date of their legal majority.

When Lydia turned eighteen, she was still in her adult education high
school program, making excellent progress. She had been eligible to
participate in the state's independent living program, which theoretically
would have helped her get housing, start a savings account, and finish
school. While this program existed on paper, it was not being administered in our area. Lydia remained for several months with her foster
parents, the Fowlers, but they were becoming less tolerant of her desire
to be independent. After an argument with her caseworker about her

choices of friends, Lydia decided to strike out on her own. She phoned her mother and told her this decision, and surprisingly, her father agreed to allow her to return home for the first time in several years. For six months she remained with her parents and completed her high school equivalency requirements, but she was soon asked to leave again. Her new boyfriend's family permitted her to move in with them. However, his mother has serious psychiatric problems, and after one psychotic incident, Lydia and her boyfriend moved several blocks away to the home of the boyfriend's grandmother, who allowed the young couple to camp out in their toolshed.

For several months I visited Lydia regularly there and delivered food packages. Her weight plummeted and her health declined. I took her to a doctor, who volunteered his services, and he diagnosed an ulcer and anxiety, as well as other problems. Without Medicaid, Lydia could not pay for her medications. Lydia expressed interest in birth control and called the health department about getting the injection that prevented pregnancy for three months at a time. However, she never could find anyone to drive her to a clinic for an appointment. I offered, but she had no way to telephone me. She was able to get a part-time job in a fast-food restaurant for several months, but lost it when she could not get reliable rides to and from work. When I came by to deliver her Christmas gifts, she confided that she was pregnant. She was tense, but happy.

"Now I can get the medical care I need," she said.

Indeed, as a pregnant mother, she was eligible for Medicaid, food stamps, WIC, and other maternity benefits. The state's Healthy Start initiative suddenly gave her the cushion she needed, and when the baby is born Lydia will be eligible for other aid. However, her boyfriend's grandparents decided that it was not good for Lydia to sleep around paints and chemicals now that she was pregnant. After a few months of living with friends, Lydia and her boyfriend were able to afford the rent for their own trailer. Lydia's mother gave her a full-time job answering phones in her office, and she thinks she will be able to keep the job because she will be allowed to bring the baby to work. She says she and her mother are getting along "better than ever" and that her mother is looking forward to being a grandmother.

"I don't want to raise a child the same way I was raised. I want this child to feel that it is worth something in life. I am determined to love my baby the right way," Lydia told me, her eyes shining with expectation.

* * *

The Stevenson siblings are still apart. Cory and Alicia finally did visit their mother, Tammy, in Washington. They enjoyed the visit, but both were anxious to return. Cory wanted to be with his father and grandfather; Alicia was too tied to her current boyfriend and Ruth to consider a change. Also, Alicia said she was uncomfortable with her stepfather. A few months afterward, though, Cory and Red Stevenson began to clash. After one heated battle, Cory called me and asked if he could go to live with his mother. Alicia was furious and tried to talk Cory out of it, but in the end she decided he was better off with their mother than their father. Mitzi Keller, his caseworker, asked Cory to pay for part of the plane fare from the balance in his savings account and HRS paid for the rest of the one-way fare. Tammy welcomed her son, but within three months he clashed with her husband. After Cory had some minor trouble with the police, she decided to place Cory in foster care in Spokane. He has remained with the same foster family for more than two years but has done poorly in school and has been arrested a few times for minor offenses.

Rich Stevenson and his young wife, Janet, continue to live together, although they are legally divorced. Both have jobs, one as a checkout cashier, the other as a laborer. Cory is planning to join them this summer if he can get the fare from Spokane, and they hope Alicia will visit them too.

Alicia's life took a difficult turn when suddenly Ruth Levy decided not to continue as a foster parent for health reasons. All the girls in her care were divided among several foster homes. In November of her senior year in high school Alicia moved quite close to me but away from her schoolmates, foster sisters, and the security she had known for the past three years. A week after she moved, Alicia turned eighteen. I asked Mitzi about putting Alicia in the independent living program. In order to qualify, Alicia had to have a job but had not found one yet in her new location. Also, Mitzi said that Alicia would never finish school because she had failed eleventh grade English and was taking two years at one time to catch up.

I bristled at Mitzi's negativity and determined to assist Alicia. One weekend she needed to type a term paper on Mozart into a computer and I loaned her mine. She brought a notebook filled with research, several good sources, and a CD of the music. I showed her some tricks of word processing, and she caught on quickly. She received an A on the paper. But while she did fine in her senior English class, she failed the junior class because of unfinished work. More and more I discovered she was cutting school, and her foster mother didn't insist that she attend. Also, she had a new boyfriend, who had invited her to move in with him when his latest jail term was up. I explained that the minute she left the foster home, she would no longer receive any subsidies or Medicaid, but if she stayed in school, she would continue to get her foster care rate and have a safe home. While she liked her foster family, she was not attached to them and was not interested in living with Tammy either.

In March I noticed that Alicia's new foster mother was so ill that Alicia had to help baby-sit the smaller children in the home. During spring vacation, Alicia took her foster sister, who was only fifteen, to a party and they stayed out most of the night. Mitzi heard about this and Alicia was blamed for corrupting the younger child. Angrily, Alicia went to a pay phone, called her boyfriend, and disappeared for the night. The next morning she was told to gather her possessions. The paperwork was processed, she was thrown out of the foster care system, and I was no longer her Guardian ad Litem. I told her I would always be her guardian in my heart.

Alicia never returned to school.

I knew where her boyfriend lived and went to visit them in a dilapidated trailer behind a shopping plaza. I tried to talk her into finishing school, even offering her money to help her stay in classes, but she said she wanted to get a job. She promised to call me and let me know how she was doing.

Two weeks later her foster mother died suddenly from a cerebral hemorrhage. Once again I went to the trailer to give Alicia the news. She asked me to take her to the funeral home. Ruth Levy was there as well, but Alicia was cool toward her. Ruth whispered to me to let her know if Alicia needed her.

Alicia started calling me several times a week. "I'm seeing you much more often than when I was officially your guardian," I told her.

"I need you now," she said. "I don't have anyone else."

When she asked me to take her to a doctor for stomach problems, she told him she needed medicine to quell hunger pangs. On the way home I took her to the supermarket.

"Let's see how many groceries we can buy with twenty-five dollars," I said, then took her shopping. Alicia had no idea how to read the pricing labels to determine the best buy. We left the store with five bags of food, enough to feed her well for more than a week with products she liked.

The following week she called and asked me to come for her because her boyfriend was going to kill her. I arrived to find her sitting on a curb with a small sack of clothing. I drove her to a girlfriend's house. A few days later, at ten o'clock at night, she needed to leave that home because they wouldn't allow her to keep a puppy she had adopted. We located another friend who worked at a fast-food restaurant and she took Alicia and the dog home.

The next late-night call was for me to meet Alicia in the parking lot of a bowling alley. There she was, a skinny waif, with an even smaller bag of clothes, and a puppy in her arms. We made some calls, but nobody would take her in. "Alicia! Look at you! You're a homeless person." I tried to convince her she needed more stability. She cried and agreed. I called Ruth Levy, who came to get Alicia.

Ruth offered to keep Alicia until she finished school, provided she would attend classes and come in at a reasonable hour. That afternoon Alicia phoned a boy she knew in the neighborhood. He came to get her that evening. I suspected that she had traded sexual favors for a bed, but soon she moved on. I found a family that was willing to give her room and board in exchange for work in their family's restaurant, but she refused.

A month after that Alicia landed with a young married couple who asked her to live in their trailer and help with housekeeping. Something about the situation made me uncomfortable, but Alicia seemed content. She didn't call me as often. Then she left abruptly and moved to South Carolina with the husband, but not the wife. She claimed that the couple had originally asked her to conceive a baby for the infertile wife, but she and the husband had fallen in love. She is still with him. Now Alicia calls me collect once a week to talk, to cry, or to ask for help getting medications. When possible her doctor here gives me free samples to send her. She qualifies for no medical care of any kind. She contacted me when she lost her wallet and needed new identification papers. HRS, the entity that had been her parent, ignored her request for a new birth certificate or Social Security card, even though they were in her files. Alicia thinks a baby will solve her immediate financial and medical problems and might give her something to love, and just maybe someone to love her. The health department, which would not fill her prescriptions, did remove her Norplant birth control for free.

When we spoke a few days ago, Alicia reported that she loved her new job as a full-time waitress at an Italian restaurant and that her boyfriend had been made assistant manager of a yogurt store at the mall. They were moving to a larger mobile home and were "happier together than ever before."

From time to time I would inquire about the foster home of Renata and Conrad MacDougal. About a year after Cory moved to Washington, Nancy called me and said, "I've just received a report from the guardian for one of the girls who is living with the MacDougals now. We're having more problems with that home and I need you to relate your impressions."

At Nancy's behest I agreed to a conference with the head of the HRS district and Cicely, the other guardian, whom I had not yet met. As Cicely read from her report, though, the similarity to my notes was uncanny.

"Kim's teacher said she had made some suicidal comments. I told Mrs. MacDougal that Kim needed to be in therapy immediately, but Mrs. MacDougal said she would settle down in a few weeks once she understood their family's program." Cicely went on to describe how Mrs. MacDougal had blocked her phone calls to Kim. When she finally drove out to see her, Kim was very tense. She said that Renata MacDougal told her that the judge despised guardians, so that having one was going to work against her getting what she wanted. Renata MacDougal also said that she sued the first Guardian ad Litem that came into her home and won.

I gasped. "But *we* sued *her!*" I stared at the administrator, who did not blink.

Cicely continued with a description of the MacDougals' home, saying it did not look as if any children lived there and that Kim's room looked like a "hotel room." She could only sit on certain chairs in the living room, and a sheet to protect the furniture had to be in place. Cicely said that the next time she saw her, Kim was very upset because after she left, Mrs. MacDougal screamed, "That bitch isn't going to tell me what to do."

Cicely read her conclusions. " 'From what I have seen this place is more like a concentration camp than a loving home and in my opinion is not suitable for Kim or any other child. The developmentally impaired boys in this placement seem to have been brainwashed into submission. Aside from requiring excessive labor, the family is emotionally abusive. A child like Kim, who is an abuse victim, should never be placed in a foster home of this type.' "

I was then asked to read the letter I sent Lillian shortly after Cory

Stevenson left the MacDougals. " 'My notes document an authoritarian approach, threatening attitude, verbal abuse, humiliation, expectations far exceeding a child's emotional and developmental level, punishments with extreme time limits, work and chores above and beyond normal household patterns, and general lack of knowledge regarding contemporary parenting skills.' " I emphasized the words that echoed Cicely's. "She missed more than a month of psychological therapy . . . more relevant in the management of a prison camp than a foster home."

Nancy leaned forward. "Gay's letter was written more than a year ago."

"Perhaps this is merely a clash of personalities and parenting styles," the administrator said, then promised that he would look into the matter.

Six weeks later I received a thick packet in the mail with copies of the report regarding the investigation of the MacDougals' foster home. Caseworkers and supervisors complimented the MacDougals' ability to structure the children and concluded that the home is "a valuable asset to the boys in that county." The head of the foster care division wrote that Renata MacDougal is a full-time homemaker dedicated to being a foster mother. Then she added, "As far as children having rights, the problem is in the definition of rights. To Renata MacDougal a right means a privilege, which must be earned. Both parents are disciplinarians who want to teach their foster children to care for themselves since they will not have biological families to support them." The official report concluded, "Although there are issues that need to be addressed, we do not believe that the evidence warrants the closing of this foster home."

Three years later, I received a call from Alicia's foster mother, Ruth Levy, who was again a foster parent. "Guess what I got last month?" she asked, then filled in, "a refugee from Mrs. MacDougal. Renata is up to all her old tricks." She explained that all the foster children had received personalized quilts from the Foster Parent Association, but Mrs. MacDougal wouldn't let him take his with him because she was saving it for another child."

"And with the kid's name right on it!" I said in amazement.

The next day I mentioned it to Nancy. "Who's the kid? Where's he now? When did he get the quilt?" she asked rapid-fire. Ten minutes later she had called me back to report that not only was the quilt on its way, but she was going to check into why the MacDougals still had their foster care license. There is a new district administrator whom Nancy has asked to review the situation from a fresh perspective because, since

Cory left the MacDougals', seven guardians have monitored that home and each one has expressed concern for the welfare of the children in their care.

The Colby sisters moved into their new home but still have not been adopted because their adoptions counselors suggested that the Slaters would benefit financially if they did not adopt the children. Theoretically the state offers the independent living program and subsidized college tuition to foster children who are still in school past the age of eighteen, so the Slaters decided to get more information before continuing with the adoption process.

Simone is doing well in school, has won awards for track and golf, and is active in the church youth group. Nicole's grades are the best in the family, but she sometimes has uncontrollable tantrums and severe squabbles with Jeanne and Vic. Clearly her problems are far from over and she continues to have regular therapy with Dr. Abernathy. Julie calls her mother often and sometimes sleeps at her house. Julie also phones me to report on what she is doing or complain about a tiny injustice. Last week Julie was annoyed because she hadn't had pizza in almost a month. I laughed and reminded her of the time when she was not getting dinner at all most nights.

Recently the Slaters realized that the state-supported educational programs for children over eighteen were rarely implemented and decided that the children needed the security of an adoptive home. They have signed the consents for the adoption, which will become final this autumn. Unlike many states, Florida does not have parity of support between foster children and adopted ones. I am working to get the Colby sisters additional subsidies if they attend college and also to change this unfair statute to benefit all adopted children in Florida.

Sharonda, one of my current cases, took her caseworker's advice to heart. Now that she is pregnant she qualifies for many forms of assistance, including medical care. She will have her first child before her seventeenth birthday.

HRS continues to have conflicts with the Guardian ad Litem program. As of April 1994, they are attempting to change the court order appointing the Guardian ad Litem program to a case as well as the individual Guardian ad Litem. We may no longer have access to records relating to parties—other than the children we are representing—without their consent or a further court order, and visitation away from home now must be prearranged with either the caretaker or the agency and can no longer be spontaneous.

The Guardian ad Litem program cannot continue to grow too fast in our area because funding to expand case coordinators and office support for the volunteers is not available. It would be foolhardy to allow poorly managed guardians to deal with the complex and life-altering aspects of familys' lives, but it is equally as senseless to deny children advocacy when such a cost effective program is available. Actually, Florida is serving a respectable percentage of its cases, although respectable is not acceptable by my standards. However, in Chicago there are four hundred advocates for 30,000 cases so that only those children in the most dire straits can be served. The whole system is overcrowded, with some case-workers trying to cope with more than sixty cases each, and attorneys representing children in certain jurisdictions juggle as many as five hundred cases apiece! There are beleaguered judges who hear forty-five juvenile dependency cases a day, allowing less than ten minutes per child in which to make their crucial decisions. Nationally 37,000 volunteers serve less than twenty-five percent of the children who need a voice in the court system, and at least five times the number of advocates will be needed to represent their best interests. This is not merely a financial problem. Regions with modest resources often have outstanding programs while wealthier areas have none. Programs in places like Kansas City, Missouri, are making an enormous difference, while some cities, such as Philadelphia, have no program in place . . . as yet.

Nevertheless, while the problems will never fade away, I am not discouraged. All my guardian children came into my life during periods of enormous upheaval and crisis for them and their families. Almost every service I offered was one they would otherwise not have received. I forged relationships with them that were unique in their experience. I was their advocate, their voice. I cared for them unconditionally and continue to do that, since I do not know how to turn off nurturing like a faucet.

Adults sometimes forget a very basic premise of child development. We often expect children to think as adults do but suppose that they feel differently. In fact, the opposite is true. As children's minds are forming, they do not process ideas in logical ways. We cannot expect them to sit still just because we say to or to make reasonable requests or thoughtful decisions. On the other hand, even infants are upset when they hear a voice raised in anger. If we told another adult that their actions were "stupid" or shouted for compliance, we would offend them, and yet we don't allow children to react in the same way. Young people should receive the same courtesy we extend to honored business associates, treasured friends, and respected relatives. We need to allow for their immaturity in behavior while being loving, supportive, and kind. My most important role as a Guardian ad Litem is to interpret this truth to both the children as well as to their assigned caretakers.

Today with so many of my guardian children's lives in flux, I am asked whether I think I made a difference in the long run. I don't know. And it doesn't matter. I made a difference on some days. I arranged a dentist appointment or got them into a special classroom or found their mother when nobody else had bothered to do so. I listened to their complaints or held their hand when nobody else was around. I told them over and over that they were worth something. I forgave their faults and applauded their achievements. These children are neither failures nor successes, they are evolving human beings.

And no matter what they become, my greatest hope is that someday, somehow, somewhere each one will remember to renew the license to care for another person in need and pass the legacy on.

The heyday of a woman's life is . . . when the vital forces heretofore expended in other ways are garnered in the brain, when their thoughts and sentiments flow out in broader channels, when philanthropy takes the place of family selfishness, and when from the depths of poverty and suffering the wail of humanity grows as pathetic to their ears as once was the cry of their own children.

—ELIZABETH CADY STANTON

Index